RHAPSODY IN GREEN

Previous books on Celtic by the authors:

Tom Campbell: *Glasgow Celtic 1945–1970* (1970)

Tom Campbell and Pat Woods: *The Glory and the Dream: The history of Celtic FC 1887–1986* (1986, updated edition published in 1987)

Pat Woods: *Celtic FC facts and figures 1888–1981* (1981)

Pat Woods: *The Celtic Quiz Book* (1987)

Pat Woods and Kevin McCarra, with photographs by Oscar Marzaroli: *One Afternoon in Lisbon* (1988)

RHAPSODY IN GREEN
GREAT CELTIC MOMENTS

Tom Campbell
AND **Pat Woods**

FOREWORD BY

Bobby Murdoch

MAINSTREAM
PUBLISHING

First published in Great Britain 1990 by
MAINSTREAM PUBLISHING COMPANY
(EDINBURGH) LTD
7 Albany Street
Edinburgh EH1 3UG

British Library Cataloguing in Publication Data
Campbell, Tom *1934–*
Rhapsody in Green : Great Celtic moments.
1. Scotland. Association football. Clubs: Glasgow Celtic
Football Club, history
I. Title   II. Woods, Pat *1946–*
796.33463091443

ISBN 1-85158-340-8 (paper)
ISBN 1-85158-328-9 (cased)

Typeset in 10 point Times
Printed in Great Britain by Billings & Sons, Worcester.

DEDICATION

This book is dedicated to Celtic fans everywhere – the true custodians of the tradition.

The Celtic are blessed with having a following that simply defy the elements, whose enthusiasm for their own side is never lukewarm!

(*Scottish Referee*: 7 September 1891)

ACKNOWLEDGMENTS

Many individuals and organisations made valuable contributions in the writing of this book. In particular, the authors would like to thank the following:

Peter Byrne for releasing his correspondence with Ferencvaros and Celtic.

Ronnie Campbell for his unfailing enthusiasm and encouragement.

Tommy Collin for the loan of the 1982 Ajax match pennant.

Bob Crampsey for verifying a couple of points.

Jim Craig for his observations and recollections of matches that he saw or played in.

Dixie Deans for his memories of the 1972 Scottish Cup final.

Ricki Fearon, dealer in football memorabilia in the 'Victorian Village' (Glasgow) for lending the *Evening Times* sports edition of the day of the 1957 League Cup final.

Bob Ferrier Jr. for providing background information on the 1931 Scottish Cup final in which his father captained Motherwell.

Gwyn Grant of Llanelli for his observations and evaluation of Jock Stein's career in non-league football in Wales.

Eugene McBride for his unfailing enthusiasm and encouragement.

Kevin McCarra for his invaluable comments and constructive criticism of the manuscript throughout.

Malcolm MacDonald for his recollections of Celtic in the 1930s, and the Empire Exhibition of 1938 in particular.

Billy McNeill for an 1984 interview in which he recalled the events of the 1965 Scottish Cup final.

Billy McPhail for observations on the 1957 League Cup final.

Bobby Murdoch for writing the foreword, and for his recollections of matches he saw or played in.

James Rafferty of Croy for providing information concerning Jimmy Quinn's mining background.

Barrie Thomas, sports editor of the *Llanelli Star*, for providing assistance about Jock Stein's career with Llanelli.

David Walker of the *Sunday Post* for his assistance with photographs.

Jack Webster, journalist and football historian, for providing background information about the history of Aberdeen FC.

Also, the authors wish to acknowledge the superb professionalism of the staff at the reference sections of the following library authorities on the phone, on research visits, and in writing, especially their unfailingly patient response to requests for volumes of newspapers:

Aberdeen, Dundee, Dunfermline, Edinburgh, Glasgow, Leeds, Liverpool, Llanelli, Motherwell and Ottawa.

Finally, our thanks are also due to the staff of the British Library (Newspaper Library), Colindale, London for their hospitable and excellent service during a four-day research stint.

Our thanks to D.C. Thomson for providing photographs.

If anyone has been omitted inadvertently from this list, we extend our sincere apologies.

CONTENTS

FOREWORD

Sometimes it's hard for me to believe that more than 30 years have passed since I first turned up at Celtic Park as a young player. It was a great thrill for me to go through the front door then, as it was for every match I played in for the club. To be honest, it's still a thrill just going to the ground as a spectator.

When I joined Celtic as a teenager, the legendary Charlie Tully was getting ready to hang up his boots – when I was moving on, young Danny McGrain was starting to make a name for himself. Like these players, I would like to think that I made a contribution to Celtic's history during my years at Parkhead. Frankly, I could never describe the feeling of putting on a Celtic jersey – except to say that it made me and the other lads feel ten feet tall.

I read this book with a great deal of interest and pleasure, especially the accounts of games I played in. Pat Woods and Tom Campbell deserve congratulations for recapturing the flavour and excitement of so many great matches. And one last word – I was delighted that they paid tribute to the part played by Celtic supporters. I'll always remember listening to Jock Stein on that subject: 'This game exists because of people, and for people. I feel most successful when I see the terraces at Celtic Park packed.'

Bobby Murdoch

1

DANCING IN THE STREETS

A CELTIC 'BAWL'

Begorra, bejabbers, who says they can't play?
Jist let him come round and we'll stap up his bray;
We'll belabber him jist as we did the Q.P.,
And make him howl out 'Ochone, let me be.'

Rejoicin' there is in the district out East,
We all ov us now hold our heads with the best;
Our bould Ciltic boys are the wans for the ball,
And of cups they will merrily jist lift them all!

They've gotten the 'City' and the 'Scottish' wan too,
And the 'Charity's' standin' to brighten their view;
Och! The 'League' it isn't a 'half mile' to fame,
And they mane to be 'kings' of the great football game.

Begorra, bejabbers, who says they can't play?
Jist let him come east and we'll stap up his bray;
We'll belabber him jist as we did the Q.P.,
And knock him about like some ould referee!

Anonymous
(The poem appeared in *The Bailie* of 13 April 1892. Presumably, the 'mis-spellings' are an attempt to recreate a form of stage-Irish. The last line perhaps refers to an incident involving Celtic fans and an umpire at a November 1888 match versus Queen's Park.)

IN THE 1950s many supporters' clubs used to hold Quiz Nights and invited players, and other personalities, to test their knowledge of sports trivia and to mingle with the fans. Jock Stein, Celtic's captain, always a popular guest at these functions, frequently raised a few smiles with his compulsive attention to detail. A recurring question was the distance of the marathon, and Stein would get the points by answering 'Twenty-six miles,' but invariably he would insist on adding, 'and 385 yards.'

He was stumped – once – by this question: 'Next to Celtic and Rangers, which team has won most Scottish Cups?' The answer, surprising to a modern generation, is Queen's Park, with ten victories. But, it has to be added, the last of these triumphs was back in 1893.

When Celtic were formed in the late 1880s, Queen's Park was still the premier club in Scotland, coping successfully with challenges from the likes of Renton, Vale of Leven, Third Lanark and Rangers. Celtic's immediate success – in bursting upon the scene, watched by huge crowds drawn from a captive audience and fielding players obtained from a number of other clubs – concentrated Queen's Park's attention. The amateur club recognised immediately that Celtic represented the greatest threat to the old order; it was prepared to put up a struggle to preserve amateurism in an increasingly professional sport. Queen's Park were also conscious that they represented the native Scots against the immigrant Irish.

Matches between the clubs at times took on some of the elements of a pitched battle, and at least one cup-tie ended in brawling among the players on and off the field. By 1892 the sides had met four times in competitive matches, and Celtic had still not managed a victory. The relatively small number of games could be explained in part by the fact that the Scottish League came into existence only in 1890/91, and the luck of the draw in the Scottish Cup, Glasgow Cup and Charity Cup determined the number of meetings.

Queen's Park had chosen not to participate in the newly formed League, because it would have meant competing against paid players, and thus condoning 'professionalism'. Although payments to players were strictly illegal, every club in Scotland – with the exception of Queen's Park – did pay players in one form or another. Celtic, the prime movers for a league in order to guarantee fixtures and to promote competition, offended the venerable Hampden club when their representative, John H. McLaughlin, an unrivalled speaker and debater in the committee chamber, consistently advocated the sweeping away of 'the Pharisaical cant of "pure amateurism"' in order to stem the flood of players to the professional game in England and place all parties on an honest footing. Of course, as Queen's Park had feared, the formation of the Scottish League was only a preliminary stage in the legalisation of professionalism among football players. As with the Scottish League, Celtic were in the vanguard of reform, and John H. McLaughlin's skill in persuasion was a major factor in achieving this most momentous of changes in May 1893. Thus, in the eyes of Queen's Park, Celtic were to be considered as a threat to themselves in particular – and to the sport in general.

To many other Scots the immediate success of Celtic was viewed with understandable resentment. Founded for charitable purposes, the Catholic and Irish club, from the very start, had emerged as a high-profile, brash organisation; it could not afford to fail, at the box-office or on the field. Such naked and aggressive ambition attracted hostility from many quarters.

The club became noted within a very short time for its business acumen, consistently leaving rivals far behind in providing 'attractions'. Large and enthusiastic crowds flocked to Celtic Park within the space of two weeks in April 1891 to see their favourites take on English teams such as Blackburn Rovers, Preston North End and Bolton Wanderers, three of the most formidable sides in the country.

Sketches at the match. The Scottish Referee's *view.*

Early in its history, the club attempted to avoid the last-minute cancellation of matches – and a subsequent loss of revenue – by covering the pitch with tarpaulin: '. . . it was considered advisable to have the Park covered to protect it from the frost', as a minute from a committee meeting of December 1892 indicates. Another item in the same minutes shows the club's enterprise: it was proposed that 'we introduce the Electric Light to Celtic Park with the object of having evening matches and holding other athletic meetings'. A year later, on Christmas Day 1893, the lights were ready for an experimental match against Clyde, their neighbours in the East End. The *Evening Times* of 26 December 1893 reported that:

> the novelty of a football match by the aid of the electric light, combined with the fact that the competing teams were such keen rivals as Celtic and Clyde, last evening attracted some 5,000 spectators to Celtic Park, Glasgow. Football previously had been played at night under the artificial light, particularly at

the Edinburgh and Glasgow Exhibitions, but this was the first match of the kind on a private field. Sixteen arc lamps are used to illumine the playing pitch, the lights being hung from high poles erected inside the racing track with a row suspended up the middle of the field. Last evening the atmosphere was foggy and not favourable to the experiment, but there appeared to be sufficient light for the players to follow every movement of the game.

An experiment – but 5,000 turned up on a wintry night and, cannily, the electric contractor was to be paid for his labour out of the stand drawings. The committee had a reputation of leaving little to chance, this time providing a back-up source of power with a hundred gas-jets along the covered enclosure. Another minute, from October 1893, recommends '[the gas-jets] to be used should the electric light fail at any time – the cost of installation not to exceed £15'. However, some practical difficulties revealed themselves with the lighting, most obviously the entangling of footballs among the overhead wires. The enterprise was abandoned early in 1894, and the stadium would not see matches played under artificial lighting until the introduction of floodlighting in 1959 .

The committee members shrugged off that particular disappointment, and looked for other means of attracting spectators and making money. For example, within five years of its inception, the club could sponsor an athletic meeting at Celtic Park that attracted a crowd of 15,000 (almost certainly a record then for such a sports event) which 'witnessed an array of athletic talent as has never been seen at any club meeting in Scotland'. (*Scottish Referee*: 15 August 1892)

It was a highly organised club, and the football team was only one aspect of it – admittedly, the most obvious and important aspect. Celtic teams in the early days were chosen by the committee, though it is clear that the members, some of whom had little knowledge of the game, sought out and welcomed the advice of seasoned and respected players such as James Kelly, the captain, and the Maley brothers, Tom and Willie. One of them wondered why Celtic played away games, since 'we have a fine field here'.

The members, according to the first set of *Rules, Constitution and Bye-Laws of the Celtic Football and Athletic Club,* paid an annual subscription of 5/– (25p), and had to abide by such injunctions as 'no gambling is allowed in the clubhouse'. They sorted themselves out into sub-committees to carry out the various aspects of the club's affairs, and it is likely that team matters were the responsibility of the Match Committee, consisting of half a dozen members. Judging by the recollections of John McCartney in his 1930 *Story of the Scottish Football League,* they were wise to seek out the advice of the above-mentioned players, especially James Kelly, the club's first captain and possibly the most famous player in Scotland. The capture of Kelly had gained the fledgling club instant credibility, exerting a tremendous influence on the other players, and it was little wonder that the

Celtic sides of the decade were built around him. McCartney remembered that, in the early days of Scottish football, committee men were never short of advice in clubhouses, where 'frenzied rabids' hollered in at the doors and windows 'what had to be done' and 'who had to be watched'.

The price of success in football is involvement, and certainly the Celtic committee (or 'Komity', as it was once described in a Glasgow-Irish term) was overworked in its first five years; the annual report submitted to the 1892 AGM revealed that in the preceding year 107 committee meetings had been held. *Scottish Sport* commented: 'Just cause for marital squabbles.'

Despite the personal jealousies and dissensions endemic of committee work in any sphere of human activity, Celtic FC was moving from strength to strength. Perhaps the personality and energy of John Glass, the chairman and the person instrumental in luring James Kelly from Renton to Celtic Park, was the main reason. His vision was such that he raided top-class English clubs, as in the case of Dan Doyle of Everton in 1891 – a potential acquisition raised and contemptuously dismissed in the Liverpool newspapers. The player, worn down by Glass's enthusiastic outline of the benefits of returning to Scotland – including the tenancy of a public house, similar to the offer made to Kelly – interrupted weakly to appeal: 'Don't put my name over the door until I've got the licence.' Doyle's decision to join the 'amateur' Celtic, a bombshell whose modern equivalent in terms of impact would be Terry Butcher's move to Rangers in 1986, was the most eloquent testimony to the hypocrisy rife in Scottish football then.

John Glass, a man totally involved in every aspect of running Celtic, took pains to show his personal interest. In November 1888 a cash-taker at the Glasgow Cup-tie against Queen's Park was reported to Glass as being the worse for liquor on duty. Glass had appointed the man to the job in the first place, and presumably was a friend, but he was incensed, attacking the culprit so conclusively that 'John L. Sullivan could not have handled his man better'.

Energetic and committed too was John H. McLaughlin, later to be regarded as the most influential legislator in Scottish football. One of his earliest responsibilities was acting as Celtic's treasurer; he always took the proceeds home after match-days, but on one occasion, after a meeting at the ground which went into 'the wee sma' hours', he left the money in 'this little wooden office forgotten until, as the treasurer was giving of his best at late Mass at St Mary's, Abercromby Street [where he was organist], he suddenly remembered the cash, and sudden illness necessitated his retiral from the choir, and a rush up to the field relieved his mind when he found the cash safe and sound.' (*Weekly Record and Mail* : Willie Maley's memoirs, summer 1915)

In that excellent 1960s' film *The Loneliness of the Long Distance Runner* a memorable scene occurs on the day of the cross-country race: a dozen public-school lads – self-assured in well-fitting blazers and flannels, resplendent in tracksuits and spikes, healthy, trained and coached for the event – meet their opponents, the inmates of a borstal. The contrast is striking: these boys wear ill-fitting singlets and shorts institutionally black in colour, running shoes rather than spikes, and have the demeanour half-defiant, half-apprehensive of the under-privileged. A symbol of the two Britains.

THINGS AIN'T WHAT THEY USED TO BE

So much for the past; let us now proceed to briefly analyse the present. And in the first place we find that the character of the players and the spectators has entirely changed during those years.

The reason for this we need not go far to seek. The enthusiasm football aroused in provincial districts, as well as the larger towns, infected a class of player almost entirely drawn from the mining and artisan classes. Now, no one can lift the finger of scorn against the respectable working man . . . but it is just at this point that the difference is evidenced. The game, instead of being pursued for the physical benefits derived, is adopted for the sordid gains of monetary advantages . . .

Is it any wonder, therefore, that so frequently we have to witness at our matches the spectacle of premeditated and deliberate foul play as a means to obtain victory?

('Scotia', *Scottish Sport*: 14 August 1893)

Confrontations between Queen's Park and Celtic in the 1890s had a similar aspect, at least among their followings, which could be distinguished readily and broadly as representatives of the middle class and the working class. Little differentiation could be made between the players; both clubs fielded healthy and fit young men. But one team was playing for the club's motto, 'the game for the game's sake', the other for both glory and gain.

Resentment still flourished about Celtic's impact, and in particular the blatant flouting by the newcomers of the code so beloved of Queen's Park. It was predictable and understandable, but the antagonism had a basis in class-consciousness. A striking feature of the Industrial Revolution was the dramatic growth of large cities, Glasgow being a prime example of rapid, chaotic expansion. Watching football matches and athletics meetings had become a major leisure activity for the working man. Thomas Hughes, author of *Tom Brown's Schooldays*, reflected the middle-class distaste for the 'vulgarity' accompanying football's increasing appeal as a spectator sport when he described the rise of professional sport as 'the child of the railways, free Saturday afternoons, and the popular press'. Queen's Park FC was a bastion of the Establishment, firmly anti-payment; Celtic, champions of the Catholic working-class, represented a threat to the status quo. A quick glance at the line-ups for the 1892 final between Queen's Park and Celtic looks as if somebody had taken 22 names and divided them into two parallel lists of Scottish and Irish names.

In the 1890s the life of the working man was precarious; no unemployment relief was available to cushion the blow of being laid off, wages were low and trade unions were in their infancy. For example, in the massive Clydeside shipbuilding complex the Amalgamated Society of Engineers had recruited only ten per cent of potential members by 1890. However, such an organisation as the Glasgow Trades Council, representing the local trade unions, was already advocating the nationalisation of the railways and the municipal ownership of the tramways to keep the fares as low as possible; by the turn of the century the socialistic thrust of Glasgow Corporation had seen the civic administration in charge of four gasworks, two electricity-generating stations, public baths and wash-houses, hospitals, markets and 72 miles of tramway lines.[1] Celtic had been formed to cash in on the growing enthusiasm of the workers for football, and to use the proceeds for the needs of the Irish Catholic community. Queen's Park's origins were different, that club having been formed as an offshoot of the Victorian ethos of 'muscular Christianity'. Their first minutes, dated 9 July 1867, read in part: 'Tonight at half past eight o'clock a number of gentlemen met at No. 3 Eglinton Terrace for the purpose of forming a football club . . .' Nobody could accuse Celtic of being founded by 'a number of gentlemen'.

The impulse behind Queen's Park throughout its first decades was expressed with the élitist (and perhaps unconscious) prejudices of a bourgeois morality. As an institution which had done so much to foster the sport in Scotland, Queen's Park deserved enormous credit, but its puritanical zeal often bordered on self-righteousness.

In December 1876, after being defeated for the first time in the Scottish Cup, at the hands of Vale of Leven at Hampden, Queen's Park officials had no compunction about travelling down to Dunbartonshire to inspect the boots of players on the winning side, claiming that marks on the Hampden turf had been made by spiked boots (which were, of course, banned). The incensed Vale officials were quick to point out that, apart from having found no evidence for their accusation, the Glasgow club's president and secretary had not even entertained the possibility that the turf marks had been created by the use of umbrellas and shooting sticks on the part of the spectators. Queen's Park, hinted the Vale officials, seemed to be a law unto themselves, and their high-handed reaction a typically imperious gesture on the part of a club which believed it had divine right to the trophy.

By the 1890s, with the rapid expansion of football, the club appeared intent on isolating itself from the dynamics of change in its resentment of the encroachment of professionalism and its attendant woes. Too many

7

matches were now crucial financially for the outcome to be a matter of disputed decisions, but shortly before the 1892 Scottish Cup final Queen's Park successfully opposed the use of goal nets in this showcase for the domestic game. Celtic had shown no qualms in introducing goal nets at Celtic Park earlier that year, reportedly for the first time in Scotland. But, once again, Queen's Park was, Canute-like, resisting the tide of change.

The 1892 final, then, would not only be a culture-clash, but also juxtapose two sharply contrasting philosophies about football.

*SCOTTISH CUP FINAL** 12 March 1892 Ibrox Park		*SCOTTISH CUP FINAL* 9 April 1892 Ibrox Park	
QUEEN'S PK 0	**CELTIC 1**	**QUEEN'S PK 1**	**CELTIC 5**
Baird	Cullen	Baird	Cullen
Sillars	Reynolds	Sillars	Reynolds
Smellie	Doyle	Sellar	Doyle
Gillespie	W. Maley	Gillespie	W. Maley
Robertson	Kelly	Robertson	Kelly
Stewart	Dowds	Stewart	Gallacher
Gulliland	McCallum	Gulliland	McCallum
Waddell	Brady	Waddell	Brady
J. Hamilton	Madden	J. Hamilton	Dowds
Sellar	McMahon	W. Lambie	McMahon
W. Lambie	Campbell	H. Scott**	Campbell

Scorers:

Campbell (60)	Waddell (20)	Campbell (49, 51)
		McMahon (65, 90)
		Sellar (og 75)

Referee: G. Sneddon (President of the SFA)[2]

Attendance: 40,000 (estimated)   23,000 (estimated)

* played as a 'friendly'   **James Lambie played under this assumed name, for no apparent reason

It was perhaps the most important match played in Scottish football up to that time. Certainly the Cup final attracted more attention than ever before, with the followers of football realising that the sport was in the process of exciting and irreversible change. One newspaper on the eve of the match said:

A fight for a cup. A struggle where it is expected the contestants will strive with a desperation hitherto unknown in club history. It is no ordinary final this. Everybody realises that, and talks of it with a zest and pleasure which convinces you of the great and sincere interest which they have in the result

. . . In the busy thoroughfares, travelling by tram, rail, or in public places where men do congregate, opinions *re* the contest are freely invited, and listened to with an attention and curiosity which is uppermost on the lips, and an insatiable desire for the latest information, the latest opinion, the latest wrinkle, seems to pervade the entire community.'

(*Scottish Sport*: 11 March 1892)

Ibrox Park had undergone extensive renovations for the occasion. In fact, back in the 1890s football grounds changed from season to season as clubs expanded their premises to cash in on the football boom. But 'the extensive arrangements for the comfort of the public' have a faded, distant look; the roadway in front of the ground was opened up, a substantial paling erected, and two extra pay-boxes provided. The total number of pay-boxes was 20, 13 to the ground and seven for the three stands. Along the full width of the pitch the ground had been banked, and two stands were erected on the banking, framed by Glengarnock steel beams and girders at a cost of £1,300 and designed to hold 2,000 onlookers. Potential spectators had already been assured that the plans for the stands had been approved by the Govan Dean of Guild Court, and that Mr A. B. Allan, Master of Works for Govan, had examined and certified the wooden stand, and would examine the steel stands in the days before the final. Banked terracing too had been built up in front of the stands and behind the goals, and 'a strong cable placed along the back to prevent the crowd being pushed over on to the fence'. It was estimated that the capacity of the ground would be in the neighbourhood of 36,000, and the last touch of modernity came with the installation of a telephone line and phone for the use of the journalists.

The preparations were inadequate. The gates opened 20 minutes after noon in time for the four o'clock kick-off, but the crowds kept pouring along to Ibrox Park in their thousands. It was estimated that more than 12,000 disembarked from the 13 'special trains' and from the regular services to Ibrox Station. The ferries and the Cluthas across the Clyde to Govan and Kinning Park were crowded; and 'Ayrshire, Lanarkshire, Renfrewshire, and Stirlingshire sent in hundreds of football enthusiasts, while Glasgow contributed thousands to swell the throng. Some of the districts within the city were almost depopulated, entire colonies wending their way on foot or by river and road, car and cab, to the scene of the great battle.' (*Scottish Referee*: 14 March 1892). In the same issue a columnist indicated that 'So great was the interest taken in the match that a great many works in and around Glasgow had to stop for the day at breakfast time for the want of men.' Around 100 spectators, it was reported, had travelled from Ireland, presumably to support Celtic. Even in England interest was expressed and one newspaper was quoted as saying: 'Several circumstances add enormously to the interest felt in the game between the best club in the League (Celtic) and the bitterest opponents of that organi-

GLASGOW & SOUTH-WESTERN RAILWAY.

FINAL TIE for SCOTTISH CUP,

At Ibrox Park, on Saturday, 12th March.

TRAIN ARRANGEMENTS—

ST. ENOCH TO IBROX.—Trains leave St. Enoch Station for Ibrox Station, calling at Main Street and Shields Road, at 12.20 1.22. 1.30, 2 20, 3.20, and 3 33 p.m, and in addition SPECIAL TRAINS will be run direct from St. Enoch to Ibrox EVERY FEW MINUTES between the hours of 2 0 and 3.0 p.m.

SPRINGBURN, BELLGROVE, AND GALLOWGATE TO IBROX.—Special Trains leave Springburn at 2.0 and 2 20 p.m., Bellgrove at 2 5 and 2 55 p.m., and Gallowgate at 2.10 and 2 30 p.m. for Ibrox.

IBROX TO ST. ENOCH.—Special Trains will be run from Ibrox Station to St. Enoch Station immediately after the Match.

JOHN MORTON, Secretary and General Manager.

Glasgow, March, 1892.

sation (Queen's Park). Given a favourable day, there should be fully 30,000 present. The Scottish Association will do well to make every suitable arrangement for the preservation of law and order. Such precautions look like being needed.'[3]

A healthy police presence of 150 officers under Captains Harding and Hamilton was present to control the crowds, and as a precautionary measure four mounted policemen were added. Despite that, the first field invasion took place shortly after two o'clock, almost two hours before the kick-off:

. . . the field was packed to overflowing, stand and terraces being unable to accommodate more . . . It was due most of all to the overcrowding at the pavilion that the spectators, forced from behind by the numbers entering pell-mell into the field, burst aside the feeble resistance of the police, and scampered over the field of play like lunatics let loose . . . The orderly spectators who, hours before, had taken up their stand around the field, annoyed at the invaders, pelted them with loose snow, but the interest in the match was such that, although pelted right and left, the crowd held to their ground and defied all efforts to dislodge them. The appearance of the mounted policeman had an appreciable effect on the disorderly, and before the prancing steeds they fell back as far as the limits of the ground and crowd behind would permit.

(*Scottish Referee*: 14 March 1892)

The authorities closed the gates an hour or so before the kick-off, and it was estimated that 20,000 people were still milling around on the streets outside the ground; it was reported that the roofs of adjacent houses were black with onlookers, that trees were covered with agile young men anxious to catch even a glimpse of the play, and that 5,000 people leaped the barricades after the gates were closed.

Celtic had made adequate and professional preparations for their arrival at the ground: the party, consisting of players, officials, and some followers, gathered at Parkhead and left in a couple of large brakes for lunch at a secret rendezvous (the Bridge Street Hotel) before making its way to Ibrox Park through the crowded streets without too much obstruction. The method of transportation is in marked contrast to the present-day 'staged' arrival in air-conditioned coaches with the obligatory motor-cycle escort. The actual arrival at the ground, however, was chaotic, and the Celtic party experienced difficulty in gaining the safety of the pavilion through the milling crowds.

The condition of the pitch remained a matter of concern. Snow had been falling in Glasgow in the days before the final, and the pitch was still snow-bound on the morning of the match. Fortunately, a thaw had set in and the ground underfoot was soft rather than hard. But it was going to be greasy and treacherous, despite being cleared of snow and sanded to provide better footing for the players. The highly professional Celts had arranged for a cobbler to be present at Ibrox, and were prepared to change at the last minute from studs to bars. The general feeling was that the difficult conditions might favour Queen's Park, a side of renowned spirit and enthusiasm, and would adversely affect the combined play of Celtic.

In the vast throng expectantly awaiting the appearance of the teams were devotees of the Parkhead club sporting pipes, specially manufactured, with the legend 'Play up, Celts', and a number of 'ultra enthusiasts' in front of the pavilion stand unfurled a banner, painted in green, with the words: 'Good old Celtic! Hurry up!'

After police, both on foot and mounted, cleared a path from the pavilion, Celtic took the field first, with Kelly leading his men out, and the tension showed through in the wording of one newspaper account: 'Kelly burst into the arena at the head of the Celts.' Many followers felt that Celtic's main weakness lay in their temperament, pointing out that, despite the club's considerable impact upon the football scene, the team had not yet won too many trophies. How would they react to a packed Ibrox Park – with spectators crowding the sidelines and already encroaching upon the playing surface? Others hinted at a hoodoo, reminding neighbours that Celtic had never managed a victory over Queen's Park in four attempts, and suggested that the newcomers might still be intimidated by the reputation of the well-established amateur club. Queen's Park, already winners of nine Scottish Cups, had never lost in a final. Tradition was on their side, and tradition is a powerful motivating force in football. Celtic, on the other hand, had appeared in only one final, against Third Lanark in 1889, and had lost.

Before the match Queen's Park suffered a devastating blow to morale with the withdrawal of their famous full back, Walter Arnott; a veteran, he organised the defence and his long clearances had earned him the reputation of being one of the best defenders in the country. His illness, which soon developed into erysipelas, a skin-condition with recurring bouts of fever, ruled him out.

Celtic opted to include Johnny Madden at centre forward, although he had a suspect ankle. In the 1890s forwards were given rough treatment from defenders, kicking and hacking being the most common methods employed in dealing with them. As one of the nippiest forwards in Scotland, Madden was a marked man.[4]

FAME IS SWEET

The *Glasgow Observer* of 13 November 1909 claimed that the treat known to generations of Glasgwegians as a 'Macallum' (or a 'McCallum') – an ice-cream with a raspberry flavouring on top – was named after the Celtic forward Neillie McCallum. McCallum, who played in the 1892 Scottish Cup final, had the distinction of scoring Celtic's very first goal (in May 1888 against Rangers). He had played also for Rangers in February 1888 against Aston Villa at Parry Barr, Birmingham, as did four other guest players. An 'amateur' with Renton, he was free to play for any club that invited him. He was thus the first footballer to play for both 'Old Firm' clubs and the first Catholic to play for Rangers.

Queen's Park won the toss and, having chosen to take advantage of the wind, dominated play for the opening 20 minutes. Their approach was muscular and vigorous, pinning Celtic down in defence; the Celtic rearguard, if not in disarray, looked decidedly uneasy on the greasy surface. Kelly, famed throughout Scotland as an attacking centre half, had little opportunity to venture forward, being fully occupied in containing Queen's forwards; frequently, he had to rely on his renowned mobility to help his full backs, Reynolds and Doyle, cope with dangerous thrusts.

Prior to the match, Kelly's current form had been questioned, and he was destined to have a miserable time in the international against England three weeks later, when Scotland suffered a 1–4 defeat; however, he was playing his customary reliable game for Celtic, as he was required to do. Consider this match report of the opening 20 minutes: 'Unquestionably, the Queen's Park showed the best football, played the best game, and were the most capable set, their handicapped condition notwithstanding. They took the game in hand right off, and played with a dash, coolness, resource and brilliance which set their supporters into raptures, while it had a correspondingly opposite effect on the other side. Finer passing and more concerted action I have not seen from the Queen's Park this season.' (*Scottish Sport*: 15 March 1892)

Eventually, Celtic settled down, but were noticeably short of their top form; the famous left wing of Sandy McMahon and Johnny Campbell showed flashes of skill but, to the surprise of many in the crowd, the Queen's Park right defensive flank coped comfortably with a seemingly daunting task.

Several times the crowd encroached upon the field, and caused delays in the game. After one prolonged stoppage on the 20-minute mark the captains of both sides consulted with the referee, Mr Sneddon, and the linesmen. It seemed clear that the topic of discussion was the conditions; the frequent interruptions, when added to the vagaries of the playing surface, had reduced the contest to a game of chance. *Scottish Sport* reported that 'the moment the ball came near one or other of the goals the spectators swayed and surged over the lines, and not until the "horsemen" were called in was it possible to take a corner kick. The players, too, came into contact with the crowd, and often in their eagerness to keep the ball they found themselves embracing the spectators.'

The captains informed the referee that they would be protesting the match, and would prefer another opportunity of settling the outcome; the linesmen, representatives of the competing teams, seconded that idea. The referee felt unable to rule on such a matter there and then, but agreed to receive notice of the protest. And so the 'final' continued.

The turning point of the match for Celtic was provided by the inspirational Kelly, who embarked on a long run out of defence in which he passed several opponents before shooting for goal; however, his fierce drive was inches over the crossbar. Fifteen minutes after the interval, however, came the only goal. After Baird had made a splendid save, the ball broke to Campbell, who scored from close range ' . . . amid a scene the like of which has never been witnessed in Scotland. The heavens were rent with the shouts of acclamation that greeted the performance. The supporters of what seemed the winning team were mad with delight, and in the exuberance of their joy verbosity found vent in roar upon roar of "Play up, Celts!". One band of enthusiasts held high a large banneret on which this encouraging motto was displayed to the amazed throng. This was the crowning scene of the day.' (*Scottish Referee*: 14 March 1892)

To their credit Queen's Park, now playing against the wind and a goal down, stormed back into the game, and two minutes later scored a goal that the referee disallowed on the grounds of offside.

At last the match was over and, in the days prior to public address systems, the crowds left Ibrox celebrating or mourning. In the 1890s the cup was presented inside the pavilion, in relative privacy, to the winning club, or at a function to which both clubs were invited . . . and so, many thousands in the record crowd left Ibrox fully convinced that the Cup had

SCOTTISH FOOTBALL ASSOCIATION.

PROTESTED FINAL CUP TIE.
SATURDAY FIRST, 9TH APRIL, 1892.
QUEEN'S PARK
v.
CELTIC,
IBROX PARK, COPELAND ROAD, GOVAN.

Admission, 1s ; Ladies Free. Covered Stand, 2s 6d ;
Pavilion Stand, 2s ; South-West Corner Stand, 1s extra
Each Person.

THE GREAT FINAL.

QUEEN'S v. CELTIC.
PARTY BADGES—" PLAY UP, QUEEN'S PARK."
" PLAY UP, CELTIC."
ON SALE AT W. G. BELL'S,
20 ARGYLE STREET, GLASGOW.

Adverts in the Scottish Referee.

been won or lost.

As anticipated, the protest was upheld, and the teams were ordered to play again for the Scottish Cup a month later on the same ground – but with the price of admission doubled, to two shillings (10p), in an attempt to control the size of crowd without reducing the profits.

One gratifying note. Despite the record crowd, the crushing and the field invasions, the atmosphere for the final was recognised as good-natured, and on the following Monday no cases were scheduled for Govan Police Court – the first time that had happened in the previous six years. Some spectators, however, had displayed a keen interest in the gathering-up of the gate-receipts, as *Scottish Sport* suggests: 'That was a terrible struggle for the money-bag that took place at the rear stair of the pavilion prior to the game. But for the assistance of Johnny Taylor, the Rangers trainer, and the water hose, some of the leading lights of Scottish football would have perished. Lachie Thomson's trainer figured prominently in the final brush with the enemy, and with stout cudgel in hand made dreadful havoc amongst the light-fingered gentry.' (15 March 1892: NB – Lachie Thomson appears to have been an athlete.)

A month later, on 9 April, the destination of the cup was settled. The SFA had changed its mind about the price of admission a day or so earlier, but the information was not relayed effectively to the football public. The end result was the same; a much-reduced crowd of about 23,000, a well-behaved gathering that scarcely warranted the 200 constables and 30 mounted policemen engaged to supervise them.

Perhaps it came to Celtic's attention that they would be the standard-bearers of the poorest part of the city, for *Scottish Sport* sniffily remarked how 'at intervals of a few yards on each side of the footpaths at Ibrox Terrace stood good-looking girls – remarkably well dressed for their position – holding out tin boxes for contributions to aid the East End weavers in their strike against lower wages. Judging from the patronage they received, the strike will not soon come to an end.'

VINEGAR HILL!

Tis night! The flare of lamps!! The shows are open!!! M'yes – the Fair, you say. Strange place. Very oily perfume. Vinegar intervening . . . Switchback – very racey – odd – ruddle uddle – hair on end – hold like mad – screams of women (ladies, beg pardon) – sort of journey. Glad when back with your spinal column unshattered. Sort of mad pleasure. When you came off, you wonder if you've got feet or are simply flying through the 'paraffin' air . . . Hobby horses – mixture of switchback, ocean wave, and merry-go-rounds. Very nice – halfpence [worth] plentiful. Ladies enjoy excitement – would go round all night and next day also. Steam whistle – also organ, very musical. No ear required, can't mistake tunes . . .

Boxing booths (not acting). Get mauled for twopence. Half dozen clean-shaven big countenanced fellows in white cotton jerseys and big gloves offer you any amount of black eyes for two browns. Not in it – can't fight – and ain't noble enough and can't paint – black eyes. Leave the ring for the outside world . . .

Circuses, wild-beast shows. Surge with crowd. Another parting shot at Sally, dolls, bells, and bottles . . .

(*The Bailie*: 20 July 1892)

The raffish Vinegar Hill was the great East End carnival centre in the summer; it was located off the Gallowgate and close to Celtic Park. The famous Glasgow show-business family, the Greens, started their career here – a career which led to their building, in Renfield Street, Green's Playhouse, Europe's largest cinema when it opened in 1927.

Queen's Park sustained yet another serious blow before the kick-off, when their captain, Smellie, was forced to withdraw, leaving the Spiders without either of their regular full backs, as Arnott was still indisposed. They made the fatal decision to move Sellar back into the rearguard, where he had rarely played; a Scottish Cup final is not the time or the place to experiment.

Celtic also had to make a change, since Madden was still affected by his ankle injury; the resulting shuffle was evidence of the club's organisation, with changes kept to a minimum. Peter Dowds, a player who could perform well·in any position, was moved from the half back line to replace Madden; the reliable veteran, Gallacher, took his place at left half.

Disquieting rumours had been spreading around Glasgow about Celtic's captain, James Kelly, but were denied: 'The report which has somehow gained currency that Kelly was to be left out of tomorrow's match is entirely without foundation, and the committee of the club feel sore at its circulation. The step, it is said, was not even contemplated. All the same, we heard it suggested several times outside club circles.' (*Scottish Sport*: 8 April 1892)

Queen's Park started brightly, but mainly because they had won the toss again and booked the assistance of a stiff breeze. Later, in the postmortems the amateurs were to state that they felt a half-time lead of three goals might be enough to hold on for a victory! Despite facing the wind, Celtic had little difficulty defending, and the Queen's Park pressure posed little real danger; more ominously for the amateurs' hopes of landing a tenth Scottish Cup, Celtic's increasingly frequent raids were stretching their defence.

Football in those days was different tactically from now. In its earliest days the sport had been a 'kick-and-rush' affair, with opponents being allowed to hack and tackle players. The more skilled – or more foolhardy – held on to the ball until dispossessed of it by one means or another. In the 1880s, teams gave some thought to combined play, though it was a primitive stage of development compared to today's 'possession play'. Preston North End in England, and Celtic in Scotland in the 1890s, were the principal exponents of the new approach.

Sides lined up in formations that best suited the abilities of their players. For this occasion, Queen's Park, famous for goal-scoring, played with six forwards, four half backs, no full backs, and a goalkeeper; Celtic countered with four forwards, four half backs, two full backs, and a goalkeeper.

Queen's Park opened the scoring in the first half, through Waddell in 20 minutes, but posed little threat to Cullen's goal thereafter. In the first match Celtic's keeper had played with great courage and agility to save and clear the ball, at the same time avoiding the vigorous charges of the Queen's Park forwards. He still had to be watchful, but did not require similar heroics or good fortune in the replay. A few weeks after it, however, he did need his full share of luck when an explosion rocked his workplace, Higginbotham's Mills, adjacent to Glasgow Green, and killed three employees.

Within six minutes of the restart, Celtic, unrelentingly professional, had moved ahead through two goals by Campbell: the first was scored following a scrimmage in front of goal, and the second followed a delightful piece of combined play with his partner McMahon that split the Hampden defence. Celtic's confidence was growing by the minute, as was the corresponding enthusiasm on the terracing. One observer noted that, when Queen's Park had scored, those in the stand applauded . . . but, when Celtic scored, the cheering came from those standing around the ropes.

Kindred Spirits:1907 ads. Campbell joined Celtic from Aston Villa, McMahon was known as 'The Duke'.

Sandy McMahon, a clever dribbler from the rugby-playing stronghold of Selkirk, scored a third goal in 65 minutes when he ran the ball through a disorganised defence in an individual sortie. The result was no longer in doubt, but Queen's Park moved Sellar up into the attack in a vain attempt at a comeback.

Celtic's attack was threatening to score with every raid: in 75 minutes Kelly took a free kick on the edge of the penalty area and his shot was deflected past the luckless keeper by a defender, and in the dying seconds McMahon scored a fifth goal with a brave header, so typical of him.

Celtic had won the Scottish Cup for the first time, their first triumph in a competition that was destined to become synonymous with their name. They had defeated worthy opponents to do so. It had been no ordinary final, and the face of Scottish football had been changed.

The celebrations were those of a whole community caught up in that heady brew of pride and joy – after years of feeling downtrodden. All over Scotland the people in the Irish and Catholic enclaves rejoiced, seeing in the mere sporting victory a symbol for the future:

> There was much jubilation on the part of the Irish population of Edinburgh and Leith when it became known that Celtic had won the Scottish Cup . . . Edinburgh and Leith people look forward with expectancy to the coming of the Celts on Monday next when they meet the Athletic . . .
>
> The half-time result of the great final was received at Cappielow Park [Greenock] with loud, cheers, mingled with groans . . .
>
> Coatbridge was *en fête* on Saturday over the victory of the Celtic. In the second half, when it was intimated that the Celts had scored three goals in ten minutes, you might have heard the cheers at Ibrox. Had the Celtic team been immersed in the whisky that was drunk to their health, the Parkhead lot would have been *non est* . . .
>
> [In Glasgow itself,] as the evening wore on, the whole East End put on an air of alleged [justified?] gaiety and a colour of deep carnation that would have given an unenlightened stranger the severe knock of astonishment. Bands!

18

You ought to have seen them. They perambulated all the district until well on in the evening, and with the aid of a liberal use of party music helped to make things hum along merrily. Of course, this caused a risk of a ruction with [King] Billy's men. But what of that?

(Scottish Referee: 11 April 1892)

The pleasantries surrounding the actual presentation of the cup to Celtic were a shade more subdued. Both clubs, officials and players, retired to the Alexandra Hotel in Bath Street after the match. Mr Sneddon, the President of the SFA – and the man who had refereed the final – congratulated the winners in a speech, then rounded off a full day's work by presenting the trophy to Celtic. The Queen's Park party accepted the defeat graciously, and all enjoyed a pleasant evening at the hotel.

A sour note crept in later when *The Bailie* printed a rumour that the Scottish Cup now adorned 'the altar of a Roman Catholic chapel in the East End', but this account was rebutted in the *Scottish Referee* a few days later at Celtic's request.

Sadly too, Peter Dowds did not live long to savour the triumph in the 1892 final; three years later he died of consumption, the deadly lung-disease that was such a scourge in those days.

PATRIOTIC FERVOUR

When Michael Davitt, the noted Irish politician, visited Parkhead to lay the first sod on the new Celtic Park – as yet unopened – and to take 'the initiating kick' of the League match against Clyde, he was greeted with the phrase 'Cead Mille Failthe to Davitt' in bold letters above the pavilion entrance. The sod contained a goodly number of 'dear little shamrocks from Ould Donegal', and the ceremony took place on Saturday, 19 March 1892. A large crowd of 10,000, attributed to Davitt's presence, attended the match.

The following lines were penned by D. A. Johnson to commemorate the occasion, and to praise the shamrocks planted on Celtic Park:

On an alien soil like yourselves I am here –
I'll take root and flourish, of that never fear;
And though I'll be crossed sore and oft by your foes,
You'll find me as hardy as Thistle or Rose,
If model you need, on your own pitch you have it;
Let your play honour me, and my friend, Michael Davitt.

The poem was published in *Scottish Sport* on 22 March 1892. On 29 March *Scottish Sport* noted that a Belfast paper had condemned Davitt's visit to Celtic Park, and his enthusiastic reception: ' . . . it is bad taste to give any club a political tinge, as independent patronage will thereby be drawn therefrom.'

Ironically, the final did much to foster a new spirit of friendship between Celtic and Queen's Park, a relationship that has endured to the present time. Both clubs came to have a grudging respect – or acceptance – of the philosophy of the other, and the tragic case of Dan Doyle illustrates the new-found good will. Doyle, a handsome, dashing figure and a hero to the Celtic following, lost through his own mismanagement the ownership of his two pubs, described as 'dram-shops, really'. He quickly became a down-and-out in the East End of Glasgow, reduced to cadging drinks before Tom Robertson, one of his opponents in the 1892 final, was able to find him a labouring job in an engineering firm. Further evidence of the accord is shown in an excerpt from *The Bulletin* of 19 May 1917 which noted that ' . . . the Celtic officials have, unasked, pledged their word never to approach a Queen's Park player, directly or indirectly, to ask him to sign a professional form, and – crowning test of fellowship – that the clubs do not check each other's gates in home-and-home matches'.

Significant also in the long run was the forging of that unique bond already developing between the club, the team and its large body of supporters, as 'Granuaile' attested to in the *SFA Annual* of 1892/93: 'The village tenor sings their prowess; the youthful artist depicts them in brilliant colours (the great left wing in particular being represented as wending through a maze of multi-coloured opponents), whilst the grey-haired patriarch rests ill at ease until he hears the final result of some important fixture . . . "Good old Celts!" Such is the cry that greets them, such is the only expression that many an ardent follower can give to his feelings, wrapped up as they are entirely in the "bhoys".'

A WOMAN'S PLACE?

A specially organised force were astonished to find that 'the band of wily highwaymen' they had finally apprehended for a series of mail-coach robberies near Salmon Falls, Idaho, turned out to be 'six robust female members of one family'. The desperadoes admitted their guilt, but claimed to be acting under their father's orders; the father managed to avoid capture.

(*Glasgow Herald*: 5 April 1892)

Footnotes

1 In the 1890s the private companies were already operating special workmen's trains with fares as low as two pence for a distance between eight and ten miles. The motive, of course, was profit. The intention of public ownership was to make low fares available, and to plough back the proceeds into expanded services.

2 In those days there were no neutral linesmen, each club providing its own. The linesmen for this final were R. Brown and J. Glass, respectively the Presidents of Queen's Park and Celtic.

3 The rivalry between the Scottish League and the SFA is long-standing. A similar situation existed in England where it was said that the Football Association represented the public schools and the Football League represented the public houses.

4 Apparently, on one occasion when being marked by 'Bummer' Campbell of Kilmarnock, a pivot notorious for hard tackling, Madden walked off the pitch and returned with a huge pocket-knife, blade open. He handed the weapon to Campbell asking his opponent to pierce his (Madden's) heart, 'as he preferred a sudden death to the slow torture to which he was being subjected'.

2

A STAR IS BORN

JIMMY QUINN, THE OLD WARHORSE

Say, Jimmie, that it is not true
That you must quit the game
For we are oh! so proud of you
And glory in your fame.
Far be the day when we must part,
Ne'er see those runs of thine
That spread dismay in many a heart,
And oft enraptured mine.

Your name is known from pole to pole,
Full many an exile sighs,
In fancy sees some thrilling goal
You scored in the 'Paradise'.
We cannot spare you, 'lad of parts',
Our daring, dauntless boy,
The idol of all Celtic hearts –
Jimmie Quinn from Croy.

(Printed in the *Glasgow Observer*, 1 August 1914, this poem com-
memorates Quinn's impending retirement.)

FEW PEOPLE in Sheffield would have recognised the tall, athletic figure
of Willie Maley, the honorary secretary of Celtic, standing anxiously under
a lamp-post outside the Victoria Railway Station. At least, that was what he
hoped, because Maley was engaged in an illegal activity; he was waiting to
meet George Allan, the free-scoring centre of Liverpool – and the meeting
was unsanctioned by the Merseyside club.

At last the player turned up, and the negotiations began with voices
lowered every time a passer-by appeared; Maley knew the risk he was taking
in 'tapping' a player under contract to another club, but Celtic, committed

to success from their founding, needed a scorer. And Allan was eager to go where financial rewards were high. The two were deep in conversation.

'Maley! I've got you at last!' Maley whirled around at the harsh, triumphant voice that he recognised immediately as belonging to John McKenna, his counterpart at Liverpool. 'I'm going to report you!'

The player looked on aghast, but Maley – not yet 30 and only seven years older than his intended catch – smiled broadly and shrugged his broad shoulders, although inwardly he was nervous: 'Can't a man have his friends without being suspected?'

It was a serious charge, and one that might have ended his career; McKenna was determined to proceed with it, and called upon Mr J. J. Bentley who was in the vicinity to testify that he too had seen the pair deep in conversation. However, Mr Bentley, the President of the Football League, and a personal friend of Celtic's secretary, declined to become involved. Without corroboration McKenna's case was useless and the threat to Maley's career was over.

George Allan did join Celtic in 1897 but within a year was back in Liverpool having failed to reproduce his goal-scoring feats at Celtic Park.[1] Maley pondered the pros and cons of buying ready-made players: *It cost money in transfer fees and in terms for star players, it provided skilled players but not always loyalty, sometimes the player did not display the same form. Would it not be better to raise your own players and introduce them when they are ready? That way you don't buy trouble and . . .*

ANYTHING YOU CAN DO . . .

In 1904 the Maley brothers, Tom and Willie, accomplished the unique feat of managing their clubs to victory in the FA and Scottish Cups in the same season. Tom guided Manchester City in their win over Bolton Wanderers, and Willie was in charge of Celtic against Rangers.

Willie Maley played the most significant role in the club's first half-century and objective historians might consider that his contribution to Celtic was the equal of Jock Stein's. Like the latter he was not an outstanding player:

> Too modest to shine on the field where he always seems to be holding himself in reserve, his light burns brightly in the council chamber . . . in Mr Maley [Celtic] has one of the most judicious [advisers], one whose opinions are admired for their soundness, heightened by a manner of expression that commands for them increased respect. Mr Maley is not an orator, and thinks before he speaks. He looks soft and pliable, but that is only a freak of nature, for he is hard – nay, clear-headed . . . To people in general he is reserved to

the point of indifference; among his friends and clubmates he is familiar, yet dignified. Men of Mr Maley's stamp are a distinct gain to the intellectual side of a physical pastime which is bound to profit by the connection.

(Scottish Sport: 25 August 1890)

Maley's career had prospered since retiring as a footballer. As a member of Celtic's first team he had been an average player although he gained representative honours.[2] However, his maturity was paying dividends off the field: in June 1897 he was appointed secretary-manager of the club, shortly after it became a limited liability company in recognition of the respect he had gained within the organisation while acting as player and match secretary from the outset. Survival within Celtic Park throughout the early turbulent years required considerable political skills. His brother Tom, more charismatic but less astute, fell foul of the more commercially-minded members over the direction of the club. As the governor of Whitevale, and later Slatefield, Industrial School(s), Tom Maley saw the ravages of poverty at first hand and felt ample justification about the club's neglect of its original mission – the raising of money to assist the poor children of the parishes in the East End. Latterly it was not a popular stand when expressed so vocally as by Tom Maley.

Willie Maley's worth to Celtic was noticed, and in January 1894 he was considering an offer to join Sheffield United as a player 'with top class wages' and the prospect that he would soon become the club's manager; he was also given the further inducement of guaranteed employment in the Duke of Norfolk's estate office 'at a very tempting salary' where his training as an accountant could be utilised.

Celtic's committee moved to offer him the post as manager of the club, but the negotiations fell through when Maley rejected the original terms. It was scarcely coincidental that Maley's decision to retain his position as secretary of Celtic was followed a few months later by his resignation from employment in a chartered accountant's office and the opening of a business as a 'hosier, hatter, glover, and athletic outfitter' in 'handsome and commodious premises' in the Gallowgate.

In the club's early days internal dissension among the committee members was frequent and virulent: one chairman, John H. McLaughlin, aired his views about the team and his colleagues in a column in the *Glasgow Examiner*, and was often critical of 'the more obstinate of the directors [who] are beginning to see the folly of sticking to the present trio [of half backs] . . . and the fact is being brought home to these irritating individuals that the present half-back line is absolutely useless.' (8 October 1898)

When Maley took over as 'manager' in 1897, the transition could not have been easy: bitterness lingered on after the prolonged limited liability debate. Maley, not yet 30, took over a group of players who had been recent and more distinguished colleagues.

WILLIAM MALEY,
Secretary Celtic F.C.

W MALEY

"Son of a soldier and a man."—Carleton.

Willie Maley, 1900 portrait.

Most importantly, he did not exert the dominant influence in team selection until after World War One, though he was not averse to a pep-talk when necessary, as this *Scottish Sport* report of a Celtic match at Dundee indicates: 'Whether the visiting team received a word of comfort from Secretary Maley during the interval I do not know, but I rather think he must have said something sharp, for on resuming there was a distinct change in tactics, with harder and more determined concentration on the charge of Ritchie [Dundee's keeper].' (22 November 1898)

Prior to the Great War the involvement of the directors was an active one, with former players on the board attending practice sessions, suggesting tactics, and helping individual players iron out faults. Maley always felt that the best way to produce a winning Celtic team was by rearing, training

25

and indoctrinating young players in a systematic fashion. He believed totally that a team had to have an *esprit de corps* to achieve consistent success, and doubted if star players from other teams would possess it. His main task was to persuade the directors of the worth of his vision, by no means an easy task.

It was inevitable that Celtic's scouting for young prospects should take Maley to mining communities, where the grim working conditions bred a hardiness and strength that produced some of the finest Scottish footballers and athletes. Smithston was a hamlet of 70-odd 'tied' houses owned by the coal masters William Baird and Company, and close to the Dunbartonshire village of Croy. The Quinn family lived in Smithston Row, almost certainly in a two-apartment dwelling lit by paraffin lamp and supplied with water from communal pumps.[3] Abe Moffat, a former president of the Scottish Miners Union, while looking back at this period, recalled how 'miners and their families were looked upon as sub-human beings whose only purpose was to produce coal and profits for the coalowners'.

Because coalmining was dangerous and ill-paid but an expanding industry in the 19th century, there were openings for waves of Irish migrants desperate to take the least skilled jobs and the worst housing. Trouble with the local Scots was inevitable; the Scots, almost as poor, saw the Irish as rivals for jobs, and often used by employers as strike-breakers or as a means to cut wages. The old antipathy lingered on in towns like nearby Kilsyth: the visit of the Anderston Conservative Flute Band (consisting of men from the Anderston, Springburn, Bridgeton and Dennistoun districts of Glasgow) provoked a notorious riot in April 1905. Disembarking at Croy Station, the band began marching to Kilsyth accompanied by a number of local followers; approaching a Roman Catholic district, the band played with gusto its repertoire of provocative tunes and some members waved Orange colours (mainly handkerchiefs). Stone-throwing, bottle-throwing and fighting broke out, and eventually the mêlée involved more than 1,500 persons. Police reinforcements rushed from Stirling and Falkirk to deal with the situation, and several hours elapsed before the police were able to escort the band members from Kilsyth back to Glasgow.

It could have been worse. Many of the able-bodied Catholic men in the area were attending a football match in Kilsyth involving Smithston Hibs and were unable to participate.

26

Jimmy Quinn, 1901/02 portrait.

Jimmy Quinn played at different times for both Smithston Hibs and Smithston Albion and soon attracted attention. He was approached by Sunderland, but the negotiations broke down when a family council at Smithston Row decided that the youngster could go to England only on condition that the whole family moved with him. Sunderland's manager admitted defeat: 'That ended it all. I left the miners' row convinced that Jimmy Quinn would never join an English club, and he never did.'

To the utter astonishment of Willie Maley he also refused to join Celtic. The club had been told of Quinn's ability and potential by his former headmaster, a friend of Tom Maley since college days, and Willie Maley had to assume that the signing would be a formality. Quinn, modest and shy throughout his whole career, felt he should remain with Smithston and took some persuading to leave his Junior side.

Maley was astute enough to sign him on a registration form, and managed to get him to join the other Celtic players for training. Eventually, the lad was signed on. It was strange that Quinn did not jump at the chance to play senior football. Working at the face of the nearby Gartshore Number Two and Nine pits, hewing coal with a pick and levering slabs away with a crowbar, all the while crouching or lying down in cramped tunnels, was the only future he could see for himself. Perhaps his family persuaded him in words similar to these: 'Christ, son. The pits! Ponies work in the pits, son. That's as many brains as ye need tae work in the pits. They go blin'. Did ye ken that? They're doon in the daurk that long that they canny see. An' they're no' the only wans. Ah've been blin' fae Ah wis ony age masel'. That's whit it does tae ye. When Ah wis your age, Ah had ideas, son. Things Ah could see that Ah wid like tae dae. But the pits took care o' that. Ah'm jist a miner noo. Ma days don't belong tae me. Ah'm doon there. An' Ah canny see beyond the seam that Ah'm tryin' tae howk.' (William McIlvanney: *Docherty*, 1975)

Compared to coalmining the life of a football player must have seemed a soft touch. For a start Quinn's wages were doubled immediately to £3. 10/– a week. He no longer had to slave at least eight hours a day for his living. Training for football was not a science, as a glance at one schedule would

---

THE WHITE MAN'S 'BURDEN'

Colonel Sandys, MP for Bootle Division, speaking at a Primrose League demonstration in April 1904, defended the introduction of Chinese labour into the Transvaal, arguing that it was 'absolutely necessary if the colony were to prosper and become what they all hoped for – a white man's country. Without Chinese labour the mines could not be worked, and either Great Britain would have to be taxed more heavily to keep the place going, or they would have to ask Mr Kruger to come back and govern the place himself.'

reveal. A typical day would begin with a leisurely six-mile walk to stretch and strengthen the legs, followed by a work-out with Indian clubs, or a few laps around the track – depending on individual requirements. Conventional wisdom frowned upon sprinting, over-indulgence being regarded as a recipe for sudden breakdowns.

Quinn, despite his reputation for strength and vigorous play, was not tall; most accounts suggest he was about five feet, eight inches but he was muscular and compact. Doctors would describe him as 'the perfect mesomorph'. At the height of his career, Barr's – situated close to Celtic Park – asked him to endorse their famous 'Irn Brew', devised to slake the thirst of labourers working in the heat of Parkhead Forge. For some reason Quinn declined the commercial opportunity, but he was persuaded later to advertise that 'truly wonderful remedy for assorted sprains and muscular pains, namely Boag's Rheumatic Rum'.

Quinn always stayed close to his roots, continuing to travel the 12 miles there and back from Croy to Celtic Park by train and tram daily; he must have been aware of the appalling conditions in much of Glasgow as described by Robert H. Sherard of the *London Magazine* in spring, 1904:

> . . . hundreds of half-naked little children lurking in the early dawn in such streets as Argyle Street, Jamaica Street and Howard Street for the opening of the shops of bakers and fishmongers. Mouldy bread and fish which is unfit for sale are welcome to those little ones . . . Enteric is common, smallpox flourishes amain in Glasgow, and from the slough and mire of the awful streets the deadly plague ever and anon raises a menacing head . . . The pay for a casual labourer at the docks is fourpence an hour, and a man may be discharged at any time of the day. In the iron foundries men working full-time are earning 18/–, 16/–, and 15/– a week. One hears of men with nine children who have to subsist on such wages. The wages of the women workers are so miserable that even the small sums that their children can earn for them are indispensable additions to the resources of the family.[4]

It was little wonder that football players, working-class lads, considered themselves lucky to be paid for participating in sport.

DISORDERS IN MACEDONIA

There was some fighting yesterday near Demir Kapu. The heads of four Bulgarians killed in the encounter have been brought to the village by Turkish soldiers.

(Despatch from Salonika, 16 April 1904)

SCOTTISH CUP FINAL
16 April 1904
Hampden Park

CELTIC 3	**RANGERS 2**
Adams	Watson
McLeod	N. Smith
Orr	Drummond
Young	Henderson
Loney	Stark
Hay	Robertson
Muir	Walker
McMenemy	Speedie
Quinn	Mackie
Somers	Donnachie
Hamilton	A. Smith

Scorers:
Quinn (37, 41, 80)   Speedie (10, 11)
Referee: Tom Robertson (Queen's Park)

Attendance: 64,323

Celtic had to resolve a crisis before the match: Alec Bennett, a highly skilled centre forward, was being linked with Rangers again, and the news broke on the eve of the Old Firm Cup final. It did not come as any great surprise, because Bennett had never made a secret of his fondness for the Light Blues. It appears certain that Rangers had discouraged Bennett from re-signing with Celtic for the next season and were confident of signing him. No matter what the outcome, the player was bound to be affected by the situation.[5]

Maley recommended that Bennett, while one of Celtic's best players, should be replaced by Jimmy Quinn; in doing so, he was prepared to overcome the reservations of directors about Quinn's failure to come up to expectations. The manager pointed out that Quinn had played at centre forward before with success, and most memorably against Rangers when he scored three times in 1902 in the Glasgow Exhibition Trophy. It was expected that Rangers, a bigger and heavier side, would rely on their physique to upset the younger and lighter Celts; Quinn's strength might help . . .

Maley's suggestions carried the day, but it was a tense Celtic team that trooped out to face Rangers on 16 April 1904 – the third Old Firm final and a rubber match, as Rangers had won in 1894 and Celtic in 1899. Rangers were the current holders, having beaten Hearts the previous year.

Rangers were bound to be grim opponents that season as both League fixtures (and a testimonial match) were drawn. The rivalry between the

THE HOOPS

The jerseys worn by Celtic in the 1904 final against Rangers had been introduced, it seems, only nine months earlier, according to a report of the Celtic v Third Lanark league match at Parkhead on 29 August 1903: 'The Celts appeared in new jerseys on Saturday – horizontal stripes of green and white, instead of vertical. For some time the change rather tickled one, but latterly the alteration was appreciated.'

(*Scottish Referee*)

It was an unhappy debut for the hoops, Celtic losing 1–3. Alec Bennett gained the honour of scoring the first goal in the famous jersey, and Celtic's team was as follows: McPherson, Watson, Battles, Moir, Young, Hay, Muir, Grassam, Bennett, Somers, Quinn.

clubs was taking on an extra edge and the immediate success of Celtic was a factor in it. The new club established an early and unpopular supremacy in Glasgow and in 1893/94 Celtic defeated the other clubs with ease, except for Rangers. This situation, according to some historians, drove 'the disgruntled supporters of Third Lanark, Thistle, Clyde and other city clubs to look elsewhere for consolation and transfer their allegiance to Ibrox, the home of the giant-killers, the four-times conquerors [that season] of the mighty Celtic. From now onwards all roads led to Ibrox. Partick Thistle were practically driven out of Meadowside by the over-and-under-river trek to Ibrox, and other clubs have seen a large section of their following making Ibrox their mecca on a Saturday afternoon.' (*Evening Times* [Sports Edition]: 8 August 1931)

In fact, on the day before the final, one newspaper, while referring to the financial rewards the rivalry was bringing to both clubs, coined a new phrase that was to enter the language of the sports pages: 'The Old Firm of Rangers, Celtic Ltd.' (*Scottish Referee*: 15 April 1904)

Hampden Park presented a splendid spectacle with a crowd of 64,323 for this Scottish Cup final – the first to be played on the present stadium. The ground was regarded with justification as the finest in the world, with twin handsome stands on its south side and its celebrated 'Classic Slopes' – 'that magnificent solid-earth terracing raised tier upon tier, until now it has reached a height on which with safety and comfort, and with a clearer view of the entire play, eighty-five to one hundred thousand people may take their stand.' (*Scottish Referee*: 15 April 1904) Such was the public's enthusiasm for football in the early 1900s that the crowd was 25 times the attendance that turned out for the first Scottish Cup final only 30 years earlier. The distribution of the 'gate' was interesting: Celtic and Rangers divided the proceeds from the terracings between them, Queen's Park retained the stand takings, and the SFA was given only enough money to pay for the medals. The crowd was a record one for a club match in Scotland, with most reports attributing the size of the crowd to the reduction in admission, down to sixpence instead of the normal shilling. However neither the official attendance nor receipts included the hundreds, if not thousands, who climbed over the tall zinc fencing at the eastern end of the ground.

MISSIONARY WORK

In 1904 Celtic embarked on the club's first Continental tour, winning all four matches against 'enthusiastic beginners' in Central Europe. W. G. Gallacher ('Waverley' of the *Daily Record*) recalled that in 1937, when he accompanied the Scottish international side that drew 1–1 with the highly rated Austria in Vienna, 'the late Hugo Meisl, the man who put Austrian football on the map in a big way, confessed to me that he had modelled the play of his country's team on Celtic, with particular emphasis on the triangular play on the wings in which the half-back moved up with his two forwards in rhythmic passing. Masters of it were the wing-triangles in the Celtic eleven that once toured Central Europe: Young, Bennett and McMenemy on one side of the field; Hay, Somers and Hamilton on the other; with the powerful Jimmy Quinn as the spearhead.'

Did someone say Rapid Vienna?

Rangers won the toss and elected to play with the wind at their backs. Apart from the breeze, conditions were ideal since rain earlier in the week had made the pitch soft but not greasy. Celtic made all the early running with McMenemy at inside right prominent in distributing the ball to the wings; young Somers at inside left was showing signs of settling into the side. Thus, Rangers were put under immediate pressure and Watson was busy from the start.

In a Rangers–Celtic match the unexpected always happens. After ten minutes Rangers had made only one or two forays into the Celtic half; after 11 minutes they were two goals ahead. The first was a mistake by Adams, Celtic's goalkeeper; Smith, on Rangers' left, broke away past Young and McLeod, and centred for Finlay Speedie to head straight at the keeper. Somehow, the latter played the ball into the net as he collided with the post. A soft goal, against the run of play, but worse was to follow . . . Smith gained a corner within another minute, and took it himself; the ball landed at Speedie's feet in a crowded goalmouth, and the Rangers forward lashed it into the net past an unsighted Adams through a ruck of players.

Astonishingly, after these setbacks, the young Celtic side continued to dominate play. The half-backs were assertive and Loney was mastering Rangers' centre, Mackie, in the air and on the ground. Rangers were mis-

SKETCHES AT NEW HAMPEN ON SATURDAY

WATSON PUNTS OUT A STRONG SHOT

JACKY THROWS IN.

DRUMMOND & MUIR.

QUINS RECEPTION ON SCORING WINNING GOAL

JOCK DUCKS

JOCK THIS WON'T MOST PULL UP A BIT.

WATSON TIPS PAST

ROBERTSON & SMITH NET REPAIRERS

"GOOD OWLD CELTS!"

COLLECTED FOR THE PERTH DISASTER

QUIN GETS BETWEEN THE RANGERS BACKS AND SCORES

THE SCOTTISH CUP FINAL - RANGERS v CELTS

sing the leadership of Hamilton, out through injury, and the substitute, hard though he tried, was making little impression. Celtic's replacement at centre, Jimmy Quinn, was beginning to influence play, and his energetic running had started to disconcert Rangers' defenders. Nobody could accuse the young ex-miner of subtlety, but he was effective. Stark, Rangers' rugged centre half, was experiencing difficulty in containing him; Nick Smith and Jock Drummond, summoned to help out, had to call on experience and all their physical strength to stop him. The concentration on Quinn allowed the other Celtic forwards more room to manoeuvre, and the pressure continued.

Quinn scored an individual goal for Celtic in 37 minutes, not long after Rangers had come within inches of taking an unassailable three-goal lead, the ball slipping past Celtic's post. Quinn's response was of the kind that turns football matches around – the stuff of legends. He gathered a loose ball near midfield, saw nobody in position for a pass and made straight for goal; he ran through a Rangers defence noted for its hard tackling, shrugging off collisions, surviving challenges from Smith and Drummond, and lashed the ball past Watson for a stunning solo goal, the prerogative of a hero.[6]

Shortly before half-time Quinn equalised; Muir, 'a speed merchant', sprinted up the right wing and, after eluding Robertson and Drummond near the corner flag, centred the ball for Quinn, with the instinctive reaction of a striker, to smash the ball past a motionless Watson.

Quinn in typical action.

SATURDAY NIGHT IN ARGYLE STREET.

THE FLOWER GIRL.

"SPECIAL"

LATEST FOOTBALL

IN THE B AND D MARKET.

THE APPLE VENDOR.

SKYLARK
CAKE WALK
MONA
HOLY CITY

LET HER DROWN

THE VETERAN WATCH SELLER.

GENTLEMEN, THE WINNER OF THE CUP, ONE PENNY

WORDS AND MUSIC, OF ALL THE LATEST SONGS.

Two goals for Quinn – scored in characteristic style – had brought Celtic back into the game. The score was level at half-time, Celtic had the wind behind them, and Rangers, already wilting under Quinn's single-minded charges, had to cope with a younger, fresher side dictating the pace – the average age of Celtic was 23 compared to Rangers' 28.

However, in the opening minutes of the second half Rangers enjoyed their best spell of the final and came close with a shot that grazed the post. Celtic shook that off as a minor irritant, and laid siege to the Ibrox goal. Watson was forced into several fine saves, and on one occasion he cut out a dangerous cross from Muir, as Somers rushed in; Somers had to be disentangled from the net which required repairs. He made another exceptional save to thwart McMenemy's shot from 15 yards. Celtic's forwards were camped in Rangers' half, and their build-up was skilful and patient as the half backs and inside men stretched Rangers' defenders with the speed of Muir and Hamilton on the wings – and the power of Quinn through the middle.

Fittingly, it was Quinn who scored the winning goal ten minutes from the end. Celtic's Willie Orr intercepted a long clearance from defence and passed the ball to Hay; the left half saw some space for Quinn to sidefoot the ball past Stark, who by now was limping; again he hurled himself at goal, and again was challenged by Rangers' full backs; he shook off Drummond but was tackled fiercely by Smith; Quinn staggered, stumbled and trailed the ball clear of the defender; he managed to straighten himself up before slipping the ball past the advancing Watson from about ten yards out. One account stated that Quinn 'ploughed with the ball into the net and Rangers were left in the lonely furrow of humiliation and defeat'.

The sequel was astonishing: '. . . he was nearly dismembered by the wild embraces of his mates, one of whom actually kissed the successful marksmen. He himself, however, remained unmoved. "Look at him!" shouted an enthusiastic Celt in the reserved enclosure. "Look at him! He's as cool as hell!"' (*Glasgow Observer*: 23 April 1904)

Celtic had won the cup for the fourth time, and continued to add to a growing reputation for fighting spirit; Quinn, even if he never kicked another ball, had gained immortality. He had scored the first hat-trick in a Scottish Cup final, a record that was to stand alone till 1972.[7]

After three years at Parkhead, Quinn had become an overnight sensation and impressions of the suitably unassuming folk-hero would be emblazoned on the cloth banners of many horse-drawn Celtic brake clubs. Perhaps the Camlachie Shamrock, wending a joyous way home from Hampden after Celtic's victory, would soon be one of them. What a colourful and noisy spectacle they presented! 'Quite suddenly you will hear a great clatter of wheels, and loud cries and shrill blasts of trumpets, and a brake full of men in cravats and bunnets rattles past you with a banner flying, and much clamour and loud chaff. These are "fitba" supporters now back from their gemme . . .' (J. H. Muir: *Glasgow in 1901*, 1901)

ADVERT

The Empire Palace Theatre on Sauchiehall Street in Glasgow in the week beginning 18 April 1904 was offering this bill:

Lelia Roze: comedienne and burlesque artiste
Prof. Dunning: the clever ventriloquist
Cinquevalli: the incomparable juggler
Mina Martino; chanteuse
Gypsy Woolf: with her six white piccaninnies

Footnotes

1 George Allan, like so many footballers of his time, died young – at the age of 24, a victim of consumption.

2 He was 'capped' against England and Ireland in both full international and inter-league matches. Jock Stein's sole honour was against the *Football* League in 1954.

3 The newspapers used 'Quin' in the early 1900s, and this was the spelling on his birth-certificate. 'Quinn' had become the common usage by 1910 and the player raised no objections when it was used throughout his 'memoirs' in a *Weekly Record* series in 1915.

4 The decimal equivalents are as follows:

18/– = 90p
16/– = 80p
15/– = 75p

Note that these amounts are conversions and not equivalents in purchasing power. In 1904, 3d (1p roughly) would buy two pounds of sugar, and 4d a loaf of bread.

5 Alec Bennett played for Celtic until 1908, when he joined Rangers. Moved to outside right to make way for Quinn, he was a member of possibly the most famous side (and forward line) in the history of the club.

6 Within a year Nick Smith, a football veteran at 31 but still a young man, was dead – one victim of an epidemic of enteric fever that killed almost a hundred people in his native Ayrshire. Our thanks to Bill Murray, author of *The Old Firm* (1984), for this information.

7 Dixie Deans of Celtic scored three times against Hibernian in a 6–1 victory in 1972. The claim for John Smith of Queen's Park in 1881 remains open to question.

3

ON THE EVE

TRIUMPHANT CELTS

Here's to the Celtic, triumphant today;
Here's their consistency, skill and fair-play.
Here's to 'Prince Charlie', of keepers the best,
And here's to Joe Dodds, who withstood Hampden's test.
Here's to our 'Iceberg', of tactics a master,
Whose coolness oft saves his great club from disaster.
And here's to McMaster, a coming great man,
And also big 'Sunny', the Chief of the Clan.
And bold Peter Johnstone we'll never forget,
Who keeps all the crack shots from bulging the net.
Here's to young Andy (what limbs he has got);
The goalkeeper squirms if he touches his shot.
Here's to 'Wee Pat'; he's our pet, be it said,
The Wizard of Football and Pride of Parkhead.
And here's to St Anthony's product McColl
Who leads every dash on the enemy's goal.
And the famous Napoleon we're quite proud to own;
With 'brains in his feet', he stands peerless, alone.
And gallant John Browning, who never would quit,
Long may he flourish, our songster and wit.
Long may the Cup 'mongst your silverware lie,
Long may the Flag float on Paradise high.
Kings of the football world, dearest and best,
Still may you prosper, the 'Pride of the West'.

Poem by J. C.
(Printed in the *Glasgow Observer*: 25 April 1914)

THE BOAT-TRAIN pulled out of Friedrichstrasse Bahnhof, leaving behind the lights and bustle of Berlin; it gradually built up power as it moved through the suburbs, and eventually out into the darkened German countryside. The young Celtic footballer yawned wearily as he climbed into the sleeping-berth – and, as the youngest member of the party, it had to be the top one.

Fighting back sleep, he mumbled something to the giant figure still framed in the doorway, and vaguely he heard his team-mate reply, 'Well, I'll away for a wee walk then, jist tae see whit's oan the train. I'll be back in a wee while, son.' The broad Ayrshire voice became more coaxing, 'Are ye sure ye don't want tae come – for a while?'

The youngster shook his head, still yawning, and watched the burly figure close the door with a cheerful grin and an understanding wink. He settled down for the long journey that would lead all the way back to Glasgow. But the excitement of the past few weeks still occupied his thoughts. Tired in body but unable to sleep, he allowed his mind to wander unchecked as the train thundered on into the night . . .

Some man, that Sunny Jim. He must be over six feet in height, broad shoulders, and an iron man, as well. Somebody – who was it, now? – used to say he was 'always the last to roost, but first to strip the next day'. An' yet, he's the friendliest man to have on your side. Well, maybe the Burnley players might not think that.[1]

Just think. Tomorrow you'll waken up in Flushing – funny name for a port, isn't it? And then the boat home. Hard to realise you've travelled more than three thousand miles in only three weeks. That was what Willie Maley figured it out, an' he knows jist about everything about figures an' calculations. Aye, three weeks ago you left St Enoch's the day after Celtic beat Thirds 6–0 in the Charity Cup. Anither great season.

Imagine being on this train, an' travelling all night, an' getting on a boat after that? Incredible. You'll have tae tell your pals everything; they'll no' believe it.

The sing-song on the boat coming over tae Holland. What was it called? Right, the Köningen Regentes. The names would make you laugh. An' it was the Celtic that started the singing, an' everybody on the deck joined in. Great.

An' imagine kidding Willie Maley? Well, he's different oan a trip like this, but who's likely to believe you when you tell them that? He wanted to meet that Princess of Pless – anither daft name – but she stayed in her cabin the whole time. Patsy Gallacher said it was because she couldnae sing; an' Sunny Jim said she was in the huff because Will Quinn the trainer made sure the Celtic baggage got oan the boat first, an' hers had to wait. Somebody else on the deck said she was only a princess, an' we're the kings o' Scotland. Remember what Patsy said? He's got an awful tongue, an' he said, out loud as well, 'Too bad, hen.' Willie Maley looked peeved at hearin' that. Somebody said he was awful partial tae royalty – well, for an

Irishman. He's always tellin' about the time he was introduced to the Princess May of Teck when he played for Scotland against England 20 years ago. You should try an' tell him you weren't born then, an' see what he says!

Look at the dark out there! Suppose those lights are wee farms an' villages. Different from Berlin, that's for sure. Some place, that Berlin. Everybody wanted to stay longer. Nothing back home like that; clean, wide streets – strasses, they called them – straight and long, great buildings, an' statues. Patsy said the pigeons were workin' overtime! An' those model housing schemes for working people, the tramway system, miles ahead of Glasgow for comfort an' cheapness. Clean tae.

The parks were smashin'. Imagine, open night an' day for everybody! An' the cafes, wi' music an' dancing, an' people havin' a great time. You can get anything in the parks: automatic cafes, they call them, where you put a coin in, an' get back tea or coffee . . . Beer tae. Imagine! An' sausages or sandwiches. Incredible. Remember that park the other day, the hoaliday. All the cafes packed, people singing an' drinkin' beer till all hours – an' niver a drunk man in sight! You don't see that in Sauchiehall Street.

It doesn't matter what the people back home say. These Germans are no' as bad as they're made out to be. Bit worrying, though, all the uniforms you see everywhere. You don't see as many back home, do you? Men in uniform everywhere, even in the concert halls. Remember the night the whole audience joined in singing all those songs that sounded like hymns or marching songs. Naw, that was worrying, an' even the youngsters were out there drilling wi' toy helmets an' swords on the day of the Emperor's parade. All the music sounds like in a parade, that's what's the matter wi it! Remember the time in the cafe they started to play 'God Save the Queen' in honour of us, an' that soldier in thae funny glasses marched up an' down in that daft marchin' style till they stopped the music.

Reminds you of that article in the Evening Times *the week before you left. Something aboot the German Minister for War telling the Reichstag that he had told the Emperor all the units in the army were ready for war. There was that major from Perthshire, the one that said German spies were in British cities stealin' secrets. It sounded like newspaper talk back then, but now . . . Naw, it's hard to believe there'll be a war; these people here are jist too civilised for that. Surely?*

Matter o' fact, when you think of it they were all friendly: the Germans, the Austrians and the Hungarians. The folk in Berlin would like you back next year, they said. They think the Celtic have given the game a rare boost. Wonder if you'll be back in Germany next year? It's good to play against foreigners like that; cheery, good-natured lads, more enthusiasm than skill, mind you, but smashin' fellows. The crowds were great as well; remember the reception after the match against Preussen? A walkover against that bunch, students an' businessmen rather than players but really good-

natured. *Fancy shakin' hands when you bumped intae them! An' they spoke English a treat. Fussball they called it. Funny.*

An' after that match goin' back to the hotel an' passing the tramcars, all crowded, an' the people a' staunin' up an' cheering, wavin' their hats as if you were royalty. Incredible. An' that translator, Werner, I think they called him, when he read out the papers. What was it the Berliner Tageblatt *said? Well, Werner said it stated that the Celtic were the finest team in the world. No' bad at all!*

So it's back to Flushing in the morning. An' three weeks ago you left there by train to Vienna. Twenty-seven hours on a train, a great train but that heat was sheer murder. Thank God Sunny Jim managed to talk the directors intae getting refreshments to cope wi' that heat! Gallons o' Pilsner a' the way across Holland, Germany an' Austria till you arrived in Vienna. You've been well-looked after oan this trip, plenty o' spending money.

It's still hard to believe that you've been tae these places, an' some of your pals have niver been as faur as Edinburgh. After Vienna you went an' travelled a' the way tae Budapest. That was incredible, no' like Scotland at a' – real Catholic countries these places, chapels in every wee village.

'An' that crowd at the first game o' the tour against Ferencvarosi Torna Club – aye, that's what they called themselves. A' those wee boys waitin' for the taxis outside the ground, an' a' rushing to help wi' the hampers. A rare sight when they opened the gate jist a crack to let the hampers in, an' about 40 o' the boys sneaked in carrying the hamper, underneath the hamper, aroon the hamper – an' the officials from Ferencvarosi hitting them wi' fists an' sticks, an' the policeman oan the horse jist about ready to draw his sword. Those wee lads must have been black-an'-blue; still, they can tell their weans that they saw the Celtic. The home team said the gate was only £800, but that's ridiculous when the cheapest price was 1/– an' there had to be at least 25,000 in the park. They must have taken in mair than double whit they declared. Terrible but, mind you, Willie Maley said that a' the Scottish teams used to do jist that. That was where the money came from to pay the players under the table - 'amateurs' they were called then. At least that's no' done nowadays.

The referee that day! The local one that patrolled the touchline *alongside oor player George Jarvis. Imagine having one o' the visiting squad as a linesman!*

Naebody was keen to play Burnley in Budapest. They should have gied us more warning than that; telling you when you arrived in Vienna, imagine. If you have to play the English Cup winners, you should be given more time to get ready. The grumbling stopped, though, when one of the directors revealed it was for charity. The Celtic an' charity, right? You have to play the game. Sometimes it's hard to credit there are poor people oan the Continent as well. The Celtic played that match for charity – and the

41

unemployed. The people here had that bad time after that Balkan War. Remember a' the headlines back home about 'Trouble in the Balkans'?

In Budapest you noticed an awful lot of people walkin' the streets in search of work after trade was hit by that Balkan War. So, the Celtic didn't have much choice – though Willie Maley was miffed that Burnley knew all about the match before they left England. A newspaper put up a Cup for the winners, an' there must have been another 20,000 crowd because it was a church holiday; they said they raised £1,500 for the fund, an' that was the best part.

Patsy said there was nae charity oan that field, specially in the last 15 minutes. You've nae idea how frustrating it can be to play oan a bone-hard pitch in that heat – an' against Englishmen. Near the end naebody was playing football, an' because they a' could speak English the swearing was atrocious. Another penalty – against Sunny Jim when the ba' hit him oan the chest! Diabolical. An' at the end when the referee wanted you to play extra time, but everybody was standin' around in midfield wrangling an' swearing at each other. An' that stupid referee jabbering away at both teams, an' naebody had a clue what he was saying. That was when Peter Johnstone got scunnered, an' had the fight wi' the Burnley player till a' the others broke it up! Naebody sneers at Big Peter an' gets away wi' it!

Remember the way the teams finally left the pitch, shoutin' at each other; it looked like another fight would break out in the pavilion, but the officials managed to sort it out. The last you saw of the Cup was it staunin' oan the track, guarded by policemen with swords, no' drawn mind you, but kept handy. One of the directors said later that the owner of the newspaper didn't want the Cup to leave Budapest until the winners were decided in a replay. Not oan your nelly duff! Ach, well, it'll turn up some time.

Somebody said you have to play in Burnley at the start of next season for it. Wonder if Burnley's as interesting a place as Budapest, or Vienna, or Berlin.

That was some journey across Hungary, the Great Plain they called it. The train was stifling, but nothing compared tae the fields. Men an' women, even weans, a' bundled up against the sun an' the heat, toilin' away. Willie Maley said they were the serfs, workin' for pennies oan the estates of rich people – magnates, he called them – while the owners pamper their racehorses. Some world, isn't it? Imagine. They still have serfs in 1914!

Nae bother in Vienna where the lads thrashed some outfit called WAC Rapide; funny bunch, every time they got a wee nudge they went down as if hit by a ton o' bricks. Still, their supporters cheered the Celtic off the field, an' Patsy got a hat-trick. One o' the newspapers there went on and on about the Scotch 'Meisters' – for five whole columns, the translator said. Just like the folk in Budapest an' Berlin, they want you back next summer.

'Meisters', eh? Sounds no' bad at a'. An' that's what the Scottish papers

were saying after you beat the Hibs in the Scottish Cup. Let's think – that was only a few weeks ago, but it seems like ages . . .

Ah, well, a great experience . . . but it's time for a wee sleep.

* * *

Celtic FC 1913/14. Back row left to right: W. Maley (manager), McMaster, Dodds, Shaw, McNair, Johnstone, McColl, Quinn (trainer). Front row: McAtee, Gallacher, Young, McMenemy, Browning.

Those newspapers could have been right. At the end of the 1913/14 season Celtic, on the brink of the double, were regarded as the best-balanced and most consistent team in Scotland, and probably in Britain. One could argue justifiably that, because the United Kingdom was the historical leader in football, Celtic could claim to be considered the greatest club side in the world.

Before asserting the claim to global supremacy Celtic had to determine who was best in Glasgow, an often more difficult task and one impossible to substantiate with unanimous approval. Most observers agreed that Celtic had made a special effort throughout the League programme in 1913/14 to prevent Rangers from winning the championship – an honour that would have meant the fourth successive title for Ibrox. Worse, it would have given the club's greatest rivals considerable momentum in their bid to match Celtic's most cherished record – the run of six successive championships won between 1905 and 1910.

Celtic, however, made a discouragingly shaky start in which two defeats were sustained within the first six matches. Much of the early difficulty was being caused by the semi-retirement of the legendary Jimmy Quinn, now slowing down because of age and hampered by cumulative injuries directly attributable to his headlong style of play. Willie Maley, the manager, was forced to experiment with several players in the early months of the campaign; he tried out first-season juniors, he moved more experienced

---

THE BEST OF ENEMIES?
Sir John Ure Primrose, Bart., former Lord Provost of Glasgow and the current chairman of Rangers, '. . . presented a handsome case of pipes to James Quinn, Celtic's world-famous centre forward, as a souvenir of memorable goal-scoring feats, especially against Rangers. Quinn, an inveterate smoker, will doubtless derive much solace from Sir John's appropriate gift.'
(*Glasgow Observer:* 18 April 1914)

---

players into Quinn's position, but was unable to find the proper blend. He watched ruefully as Quinn made one of his rare appearances at Greenock to score two goals in a 4–0 win over Morton.

The one Celtic tradition that was preserved throughout the season was success, and it was based on a remarkable consistency. To ensure this primary purpose some changes evolved in the playing style of the team. The key factor was the role chosen by Patsy Gallacher, an incredible dribbler and considered by many as the greatest forward in the entire history of the club. Gallacher, a leader on and off the field, realised that subtle changes were required now that circumstances had altered; he made the decision that he would have to help out in defence not just when necessary but as a matter of conscious policy. Willing to subordinate his prominence and crowd-pleasing skills in the interests of teamwork, Gallacher assumed the responsibilities and job-description of a modern midfield player.

It was a most pragmatic Celtic side. The cornerstone of their success was a superb defence – so drilled, competent and organised that it gave up a miserly 14 goals in a 38-game schedule. Not surprisingly that constituted the best record in Scottish football; from 11 October 1913 to 28 February 1914 Celtic gave up only one goal in a run of 20 matches. In fact, only seven goals were conceded in the last 32 games of the campaign, and the only defeat in that sequence came at Falkirk, where Celtic played without the regular full-back combination of Alec McNair and Joe Dodds, and the left-wing partnership of Jimmy McMenemy and John Browning. McNair was sidelined through injury, and the others were playing for Scotland against Wales at Celtic Park in a 0–0 draw.

Throughout every aspect of the running of the club, organisation manifested itself. In June 1913 Lord Kinnaird, the widely respected President of the FA, described Celtic as one of the two best-managed clubs in Britain; the other he had in mind was Aston Villa. An article in the 17 May 1917 issue of *The Bulletin* was even more emphatic, labelling Celtic as 'the most consistently successful and best-managed professional club the world has ever known'.

Certainly the contemporary press was prone to hold the Parkhead club up

---

A GUID NEW YEAR

On Hogmanay 1913 a large crowd gathered at Glasgow Cross to hear the old year being rung out and the new one rung in by a carillon of bells in the Tolbooth Tower. At the stroke of midnight there was a huge cheer and there was much hand-shaking among the spectators before they went their separate ways to first-foot their friends, to the sound of factory hooters and the sirens of Clyde shipping heralding the advent of 1914. One newspaper commenting on the scene remarked that:

> The continued prosperity in trade has brought with it more spending money and banished almost entirely the depression which over-shadowed the occasion a few years ago. The city never bore a more festive appearance . . .

Celtic hanselled the festivities by defeating Rangers 4–0 at Parkhead in the now traditional Ne'erday fixture, watched by a crowd estimated at 75,000. The scorers were Young, McMenemy, and Browning (2).

---

as a model for the rest. Using the gathering in the pavilion held to celebrate the winning of the Scottish Cup and the League Championship as his starting point, a columnist in the *Scottish Weekly Record* commented: 'It is by the way they come into close touch with their players that the Celtic directors have had so much success.' (25 April 1914)

Rangers' reputation suffered in comparison, most frequently in the columns of the *Glasgow Observer,* whose sports page was very much the *Celtic View* of its day. The paper's correspondent, never one to resist temptation, was given the opportunity to gloat when he examined the contrasting balance-sheets of the Glasgow giants in June 1914. The figures revealed that Celtic had a roster of 16 players and Rangers 25, that Celtic's wages had come to £5,802 and Rangers' had amounted to £5,387. The partisan columnist explained that the Celtic directors did not believe in tagging a player as a reserve and treating him accordingly. He argued 'better to have 16 first-class players at £6 a week than 25 moderates averaging half that sum'. He volunteered another observation: 'The result is that the well-paid Celtic player is always anxious to do his best for the club, that jealousy is a thing unknown, and harmony on and off the field a feature . . . When players get to know that in the eyes of their directors they are all equal, that the youngest recruit is as much appreciated as the oldest veteran, and that there are no stars with extravagant salaries, nothing but good feeling is engendered . . . Contrast this with the strife that has been one of the causes of Rangers' failure last season, and the grumbling of a certain section because others were favoured or were thought to be . . . two rival camps were set up at Ibrox last season, home-Scots and Anglo-Scots.'

In this way the newspaper – and the club – were able to deflect any possible criticism about the club's not fielding a reserve side, an economic move of dubious value in the long run.

Without a doubt much of the credit was due to the practical, working relationship that had been evolving between the manager and his directors. In 1914 Willie Maley was in his mid-40s, arguably at an equilibrium between mental and physical powers, and thus at his best in the role determined for the manager of those days. At training, he could rely on the presence and practical help of two directors, James Kelly and Michael Dunbar, who had played for the club and remained eager to help the younger players with the benefit of their experience; the other directors concentrated on the more mundane aspects of running a football club – the finances and business end of the organisation. The working relationship among players, manager and directors was a harmonious one, and apparently unique in professional football.

Maley operated on a deceptively simple philosophy – his conviction that, by selecting carefully players of talent or potential from Junior ranks and by blending them with experienced men capable and willing to impart on-field coaching, Celtic could only benefit from a continuity of playing strength and the nurturing of loyalty. Maley's greatest asset in realising his aims was that he embodied the Celtic tradition. Physically imposing, he remained fit enough to impress his players, and his efforts on Celtic's behalf were tireless. A member of Celtic's first-ever side, he retained an aura of past glory and, although by 1914 an institution at Parkhead, he was not too removed from the players by age. The delicate task of 'managing' a squad, maintaining control and achieving results while adjusting to the needs imposed by Quinn's absence he accomplished with characteristic assurance. In general, he had earned the respect of the players, as well as the confidence of the directors, who awarded him an honorarium of 300 guineas to mark his silver anniversary with the club in 1913. However, he could be authoritarian and David McLean, a forward at the club between 1907 and 1909, insisted (much later) that Maley was a tyrant who imposed his will so forcefully that established players such as Jim Young, the team's captain, and even Alec McNair were apprehensive upon leaving the field after a defeat.

It was not surprising that Celtic had compiled the best record in Scottish football; by contrast Hibernian's history was less distinguished. Both clubs had reflected the Irish and Catholic contribution to Scottish sport. Hibernian had been formed in Edinburgh to represent the capital's Irish community, and its first 'manager' and greatest influence was Canon Edward Hannan; Celtic, with Brother Walfrid to the fore, performed the same service in Glasgow.

Ironically, the first impetus to forming Celtic as a football club lay in

Hibernian's success in winning the Scottish Cup in 1887, after which they were fêted in St Mary's Hall in Glasgow by the Catholic community, and later welcomed back to Edinburgh in another church hall with a banner that read 'God Save Ireland. Hurrah for the green jerseys'. The start of another 'Catholic club' later that year, although based in the West of Scotland, marked the death knell for the 'first' Hibernian, who were, if anything, more Catholic than Celtic. The new club, whose name 'Celtic' was chosen in preference to 'Hibernian', were in a financial position to offer better wages to the best 'amateurs' on Hibernian's books; consequently, six members of the Hibs squad moved to Glasgow to join the new club, and four of them had played in the cup-winning side – Gallacher, Groves, McKeown and McLaren.

This piracy ensured that any future Hibernian-Celtic matches would be played in an atmosphere of anger and tension: a lingering resentment permeated the Edinburgh club, and Celtic's visit to Easter Road in October 1888 had to be curtailed when local fans rioted and halted the game by invading the field. The defection of so many star players to the west led eventually to the disbanding of the club in 1891; fortunately, it was re-formed a year later, and re-entered Scottish football, soon shedding its overwhelmingly Catholic orientation.

During the week of the 1914 Scottish Cup final – or more than a quarter of a century after the original squabbles – the *Edinburgh Evening News'* preview of 'Scotland's "Irish" final' carried a sting in the tail when reminding its readers of the earlier disputes: 'They [Celtic] began by helping themselves to the greater part of a team. The old "Hibs" were the victims. The Celtic laid their foundations on the wreck of the Easter Road club and, when the final smash came, they took over that bright and shining light in the forward play of his day, Sandy McMahon . . . Other times, other manners; the Celtic nowadays raise their own players.'

Hibernian's record was a highly respectable one. They had reached the Cup final two other times: in 1896 when they lost 1–3 to Hearts in the only final played in Edinburgh, at Logie Green, and in 1902 they had upset Celtic 1–0 in a match played at Celtic Park because the original venue, Ibrox, had been the scene of a disaster at the Scotland-England fixture earlier in the month. And, on one occasion they had managed to win the League championship, in 1902/03 when they sustained only one defeat in a 22-match schedule.

Throughout the 1913/14 season, however, the difference in class was apparent. Celtic would lift the League title in impressive fashion, helped by winning 2–0 at Ibrox in October and by a splendid 4–0 victory over Rangers at Parkhead on New Year's Day; Hibernian were entrenched in the lower half of the table, but a recent meritorious draw by them at Ibrox had brought Celtic one step nearer the flag. Celtic's march to the final was steady, the team shrugging off the luck of the draw that saw every tie played on opponents' grounds. The only side to give Celtic trouble was Clyde, who salvaged a 0–0 draw at Shawfield before yielding 2–0 at Parkhead. On the other hand, Hibernian had struggled through against Morton in a replay, but eliminated Rangers 2–1 at Easter Road in the next round. Further hard-won victories, both by 3–1 scores, over Queen's Park and St Mirren earned them their place in the final.

Hibernian's hopes rested on the shaky premise that it was a Scottish Cup tie – a traditional place for a reversal of form, for an upset. Certainly, they had the credentials for a cup-team: a settled lineup, a resolute defence, and a physical approach, a side described by one critic as 'a hardy lot of bustlers and hustlers'. However, logic dictated that Celtic would start as favourites, and their defensive record figured as a major factor in the calculations of the punters and bookies – in League play Hibernian had given up more than five times as many goals. As always, eccentrics spoke of the possibility of an upset, but one Celtic follower, resident in the United States, dismissed this form of speculation by quoting 'Teddy' Roosevelt's comment about his presidential opponent in the 1904 election: 'You don't beat a somebody with a nobody. '

Another Edinburgh newspaper, the *Evening Despatch,* conceded on 10 April that Hibernian's task would be a daunting one, admitting that Celtic's consistency would present the major obstacle, and paid the ultimate, if grudging, tribute to the Glasgow club's professionalism: '. . . remarkable knack of muddling through even when they have had the worst of the game.'

SCOTTISH CUP FINAL		*REPLAY*	
11 April 1914		16 April 1914	
Ibrox Park		Ibrox Park	
CELTIC 0	**HIBERNIAN 0**	**CELTIC 4**	**HIBERNIAN 1**
Shaw	Allan	Shaw	Allan
McNair	Girdwood	McNair	Girdwood
Dodds	Templeton	Dodds	Templeton
Young	Kerr	Young	Kerr
Johnstone	Paterson	Johnstone	Paterson
McMaster	Grossert	McMaster	Grossert
McAtee	Wilson	McAtee	Wilson
Gallacher	Fleming	Gallacher	Fleming
Owers	Hendren	McColl	Hendren
McMenemy	Wood	McMenemy	Wood
Browning	Smith	Browning	Smith

Scorers:

McColl (8, 11)   Smith (65)
Browning (40, 60)

Referee: T. Dougray (Barrhead)   T. Dougray (Barrhead)

Attendances: 56,000 (estimated)   40,000 (estimated)

Even before the kick-off Hibernian encountered some difficulties: the brake carrying the Edinburgh party through the congested streets around Ibrox was halted by the police in Copeland Road and refused permission to continue. It took some time for their manager, Dan McMichael, to convince the sceptical police that they were delaying the arrival of Celtic's opponents. Despite the smiles and banter, the reception could not have been reassuring to the outsiders.

Ibrox had won the annual contest for the venue of the Scottish Cup final, and that represented pleasant news for Rangers' treasurer, as the hosts received a lucrative percentage of the 'gate'. In recent years it had become the custom for Celtic-Rangers finals to be held at Hampden Park, and other finals to be held at Ibrox or Parkhead depending upon which Old Firm team, if any, participated. Ibrox Park had been selected for the past three years, with Celtic appearing in two of those finals; Celtic Park was the venue selected for the Falkirk-Raith Rovers clash in 1913.

On this occasion, the Easter weekend, the weather co-operated, and the day was sunny and bright, although windy conditions threatened to make ball control more difficult; a fine crowd, not much short of 60,000, flooded into Ibrox Park prepared to enjoy the occasion, but anticipating a one-sided contest.

ON THE MOVE

'The motor car is now inseparable from shooting and racing, but its power has extended to the "sports of the people",' said *The Scotsman* of 16 April 1914, adding that it had gained ground in an unexpected quarter:

> In order to attend the recent Association International, a large company of football enthusiasts motored all the way from the English Midlands to Glasgow, and others journeyed by special train to Edinburgh, and thereafter drove across country by motor charabanc. This is only symptomatic of a growing tendency among football followers. The day of the old-fashioned brake-club may be said to be drawing to a close, and the dawn of the new era of the 'motor club', with its greatly increased facilities for travelling throughout the country, has already been extensively heralded, and is already quite ushered in the West of Scotland.

To the consternation of most Celtic supporters, the club decided to persevere with the Englishman from London, the quaintly named Ebenezer Owers, at centre forward. The gangling, robust forward was one of seven players tried in that position during the season in attempts to fill the gap left by the redoubtable Jimmy Quinn. The Englishman was experienced, a straightforward, unsubtle player, who managed a respectable nine goals in

First match.

14 League matches. Still, he had been struggling despite the promptings of such inside forwards as Gallacher and McMenemy, and his form against Kilmarnock prior to the final had been so wretched that the propagandist 'Man in the Know' of the *Glasgow Observer* suggested openly that he would be dropped for the final.

Many supporters felt that Celtic had another option. Young Jimmy McColl, signed from St Anthony's, had made a promising debut at outside right against Dundee back in October; Maley, noting his sharpness, switched him to centre shortly afterwards with a degree of success. His champions could point out his seven goals in 17 matches, a creditable output for a first-season player.

In the end it boiled down to a clear-cut choice between a youngster and a veteran, between speed and strength, between the rapier and the claymore. In a Scottish Cup final, and faced with resolute opponents, the manager opted for experience.

In the team selection Willie Maley and his directors erred on the side of safety; on the fiery pitch the players displayed a similar conservatism as they concentrated on defence. That was not such a surprising approach, for the basic strength of both teams resided in their rearguards.

Celtic's defence was the most formidable in the country: Charlie Shaw, bought from Queen's Park Rangers, while smallish and solidly built, was as agile as a cat when called upon; Alec McNair at right back was an 'all-purpose' football player, capable of playing effectively anywhere, and cleared the ball so constructively and calmly that he was nicknamed 'the Icicle', but his partner at left back was the energetic Joe Dodds, a fierce competitor; the half-back line could only be described as 'formidable', noted not so much for creativity as effectiveness with the veteran captain, Jim Young, ungainly, awkward and vigorous, still a potent force, Peter Johnstone at centre half, commanding in the air and uncompromising on the ground, and Jimmy McMaster, consistently under-rated but now fully established in the left-half position.

Alec McNair (left) and Joe Dodds (right) in action during a friendly against Aston Villa at Parkhead.

Man-for-man the Edinburgh defensive complement could not compare with their opponents. However, football is a team game and Hibs' rearguard was competent, well-organised and hard: Neil Girdwood and Bob Templeton were capable, no-nonsense full backs in front of Willie Allan, a steady goalkeeper; Peter Kerr, Matt Paterson and Sandy Grossert formed a solid half-back line. It was a defence capable, on the day, of saving any Cup-tie.

Celtic had additional advantages in the forward line: Patsy Gallacher at inside right was a genius, unpredictable and brilliant but consistently productive either as a scorer or goal-maker, while Jimmy McMenemy was a masterly tactician, adept at redirecting the thrust of attack with one adroit pass. With inside forwards of such calibre Celtic could outwit any defence.

The goal-less final had to be termed a disappointment; it was not a classic since both teams were riddled with tension, and naturally put the emphasis on defence. Celtic were the more constructive side and had the better of the play, retaining the territorial advantage throughout but never fully establishing control; Hibernian, as predicted, fought hard and seemed relieved not to have fallen behind, and the longer the match went without a goal the more they grew in confidence. However, it had become a stalemate; as a sporting spectacle it had the fascination of arm-wrestling or a tug-of-war. Nothing appeared to be happening, but the tension was such that the spectators remained unwilling to look away in case something did occur.

Celtic's main misfortune was that the chances they managed to create fell to the unfortunate Owers; the centre, an honest trier, had another miserable afternoon, contriving to miss three chances throughout the 90 minutes. Awkward at the best of times, but his miseries compounded by poor form, he snatched at the opportunities, sending the ball wide of the posts each time. The *Glasgow Observer* later predicted that 'the supporters would not have the opportunity of seeing the player in a green-and-white jersey again'.

Although pressed back into defence for much of the contest, Hibernian also created chances. In the first half Alec McNair scrambled – if that word could ever be used of McNair – a shot from Wilson off the line with his knee; and very late in the match Smith drew Shaw from his line, managed to round him, but was unable to find the empty net from an awkward angle.

All sorts of excuses could be provided for the disappointing contest: the wind had affected the play, the hard, fast conditions underfoot hampered control, two solid defences had coped with most threats towards their goal . . . but rumours started to circulate that the result had been arranged, with the cynics recalling past scandals in the Cup, allegations that the *Scottish Referee* was quick to denounce.

VOTES FOR WOMEN

One woman, espousing the Suffragette cause in the spring of 1914, claimed that they desired the vote 'for the abolition of sweated labour, whether of man, woman, or child, a living wage for every working man, sufficient to enable the wife to stay at home and look after the children and the women, the suppression of the White Slave Traffic, the regulation of the Drink Traffic, and other social evils from which the poor suffer'.

Celtic's formidable captain, Jim Young, stands guard (on right) as his goalkeeper clears the ball.

The replay was arranged for the following Thursday at the same venue with a 5.45 p.m. kick-off. The extra match involved some shuffling of the League programme: apparently, the schedule had to be completed by 30 April and both clubs had commitments to fulfil in order to catch up on the backlog. Only two days after the first match at Ibrox, Celtic lined up against Queen's Park at Parkhead, and exorcised the frustration of the Saturday with a 5–0 romp. To the delight of the supporters young McColl was chosen as centre forward and he responded to the cheers by scoring twice. Hibernian were due to meet lowly Dumbarton in a League fixture devoid of any importance because relegation (and promotion) had not yet been introduced; accordingly, on the day before the replay, they fielded a side that contained only one regular, the keeper Allan. The other members of the side continued to rest at Gullane in preparation for Celtic. Thus, neither side was at a significant disadvantage for the resumption of hostilities.

The outcome was more predictable in the replay; the law of averages indicates that stronger sides will prevail eventually, and their chances increase with the opportunity to play. That was the case on the Thursday. The fact that Hibernian chose to field the same team indicated the limits of their strength; Celtic could make changes and improve the odds in their favour. The only change made in both line ups was the replacement of Owers by McColl, but it made a considerable difference.

McColl, in his first year as a senior player, had made a good impression – and was being considered a 'lucky' player. Very shortly after signing for Celtic he was loaned to Peebles Rovers for a local cup final against Gala Fairydean; in his first senior match, he scored a goal that helped Peebles win the cup, and gained for himself a medal. By the end of that season he had also earned a League medal, a Scottish Cup medal and a Charity Cup medal. He had started off a distinguished career on a high note. For a while he replaced Jimmy McMenemy at inside left, when the veteran was out with a broken collar bone. The reaction of the Celtic fans was mixed – according to the Hibernian match programme for 4 February 1950, when the profile featured McColl, who had been trainer at Easter Road since 1937: ' "Ach, he's far ower wee!" said the Parkhead faithful. Later it was "He's wee, bit game!"And still later, when McMenemy was fit, "They canna leave him oot, or the team'll gaun tae bits!" So, he moved to centre forward, displacing the famous Jimmy Quinn . . .'

Hibs set off briskly in the replay, exerting pressure on a Celtic side which had to cope with being faced by brilliant sunshine, but it was the Parkhead men who struck early, with a quick 'one-two' which all but demoralised their opponents. The account of the first two goals in *The Scotsman* captures the flavour of the sportswriting of the period. First, the eighth minute, after Browning forced a corner kick which he took himself: 'The first point was the outcome of a corner kick by Browning. The ball travelled across the goal mouth. McAtee returned it with his head and McColl tapped the ball into the net far out of Allan's reach, with nobody near to frustrate him or say him nay.' Second, after 11 minutes: 'McColl shot into Allan on the run, and the goalkeeper could only palm the leather out. Then the centre got in between the backs and again beat the custodian with a simple-looking shot which, however, Allan had no chance of saving.' (Actually, this does scant justice to McColl's alertness since, according to at least one other account, he had stumbled after his first effort before quickly recovering to dash in and net the rebound from 'a very awkward position'.)

Creditably, a shaken Hibs side found their bearings again after these hammer blows, but their exertions were to no avail against a rock-like Celtic defence guided by the commanding figure of captain 'Sunny Jim' Young, who could be heard from the press box shouting instructions such as 'Take a man apiece!'. When Hibs' attacks fizzled out, Celtic assumed control and had the better of the exchanges as the interval approached, repeatedly threatening the Edinburgh side's goal with fast, dangerous thrusts. Gallacher and McMenemy were spreading the play with incisive, defence-stretching passes and feeding the stocky speed-merchant on the right, Andy McAtee, a winger with a vicious shot and an excellent crosser of the ball, and on the opposite flank, John Browning, a comedian in the dressing-room but a dangerously direct left winger on the field. It came as no surprise when, five minutes from half-time, the latter gave Girdwood the slip. Although Browning was fouled, the referee allowed the Celt to go on and he 'popped in' the third with a fast, low shot which left Allan helpless. The final was effectively over as a contest, and all that remained in the second half was to conduct the last rites on a stuffy Hibs outfit which had never been in the hunt against Celtic's slick, effective football. Celtic oozed class as they settled down in the second half to give a delightful exhibition of the game's art and crafts. As if to remind their opponents of the hopelessness of their task, this superb Celtic team struck again on the hour, when Browning accepted a pass from his right-wing counterpart McAtee and shot the ball past Allan for the fourth. Hibs gained some consolation for their endeavours when, five minutes later, a bit of slackness crept momentarily into Celtic's play with the game well won, allowing Smith to beat Shaw with a rasping shot which grazed the upright on its way into the net. Celtic dominated until the finish, content merely to await the presentation of the trophy in the Ibrox pavilion.

While everyone at Parkhead basked in the plaudits of the football writers for the manner in which they had totally outclassed – and outgunned – a gallant Hibs team, young Jimmy McColl could take especial pride in a performance which clearly demonstrated that he had 'arrived'. It was both Celtic's good fortune and a credit to their system that with Quinn's impending retirement they had someone to step in and lead the line, one who 'subordinated mere galloping for close passing and neat trapping' and who could finish off the chances that had to come from such combined play. Energetic and tenacious too, McColl would underline his claim to be a worthy successor to the great Quinn by scoring 115 goals in 165 League appearances for Celtic.

At the end of the day – 16 April 1914 – all appeared normal. At Ibrox Park the most consistent and successful team in Scotland had emerged on top again after a momentary hiccup. Everything else seemed in order too: the Tsar still ruled in Russia as in centuries past, the British Empire printed in bold red ink on world maps constituted almost a quarter of the globe, the Labour Party – founded in 1900 – was working peacefully for controlled change in the fabric of society, the public was queuing up to see the marvels of motion pictures. But, in Europe events were unfolding with a tragic inevitability, and on 28 June 1914 the assassination of a fairly minor royal couple, the Archduke Ferdinand and his wife, at Sarajevo in the Balkans would change the world. It became the pretext for war . . .

Forty years on . . . Willie Maley doffs his hat as he steps off the Celtic Park turf for the last time, flanked by his players (left to right: Jimmy McMenemy, Willie Loney and Joe Dodds). Before the Maley Testimonial match, August 1953, Celtic v Bohemians select.

POSTSCRIPT

During the so-called Christmas Truce of 1914, when British and German troops fraternised briefly in 'No Man's Land' on the Western Front, an

---

GET STUCK IN!

Remarking that at least half of the 20,000 who attended the St Mirren versus Celtic League fixture were eligible for military service, the *Scottish Referee* of 31 August 1914 argued that 'to stand idly by at the present crisis is almost criminal . . . Football is a mere side issue when the glorious British Empire is at stake.'

The sport was coming under pressure, particularly in the press, to abandon its competitions in the national emergency, not least because its thousands of fit young men seemed ideal fighting material. This pressure was largely resisted, though the players clearly felt obliged to underline their patriotism.

On his return from London, where he represented the Scottish League against the Southern League, Jimmy McMenemy was clearly moved by the pitiful sight of the Belgian refugees there – described as 'all huddled together at the stations, old men and women and children, with that strung look which their terrible experiences have brought them'. McMenemy told the *Weekly News*: 'Vengeance is mine [I will repay, saith the Lord], but I hope Kaiser Wilhelm gets his reward on this earth, and that when he does it is a good old British bayonet that gives him it.' (17 October 1914)

---

officer of a Highland regiment engaged in conversation with a German sergeant. The German deplored the 'spoiling effect' that the war was having on his favourite sport of football, adding that he had been a member of the Leipzig side that beat Celtic earlier that year. Probably as a result of a language misunderstanding on the part of the British officer, the game was cited as having been played in Scotland.

Celtic had enjoyed a better tour in the same part of the Continent than Tottenham Hotspur; the English side won a rough encounter with Pforzheim in May 1914 but were assaulted at the whistle by opponents and spectators. Their goalkeeper had his head cut by an umbrella wielded as a weapon, another outfield player was struck by stones – and their chairman, after being stoned by fans, was chased and robbed of £15 (a considerable sum in those days).

Celtic's popularity in Central Europe can be gauged by the contents of a letter sent home to Castle Douglas by a Private Kelly, who celebrated Celtic's winning of the 1915 Championship by holding an impromptu concert in the dug-out with his pals near the German lines; they used biscuit-tins and mouth organs for musical accompaniment. He wrote home: '. . . only 90 yards from the German trenches, and they started to shout over to us in good English "Good old Jimmy Quinn".'

On a more sombre note, that stalwart Celtic player, Peter Johnstone, who had been a member of the 1914 tour, was killed in action during the severe fighting in mid-1917 on the Arras section of the Western Front.

Footnotes
1 Celtic's captain, the redoubtable Jim Young, was always known as 'Sunny Jim' –
to the bemusement of opponents. The nickname originated in the ads for Force
breakfast cereal in 1903 featuring an energy-filled character. One sample jingle ran
as follows:

>*'Vigor, Vim, Perfect Trim –*
>*Force made him – Sunny Jim.'*

Tragically, Young died in a motor-cycle accident in 1922, aged 40.
2 In 1986 Peter Byrne, a member of the Ottawa (Canada) Celtic Supporters Club
was re-reading a Celtic history, and came across the reference to Ferencvarosi
Torna. He checked with a friend, Steve Bedok, who had fled Hungary in 1956 after
the uprising against the Soviets. He found that the modern club, Ferencvaros, were
the same organisation, founded in 1895, and favoured the original Celtic strip of
green-and-white stripes (rather than hoops), and like Celtic were sometimes referred
to as 'the people's team'.

Peter Byrne composed a letter to Budapest, suggesting that it might be an
appropriate gesture if Ferencvaros could find the original trophy and present it to
Celtic in their official centenary year. Steve Bedok translated the letter into
Hungarian, and volunteered to deliver it personally in April 1987 when he would be
visiting Hungary for the first time since 1956.

Ferencvaros were intrigued by the approach, and checked their records; it was
agreed that the trophy had been raffled in order to raise money for the Red Cross in
the early days of World War One, but the turmoil of two world wars and the passage
of 73 years had obliterated the trail. The Hungarian club were pleased to accept the
suggestion of the Celtic supporter, resident in Canada, that they offer Celtic a
modern equivalent of the original cup in belated recognition for the drawn match in
Budapest – and the replay at Burnley in September, won 2–1 by Celtic.

At the end of season 1987/88, shortly after Celtic had gained a memorable
double with a dramatic victory over Dundee United at Hampden, Zoltan Magyar, the
chairman of Ferencvaros, presented his Celtic counterpart, Jack McGinn, with a
specially commissioned 'trophy'. The delicately wrought, glazed-china vase now
has an honoured place at Parkhead among the many trophies held by the club –
thanks to the efforts of one supporter.

4

RIOT!

THE PARADISE

There's a football combination the finest in the land,
To see them play on Saturday – why boys, it's simply grand.
Their play is quite the neatest, their goals are just the same,
They wear the dear old green-and-white,
And Celtic is their name.

Charlie Shaw's the goalie, a good 'un you can bet –
Never lost a goal unless the ball went in the net,
There's no swank about The Tank, McStay,
Our famed big Willie;
Of all the backs that play the game,
There's none like Hughie Hilley.

Hail Cassidy and Cringan! Hail Gilchrist and McFarlane!
Pat Connolly and Murphy, and McNair the brake-clubs' darlin'!
There's dainty young McLean. Oh! the halves and backs I pity;
He'll get his national honours yet, and the freedom of the city.

Other stars heard of our Patsy and came to see him playin';
Jack Dempsey simply roared and laughed, Geo. Robey did the same.
Harry Lauder spent a saxpence, De Valera took a fit,
His dodges and antics on the ball are simply IT.

A forward line invincible, defence that's grim and fearless,
A team with every honour won, a record that is peerless,
Our reputation has foundation on football clean and clever,
For teams may come and teams may go, but Celts go on for ever!

A lay, or song, by 'J. R.' of Sister Street, Mile End, adjacent to Celtic Park.
(Printed in *The Glasgow Star and Examiner* of 9 December 1922)

FROM ITS founding in 1887 – and its first appearance on a field in 1888 – the Celtic Football Club held an ambivalent position in Scottish sport. Many Scots recognised the skill, flair and fervour of Celtic sides, but continued to withhold total acceptance because of their widely held belief that Celtic were still more Irish than Scottish.

Celtic, through continued success on the field, had become a potent symbol for the large Irish Catholic community in Scotland, although the tenuous links with Ireland and Irish politics were becoming more frayed with each passing decade. Events in Ireland, however, kept intruding and represented the major stumbling-block to assimilation with the rest of Scotland. It seemed that the issue of Irish Home Rule might be resolved finally in September 1914 with an Act passed at Westminster; but the outbreak of war a month earlier delayed the implementation indefinitely. The Irish in Scotland felt overwhelmingly that the way to ensure self-determination for Ireland was through participation in Britain's war effort. The enthusiasm of the *Glasgow Observer* for the war was boundless in the early stages, a policy justified by the editor, Charles Diamond, in these terms: 'Since the acceptance of the Irish people at large of the Home Rule Bill, the vast mass of Irishmen everywhere are, and will hold themselves, loyal to the Empire with which they have concluded an act of partnership.' (29 April 1916)

The Easter Rebellion of 1916 changed everything. The uprising was short-lived, and unsuccessful; but, by executing most of the leaders, Britain elevated them to the status of martyrs, and ensured that the struggle would be prolonged. In Scotland the leaders of the Irish community were dismayed at the violent turn of events; the *Glasgow Observer*, within a week of the Rising, endorsed the feeling, describing the rebels in Dublin as 'impracticable theorists and dreamers', 'anarchists', and 'misguided instruments of German intrigue'. Bailie McCabe, the senior magistrate for Dundee, felt that the actions of the revolutionaries would be construed as an act of back-stabbing, and might cast doubt on the loyalty and sincerity of the Irish community in Scotland.

The reaction of the native Scot was one of renewed suspicion, and inevitably the thinly-disguised prejudice emerged again. One war-time novel has a Glasgow shop-steward complain: 'Glasgow's stinkin' nowadays with two things, money and Irish . . . I'm not speakin' about Ulster, which is a dour, ill-tempered den, but our folk all the same. But the men that will not do a hand's turn to help the war, and take the chance of our necessities to set up a bawbee rebellion are hateful to Goad and man. We treated them like pet lambs and that's the thanks we get. They're coming over here in thousands to tak the jobs of the lads that are doing their duty.' (John Buchan: *Mr Standfast*, 1919)

The prejudice was not limited to the factories and shipyards; some of the most vitriolic came from distinguished sources. A noted academic,

Professor Andrew Dewar Gibb of Glasgow University, worried about the threat posed to the Scottish identity, ranted:

> . . . in Glasgow, they are fast developing a monopoly of the priest-hood, the pawnshops, and the public houses. They form an appreciable proportion of the population of Scotland, breeding as they do, not merely unchecked but actually encouraged by their own medicine-men. [Warming to the theme that the Irish community was responsible for most criminal activity in Scotland, he asserted:] Wheresoever knives and razors are used, wheresoever sneak thefts and mean pilfering are easy and safe, wheresoever dirty acts of sexual baseness are committed, there you will find the Irishman in Scotland with all but a monopoly of the business.
>
> *(Scotland in Eclipse*: 1930)

In the spring of 1922 the Reverend David Ness, the Most Worshipful Grand Master of the Orange Order of Scotland, still angered at the Government's passing of the Education Act of 1918 – whose provisions allowed for the incorporation of Catholic schools within the state system while retaining their religious identity – thundered of 'a more clamant need than ever for the organisation to stem the tide of Roman Catholicism'. Other opponents of the Act complained bitterly, seeking a rallying-point in the slogan: 'Rome on the rates!'.

Another, and perhaps more pressing, issue was engaging the Government – the maintenance of public order. After the slaughter in the trenches ended in 1918, the statesmen and politicians met at Versailles to redesign a world 'fit for heroes'; they failed miserably in the attempt. Mr Shortt, the Home Secretary, was sufficiently agitated by the spectre of an unemployment level of almost two million to voice his fears at the end of April 1922 for a Britain 'in the midst of a great industrial struggle. Abroad there are the grim signs of internecine strife, and at home of civil war in Ireland . . . since the end of the 18th century in France there has not been so much working for revolution as there is today. We know what the people are who are so working and what they are doing, and I can assure you that, so far as this country is concerned, the secret service was never more efficient than it is today, but it was never more necessary. Working throughout the world everywhere there are revolutionary elements who know that the British Empire is the one great obstacle to their revolutionary desires.'

Certainly, the Government of the day was concerned, unjustifiably as it turned out, about the potential risks that the Irish situation was posing for the west of Scotland. Civil war was brewing in the Free State newly created by the 1921 Treaty; the forces of those who supported the Treaty were lining up against those who opposed it, and the stage was set for the most tragic and long-running of conflicts.

MAY DAY ON GLASGOW GREEN

Glasgow labourists observed May Day with the usual demonstration on the Fleshers Haugh [Glasgow Green] . . . There was no lack of music, numerous brass, pipe and flute bands cheering the demonstrators on their long march, which was accomplished in good order. At the Haugh the processionists formed into a great circle, at intervals in which platforms had been placed and labelled. There were no fewer than fifteen of these included on the programme, beginning with that for Glasgow Trades and Labour Council, and followed by those various trades and co-operative societies, Communist bodies, National Workers' Committee, the Unemployed Workers' Committee, Glasgow and District Socialist Sunday School Union etc.

From these platforms speeches were delivered on a wide range of subjects. One could hear the Versailles Treaty denounced here, the Genoa Conference attacked there, the Bolshevists of Russia praised over there, the Crown and Kirk verbally cast down at another stance, Parliament ridiculed at yet another, or defended as a useful instrument a little further on . . .

(*Glasgow Herald*: 2 May, 1922)

After partition, anti-Treaty forces made attacks on the border to prevent co-operation between Ulster and the Free State, and in Belfast sectarian warfare escalated dramatically with bombs in the streets and murders. The fighting in Belfast produced the only significant outcome of the crisis for Scotland. In June 1922 a thousand homeless and destitute refugees from Belfast were billeted in the Partick, Govan and Calton districts of Glasgow. In fact, the parish hall of St Mary's in Abercromby Street – the hall that witnessed the birth of the Celtic Football Club – was converted into an information bureau, hostel and distribution centre for the unfortunates, men, women, and children, fleeing, in the words of the Catholic press, as 'victims of Orange gunmen and "Special" bullies'.

Daily the refugees off the boat-train or at the Broomielaw were met and directed to the hall, where they met with every assistance possible. At the midday meal hour, the poor of the district were fed alongside the refugees, maintaining a magnificent tradition of charity – and an echo of the Poor Children's Dinner Table, the primary purpose for which Celtic had been founded.

As civil war loomed across the Irish sea, Glasgow managed to find a more acceptable alternative in the football rivalry between Rangers and Celtic, by then firmly entrenched as the standard-bearers of Protestantism and Catholicism. And, as the 1921/22 season drew to a close in April, the bitter rivals were battling for the League Championship as so often before.

The situation was highly intriguing. On the morning of the last Saturday in the campaign the standings were as follows:

	P	W	D	L	F	A	PTS
Celtic	41	27	12	2	82	19	66
Rangers	41	28	9	4	83	26	65

Both Old Firm sides had to play their last match away from home; Rangers were due to face Clyde at Shawfield and Celtic had to travel to Greenock to take on Morton. Rangers, one point behind Celtic, seemed to have the easier task, with Clyde being a middle-of-the-League team; Morton, Celtic's opponents, had a similar League position, but two weeks previously had won the Scottish Cup for the first time by beating Rangers. They would be a side keen to add another Old Firm 'scalp' to their tally, and to live up to their new-found prominence in Scottish football.

Opinions varied about the value of goal-average in determining positions in the League; although nothing had been decided, the feeling was that a play-off match would have to be staged on neutral ground to decide the Championship if the teams ended up tied in points. A fairly recent precedent was the decider, won 2–1 by Celtic over Rangers, at Hampden Park at the end of the 1904/5 season.

Earlier in the 1921/22 campaign Rangers looked to have the title firmly in their grasp, when they opened up a substantial lead over Celtic; but the Parkhead men, by capitalising on an exceptional home record, whittled away at the deficit with grim determination. Celtic went through the League programme undefeated at Parkhead in 21 matches, and gave up only four goals there. The Celtic goal, tended by Charlie Shaw, was considered so inviolable that many supporters referred to it as 'the Holy City'.

JUST DANDY!

Throughout his lengthy tenure as Celtic's manager, Willie Maley had to deal with all sorts of temperaments. John Gilchrist, a stylish half back of the early 1920s and off-field always impeccably turned out, was an independent individual who often proved difficult to control. When the manager, a noted authoritarian, on one occasion thought to reprimand the player, he was himself rebuked in these words: 'Speak to me when you are better dressed!'

Not surprisingly, Gilchrist was transferred to Preston North End after his next breach of discipline; he lasted only one year at Deepdale before leaving in the aftermath of another lapse in discipline.

In the closing phase of the season Rangers were starting to struggle, although they had advanced to the final of the Scottish Cup against Morton, though needing two replays *en route*. Celtic 'enjoyed' the advantage of having been eliminated at home in the third round by Hamilton. By 1 April Celtic had built up a six-point lead, but Rangers had three matches in hand. The Ibrox club faced the prospect of three away games within six days: on the Monday they travelled to Kirkcaldy and beat Raith Rovers 3–0, on the Wednesday they went to Pittodrie and dropped a vital point in a 0–0 draw with Aberdeen, and on the Saturday thrashed Dumbarton 4–0 at Boghead. The victory over Dumbarton was of little consolation, because Rangers now trailed Celtic by one point.

Celtic had settled to an impressive consistency and continued to win the difficult matches. Their gritty, rather than brilliant, performances and victories were described quaintly by one commentator as 'tholing a stiff assize'. The uncontainable talent of Patsy Gallacher was the major factor in a 2–1 win at Tynecastle against a Hearts threatened with relegation: the Edinburgh defenders meted out some uncouth tackling to Celtic's star who, according to the *Glasgow Observer*'s 'Man in the Know', should have earned 'a martyr's crown for the heroic restraint under brazen provocation'. On 15 April Celtic supporters danced with joy as their team defeated a rugged Albion Rovers by 2–0; the celebrations on the terracings were as much due to Rangers' shock defeat in the Scottish Cup final – a result that confirmed the existence of a hoodoo at Ibrox, at least in the Cup.

Two days later Rangers renewed the pressure on Celtic by defeating the doomed Queen's Park at Ibrox in controversial circumstances. Carl Hansen, Rangers' Danish centre, drove a free kick into the roof of the net – a shock to the Hampden men who had been informed by the referee that the kick was to be indirect. On the same night Celtic retained their momentum with a convincing 3–0 win over Partick Thistle at Parkhead. The *Glasgow Observer* again praised Gallacher's contribution, this time of two goals, marvelling at his 'blazing into dazzling radiance, jazzing and capering at will around the mortified Thistle men'. (22 April 1922)

The stage was set for a knife-edge finale.

Greenock has always been a grimly working-class town, with a reputation for rain and drizzle, and its football team, Morton, has always matched its virtues: determination, dourness, whole-hearted effort and a commendable reluctance to accept defeat from a Glasgow side. Recently, Morton had given Greenock its greatest football day by lifting the Scottish Cup, and the locals anticipated the exhilarating prospect of defeating the other member of the Old Firm in another vital match. As Tom Robertson, Morton's historian, expressed it: 'With the triumph at Hampden Park fresh in the minds of the Morton players and supporters, Greenock was going to be a difficult place for even Celtic to avoid defeat.'

FROM BRAKE TO BUS!

John McFadyen, who believed that his Sarsfield Club (in 1968 almost 55 years old) was the oldest Celtic supporters' club in existence, recalled the demise of the brake-clubs in the 1920s:

> Supporters' clubs are a product of the modern society and it is only in the past 20 or so years that they have got really into the swing, with the advent of the modern omnibus and the new affluent society . . . In the World War One era we had the brake-clubs when money and transport were not nearly so plentiful. The supporters travelled in horse-drawn carts, gaily decorated with colours and each having its brake-club banner. Those carts left for the game from all over the city. Between the wars there was a gradual fall away of this type of club. People who wanted to see their team went by train and the clubs as such fell by the wayside – at least nearly all did.
>
> One, at least, continued, however. We have in our possession the 'Sarsfield Brake-Club' banner which was acquired from a skirmish with the Orange Walk in the Gorbals in the First World War period. This banner was repainted and two huge paintings of Celtic favourites imposed on it. With the passing of the years these players were changed; today the banner carries the paintings of Joe Dodds and Stevie Chalmers. We have people in the district [the Gorbals area] who still remember the brake-club leaving Teacher's Pub at the corner of Rutherglen Road and Lawmoor Street, gaily decorated, and being led off by the Sarsfield Flute Band. At times Celtic players returned from the away games on the cart.
>
> (*Celtic View:* 31 July 1968)

Local fervour and enthusiasm were running high, and the thousands of Celtic followers were preparing to travel and add their support. Willie Maley, while aware that Celtic had not lost a fixture at Cappielow since 1909/10, also knew that Celtic's recent record at Greenock – in the past six seasons – consisted of three draws and three wins, each of the latter by a single-goal margin. He arranged for two special trains, apparently at reduced prices, to carry Celtic fans from Glasgow to Cartsdyke, close to the ground, at a return fair of two shillings (10p). Many in Celtic's support would be journeying to Greenock by motor charabanc.

An extra dimension of tension – entirely inappropriate to a football match – was added when the newspapers bore headlines of yet more troubles in Ireland. The *Bulletin*, a national daily newspaper published in Glasgow, reported on the growing turmoil: 'Battle resumed – Regulars and Rebels clash again at Mullingar . . . Awful crimes in Cork . . . Outrages in County Down . . . Turmoil in the Dail.' On the morning of the match the same newspaper carried further reports: 'Dail preparing . . . Grave Irish situation . . . the Army split . . .' The *Greenock Telegraph* reported that five more people had been shot dead in further outrages at Cork, and two days later – in the issue that covered the match – would give graphic accounts of activity on the Derry-Donegal border where 'gangs of IRA mutineers' were holding up motorists coming from Londonderry into the Free State; it described the sabotage of railway tracks, bridges, and roads in Tipperary, and the warnings given to Protestants to leave several districts in the Free State, now clearly on the brink of civil war.

On the sporting scene the authorities were concerned with sporadic outbreaks of football hooliganism in the west of Scotland; unfortunately violence and football have gone together for a long time – decades before 'Casuals'. No place had a more fearsome reputation than Greenock in a region described as 'a hard place that bred hard men'. Back in April 1899 the Morton-Port Glasgow fixture had degenerated into a full-scale riot, according to the official police report, when about 1,200 'of the roughest class of shipyard workers from Port Glasgow, many of them in a drunken condition' fought a running battle with police who sustained 32 casualties in the affray. Football seemed of secondary interest, as the Port Glasgow followers stayed outside the ground to drink in a field adjacent to Cappielow Park and placed bets on the outcome of the match. A second goal for Morton ruined too many wagers, and the crowd outside stormed over a fence and attacked the police. In the mêlée any lingering interest in football was forgotten, as two mounted police galloped towards the invaders, lashing out with riding crops, while reinforcements were being called; in retaliation, the mob tore down the fencing and used the wooden stakes as weapons against the police. In the aftermath a Port Glasgow bailie blamed the police for the trouble, and the Morton directors said that the fixture would be terminated unless Port Glasgow fans were banned from attending it.

The brake-clubs in their lighter moments: Daily Record & Mail, *2 April 1923.*

Only a fortnight before the Morton-Celtic League decider, four youths from Renfrew were sent to prison – three sentenced to 30 days and one to 60 days, all with hard labour – after being found guilty of stoning a special train carrying the team, officials, and supporters of the visiting Rutherglen Glencairn after a Junior Cup-tie, a hooligan act which caused several injuries in addition to smashed windows. The sentences would have gratified many modern football administrators.

In another part of Renfrewshire – Paisley – a section of St Mirren's ground, Love Street, was called 'Cairters' Corner', a spot where local carters gathered on match days; it was described by the club's historian, Willie Hunter, as 'the most noisome stretch of terracing in Scotland, perhaps the world'.

The followers of the two Glasgow rivals, Rangers and Celtic, did not escape censure and suspicion. The main worry derived from the threat to public safety posed by the brake-clubs in the early 1920s. Rangers' brakes, returning from a defeat at Falkirk, were involved in violent scenes in a mining district after stones were hurled at a vehicle, and one newspaper account mentions that the members of the brake-club had armed themselves with 'heavy iron bars, swords, and bayonets'. The Kent Star brake-club, leaving Calton for a Celtic match at Hampden Park, was surrounded by police in London Road and the occupants detained in the Central Police Station while they were searched (in vain) for revolvers; the police had acted on an anonymous tip that such weapons were being carried.

The Chief Constable of Glasgow was approached by the city's magistrates to look into 'the serious results of disturbances caused by a section of football brake-clubs'. The police exasperation at the situation was shown in his intimation that admission to grounds would be refused to anybody carrying bugles, flags or rattles, and that plain-clothes officers would be posted among spectators with the authority to arrest anybody violating the regulations.

A BEEHIVE OF ACTIVITY!

In the 1920s, and for a few decades thereafter, the close (the shared entry for the inhabitants of a Glasgow tenement) was also a thoroughfare for delivery and other traffic:

> Postmen brought letters that all the neighbours knew about, even before they fell through the right letter-box. Messenger-boys puffed up the stairs with great baskets of groceries on their heads, carrying dawds of butter spaded-out from big slabs behind shop counters, steeping-peas for soup, sugar and soaps and sodas, Belfast ham, home sausage and mouse-trap cheese. Tinkers came, selling clothes-pegs and looking for 'pieces' for the peely-wally offspring wrapped in their shawls. Milk-boys clattered and whistled, up and down, carrying maybe a dozen long-handled milk-cans over each arm. In hoity-toity closes even newspapers were delivered.
>
> (Anna Blair: *Tea at Miss Cranston's*, 1985)

And so Celtic set off for Greenock for a football match that would decide the championship but, as so often happens, it was more than a game. All the ingredients for trouble were present: a history of hooliganism in the area, a festering hostility between the followers of the clubs, an outbreak of hostilities in Ireland. Celtic's Irish and Catholic supporters would be resented by Morton's, drawn primarily from the shipyards, overwhelmingly Scottish and Protestant.

SCOTTISH LEAGUE CHAMPIONSHIP
29 April 1922
Cappielow Park, Greenock

MORTON 1	**CELTIC 1**
Morton	*Celtic*
Edwards	Shaw
McIntyre	McNair
R. Brown	Dodds
Gourlay	Gilchrist
Wright	Cringan
McGregor	McStay
McNab	McAtee
McKay	Gallacher
French	Cassidy
A. Brown	McFarlane
McMinn	McLean

Scorers:
A. Brown (35)   McAtee (82)
Referee: P. Craigmyle (Aberdeen)

Attendance: 23,500 (a ground record)

The atmosphere in Greenock was fraught with tension. The home fans thronged to Cappielow in their thousands, boosted by that success in the Cup and hoping to see Willie Cringan – Celtic's captain and a spectator at the final – eat his words. Unwisely, the Celt had expressed the opinion that Morton's success owed more to Rangers' deficiencies than to Morton's virtues. The Celtic legions marched to the ground from charabancs and trains, and some may have noticed that a quasi-nationalistic, quasi-religious dimension had been added, inadvertently or not, by Morton's flying of a brand-new Scottish Standard from the flag pole of the pavilion.

The pre-game ban on flags and banners was ignored by many in the Celtic following, who circumvented the efforts of the police to confiscate the bunting by throwing them over the wall to friends already inside the ground. Many supporters congregated near the flags, more often than not the colours of the infant Irish Free State, although they appeared more sympathetic to the aspirations of the anti-Treaty forces as indicated by their adoption at this period of the young IRA member, Kevin Barry, hanged by the British in 1920. The young rebel, taken up as a lay patron-saint, was frequently eulogised in song from the terracings. Doubtless the same supporters would have subscribed to the lyrics of the rebel song *Soldiers of '22*, one of the many chanted on the Parkhead terracings down the years:

Take it down from the mast, Irish traitors,
The flag we Republicans claim.
It can never belong to Free Staters,
You've brought it nothing but shame.[1]

As the time for the kick-off neared, the Morton supporters were not will-ing to be out-sung, or out-shouted, nor were they prepared to be out-fought if matters came to a boil. Already a few skirmishes had broken out on the West Terracing – known locally as the 'Wee Dublin End'.[2] The emergence of the teams on the pitch ended momentarily the scenes of disorder.

The crowd, still in 1990 the official record for the ground at 23,500, was described as 'a seething, solid, noisy mass'. Many fans, however, had gained admission by forced entry, and hundreds of youngsters had to seek the safety of the track, or the areas behind the goal, to avoid being crushed.

The frenzied atmosphere did not affect Morton adversely in any way, as straight from the opening whistle they took the game to Celtic with refreshing enthusiasm and a surprising degree of skill. Predictably, their defence was solid and hard-tackling, but their young forwards were a revelation. Both inside forwards, McKay and Brown, were only first-season players but they had quickly blossomed. Known by the Morton supporters as 'The Twins', the youngsters remained fresh at the season's end, full of running and dangerous near goal: 'For once the Celts were outdone in nippy forwards. McKay and Brown were full of it. They manoeuvred about, dodged, swerved, and did all the other things that are generally credited to the inimitable Patsy Gallacher . . . ' (*Greenock Telegraph*: 1 May 1922)

Morton's main scoring threat normally was George French, the centre forward; he had missed the Cup final because of injury, but he had recovered to play against Celtic in the League decider. He showed early signs of being in form, and Cringan was soon forced to pay him close attention.

Although the match had started off at a furious pace with keen tackling, it was being played in a sporting manner – on the field. Nobody com-plained, then or later, of any undue animosity among the players.

To the dismay of the vast Celtic support, Morton established control of midfield, where their half backs' incisive tackling and close marking gave the Celtic forwards little time to control the ball. Gallacher, the Celtic

Celtic F.C. 1922/23. Back row (left to right): Ed McGarvey (asst trainer), McNair, W. McStay, C. Shaw, Hugh Hilley, W. Maley (manager), J. McStay, J. McFarlane and W. Quinn (trainer). Front row: A. McAtee, J. Cassidy, A. McLean, W. Cringan, P. Gallacher and P. Connolly.

playmaker, showed a few touches of artistry in early attempts to settle his colleagues, but soon he was forced back into a defensive role. In fact, in the whole first half Celtic had only two efforts at goal: a run by Adam McLean on the left that ended with him being crowded out as he shot, and a typical corkscrew dribble past several opponents by Gallacher that was thwarted by a desperate tackle.

The action was totally in Celtic's half, and all the Parkhead heroes were in defence. Their heroism was quiet, effective and professional rather than flashy. Charlie Shaw, a reassuring figure in goal, calmed down his outer defenders in the penalty area and raced quickly from his goal to clear up any threats to his charge. He was ably supported by the veteran full back, Alec McNair, in a situation tailor-made for him. McNair was the epitome of coolness, allowing nothing to disturb him. The uproar of the crowd on the terracing or their proximity on the track, the speed of his opponents, the realisation that a championship was at stake . . . he continued to play his normal game, totally alert , utterly competent.

However, Morton's pressure deserved a reward, and ten minutes from the interval the home side scored: a combined attack appeared to have broken down, but the ball found Alf Brown in a ruck of players in the goalmouth and he shot past an unsighted Shaw to give Morton the lead.

REFEREES!

Fifty years after travelling with Celtic to Prague in 1922 as a raw recruit from St Anthony's Juniors, Hugh Hilley recalled the event:

> The two Prague teams, Slavia and Sparta, had a rivalry every bit as keen as Celtic and Rangers and, when Sparta beat us 2–1, Slavia were on the spot. They just had to get as good a result against us. It was very hot and it was agreed that the ground on which we were to play should be watered for several days beforehand. It was also settled that the game would be played with our T-type ball rather than the lighter Continental ball, and that the home side would arrange for the studs on our boots to be replaced with cross bars.
>
> When we got to the ground, we found it hadn't been watered, nothing had been done about our boots, and when we produced the T-ball it was replaced by the Continental type. We were holding on to a one-goal lead into the second half, but the Slavia side were getting away with everything short of murder. Eventually, Gilchrist and Willie McStay were sent off for ridiculous reasons, and in the end we lost 3–2. Afterwards we learned that there had been a lot of heavy wagers on the game and that some of the betting men had 'nobbled' the referee at half-time.

Ironically, the coach of the Slavia club was Johnny Madden, the famous ex-Celt.

Cappielow erupted at the goal and thrilled at the prospect of another upset victory, at David beating Goliath again . . .

Even as the players were trooping off the field at half-time, the troubles with the crowd escalated alarmingly.

Behind the goal in the same terracing where the pre-match skirmish had broken out, the crowd suddenly split into two as a large gap appeared; hundreds of spectators fled on to the playing surface to join the boys rushing from the track as the factions confronted each other. Amid the charges and counter-charges flags and banners could be seen as rallying-spots and, after one determined rush by the Morton supporters, several flags were surrendered. Stones and other missiles were hurled in every direction. The situation worsened when another group of Celtic followers invaded the pitch from the other end of the ground, the Sinclair Road terracing, in an attempt to reach and help their out-numbered co-supporters behind the other goal. Confronted by locals, they had to retreat in some confusion.

In the pavilion the decision was made that the reappearance of the teams might help restore order, and both teams, along with the referee, returned to the pitch. The players helped in clearing the field, and in assisting some of the injured to the pavilion for treatment. Eventually, when it was cleared of spectators, flags, bottles and other debris, the football resumed.

Celtic's position was starkly clear – they had to match whatever Rangers were doing at Shawfield. If Rangers gained one point on Celtic, a play-off match would have to be arranged; if Rangers gained two points and Celtic lost, the title would be theirs . . .

What was happening at Shawfield? Rangers were favoured to win, and had dominated the first half, played before a 30,000 crowd that taxed the ground's resources. However, Clyde were holding on grimly, aided by a little luck when Tommy Cairns, Rangers' inside forward, failed to deflect a shot into the net from close range. The news that Celtic were losing at Greenock acted as a shot of adrenaline for Rangers, as they saw the possibility of another title for Ibrox, their third in a row.

At Cappielow the pace did slacken a little in the second half; after the frenzy of the opening period it had to slow down. Celtic came more into the match, aware of all the possibilities in the tense situation. Gallacher, although well marked, was a constant threat but Morton's frequent counter-attacks carried more danger. Alec McNair, never noted for speed, saved Celtic when he overtook French in one breakaway and managed to get the ball clear from the centre forward just as he prepared to shoot.

It was not until midway through the half that Celtic established any form of control over the match; gradually, the Celtic half backs had come to grips with Morton's inside men, but it was late in the struggle before they could add much weight to the attack.

Eire flag at Parkhead (early 1950s).

But, as the minutes started to slip past, Celtic had to call upon every ounce of effort and the struggle was accompanied by noisy encouragement from the terracings. One sustained period of attack gained them several corners in quick succession, but Edwards' goal held out . . . until eight minutes from time. A ball was crossed high into Morton's goalmouth, and it appeared a goalkeeper's ball; Edwards rose for it but fumbled his clearance, and Andy McAtee, hovering nearby, got his head to it.[3] A scrambled goal, an inelegant goal . . . but priceless for Celtic. The relief brought increased confidence to Celtic, who pressed for a late winner, and in the remaining minutes Morton's goal was under siege.

Meanwhile, at Shawfield, Rangers continued to dominate the proceedings – but still had not scored. Six minutes from the end of that game they contrived the best opportunity when Davie Meiklejohn, a powerful, dominating half back, retained possession of the ball until he had a sight of goal; he drove the ball fiercely towards Clyde's net. Nothing could have stopped it, but the luckless Cairns again attempted to make sure and, from under the bar, deflected the ball over.

Minutes later both matches ended: Rangers and Celtic had each obtained one point, and Celtic had won the Championship by the slimmest of margins.

The excitement was not over at Cappielow. As the crowd, emotionally drained with the excitement of the match – described as the best seen in Greenock all season – poured out of the ground, hostilities between the fans broke out again. The Celtic charabancs were drawn up in Port Glasgow Road for the journey back to the city, and the travellers decided to arm themselves to run the anticipated gauntlet. As the vehicles started to move off, stones and bricks were thrown in both directions, resulting in casualties among both sets of supporters, while bystanders (many of them women and children) took refuge in shop doorways; numerous windows were smashed. Those supporters who had travelled by train had to fight their way to Cartsdyke Station to board the special trains; in the skirmishes and brawls Morton supporters gained possession of banners which they later destroyed by burning in the streets. Some violence broke out on the trains, which made some unscheduled stops, and a man, bleeding from a slashed face, was removed from one compartment and transferred to the guard's van at Gilmour Street in Paisley for treatment; on arrival at Glasgow Central Station another man was taken into custody and charged with the assault.[4]

Most newspapers apportioned the blame equally, apart from the *Glasgow Observer*: 'As for the so-called riot, those who know Greenock and have had experience of the local crowd, were not surprised to hear that the Celtic brake-clubmen, being a comparative minority, were attacked by the big battalion of Orange hooligans.' (6 May 1922)

Fittingly, the last word should be given to Morton's official historian: 'Some accounts have suggested that Morton supporters had taken enough over the preceding years, and sick of the confusion caused at Cappielow by the city fans, had organised themselves for a confrontation. Local shipyard workers had been seen to come to Cappielow armed with bags of rivets and other missiles. Whether this was true or only an attempt to romanticise a public disgrace is uncertain.' (Tom Robertson: *Morton 1874–1974*, 1974)

Football, they say, is only a game. . . .

SO WHAT'S NEW?

The 1990s panic about drug-abuse, especially the publicity about cocaine, has been in evidence before:

> This drug, which is working such havoc in all classes of society, in all great cities of Europe and America, is a simple substance, simply prepared, from a vegetable known as the coca plant, which grows particularly in South America . . . Opium produces sleep, cocaine produces exhilaration, the effect being produced very rapidly . . . When the reaction sets in, a cigarette leaves a 'tang', a drink is irritating, the liveliness ebbs, and the nerves become unsteady . . . A drug-fiend will stoop to any meanness, to any criminal act, to obtain the drug and, when under its influence, will not trouble to hide indiscretions but will often openly boast of the strategy used in obtaining it. Cunning, deceit, all the most loathsome characteristics of the lowest types will take possession and then, finally, insanity and death.
>
> (*Greenock Telegraph*: 1 May 1922)

Footnotes

1 The question of the Eire tricolour being flown at Parkhead by the club, and on the terracings by supporters, is a controversial one. From the foundation of the club, Celtic flew the flag of Ireland – a golden harp on a background of green – to honour the country of the founders. In 1921 Celtic substituted the flag of the new state – the tricolour of green, white and orange.

In 1952 the SFA, acting on the assumption that the displaying of the flag contributed to crowd trouble, ordered Celtic to stop flying the flag. Celtic refused, and at the end of months of discussion and argument won their point largely by default, and continued to fly the tricolour.

However, the club has always kept up its efforts to discourage the fans from waving and displaying the same colours, as shown in frequent articles in the official newspaper, the *Celtic View*.

An article in *The Celt* in February 1985 also suggested that not all Celtic supporters are enamoured of the practice. The opening paragraph read as follows:

> Anyone who attended the Rapid Vienna match at Old Trafford or who even saw highlights of the game on TV could not have failed to notice the incredible number of Irish national flags, displayed by Celtic fans. Some were green, white, and orange; some were nearer brown or red than orange; some were defaced with names of clubs and towns, or even the odd slogan or two . . .

It is my opinion that, generally, the use of the Irish national flag by Celtic fans is without regard or respect to the Republic of Ireland. There has probably never been such a gathering of tricolours anywhere in the world at any time as at Old Trafford that evening.'

2 Cappielow's west terracing was nicknamed 'Wee Dublin' because it was adjacent in the 1880s to a number of cottages occupied by a community of Irish families. The name persisted for several decades.

3 Andy McAtee, the Celtic right winger, was noted for his ability to cross the ball perfectly, and for 'shooting of deadly velocity'. Sadly, only three years after his goal secured the Championship for Celtic, he was working in the coalmines and virtually out of football. In 1925 he travelled to America for a brief spell as a player with New Bedford FC who were managed by Charlie Shaw, his former clubmate at Parkhead.

4 On the same day as the riot at Cappielow there was trouble at Love Street. Referee Tom Dougray, an experienced official, was stoned by spectators after he had ordered off two players, and had to be escorted to the pavilion by members of the teams, St Mirren and Partick Thistle.

POLITICS AND SPORT

After being criticised because Celtic visited Germany on the trip to the Continent in 1922, Willie Maley replied as follows:

> We went to Berlin by permission of the ruling football body of Scotland, and any English club can do the same thing. Trading is going on now with Germany, and rightly so if the world is to be rehabilitated. Wherever we went on the Continent we received from the British colony their gratitude to us that we had broken the ice and made possible again the intercourse of pre-war between Germany and ourselves . . . We feel we have done the country a service in going out, and sport is the first thing to break down barriers which diplomacy has been trying for years to do, and the years to come will prove our intentions.
>
> (*Glasgow Observer*: 17 June 1922)

In Cologne, where Celtic were hailed by the British Army of Occupation's newspaper, the *Cologne Post*, as 'the greatest football team in the world', the club donated 100,000 marks for poor relief in the city.

5

SHEER MAGIC!

THE QUESTION

By devious ways where the exile strays,
In many a land afar,
Their fancy flies to the Paradise,
No matter where they are.
The Green and White, like a beacon light,
Upon their path has shone –
The question slips from Celtic lips,
'How did the Bhoys get on?'

Tho' seas divide we think with pride
Of the team we left behind;
We are faithful still, through good and ill
We bear the Celts in mind.
So memory clings in their wanderings
To lighten an exile's load –
The tramp of feet down Janefield Street
Or a vision of London Road.

Far across the surf we can see the turf
That came from the shamrock shore,
The team tripping out, the welcoming shout
We heard in days of yore.
We read with zest of Britain's best
And the mighty deeds they've done;
One thought in view when the mail comes through –
Have the dear old Celtic won?

Poem by J. C.
(*Glasgow Observer*: 23 January 1926)

LATE IN April 1925 Willie Maley, Celtic's manager, was reading his mail with understandable satisfaction; Celtic had won the Scottish Cup yet again, salvaging a disappointing season with a dramatic victory in the final. From all over – Scotland, Ireland and the far outposts of Empire – the congratulatory letters were pouring in. But Maley kept returning to one particular epistle time after time.

After a truly astonishing 5–0 rout of Rangers in the semi-final Maley had arranged for the match-ball to be taken to Rome. The gift had been received, and Maley was rereading the letter of thanks from the Monsignor of the Catholic seminary with pleasure:

> Collegio Scozzese,
> 161 Via Quattro
> Fontane,
> Roma (5)
>
> 14 April 1925
>
> Dear Mr Maley,
> Many hearty thanks for the football which just arrived safe and sound. It will be greatly appreciated by the boys, who are very proud to possess such a relic; it is a great trophy and all the more enhanced by the victory of last Saturday. Well done, Celtic! Congratulations and sincere thanks. May you have another such victory!
>
> Yours very sincerely,
> Wm. R. Clapperton

Was it not surprising, to say the least, that the manager of a Scottish football club would send the ball used in a match to the Eternal City? Even if it were used in a famous victory over its keenest rivals? And was it not surprising that the Monsignor, presumably conscious of the nuances of language, chose to describe the ball as 'a relic'?

Maley would not have found it extraordinary – and nor would most of the supporters of the club. Celtic's heritage as an Irish and Catholic club had been consciously preserved from its founding and, apart from success on the football field, remained its most enduring tradition. A club and an organisation different in kind from all others, it symbolised the hopes and aspirations of a whole community, and it was aware that it did so. This mystical bond – a merging of religious, national and social factors – accounts for the ambience that permeates Celtic Park, affecting directors, players, officials and supporters. It has been there from the start, and more than a hundred years later it remains – transfigured, and modified, but still present.

Brother Walfrid, the man behind the founding of Celtic, saw the club as a worthwhile concern, but chiefly as a means of raising money to help cope with the crippling poverty in Glasgow's East End parishes. At the time of his death in 1915 he must have marvelled at its growth into one of the most famous football clubs in Britain and taken satisfaction in its continuing interest in charity.

Tom Maley, perhaps the most fiery and inspiring of speakers among the early committee-members, was one layman who identified the club's early association with Ireland and Catholicism as the cause of 'Faith and Nationality' – a heady slogan at the best of times. His eloquent words and passionate speeches helped turn support for the club and team into a crusade.

Equally devout, his brother, Willie Maley, hard-headed, pragmatic manager though he was, felt (and expressed his views often in conversation and writing) that Celtic FC was being 'looked over by a guiding hand'. Frequently he made visits to the famous Catholic shrine at Lourdes, sometimes accompanied by some of his players.

Later managers, such as Jock Stein and Billy McNeill, have been aware of the mystique that surrounds the club and often inspires its teams. Stein, once memorably described as 'a Protestant chieftain in a Catholic stronghold', when asked what set Celtic apart from the others, would nod his head sagely and confine his thoughts to the observation that 'Celtic are a very special club', while McNeill, described by one of his players as 'a man with a stake driven through his heart at a Celtic defeat', insists that 'Ours is no ordinary club'.

A MAN'S WORLD

The National Association of Schoolmasters, at a conference held at Nottingham in 1925, pledged financial support 'to any member who suffered through refusing to submit to inspection by women inspectors of the physical training of boys under his charge'. Mr H. D. Cleave of Birmingham moved a resolution declaring that 'manhood is insulted when such requests are made by women inspectors'.

On 25 May 1967, enshrined as the day of the greatest accomplishment in the club's history, while celebrations went on in Lisbon, the chairman, Bob Kelly, brimful with joy, retired early to his hotel room after confiding his lifetime belief in 'a special guiding influence over Celtic Park looking after our club'. Certainly the Celtic supporters who travelled to Portugal were doing more than attending a football match; they were the current upholders of a tradition, taking part in a pilgrimage, as it were.

The relationship between Celtic teams and spectators at Parkhead is a personal one – passionate and committed, so much so that the word 'spectator' is clearly inadequate. 'Supporter' might convey more, and 'follower' would capture another aspect, but neither term is wholly satisfactory. One parish priest in Glasgow suggested jocularly that attendance at Celtic matches might be considered as 'an eighth sacrament'. If, during the early decades of the club's existence, the relationship had a pseudo-religious aspect, support for the club since Lisbon has taken on the appearance of a cult: 'It is well nigh impossible to support Celtic without being fanatical about them. That's the way God planned it. We who have seen the Truth accept it, our children accept it, our wives have to accept it. There is but one Truth under Heaven, and its name is Celtic. All other loves are, ultimately, graven images . . . As any Biblical scholar will tell you, the only reason Celtic are not mentioned in Scripture is because God, in His infinite wisdom, kept the good wine until a hundred years ago.' (Pat McGoldrick: *Irish Times*, 23 April 1988)

As in all militant faiths, following Celtic means distorting reality – the considering of football matters as moral issues, and mere football games as conflicts between Good and Evil. Some supporters insist that 'you don't need four at the back with God on your side'; others claim that referees dress in black 'because they are agents of the devil'. One veteran supporter, whenever a Celtic keeper went for a high ball, used to breathe piously, 'Safe in the arms of Our Lord', and his faith was such that he carried on saying it even with Haffey in goal. Haffey in goal! Not for nothing are Celtic's fans blessed with a sense of humour, for the terracing enthronement of Celtic teams in the 1950s as 'the Pope's Eleven' co-existed with some forward lines being dubbed 'the Five Sorrowful Mysteries'.

No matter what the explanation, one thing is clear. Every Celtic team plays in an atmosphere in which nothing is impossible. Tradition, and the imaginative force of mythology, exert a powerful hold on the minds of the Celtic support and acts as an inspiration on the field. This emotional bond was illustrated most dramatically in the Scottish Cup final of 1985 when Celtic entered the closing stages of the match a goal down to Dundee United, a side noted for sound defence and possession play designed to disrupt the flow of the game. The supporters on the terracing continued to roar in a frenzy, urging on and encouraging the players for an even greater effort; David Hay, the manager, decided on a bold double-substitution – off came the skilful Tommy Burns and Paul McStay, and on came Brian McClair and Pierce O'Leary. Skill and finesse were making way for power and spirit. Other players found new reserves of stamina and determination, most notably Roy Aitken, and in yet another astonishing finale Celtic snatched the cup from Dundee United.

Could that be the secret of Celtic's recurring success in the Scottish Cup? An awareness by players and supporters alike of the club's tradition, an instinctive and spontaneous response by the players on the pitch to the expectations of the supporters on the terracings – but possible only when a unique blend of skill and spirit is present?

In every era Celtic sides have been blessed with performers of skill and artistry, as well as men of spirit and courage. Any list of Scottish players characterised by skill and talent would have to include Sandy McMahon, Patsy Gallacher, Jimmy McMenemy, Malcolm MacDonald, Willie Fernie, Charlie Tully, Jimmy Johnstone, Kenny Dalglish and Paul McStay. Any list of players characterised by spirit and enthusiasm must include Dan Doyle, Jimmy Quinn, Jim Young, Jimmy McGrory, Jimmy Delaney, Bobby Evans, Tommy Burns and Roy Aitken. And it has to be made clear that the men of spirit had talent to spare and the men of skill had courage in abundance.

Against that array of legendary figures every Celtic player is measured, and as a Celtic player he assumes a role in an on-going pageant of football greatness. In becoming a successor to folk heroes, and in performing before fans whose loyalty borders on religious fervour, a Celtic player inherits the legacy of a reputation accumulated through the decades, an expectation of success.

In such a context no Celtic team has ever accepted defeat willingly; when talent and skill meet their match, Celtic teams can call on reserves of inspiration and courage – a surge of adrenaline that has often produced performances and results that transcend probability. It is a myth made tangible.

Therefore, it should have come as no great surprise that in 1987/88, the season designated as the official centenary year, Celtic managed to win 'the double', and in the latter stages gained results with a subtle alchemy of skill and passion which proved irresistible. So many goals were scored in the last minutes of so many matches that one terracing wag was convinced that Brother Walfrid himself was kicking every ball.

A WOMAN'S BURDEN

On arriving home in the spring of 1925 from a thousand-mile caravan journey through Abyssinia, traversing country never previously explored by a white woman, the intrepid Mrs Rosita Forbes revealed she had been attacked twice by brigands on her tortuous expedition. She had also lost one man who died 'through drink', 25 of the mules were worn out, and one man had half a leg bitten away by a crocodile while crossing the Nile. The natives were particularly interested in 'the White Angel' (Mrs Forbes), one warrior asking if she was real flesh and blood, and desiring 'the same kind of soap which would wash him white'. The natives thought the cinema was a new form of religion, according to the explorer, since when the cinema photographer accompanying her took shots of harvesters, some downed tools and bowed their heads while others 'took the camera for a Maxim Gun and threw stones and spears at us'.

---

*　　*　　*

In April 1925, had Dundee been able to read the omens correctly, they need not have bothered turning up for the Cup final at Hampden – for all the signs pointed to Celtic having another date with destiny.

The abiding memory of Jimmy McGrory – heading a goal (against Partick Thistle).

In January nobody could have anticipated that the finalists would be Celtic and Dundee. Both teams were drifting in the League standings, with Celtic in fourth place, a distant 16 points behind Rangers, the eventual champions. Throughout this era Rangers, superbly organised on and off the field, were the dominant team in Scottish football, winning the championship in 1924/25 for the sixth time in eight seasons. The major consolation for Celtic was that the Ibrox club was experiencing difficulty in the Cup in a span that was lengthening year by year to such an extent that people were talking of it as a hoodoo.[1]

In the League Celtic's indifferent form could be explained partly by the absence through injury of Jimmy McGrory and Adam McLean. McGrory, signed from St Roch's and loaned to Clydebank for a season, had established himself as an old-fashioned centre forward in the style of Jimmy Quinn; he was direct in his approach, tireless in chasing every ball, and had the knack of the true opportunist with head and foot. McLean was an unfortunate player, because he was a contemporary of Rangers' Alan Morton; he could dazzle a full back with his wiles, could cross the ball sweetly for the front runners, and was a proven goalscorer. The harmful effect of their absence was compounded by the astonishing and unpalatable fact that Celtic – for economic reasons – did not field a reserve side at the time.

The bookies, ignoring Celtic's tradition in the Cup, looked at current performances and rated them as outsiders behind the favourites Rangers, a highly skilled Airdrie, Hibernian, and even the always unpredictable Partick Thistle.

The turning point in the season for Celtic came with a 7–0 thrashing of Third Lanark at Parkhead in the League; the players were confident when the draw for the Cup sent them to Cathkin two weeks later to play the relegation-bound Thirds. It turned out to be 'no contest' as Celtic played vintage football to win 5–1 and McGrory led the way with three goals.

The dashing McGrory scored the only goal at Ibrox against St Mirren to end a three-match epic with the Paisley side; the first match at Love Street ended 0–0, and an equally hard-fought replay finished 1–1 at Parkhead. The last seconds of the decider were played out in high drama after St Mirren's Gillies was upended on the 18-yard line; the referee, Peter Craigmyle, awarded a free kick inches outside the box despite frenzied and prolonged appeals for a penalty. The outraged St Mirren players refused to take the kick, insisting that a penalty should be awarded, but Craigmyle stood by his decision and ended the impasse by blowing for full-time.

If luck had been with Celtic, it was calculated that a miracle would be required in the semi-final against Rangers who were bidding for a clean sweep of the honours in Scottish football. In the opinion of every writer and follower of the game, Rangers were 'absolute certainties'. For one thing they had handled Celtic with ease in the previous matches that season with a comfortable 1–0 win in the League at Parkhead and a routine 4–1 victory at Ibrox at Ne'erday. Even more humiliating for Celtic was another Rangers 4–1 romp at Parkhead in the Glasgow Cup final, a loss the more difficult to accept because Rangers' captain, Tommy Cairns, with his side leading so easily, called for a halt in the scoring with still 30 minutes left to play.

It is a truism to state that every Old Firm clash is different, and the crowd of 101,714 at the Hampden semi-final witnessed a totally different outcome. Before the match Patsy Gallacher, a law unto himself – a man allowed to train alone in the afternoons at Parkhead, to suit his business interests – decided that a tactics talk with his colleagues would be in order: he felt that Rangers, despite being overwhelming favourites, had to be apprehensive about that Scottish Cup hoodoo; they would become more nervous the longer the match continued without them scoring. Patsy's plan was simple: for the opening 15 minutes of the match, he and Alec Thomson would fall back into defence until Celtic settled, then both would spring the wingers and McGrory loose with long passes. The result was a 5–0 rout for Celtic, McGrory and McLean scoring twice and Thomson adding a fifth.

At the end of an amazing 90 minutes the Celtic supporters were revelling in a victory, still celebrated in a song heard even 30 years later on the Parkhead terracing:

By one, by two, by three, or four or five
We'll beat the Rangers in the Cup
As sure as you're alive . . .
By one, two, three, or four or five.

Patsy Gallacher in action against Airdrie at Celtic Park.

Rangers' broken-hearted followers, in a state of shock, were making bonfires of their flags and banners. The trauma of the result may be gauged by the sentence in John Allan's history of Rangers, *Eleven Great Years: 1923–34*: 'The world heard the news in amazement. Many refused to believe it until confirmed in print.'

Rangers, burdened with pressure, were described by one critic, borrowing a metaphor from World War One, as having been hit, seemingly, by 'a whiff of tear gas'. Celtic, growing in confidence by the minute, had swept forward in speedy attacks. Paddy Connolly, Celtic's right winger, played the game of his life with his runs and dangerous crosses to destroy what he described as 'the greatest eleven I have ever seen wearing Rangers colours'.

CELEBRATIONS

Celtic fans could not resist gloating after the sensational 5–0 defeat of Rangers in the Scottish Cup semi-final. The brake-clubs 'formed a beflagged procession citywards' and their occupants 'raised their chorus-singing by counting the score in a sort of crescendo thus – one, two, three, four, *five!*' while 'the Rangers crowd hid their Orange flags and crept home by obscure byways.

(*Glasgow Observer*: 28 March 1925)

Celtic's opponents in the final, Dundee, after flirting briefly with the spectre of relegation, had run into form at exactly the right time. The defence was solid, rugged and hard-tackling, and a weak forward line was greatly improved by the signing of John Rankine from Doncaster Rovers and a welcome return to form by Dave McLean. Indeed, the Dundee newspapers felt that McLean was a greater goal-scoring threat than young McGrory, and the veteran forward had all the credentials to back the claim.[2]

Now safe in the League, Dundee had been helped repeatedly in the Cup by the luck of the draw in getting home advantage. The highlight of their Cup run was a splendid 3–1 victory at Dens Park over Airdrie – the only team to challenge Rangers seriously for the Championship that season. It had taken two matches to overcome a stuffy Hamilton in the semi-final, but confidence was growing on Tayside that the Cup might be won for the second time.[3]

The obstacle was a Celtic team which, if not generally regarded as being of the highest Parkhead standard, could draw upon a proud history of success in the Cup; playing in Glasgow before their fanatical following, Celtic would be difficult to beat. Gnawing at the confidence of the Dark Blues was the awareness that their only defeat (0–4) in the previous six weeks had come at Parkhead, although the captain, Jock Ross, dismissed that gamely as 'a freak result'.

The Dundee newspapers gave in-depth assessments of the chances of their favourites in the days prior to the Cup final, and it seems clear that Tayside was growing in cautious optimism. Based on statistics, not much could be detected between the teams: Celtic's higher League position could be explained by a better start to the season, but Dundee matched them in current form; Celtic might be conceded an edge in constructive play, but Dundee's more rugged style would counter that. The final, it was concluded, could hang on an intangible: a player on form, a bounce of the ball, a matter of luck . . .

The *Dundee Advertiser* spotted a major threat to Dundee's hopes: 'The great Patsy is a marvellous player, and his dribbling and generalship have won many games for his club. Gallacher, however, suffers, as all football geniuses suffer, by his own super-cleverness, for he is apt to bewilder the man alongside of him by his over-astute moves. Nevertheless, he is the man whom Dundee have to watch.' (9 April 1925) The same newspaper, on the morning of the match, summed up: 'What superiority Celtic possess in football and combination will be greatly counteracted by that whole-hearted zeal which the Dundee men can and must produce today . . . [Dundee] are insatiable as far as work is concerned and in football, as in everything else, honest endeavour is sure of its reward.' (11 April 1925)

SCOTTISH CUP FINAL
11 April 1925
Hampden Park

CELTIC 2	**DUNDEE 1**
Shevlin	Britton
W. McStay	Brown
Hilley	Thomson
Wilson	Ross
J. McStay	W. Rankine
McFarlane	Irving
Connolly	Duncan
Gallacher	McLean
McGrory	Halliday
Thomson	J. Rankine
McLean	Gilmour

Scorers:
Gallacher (74)   McLean (30)
McGrory (87)
Referee: T. Dougray (Bellshill)

Attendance: 75,137

Dundee put on a brave front for the final. Around 6,000 followers travelled to Glasgow for the match; five special trains had been laid on at

The cup-winning side in Ireland, pictured before a match with Belfast Celtic.
Top row: Wilson, J. McStay, Shevlin, W. Maley (manager), Hilley, McFarlane.
Front row: Connolly, McLean, W. McStay, Gallacher, McGrory, Thomson.

Dundee West Station, and an extra train was required, leaving Dundee at 12.20 and arriving at Mount Florida, close to Hampden, 15 minutes before the kick-off. Other supporters travelled by road, and their following was increased by former Dundonians resident in the west of Scotland.

Arriving at Buchanan Street Station the Taysiders had the opportunity to buy rosettes and 'Dark Blue' cockades from the enterprising Glasgow street-sellers; hundreds spent time in strolling around the city centre admiring the sights of Sauchiehall Street and Renfield Street before walking the three miles to Hampden Park. The *Dundee Advertiser* was caught up in the excitement of the occasion, and its reports included the most minute detail: 'Round the Hampden enclosure the police surveillance was even stricter, and mounted police lined up the queues in front of the numerous turnstiles, and kept late-comers from breaking into the line. All rosettes, decorated hats, etc. had to be pocketed before the wearers were allowed to enter the ground, and this rule was strongly enforced. In spite of the precaution, however, many Celtic banners were observed in the dense throng round the area. Inside the ground, corps of stewards directed the newcomers to the least densely packed areas. A giant four-mouthed electrically-driven megaphone placed on top of the grand stand directed the operations in stentorian tones.' (13 April 1925)

Dundee must have been dismayed at the conditions which favoured their smaller, lighter opponents. The sky was overcast and with only a vague threat of rain; not a breath of wind stirred the corner flags, and the weather was sultry and humid. Any physical advantage Dundee might have anticipated was undone by these factors; one newspaper had listed the Dundee men as enjoying an average 'edge' of two inches in height and a stone in weight.

The Dundee side had travelled to Glasgow on one of the earlier trains packed with their fans; but now at Hampden their following was dwarfed among the 75,000 spectators, and their dull, dark-blue colours faded in contrast to the Celtic green-and-white. 'The Dundonians may have been making their presence felt, but it was certainly not seen on the great terracing. Of course, many of the douce folks from Tayside were seated comfortably in the stands; yet, taken all in all, it was a very Glasgow atmosphere.' (*Dundee Sporting Post*: 13 April 1925)

NO PLACE LIKE HAMPDEN

What most impressed the English visitors to Hampden, after the magnificent arena and the excellent organisation shown everywhere, was the orderly nature of the crowds both coming and going. The Circle trains back to the city held a large complement of Sassenachs, who commented on this, and drew comparisons with Wembley in particular. Getting away from the British Empire Exhibition seems to have been a harrowing experience at times.

(*The Bulletin*: 6 April 1925)

Celtic's first raid was filled with danger: Connolly showed a hint of his speed on the right and swept over a dangerous hanging cross for McGrory and Gallacher racing in. Britton decided to punch clear and did so cleanly, as Gallacher immediately behind him went flying into the net. Britton's confident handling of the situation was what Dundee needed, and they settled down to play competently.

To the delight of their followers Dundee took the match to Celtic, but found it difficult to create clear-cut chances. In the first 20 minutes their determined play produced three half-chances but all were scorned. Celtic were faster to the ball but their attempts to mix up the play in order to unsettle Dundee foundered on a cast-iron defence. Gallacher was being marked tightly by Dundee's Irishman, Irving, and could not work loose. However, one flash of Gallacher caused near-panic in Dundee's rearguard; he drew two defenders with him before releasing McLean on the left wing, and the winger turned the defence with a cross to the far post where Connolly's shot hit the side net.

Dundee opened the scoring in 30 minutes: Duncan crossed into Celtic's goal and Shevlin tried to punt clear, but his attempt was partially blocked and reached the lurking John Rankine, who headed for goal past the helpless Shevlin only to see his attempt strike the bar and rebound for McLean to scoop into the net. The Dundee supporters came to life and celebrated noisily; the Celtic following growled in consternation and before the kick-off could be taken were demanding retribution in a growing tumult.

The ten minutes before half-time were desperate ones for Dundee; Celtic, stung into retaliation, swarmed around Britton's goal. In one mêlée Ross bobbed up on the goal-line to clear a header that had beaten his keeper, but Dundee managed to hold on till the interval. Credit had to be given to every member of Dundee's defence, and in particular to Thomson and Brown: 'The Celtic attacks broke over the pair [Thomson and Brown] like a series of waves and, when they came off at half-time with the score unchanged, they must have felt a thrill of pleasure at what they had achieved.' (*Dundee Advertiser*: 13 April 1925)

Once more Dundee's nerve was tested – even before the re-start. Both sides came out within a minute of each other and lined up waiting for the referee, Mr T. Dougray, to appear for the second half.[4]

Before the match, the Dundee party had arrived at Hampden much earlier than Celtic's, and the resultant wait could not have done frayed nerves any good; indeed, some Dundee supporters who accompanied them on the train claimed later that the players had been withdrawn and subdued on the journey to Glasgow, and had smiled only nervously at the good-natured banter tossed their way.

Accumulated pressure can crack even the strongest nerve, and the Celtic supporters added to it by singing lustily on the terracings during the half-time delay. One particular favourite filled the air:

There's a dear little plant that grows in our isle –
'Twas St Patrick himself, sure, that sent it,
And the sun on his labour with pleasure did smile,
And with dew from his eye often wet it.
It thrives thro' the bog, thro' the brake, and the mire-land,
He called it the dear little Shamrock of Ireland.

Gallacher had assumed the responsibility of his greatness, and was clamouring for the ball; Wilson and McFarlane, highly constructive wing halves, were joining in the Celtic attacks; McGrory was chasing every ball, challenging every defender; the wingers, Connolly and McLean, were stretching the Dundee defenders to the limits trying to create a half-chance for McGrory. The noise from the terracing was deafening, and the spectacle of the King's Park terracing packed with Celtic supporters was enough to daunt the most courageous: 'The excitement of the onlookers found vent in one mighty, many-throated roar, deafening, unending, tempestuous as the growl of a wrathful sea.' (*Glasgow Observer*: 18 April 1925) Yet Dundee's defenders were magnificent in their defiance. Britton had become the busiest player on the field, but was fortunate when he scrambled another dangerous cross from Connolly on to the crossbar and managed to flop on the ball in the ensuing scramble. The goalkeeper had emerged from the dressing-room after half-time clutching a 'lucky horseshoe' mascot that he placed carefully in the back of his net; perhaps he was gaining the reward for his foresight.

The role of the goalkeeper was different in the 1920s. He was considered much the same as an outfield player in most respects, and thus was liable to be tackled, challenged, charged and dunted more than at present; the old films showing keepers kicking the ball from hand with indecent haste were not the result of defects in the film – it was self-preservation: ' . . . and time and again [Britton] took the ball in his capable hands and wormed his way clear with a cluster of Celtic forwards hanging on to him. None of the Parkhead raiders were particularly careful in their treatment of the Dundee custodian, and after the game the ex-Albion Rover must have been sore, both mentally and physically.' (*Dundee Advertiser*: 13 April 1925)

One save after 15 minutes of the second half from Adam McLean deserves mention; McLean was a clever winger but he had earned a reputation as a scorer. The Celt thought about crossing but decided to make

Patsy's goal, as seen by 'Fonn' in the Glasgow Observer, *18 April 1925.*

for goal; he shot from an angle, but Britton smothered his fierce shot at the post in spectacular style.

The equaliser came with quarter of an hour left. Celtic, despite Dundee protests, were awarded a free kick just outside the penalty area, and Connolly looked first for McGrory's head. However, in the crowded goalmouth the ball dropped for Gallacher. Celtic's legendary inside forward produced a flash of magic in getting control of the ball and finding a way with it through the scrum. Even the *Dundee Advertiser* marvelled at how 'The "Mighty Atom" wriggled and pushed his way through a litter of friends and foes to stagger into the back of the net with the leather.' Accounts vary as to how Gallacher ended up entangled in the net, but most reports state that his last leap was with the ball between his feet and involved a partial somersault: '[Gallacher] crowned a daring and devious bit of play by throwing himself bodily into the net and carrying the ball with him. It was a positive relief to a great section of the crowd, who were wrought up to an almost painful degree of excitement over the long-continued battle between the Celtic attackers and Dundee's unflinching defenders.' (*Glasgow Herald*: 13 April 1925)

A goal destined to be recalled for decades! A touch of magic to continue the legend of Celtic's invincibility in the Cup! A few decades later, Charlie Tully, a legend in his own right and no mean raconteur, commented wryly on this famous goal: 'According to all the reports I hear from Chairman Bob Kelly and Jimmy McGrory about the number of men Patsy beat, he must have started his run at Melbourne, hopped on a plane to London, jumped a helicopter to Hampden Park, and grabbed a taxi up the left wing to score. That's the only possible way he could have passed all those people!'

PEERLESS PATSY

Patsy Gallacher was widely regarded as the greatest player of the day in Scottish football, an opinion endorsed by an old adversary, Tommy Cairns of Rangers, at Patsy's funeral in June 1953. Asked by somebody just how good Patsy was, his former opponent replied that Gallacher was 'the greatest f***** who ever kicked a ba''.

Gallacher donned a Rangers jersey on 25 April 1922 to play in Andy Cunningham's benefit match against Newcastle United, and helped to swell the crowd to a bumper 20,000. His equaliser in the 1–1 draw appears characteristic:

> Beaten by Mooney, he recovered the ball in his own half, twisted his way past half a dozen opponents, neatly side-stepped the oncoming goalkeeper, and cantered in to place the ball in the net.
>
> (*The Bulletin*: 26 April 1922)

Dundee tried valiantly to stem the tide, but were left only holding on grimly for a replay. A few minutes later Gallacher beat several defenders in a swerving run from the centre-circle, but Britton held his ground and position to save the final shot.

Celtic were not to be denied. With three minutes left, the overworked Dundee defence conceded another free kick, this time on the left; McFarlane sent a high ball dropping into goal and McGrory, eluding his marker for the first time in the match, dived full-length to head low past Britton. It was a spectacular goal – the sort of goal to be associated for ever with Celtic's centre forward – but he never saw it. He landed painfully and, half-stunned, heard only the acclaim of the crowd: 'I never saw that goal to this day – they had no television cameras and action replays in those days – yet it was the greatest of my life. I was only a boy and I had a Scottish Cup medal', he recalled 50 years later.

McGrory was mobbed by his team-mates, while the joy was duplicated on the terracing behind the goal; a memorable sight was that of the youngster shaking his head to clear it, then indulging 'in spontaneous hops and skips' after realising that he had scored what had to be the winning goal.

The goals were memorable and, aptly, characteristic; Gallacher's was the culmination of wizardry, and could not have been scored by any other player in Scotland; McGrory's was the result of bravery in snatching at a half-chance, and could not have been scored by a lesser opportunist. It was McGrory's first Scottish Cup final, and Gallacher's last; if the style of McGrory's header was to become his signature-tune, Gallacher's incredible dribble was his swan-song.

The mantle of greatness – and Celtic's tradition – was passing into younger and stronger hands. On the carriage coming back into the centre of Glasgow through crowds of cheering supporters Celtic's manager recognised the succession by handing the Cup to young McGrory for him to hold and show to the throngs.

The Cup had been presented to Celtic in Queen's Park's library inside the Hampden pavilion by Mr R. Campbell, the Vice-President of the SFA, who paid tribute to the winners' uphill fight and victory. He mentioned that the club had established another football record in winning the Cup for the 11th time, thus surpassing Queen's Park's ten. Tom White, Celtic's chairman, in accepting the trophy, praised Dundee for their 'able and manly opposition', while his Dundee counterpart, Mr Jackson, admitted freely that the better team had won.

That was the general consensus as evidenced by *The Bulletin* match report on the Monday, an account which also suggested that Dundee had the misfortune to contend with forces beyond their control: 'We have to confess an unbounded admiration for a side which played so vigorously, so gallantly, and with so much determination as Celtic did when it appeared as if the fates had ordained that commonplace – but gritty – defensive play was destined to conquer over all the artifice and guile of an attack which was often dismayed, but never disheartened.'

And, after all, defeat was never a word in Patsy's vocabulary . . .

Footnotes
1 The rabidly pro-Celtic columnist 'Man in the Know' could not resist gloating after the Cup final: 'And talking of crowds, I may remark that the 80,000 assemblage at Hampden last Saturday behaved throughout in perfectly orderly and decorous fashion. There was terrific excitement, frenzied enthusiasm, but not a trace of hooliganism. The reason was obvious. The undesirables were elsewhere. That [League] game at Ibrox, regarded as a reprisal for the final going to Hampden, attracted the unwanted element to Govan.'

Commenting on an incident where a Celtic brake-club became involved with Rangers supporters after the match, he added: 'At Tuesday's Sheriff Court some of the brake-club boys were fined for their wickedness in defending themselves when attacked, and their replica of the Scottish Cup, seized by the police, was declared forfeit. What will the authorities do with this imitation trophy? I suggest they give it to the Rangers who haven't seen the original for nearly a quarter of a century.' (*Glasgow Observer*: 18 April 1925)

2 Dave McLean started his senior career with Celtic, and spent some time in England before returning to Scotland with Dundee. He gained one cap while with Sheffield Wednesday, and was a veteran of 35 when he played in the 1925 final. His record of 412 League goals was marginally more than McGrory's 410, but some were scored in lower divisions. He ended up a lengthy career by playing some seasons for Forfar Athletic.

3 Dundee defeated Clyde by 2–1 in a second replay to take the Cup in 1910.

4 It was estimated that the interval lasted only four minutes. Apparently greater flexibility applied in those days; for example, the interval in the 1904 final was prolonged to allow for a collection in aid of victims injured at a grandstand collapse during a recent Perthshire versus Forfarshire cricket match.

6

A DAMNED CLOSE RUN THING

REALIZED YOUR DREAMS

So you never left the small town
With your friends, when things got way down
You stood between the tall trees
Threw all caution to the cool breeze
You stayed home on the island
And you watched the evening sunrise
And you never thought of leaving
Even when the winds blew cold

And I've seen you at the station
With your arms outstretched and waiting
To welcome home the travellers
Who went searchin' after dreams
And they never fail to mention
How your life's been one dimension
And you smile at good intentions
Knowing well they'll never see

All you want or ever needed
You found here without leaving
It's the drifter and the dreamer
Who often fail to see
In the heart that never wanders
Lies a peace that comes with morning
It's knowing when the day is done
You've realized your dreams

Rita MacNeil[1]

A FAMOUS novelist and playwright – and a Yorkshireman – once attempted to capture some of the fascination of football for the working man:

> To say that these men paid their shillings to watch twenty-two hirelings kick a ball is merely to say that a violin is wood and catgut, that *Hamlet* is so much paper and ink. For a shilling the Bruddersford AFC offered you Conflict and Art; it turned you into a critic, happy in your judgement of finer points, ready in a second to estimate the worth of a well-judged pass, a run down the touchline, a lightning shot, a clearance kick by back or goalkeeper; it turned you into a partisan, holding your breath when the ball came sailing into your own goalmouth, ecstatic when your forwards raced away towards the opposite goal, elated, downcast, bitter, triumphant by turns at the fortunes of your side, watching a ball shape *Iliads* and *Odysseys* for you . . . And what is more, it turned you into a member of a new community, all brothers together for an hour and a half, for not only had you escaped from the clanking machinery of this lesser life, from work, wages, rent, doles, sick pay, insurance-cards, nagging wives, ailing children, bad bosses, idle workmen, but you had escaped with most of your mates and neighbours, with half the town, and there you were, cheering together, thumping one another on the shoulders, swapping judgements like lords of the earth, having pushed your way through a turnstile into another and altogether more splendid kind of life, hurtling with Conflict and yet passionate and beautiful in its Art.
>
> (J. B. Priestley: *The Good Companions*, 1928)

It must have intrigued many economists where all those shillings came from in the early 1930s, when heavy industry in Britain was being hammered by the Depression. Two out of every three males, it was

---

DIRE STRAITS

The poverty of the early 1930s in industrial Scotland is described by David Stephen in graphic terms:

> There were the Means Test butchers, who specialised in the cheapest cuts of meat, and the lousiest sausages. They had queues at their door every day. The orders were huge – 2 ounce of this, and 4 ounce of that, and the inevitable dripping. When a family had been a certain time on poor relief, a clothing issue was granted (in the jargon of the time). The amounts, in cash, were fixed, but there was a little elbow room for choice of articles. There were also strict rules: wool was for nursing mothers, fine boots only for men over 70. The Means Test was iniquitous and a shatterer of home. It broke up families, it penalised the tryers, it starved the children, it drove people to suicide and insanity.
>
> (Quoted in Tom Steel: *Scotland's Story*, 1984)

---

estimated, were unemployed in parts of industrial Lanarkshire, and Motherwell was one area most gravely affected.

The *Motherwell Times* of 24 April 1931 reported that almost 100 youths had been forced to cross the Atlantic to find work – mostly farm labour on the Canadian Prairies; it deplored the situation: ' . . . these boys are likely to become great travellers before their life work is finished, one might well guess, from the fact of their long trek to their first job. It is changed days from the time when the average Motherwell boy on leaving school had only to put in his name at the "office", or see the "gaffer" in order to get a start in some pit, workshop, or factory; but today it is a pathetic fact that each large work has hundreds of names of young people for whom there is absolutely no prospect of ever being able to offer employment.'

In 1931 Motherwell, making a first appearance in the final, were Celtic's opponents and, for once in a Scottish Cup final, Celtic's support, although in the majority, were being clearly upstaged. Thousands of Motherwell fans had poured into Glasgow from mid-morning gaily bedecked in their team's colours – the famous broad claret-and-amber hoops that the club had adopted in 1928 as a means of projecting a more cheerful outlook in dismal economic times. One Celtic diehard refused to be impressed with the racing colours of Lord Hamilton of Dalzell: 'Claret 'n' amber? Looks like rid 'n' yella tae me!'

Near the top of the Mount Florida terracing at Hampden one large group of Motherwell supporters, known as 'the Knowetop Laddies',[2] was holding up large cardboard signs that spelled out M-O-T-H-E-R-W-E-L-L, and flashing them at frequent intervals, with a fair degree of professionalism – the result of hours of practice. Enthusiastic chanting and cheers accompanied the raising of each letter.

A FAMILIAR COMPLAINT

Ex-Bailie William Thomson, presiding over a Scottish Nationalist Party meeting at Gourock, called for a Scottish National Development Board to bring in new industries to compensate for the decline in the old, and lamented that:

> Among the people of the British Empire, Scottish people are the only people who have no say in their own affairs. The very smallest state in the Empire has sole control of its own affairs, Scottish people have none . . . Scotland is recognised as one of the best-educated nations in the Empire, it has some of the most outstanding men in literature and science, and men who have built the British Empire, and yet they have to ask for freedom to manage their own affairs, while the most ignorant people in the Balkans already have that freedom.
>
> (*Daily Record*: 27 March 1931)

FAITHFUL THROUGH AND THROUGH

One hint that the Depression was taking a heavy toll was conveyed in the *Evening Citizen*'s report of Celtic's Scottish Cup-tie at Perth against St Johnstone on 30 January 1932. The match report was prefaced by a mention that Celtic fans, about 200 in number, had walked throughout the night to reach Perth in time for the match – a round-journey of 120 miles. The newspaper mentions that such loyalty was not unusual among Celtic supporters at the time.

The mood on that terracing was one of civic pride – and it was entirely justifiable. Motherwell's success on the football field was an inspiration to the Scottish region hit hardest by unemployment during the Depression years. The football team was proving to be the most potent symbol of the burgh's resolve in the face of adversity, and a boost to the morale of the community.

Nicknamed 'the Steelmen', after the town's major source of employment in more prosperous times, the club was described then as ambitious, progressive and outward-looking in a grim era. At a period when the four British Associations were withdrawing from FIFA (in 1928) over the definition of 'amateurism', provincial Motherwell were spreading the gospel of football in foreign tours: Spain in 1927, South America in 1928, South Africa in 1931 and 1934, as well as exhibition matches in France and Belgium. At home the directorate had earned a deserved reputation for positive thinking by constant ground improvements so that Fir Park lived up to the promise of its name as a neat, well-maintained ground.

The most commendable of its policies was the holding on to players despite the temptation of English money. During the Depression, 'gates' were understandably low, but Motherwell FC did not waver in its determination to retain its better players – a policy that could have been followed by richer clubs in Scotland (notably Celtic) with beneficial results for the game.[3] Herbert Chapman, manager of Huddersfield and later at Arsenal, was interested in the famous left-wing partnership of Stevenson and Ferrier; while with Arsenal, the 'Bank of England club', he approached Motherwell with a blank cheque, but he was turned down emphatically.

Their long-time manager, John 'Sailor' Hunter, was the epitome of 'shrewd'. Working within a budget considered laughable by Old Firm standards, he was the official responsible for Motherwell's consistent success during the decade. His reputation has been overshadowed by Old Firm contemporaries, Willie Maley and Bill Struth, but it was based on an unfair comparison. Like Alex Ferguson at Aberdeen and Jim McLean at Dundee United in more modern times, he was rarely given the full credit due his achievement in mounting a sustained challenge, with limited resources, to Rangers and Celtic.

Between 1927 and 1934 Motherwell fielded sides that never finished worse than third in the League Championship. This period in Scottish football was dominated by a powerful Rangers – at least in the League. Rangers' hold on the Championship was so firm that the newspapers of the time commented frequently that all the other teams in the country (including Celtic) were suffering from an inferiority complex. In reality it was no complex; they *were* inferior.

However, in 1931/32, playing an elegant, attractive brand of football, Motherwell broke the Old Firm monopoly on the Championship dating back to 1905 and scored an astonishing 119 goals in the process. That one title, magnificent accomplishment as it was, constituted a scant reward for Motherwell's contribution to the football scene in Scotland.

A closer look at the finances would reveal Motherwell's precarious position. On 25 May 1930 the *Sunday Mail* reported that the Lanarkshire club had lost £1,439 on the year's working despite an impressive playing record. A few weeks later the same newspaper revealed that Celtic had shown a handsome profit of £3,500 despite a trophy-less season with little income from the Scottish Cup. The other member of the Old Firm had swept the honours and enjoyed revenues from a replayed Scottish Cup final but could make only £3,000 more than Celtic.

Every reasonably objective follower of football in Scotland had a soft spot for Motherwell, attracted by their polished play and admiring their refusal to become another nursery for wealthy English clubs. The appeal for the neutrals – as it did with the popularity of Hibernian two decades or so later – lay in a legendary forward line. The right wing comprised of Johnny Murdoch, famed for his 'poaching' ability, and John McMenemy, the son of Celtic's famous 'Napoleon' and bought from Celtic for £1,100. He was a consummate inside forward, playing a little behind the other forwards and spreading the play intelligently. At centre the robust Willie McFadyen chased goals with determination, scoring 52 in the Championship season. His strength took some of the weight off the other players. The left wing consisted of George Stevenson and Bobby Ferrier – described as 'the Rolls and Royce of Scottish football'. Stevenson was the embodiment of the classical inside forward: a skilled dribbler, an exceptional passer and a deadly finisher, he was the 'general' of the side. His partner, and Motherwell's captain, was Ferrier, the personification of danger for defences. A player who could gather the most awkward ball and control it with ease, a forward who could pass defenders on the inside and outside, and a winger who could shoot venomously and from the narrowest of angles, he scored 256 League goals from 626 appearances in a playing-career of 20 seasons.

They had established a wonderful understanding, and their admirers claimed they could find each other blindfolded. Schoolmasters made a point of taking their charges to Motherwell matches so that the youngsters could draw football lessons from watching the pair in action. Quite simply, they

Celtic players take a breather during training for the 1931 final. Top row: Cook, McGonagle, J. Thomson. Middle row: Geatons, Scarff, Wilson, A. Thomson. Front row: McGrory, Napier, McStay, R.Thomson.

had elevated wing-play to an art form. The abiding memory for spectators of the time is of a cunningly flighted ball from Stevenson inside the full back for the speedy Ferrier who had anticipated it. The options were endless: Ferrier could cut in and shoot for goal, he could return it immediately to create a chance for the gifted Stevenson, he could cross into the goalmouth for McFadyen or the lurking Murdoch to score, or he could play the ball over and back for the waiting McMenemy.

This partnership posed the greatest threat to Celtic's winning the Cup for the 13th time, and the players with the unenviable task of marking them were Peter Wilson and Willie Cook. Wilson, a most constructive wing half, had reached the veteran stage but his skills in anticipation and passing were unsurpassed, and his youthful partner Cook was gaining a reputation for coolness under pressure. A cosmopolitan touch was added in the fact that the duels between Cook and Ferrier would be between players ineligible to play for Scotland; Cook was an Irishman, and Ferrier had the misfortune to be born in England.

Confidence was high in Lanarkshire about the prospects of a Motherwell victory, and the local authorities decided to retain all policemen on duty (including the Chief Constable) on the day of the match in the expectation they would be needed to maintain order in the town upon the return of the team with the Cup. A dozen special trains left Flemington Station and Motherwell Station on the London, Midland, and Scottish line to King's Park Station, close to Hampden, and each train was packed with supporters who had paid ninepence (approximately 4p) for the return fare.

The roads too were crowded: 'The roads from Lanarkshire leading into Glasgow presented an amazing spectacle. It seemed as if every motor car in the county had been pressed into use. The Lanarkshire County Police had made special arrangements to pass all traffic through as expeditiously as possible . . .' (*Sunday Mail*: 12 April 1931)

A few Motherwell fans might have travelled even further, and at greater expense, to attend the final, with the *Motherwell Times* suggesting that some might have come back across the Atlantic to cheer on the 'Well. Others would have to wait for the result: 'Tremendous interest is being taken in this match by the many thousands of Motherwell people scattered over Canada and the States, and when the result is flashed over the Atlantic after the match thousands from the East to the West of the great American Continent will be hanging on expectantly, waiting for the news.' (10 April 1931)

Thousands who were unable to attend the match started to gather in Motherwell's Clyde Street outside the office of the local newspaper, hoping to check on the progress of the club in bulletins posted on the window. The *Motherwell Times* had a local monopoly of information until the BBC wireless coverage which consisted of a 15-minute eye-witness account by

99

Campbell Bilney, a former referee, and was scheduled to start at six
o'clock, over an hour after full-time.

<table>
<tr><td colspan="2">SCOTTISH CUP FINAL
11 April 1931
Hampden Park</td><td colspan="2">REPLAY
15 April 1931
Hampden Park</td></tr>
<tr><td>CELTIC 2</td><td>MOTHERWELL 2</td><td>CELTIC 4</td><td>MOTHERWELL 2</td></tr>
<tr><td>J. Thomson</td><td>McClory</td><td>J. Thomson</td><td>McClory</td></tr>
<tr><td>Cook</td><td>Johnman</td><td>Cook</td><td>Johnman</td></tr>
<tr><td>McGonagle</td><td>Hunter</td><td>McGonagle</td><td>Hunter</td></tr>
<tr><td>Wilson</td><td>Wales</td><td>Wilson</td><td>Wales</td></tr>
<tr><td>McStay</td><td>Craig</td><td>McStay</td><td>Craig</td></tr>
<tr><td>Geatons</td><td>Telfer</td><td>Geatons</td><td>Telfer</td></tr>
<tr><td>R. Thomson</td><td>Murdoch</td><td>R. Thomson</td><td>Murdoch</td></tr>
<tr><td>A. Thomson</td><td>McMenemy</td><td>A. Thomson</td><td>McMenemy</td></tr>
<tr><td>McGrory</td><td>McFadyen</td><td>McGrory</td><td>McFadyen</td></tr>
<tr><td>Scarff</td><td>Stevenson</td><td>Scarff</td><td>Stevenson</td></tr>
<tr><td>Napier</td><td>Ferrier</td><td>Napier</td><td>Ferrier</td></tr>
</table>

Scorers:

McGrory (83)   Stevenson (6) McGrory (30, 86)   Murdoch (26)
Craig (90, o.g.) McMenemy (20) R. Thomson (10, 35) Stevenson (70)
Referee: P. Craigmyle (Aberdeen)

Attendance: 104,803   98,579

Motherwell trooped on to a sun-drenched Hampden Park in front of the
104,803 spectators. It was the largest crowd ever to see a Motherwell team.
The Lanarkshire side, making their debut in a Scottish Cup final, were
faced with the most feared Cup side in the country – Celtic, appearing in a
21st final and with 12 triumphs to their credit. Sensing that Motherwell
were slight betting favourites, and the sentimental choice of every neutral,
the Celtic support rallied behind the team, welcoming 'the Bhoys' with a
deafening roar of anticipation that surpassed the welcome for Motherwell.

It was expected to be a close match between two sides noted for clever,
attractive play, and to judge by the League standings the outcome could be
a toss-up:

	P	W	L	D	F	A	PTS
Rangers	35	25	5	5	90	28	55
Motherwell	35	23	5	7	98	39	53
Celtic	34	22	4	8	94	32	52

A Scottish Cup final is rarely the place for controlled, sophisticated
football when the adrenaline begins to surge and the frenzy on the

terracings starts to fray the nerves. Beforehand, the expectations were that the 1931 final would produce a 'classic', with so many skilled players on the field; however, this final was destined to be remembered for raw excitement and unbearable drama.

To the surprise of many who had expected Motherwell to be more affected by the atmosphere and reveal hints of nervousness, the Lanarkshire side settled down first. Their early play was bright and constructive with dangerous forwards, led by the prolific and hard-running McFadyen, threatening Celtic's goal repeatedly. John Thomson had difficulty in holding on to a drive from Stevenson, and murmurs of apprehension from the Celtic support behind the goal indicated the concern.

Motherwell, unlike Dundee in 1925, were at Hampden to win the Cup. Dundee had put up a brave fight, dour and determined, but satisfied not to be disgraced; Motherwell were showing the form that made them the most attractive side in Scotland, and Celtic's reputation alone would not save them.

After a few minutes Motherwell, with a stiff wind at their backs, had taken complete command of the match, setting the pace and dictating the course of events. Several times only the unexpected bounce of the ball on the fast, fiery Hampden pitch stopped promising attacks, but they fully merited the touch of luck that came their way in six minutes.

McFadyen's shot cannoned off McGonagle, and Celtic's defence relaxed momentarily, but the ball broke in the direction of Stevenson and McMenemy; Stevenson did not hesitate and hit a long 'swishing daisy-cutter' that deceived Thomson in Celtic's goal although he did get his fingers to it. Thomson had not looked comfortable in the opening minutes, and some spectators blamed him for the loss of the goal but, in fairness to him, he appeared unsighted as Stevenson shot, and Celtic's captain, Jimmy McStay, admitted later that the shot had taken a deflection off his foot.

The terracing at the Mount Florida end of Hampden erupted with the bright colours of Motherwell, and back at the steeltown's Clyde Street a few minutes later the thousands of men, women, and children unable to travel to Glasgow for the match cheered and applauded.

Celtic tried to regroup, but they were rattled by the early goal and Motherwell kept up the pressure; time after time the forwards carved open Celtic's outer defence, but the last pass or cross was a little off target. McFadyen was presented with the sight of an open goal, but reacted with uncharacteristic slowness and missed his shot completely. However, the one-way traffic forced another goal in 20 minutes. Thomson had to scramble away two shots, from Murdoch and Stevenson, but the defence in front of him could not clear and McMenemy's decisive shot gave Thomson no chance, the ball striking McStay's left leg and being diverted away from the keeper who had already committed himself.

On a more normal day the interventions of Celtic's captain might have

'Peter' McGonagle and John Thomson.

led to two corners for Motherwell; instead, after only 20 minutes in a Scottish Cup final, Celtic were now two goals down. Motherwell's goals may have been tinged with luck, but they deserved the two-goal lead because of their more constructive, and positive, approach to the match. Half backs and forwards were combining beautifully and every raid threatened Celtic's goal; Celtic's only response to the frantic encouragement of their supporters was a series of unimaginative thumps in the general direction of Jimmy McGrory, who as always chased every ball gamely but was being marked closely by Craig.

The Celtic support was galvanised into outrage when the referee, Peter Craigmyle, refused to allow a claim for 'hands' against Craig; the referee judged correctly that the ball had been driven against the player's arm, and that he could not prevent the contact. However, the sense of injustice among Celtic players prompted a short-lived spell of dominance.

Celtic had managed to get into the match, but Motherwell were dangerous on the break and just before the interval McFadyen was desperately unlucky to see his header, aided by the wind, curl over the bar with the Celtic defence again in disarray.

At half-time the Motherwell supporters celebrated noisily: the Knowetop Laddies raised and re-raised their letters to great cheers, pigeon-fanciers on the terracing despatched their birds back to Lanarkshire with the glad tidings, and in Motherwell itself, outside the newspaper office, the crowd was swelling as the news was spread around the town.

Celtic's performance could only improve in the second half, so disjointed had it been in the first 45 minutes. Right from the restart they attacked, but it was effort without much subtlety, and Motherwell's defenders, resolute and composed, withstood the opening burst of pressure with relative ease. The final had degenerated into a typical Cup-tie, as Celtic attacked frantically and Motherwell defended grimly.

Motherwell, facing the wind and anticipating a Celtic revival, pulled back their inside forwards, leaving only McFadyen and the 'poacher' Murdoch up front. Celtic had improved, but it was not a vintage performance; much had been expected of the right-wing triangle, but Wilson was nervous and tentative, Alec Thomson virtually invisible, and only Bertie Thomson was threatening Motherwell's goal. The left-wing triangle, while displaying individual touches, were not combining well; Geatons had come to grips with McMenemy and was now pressing into attack, Peter Scarff and Charlie Napier looked dangerous in the midfield but were not threatening the Motherwell goal. McGrory was stretching the Motherwell defence, and challenging Allan McClory in Motherwell's goal for every ball, but his menace was still being blunted by Craig.

Despite the Celtic pressure and territorial advantage, it was becoming clearer with each passing minute that Celtic were not breaking down this stubborn defence; the fleeting minutes were being chronicled by the clock on the stand at Hampden, and Celtic's supporters, once so noisy, had lapsed into a gloomy silence.[4]

Another incident with the referee produced a memorable – and disgraceful – scene. Certainly a Motherwell defender did appear to handle the ball deliberately, but Mr Craigmyle dismissed the frantic appeals for a penalty and awarded a corner instead: the referee suffered the indignity of having to run behind the goal, pursued hotly by Bertie Thomson and Peter Scarff. The Celtic players were lucky to escape punishment for their persistent badgering of the official, whose jacket, it was claimed in one match report, was almost torn off his back. The referee's post-match claim that he was sprinting to take up position for the corner kick, and was thus unaware of being pursued, convinced nobody.

Mr Craigmyle was a popular yet controversial referee. More than most referees, he refrained from booking players, believing that at times it was his responsibility to keep players on the field. When meeting with the captains for the toss-up before this final, he had asked that they alone should approach him in appealing decisions. That season's play had been characterised by several examples of poor discipline by players. In Craigmyle's defence, he was congratulated by the officials of both sides afterwards for his handling of the match.

The strain was beginning to tell on some Motherwell defenders: both wing halves, Wales and Telfer, were largely inexperienced, and *this* was the biggest occasion in the Scottish game. McClory, a tall, gaunt figure in goal, was using up the seconds in placing the ball for his goal kicks, ignoring the howls of protest from the Celtic supporters. The backs were now starting to clear the ball by kicking out of play, in stark contrast to their more positive efforts in the first half. Most revealing, however, was the number of free kicks conceded by Motherwell, some in dangerous positions. The most frequent offender was Alan Craig, Motherwell's centre half. Why Craig continued to handle the ball so flagrantly remains a mystery, as he had contained the dangerous McGrory throughout the match. It had to be nerves manifesting themselves, but perhaps Craig was still suffering the lingering effects of flu that had caused him to miss the previous week's League game against Partick Thistle.

This growing anxiety on the Hampden pitch and terracings was hidden from those citizens of Motherwell gathered in front of the town's newspaper offices: 'Being one of those who had perforce to rely on the window of the *Times* shop for our information as to how our lads were getting on against their mighty foe, visions of a cheery town were in our minds when a note was posted up on the window that, with fifteen minutes to go, our stalwarts were still holding the enemy at bay, and being unable to content ourselves by standing idly by awaiting the next message being posted up we took a bus to Knowetop, and on our way we observed great crowds of people, the majority of whom were women folk, making their way to the Cross.' (*Motherwell Times*: 17 April 1931)

At Hampden Park a large band of Motherwell supporters decided to leave early in order to catch a train back to Lanarkshire – and to give the first eye-witness accounts of a famous victory.

In the centre of Glasgow the editor of one newspaper, anxious to steal a march on his rivals, made a decision: the presses started to roll, and the headline proclaimed Motherwell as Scottish Cup winners.

On the field, following yet another handling offence by Craig, Celtic were awarded a free kick on the edge of the box. Motherwell pulled everybody back, and formed a 'wall' to protect the goal against Napier's shot. This time Napier changed his approach; craftily he lobbed the ball over the defence for McGrory, ever alert, to lunge forward free of markers in a desperate effort to get a toe to the ball. His touch was enough to divert it into the net off an upright and, as the ball rolled around the back of the net, the Celtic support came back to life.

Jimmy McGrory's goal throws Celtic a lifeline.

McGrory picked himself up quickly and rushed to retrieve the ball; dismissing the congratulations of his colleagues, he raced back to the centre circle with the ball and pointed to the clock, gesturing unmistakably that with seven minutes left Celtic still had enough time to save the match. A constant din was erupting from the King's Park end of Hampden; green flags and handkerchiefs waved in the air. The fight had been resumed.

Celtic's players responded to McGrory's show of spirit and redoubled their efforts to break down the Lanarkshire defence, and as they pressed forward in waves to the swelling accompaniment of their thousands on the terracing, Motherwell had to abandon the studied calm of their early play, clearing the ball in any direction and at all costs while the minutes ticked away.

Wave after wave of Celtic attacks were beaten back and one long clearance from defence reached as far as John Thomson in the Celtic penalty area: behind him the Motherwell fans were whistling, trying to influence the referee into blowing for time; at the other end the Celtic supporters were roaring encouragement for one last charge.

The Knowetop Laddies, seeing the referee glance at both linesmen to verify the time, decided to tempt fate and started to raise their letters one by one; the reporters in the press-box started to fold up their notebooks; the Celtic directors were beginning to congratulate their Motherwell counterparts . . .

Thomson had cleared the ball as far as he could and down the right wing. Bertie Thomson, the most dangerous Celtic forward on the day, gathered the clearance and made his way along the touchline, beating Telfer with a neat sidestep; he neared the corner flag and tried to cross the ball, but Hunter was blocking the attempt; Thomson doubled back fom the bye-line to gain space and shake off Hunter, before sending over a hard, high centre that started to swerve towards Motherwell's goal, aided in its flight by the infamous 'Hampden Swirl'.[5] McClory started to leave his goal, eyes fixed on the ball, and confident in his ability to intercept and clutch the cross.

Jimmy McGrory takes up the sequence of events in an interview given 20 years later: ' . . . as I positioned myself to meet it with my head, I saw Alan Craig was in front of me. We both went up for it, but I never connected – and as I came down to earth again, the ball was spinning into the far corner of the net, headed there by Craig in his effort to keep it from reaching me.'

Craig, clearly worried about the threat from McGrory's heading ability, had made for the ball intending to head it past for another Celtic corner. Probably it was a goalkeeper's ball, and McClory was stretching for it. But somebody in Motherwell's defence had called out 'Go for it, Alan!' Both Craig and McClory shared the same first name – Alan. The swirling cross glanced off Craig's forehead as he bobbed up in front of his goalkeeper – and the ball crashed into the roof of the net. Ivan Sharpe, the vastly experienced correspondent of the English-based *Sunday Chronicle*, recalled the moment as the most dramatic and poignant he had ever witnessed in football, and evoked the wild excitement that broke out after an initial disbelief: 'Celtic saved on the post! Pandemonium! Down in a heap falls the unlucky Craig. He's in tears, he's rolling over and over in mental agony. Before he can recover the whistle sounds for time, and over the fences come the Celtic followers, swarming around their players, grabbing their jerseys, seizing arms and hands in tumultuous congratulation while one man, Craig, walks slowly and sorrowfully off the field half-dazed by his single error.'

Days later 'Man in the Know', that most indefatigable of Celtic zealots, was still overcome with emotion when penning his account of the drama:

... Craig flung himself face downwards on the turf in a very agony of self-reproach. The Celtic players dashed towards Bert Thomson who was simply overwhelmed under an avalanche of hysterical congratulations. The great little Celt was seized, hugged, patted, kissed – and I don't know what, while the Motherwell players, astounded, incredulous, made their way heavily to midfield. *Three seconds* remained for play . . . But, if the incidents on the field of play were remarkable, how shall I describe the scenes on the terracing? It would take Dante or Milton to do justice to the unforgettable spectacle. I never witnessed anything remotely approaching the scene and probably never shall. Talk about earthquakes, landslides, tidal waves, and what not! The upheaval on the terracing suggested the sudden, furious awakening of a slumbering mammoth . . . The crowd went mad. The air was black with upflung hats and caps. Men, utter strangers, seized each other, thumped each other, wrestled, danced, shook hands, shouted, laughed, cried, cheered and, in a word, went plumb crazy with joy.

(*Glasgow Observer*: 18 April 1931)

On the opposite terracing the Knowetop Laddies had reached M-O T-H-E-R-W-E- but, in stunned, disbelieving silence, they lowered their signs. A train had already left King's Park Station packed with cheerful and excited Motherwell supporters rehearsing their accounts: 'Ah've loast ma voice wi' cheerin'. . . Aye, mind you, Celtic were gey desperate in that second hauf. They were throwin' everything intae it, but they nivir looked like scorin'.'
A short while later, back in Motherwell:

What a glorious feeling it was to think that at last our boys had succeeded in landing the blue riband of Scottish football! We were amazed, however, when we arrived back at the *Times* shop in time to see the gentleman posting up the last notice which contained the final score. Did our eyes deceive us or was this some prank of our worthy townsman? It seemed utterly impossible that the cup which but a short quarter of an hour ago had been raised to our lips should be so ruthlessly dashed from us in so short a space of time. Our question soon dispelled any doubts and, like our fellows who but a short time ago were preparing to give a cheer, which we have no doubt would have been heard almost at Hampden, we were cast into an abyss of despondency.

(*Motherwell Times*: 17 April 1931)

Alan Craig? As Motherwell's pivot lay on the pitch, inconsolable and oblivious to the tumult around him, Peter Craigmyle moved towards him to offer assistance. The wretched player could only stare in incomprehension and mutter in a monotone, 'I've done it . . . I've done it.' Craig's anguish drew widespread sympathy, including that of his opponents, but, interestingly, Bob McPhail, the famous Rangers forward and the Ibrox club's all-time leading scorer, makes some observations about Craig in his autobiography, describing his frequent opponent as 'a classic, no-nonsense stopper . . . who just made sure that he cleared his lines as quickly as he could, even if his direction was a wee bit off at times'.

'I've done it . . . I've done it.' And, indeed he had.

POOR TIMING

Under the auspices of the Lanarkshire Labour College, a day-school will be held in the ILP Hall, Miller Street, Motherwell on Sunday first . . . At the afternoon session, Mr Gibbons will lecture on phrenology, his subject being, 'Heads, and what they teach us,' and at the evening session his subject is 'Crime and its Punishment . . .'

(*Motherwell Times*: 17 April 1931)

Apparently, the subjects were not intended as a comment on the closing seconds of the first match of the Scottish Cup final.

Dr Johnson once described a second marriage cynically as 'the triumph of hope over experience'. The same truth might be applied to a Cup replay against Celtic in those days. A Celtic team with renewed vigour in a Scottish Cup final replay is not a soothing prospect.

Motherwell could take little comfort from the confident forecast of a Dr Duncan Finlayson – who had played for them as a student – that the Scottish Cup would soon be gracing the Fir Park pavilion, a prediction that followed a consultation with a soothsayer in India.

The managers stuck by the same sides for the replay which was sche-

---

THE REIGN IN SPAIN

On the eve of the replay of the Scottish Cup final King Alfonso of Spain abdicated. The reaction of the citizens in Madrid was described as follows:

The capital went wild. Every department store and every drapery shop in Madrid were sold out of red, yellow, and purple cloth in a few hours . . . so great was the rush of the people to make Republican flags. People clambered on whatever vehicle was passing and drove it through the streets cheering and waving Republican and red flags. Taxi-cabs, motors and lorries, loaded with youths and young girls, drove through the city streets. Thousands of people assembled on the pavements waving flags, and shouting and cheering.

(*Daily Record*: 15 April 1931)

The celebrations were doomed to be short-lived, as the abdication set in train the events leading to the Spanish Civil War.

---

duled for 5 p.m. on the following Wednesday (the Hampden floodlights were not installed until 30 years later). The team selection attributed to the Celtic directors by the press was in reality little more than a formality, since it seems clear that Willie Maley had asserted full control in that sphere by the 1930s.

Another huge contingent made its way to Hampden from Lanarkshire, many works having closed early and it being the Merchants' Holiday in the town; many Celtic supporters turned up at the stadium directly from work. The *Glasgow Herald* reported that 'it was not the well-groomed crowd, dressed in holiday clothes, which attended Saturday's match. Instead, one saw hundreds whose dungarees proclaimed that they had come direct from bench and forge, and mingling with the crowd were others whose grimy hands and faces spoke eloquently of penetrating coal dust.' (16 April 1931)

The conditions were different: the skies were overcast, and rain had been falling for two days thus making the pitch sodden; the wind was gusty and would affect play.

Celtic trotted out first to be greeted by a tumultuous reception from the crowd of 98,579 and when Motherwell followed a few seconds later, one spectator made a bee-line for Alan Craig to present him with a lucky horseshoe and an encouraging pat on the back. This time McStay won the toss, and without hesitation he booked the assistance of the breeze.

Celtic, even more than Motherwell, welcomed the changes underfoot and from the opening minutes the wing-halfs were establishing control; the momentum was now with Celtic, and their play was bright and confident. Motherwell settled for containment, but within ten minutes Celtic took the lead. Peter Wilson, much more effective on the holding surface, threw a high lob into Motherwell's goal area, and Alan McClory, jumping along with the eager McGrory, misjudged the ball and lost possession.

In the resultant scramble Bert Thomson netted. McClory was incensed and chased the referee all the way to midfield, claiming that McGrory had handled the ball, but Mr Craigmyle ignored his appeal.

A few minutes later the rattled Alan McClory was in all sorts of trouble before another hanging cross from Wilson was cleared, and it was obvious that the replay would be different in atmosphere from Saturday's encounter. Behind much of the confusion in Motherwell's defence lay Jimmy McGrory, Celtic's dashing centre forward. Two goals down and with only seven minutes left in the first match, he had refused to admit defeat although the ball had never run for him in the match. He was a fast centre, always moving, and challenging defenders; he was brave, always found in the most dangerous situations; he was perhaps the greatest header of the ball in the whole history of Scottish football, but he was a leader in the true Celtic spirit. A man constitutionally unable to stop trying, a man incapable of accepting defeat until the final whistle – a genuine and humble folk-hero. On the Saturday he had scored Celtic's first goal in the 83rd minute to start a memorable rally, and his lurking presence had caused Craig's fatal error; now he was creating havoc, compounding the lack of confidence manifesting itself between Craig and McClory.

However, Motherwell equalised in 26 minutes: Ferrier's curling corner, a greasy ball and the physical challenge of McFadyen all forced Thomson to palm the ball out to the right for Murdoch – inevitably – to run and score. Four minutes later Celtic went ahead again when McClory left his goal and completely missed a cross, allowing McGrory to tap the ball into a gaping net. Two mistakes by the goalkeeper – an outstanding performer on the Saturday – eroded any remaining confidence in Motherwell's defence. The rearguard was in tatters, and ten minutes before half-time Geatons' free kick eluded the whole defence for Bert Thomson to drive into the net from a most acute angle.

To their credit Motherwell fought back and John Thomson did well in turning a fierce shot from Ferrier over the bar a minute before the interval. Motherwell had the wind behind them, and were two goals down – a situation reminiscent of the Saturday, but now in reverse. Motherwell attacked from the restart, but were rarely as penetrative as Celtic; they were guilty of overelaboration, and Celtic's free-running forwards were posing a greater danger. Both Napier and Scarff on the left wing had struck a game, and Motherwell's defenders could not risk the breakaway; McGrory continued to prowl looking for goals.

But Motherwell were putting up a fight, showing spirit as much as skill and Celtic were forced back to defend. Twenty minutes from the end Motherwell reduced the deficit to 2–3 when Stevenson took advantage of a neat dummy by McMenemy to beat Thomson conclusively from 20 yards.

Motherwell committed men to attack but, as in the first match, McStay, although small for a centre half, was outstanding; he covered the middle, challenging for every ball, and moved to help his backs when in trouble. Behind him John Thomson was busy: he had to risk injury in diving at McFadyen's feet to touch the ball away, although Ferrier picked up the loose ball and fired it across the goalmouth, coming agonisingly close to netting. Later, he had to be alert to deal with a short passback from McGonagle, and he made a diving save from the high-scoring McFadyen. He was a shade lucky when another low drive from Ferrier struck the outside of his post and went safely past for a goal kick.

With Celtic's forwards a continual threat on the break, the inevitable happened with only four minutes to play. To the roars of the Celtic support, Charlie Napier broke away on the left and his mis-hit shot went out to Thomson, who crossed high into goal; poor McClory, in the midst of a personal nightmare, missed the cross completely and McGrory found himself free to head the ball into an empty net.

Soon it was all over. The newspapers would carry the reasons for Celtic's victory: the shambles in Motherwell's defence, the opportunism and strong running of McGrory, the heavy pitch that favoured Celtic's 'off-the-cuff', less studied approach . . . It remains the most famous Scottish Cup triumph against the odds by that intangible but psychologically powerful factor – the Celtic spirit and determination.

The Cup was presented once again inside Hampden in the Queen's Park reception room by Mr R. Campbell, now the SFA President, to Tom White, Celtic's chairman, who jokingly mentioned that Celtic had to win the trophy in order to fulfil the conditions of his club's forthcoming American tour.

Afterwards Celtic adjourned to the Bank Restaurant (Proprietor: Mr Wm. Maley, Esq) to celebrate their 13th Scottish Cup victory. Thirty policemen had to be summoned to the restaurant to control the crowd of more than a thousand who had rushed the doors to catch a glimpse of the trophy and to congratulate their heroes.

When young John Thomson left early to make his way home, he was mobbed by a large crowd which followed him to the station cheering and shouting. Universally admired for his youthful grace and daring (and clearly forgiven for an uncharacteristic performance in the first match), he was considered by most followers to be the best keeper in the country, established as the last line of defence in another potentially formidable side being forged at Parkhead – a new young team that promised so much for the future.[6]

The gleaming Scottish Cup, still being passed around the Bank Restaurant by waitresses bedecked with green rosettes, was taken later by Celtic on their American tour. The Cup became the object of veneration for many exiles who had travelled vast distances to see the team. The club could have been forgiven if they were starting to consider it as their property, because 'Celtic' was becoming synonymous with the Scottish Cup.

The American tour, 1931 – Jimmy McGrory shows the Scottish Cup to exiled fans.

WHOSE BALL IS IT ANYWAY?

When Peter Craigmyle blew for the end of the replay, Bob Ferrier, Motherwell's captain, was closest to the ball, and nabbed it for a souvenir. Bertie Thomson pleaded for it, but Ferrier's response was less than polite – but understandable in view of the ordeal Motherwell had undergone. Bob Ferrier Jr, a much respected sports journalist, recalled what happened to the ball (in an amusing letter to one of the co-authors dated July 1989):

> The ball came home to Dumbarton. My father took the view that footballs were for kicking, and not for looking at, tucked up in some display case. So, I was given the ball, but it was not to be kicked to death in street football [as was later reported]. It had a long life on grass, used by myself and my contemporary super stars, and in a public park by Dumbarton East station. We played on grass in the 'Swinging Park' as it was called, since it had swings and roundabouts. It was known to us affectionately as 'Doon the Wingy'. The park remains there, with grass pitches, to this day.

Footnotes

1 Rita MacNeil, a Canadian singer and composer, writes here of a Cape Breton man who chose to stay on his poor but beautiful island rather than head to the mainland for 'a better life'. The authors consider that the sentiments reflect admirably the career and character of Jimmy McGrory.

2 The terracing behind one of the goals at Fir Park was called the Knowetop.

3 Celtic were anxious to sell Jimmy McGrory for a record fee to Arsenal despite the player's objections; on the eve of the 1931 final the Celtic Board was denying, amid growing scepticism, that John Thomson was available to the same club.

4 The clock remained a feature of Hampden until a fire at Christmas, 1945.

5 Hampden has always been cursed with wind problems, a situation aggravated by the fact that, until the erection of the North Stand in 1937, the stadium consisted of vast open terracing on three sides of the pitch. In 1929 England's goalkeeper, Hacking, was completely deceived by a corner from Alex Cheyne in the last minute to give Scotland a 1–0 win. Many Celtic supporters will recall Bonnar's difficulty with Robertson's corner, and the subsequent goal that earned Clyde a replay in 1955.

6 Sadly within a few years three members of Celtic's side had died: John Thomson died of head injuries sustained at Ibrox in 1931, Peter Scarff died of consumption in 1933, and Bert Thomson, who had been transferred to Blackpool and later, ironically, to Motherwell, died in 1937. At the time of their deaths John was 23, Peter 25, and Bertie 28.

DISTANT FIELDS

An unidentified but observant Celtic player (or official) sent a columnist his impressions of New York, one of the club's stops on the North American tour in 1931:

> It is rush and rattle, bang and bustle all the way and all the time. Everybody seems to be in a deuce of a hurry. It is too strenuous. The pace is absolutely killing. All the same, it is a wonderful city. The sights are arresting. The buildings are marvellous. Wealth parades. But there is the other side of the picture. There are poor. There are slums, and the life of the poor must be awful in a place where the cold and heat are extremes.
>
> (*Daily Record*: 28 June 1931)

Tom Maley, a prominent early player and the manager's brother, was 'invited' to be a member of the party on the club's first tour of North America in 1931. Later that year he recalled some of the problems the players experienced on the field:

> The 'diamond' in the field of play and the existence of confusing ground marks associated with baseball and kindred games made for confusion and handicap for our players and they suffered thereby. Very much lighter are the balls used in match games. In the interpretation of many of the rules of the game there is a difference. The habit of substitution caused no little bother. In our country it is forbidden; in one match our opponents had a muster-roll of seventeen! . . . Our biggest grouse lay more against the linesman [than the referees] (I am fearless! For was not I a linesman at Montreal?) These worthy chaps at times amused more than annoyed. In one notable match it was no uncommon sight to see them mixed up with the play even in the goal area!

(This extract comes from an article written by Tom Maley for the October, 1931 issue of *All Aboard*, the journal of RMS *Transylvania*, the Anchor Line ship on which he travelled.)

7

A TIME TO LIVE

SONG OF THE CELT

Oh for the days of Celtic glory,
Oh for the team that once could win.
Oh for a touch of the old-time masters –
Shaw, McNair, Dodds, and Quinn.

Once we used to cheer our heroes,
Urge them on with all our might.
And the slopes of Paradise
Would ring with wild delight.

Oh to think of it,
Oh to dream of it,
Fills our hearts with tears.
Oh for the days of Delaney prancing
Down the field with his mates in tune;
Oh for one of those hours of gladness –
Gone, alas, like our youth – too soon . . .

(Written by 'Columncille', and undated, but believed to be of late 1940s origin, the poem expresses a yearning for 'the good, old days'. The side of the late 1930s, with Delaney and company still fresh in his memory, he obviously cherished!)

IN THE last years of the 1930s, a deceptively placid time, football was not immune from the conspiracy of silence that enveloped much of British life. A little-known episode in Scottish football history symbolises the prevailing ostrich-like willingness to suspend belief, the tacit self-deception.

In October 1936 the SFA had invited Germany to play a friendly international at Ibrox Park against Scotland; the German party became the first football side to fly into Scotland for a fixture, landing at Renfrew Aerodrome after a six-hour flight from Cologne. The aircraft was a Junkers: a 16-seater, all-metal, three-engined Junkers decorated with the infamous swastika, the symbol of Nazi Germany.

With the red-white-and-black flag of Nazi Germany (incorporating the same swastika) flying above the Ibrox enclosure, the visitors were cheered before, during and after the match by most of a 60,000 crowd. The Germans emerged from the tunnel in single file, marched proudly to the centre circle, lined up with military precision, and recognised the applauding crowd with the Nazi salute, first to one side of the stadium and then to the other. Shortly afterwards, the enthusiastic singing of the German national anthem could be heard accompanying the Govan Burgh band; the singing came from 500 'fans', most of whom had disembarked from a cruise-liner in the Firth of Forth.[1]

Scotland won the match by a score of 2–0 through two opportunist goals by Jimmy Delaney of Celtic, and the victory was attributed to poor finishing by the visitors – a characteristic flaw in the play of most Continental sides, it was felt. Commenting on the lack of hostility among the crowd, George Blake, a celebrated journalist, cited the cry of one spectator: 'C'mon Jerry! Cut out the Hitler stuff, and do it on the ba'!' He added: 'The two teams were as brothers. To the men on the terraces the fellow in the white jersey was just "Auld Jerry".'

It was scarcely surprising that 'the men on the terraces' did not make more of a political statement. Throughout that 'low, dishonest decade' the Government's tactic of appeasement had shut out reality most effectively, and the policy was an accurate reading of the mood of the public in whose collective memory the horrors of World War One remained too fresh. The rise of Hitler, the emergence of the Nazis in Germany, the seizing of power by Mussolini in Italy, the growing power of the Fascists; the Civil War in Spain, the march into the Rhineland, the invasion of Ethiopia, Japan's war with China . . . all these were documented, described and discussed but Britain continued 'to sleepwalk through the 30s'.

Everybody wanted peace, and hoped that Germany would be sensible; but Hitler, encouraged by the compliance, continued his acts of aggression. Each fresh manifestation of Nazi belligerence created more alarm and fear than the one before. In 1940, when events had reached an inevitable conclusion, Malcolm Muggeridge could describe the time as 'bursts of fear, crises, with uneasy lulls in between'.

As the decade wore on, more and more Britons were starting to talk openly about what they would do if war broke out. However, many still believed or hoped it would never happen. Alastair Borthwick has the key to the Orwellian 'doublethink' of the decade when Fascism went on the rampage unchecked: 'We lived from one broken promise to another; and though it was obvious that time was running out, we always hoped it would be better tomorrow . . . We did not want to believe facts; so, we did not believe them . . . We knew and yet we refused to know.'

An editorial in the Glasgow *Evening Citizen* the day after the match observed complacently that the forms of government adopted by people abroad were of no concern to Britain and claimed an apparent ignorance of reports of intimidation; Hitler and Mussolini owed their power to 'votes as fair and as secret as those cast by the British electorate'. (15 October 1936) And yet on 14 October the Bavarian cabinet had dismissed 1,600 Catholic teachers, replacing them with 'reliable Nazis'; Sir Oswald Mosley, Britain's leading Fascist, had led a march of 2,000 of his Blackshirts through the poverty-stricken East End of London. Needless to say, Otto Nerz, the German team-manager, was delighted with the propaganda value of the friendly reception in Glasgow . . . 'that should do more to dispel the cloud of political misunderstanding than anything I know'.

However, some voices were raised in protest against the German visit. Two young men, Frank Sanderson and John Dollan, were arrested for inciting a breach of the peace by shouting 'Down with Hitler' and 'Down with Nazis'; they had also brandished placards reading 'Who murdered the Jewish footballers?' and 'The best German players are in concentration camps.'[2] When the pair appeared before the magistrate at a packed Govan Police Court the next morning, they pleaded 'Not Guilty', and were ordered to reappear one week later. Curiously, no mention is made in later Glasgow papers of any subsequent trial. Perhaps the charges were dropped quietly, or the newspapers 'chose' to ignore a trial of sensitive and controversial nature.

Another protest of sorts was made by the Glasgow Corporation; the Labour-controlled council declined to arrange a civic reception for the visitors and instead held a function honouring the organisers of the Glasgow Charity Cup competition. The SFA claimed that the Corporation knew well in advance of the proposed visit, and the President, Mr James Fleming, and the Secretary, George Graham, chose to return their invitations to the function – with Graham saying that he had to play host to the Germans.

DISASTER!

> It was on the showery evening of May 6, 1937 that the great German airship *Hindenburg*, nosing toward the mooring mast at Lakehurst to complete its first transatlantic flight of 1937, suddenly became a torch flaming in the dusk, and the cheerful inconsequentialities that poured out of American radios were broken by staccato reports of the horror on the New Jersey plain. Down went the hopes which had built a mooring mast on the Empire State Building, and had risen high as the *Hindenburg* made crossing after crossing safely in 1936.
>
> (Frederick Lewis Allan: *Since Yesterday*, 1939)

116

It was a most ambivalent era. The worst of the Depression was past and the economic prospects were improving. Beardmore's Forge was certainly in the mind of the editorial-writer of the Glasgow *Eastern Standard* who rejoiced in the fact that 'Parkhead, an industrial district of the East End, which a few years ago was practically idle, is now resounding to the clang of hammers, denoting that prosperity is no longer round the corner but is now here'. (11 June 1938) The revival in Britain's heavy industries, however, was inspired by the growing need to catch up in the armaments race with Germany. Preparations were being made for war, and the average man was realising it. He had been warned in newspaper articles by 'experts' that whole cities and their populations would be wiped out by aerial bombardment. Indeed, only a few days after the 1937 Scottish Cup final, the people of Scotland awoke to newspaper headlines bearing the grim news of the razing of the Basque town of Guernica, the victim of German dive-bombers using the Spanish Civil War as target practice for the main event.

It is surely no coincidence, therefore, that so many British attendance records were set in those uneasy pre-war years when football spectating reached a feverish, almost desperate, pitch.[3] Consider some of the evidence: the record attendance for Ibrox Park was set in January 1939 when 118,567 saw Rangers beat Celtic 2–1, and the record for Celtic Park was 'established' in January 1938 when 92,000 saw Celtic beat Rangers 3–0. Some doubt has to exist about the latter figure; *The Bulletin*, for example, gives the attendance in its match report as 83,500 and no other newspaper at the time reported it as substantially different.

The frantic determination of Celtic fans to be present at Parkhead for the third-round replay in the Scottish Cup between Celtic and Hearts in February 1939 has a fatalistic ring to it – as if this might be one of the last football matches to be seen. With thousands locked out and crowds rushing around from Janefield Street (where the gates were shut 15 minutes before the kick-off) to London Road (where they were closed as the match was starting), a crowd of 80,840 attended officially. Many excluded supporters perched uneasily on the ground's perimeter walls and fences, while others balanced on the roofs of the Delburn Street tenements that overlooked part of the ground. Many buses nearing the ground did not bother to stop to unload their passengers, but turned back, the drivers saying the situation was chaotic and hopeless with thousands milling around the stadium.

One trainload of fans tried desperately hard to gain admittance. When the train, travelling on the line adjoining Celtic Park, was slowing down but not yet stopped, impatient, would-be spectators started to open compartment doors and prepared to jump out; the driver assessed the danger quickly and stopped his train, whereupon almost every passenger leapt out on to the line and scrambled up a steep embankment to clamber over high 'sleeper' fences. Such heroics deserve success, but most of those hundreds were unable to enter the ground to see Celtic defeat Hearts by 2–1 in extra time.

The mania had manifested itself first – and most dramatically – within the space of one week in April 1937, with the setting of records for attendance for an international match (Scotland versus England) and a club match (Celtic versus Aberdeen in the Scottish Cup final). In the wake of recent disasters in England and on the Continent, and the belated concern for public safety resulting in lowered ground capacities, those figures are never likely to be surpassed.

On 17 April, only four days after the aircraft-carrier HMS *Ark Royal* was launched at Birkenhead, and a week after a local MP, John McGovern, had told an audience at the Parkhead Picture House that everything pointed to war within two years, a mammoth crowd of 149,547 at Hampden Park saw Scotland defeat England 3–1. Although it was Hampden's first all-ticket international, possession of a ticket for the ground did not guarantee the owner a spot on the terracing but merely 'the "open sesame" to the men at the turnstile'. *The Bulletin* expressed general satisfaction with the system, but complained: 'Experience has shown that spectators will not move down to the front where there is generally some elbow-room, but remain doggedly higher up.' (19 April 1937) The same complaint was to be repeated one week later following the Scottish Cup final between Celtic and Aberdeen (and at the Old Firm clash at Ibrox in January 1939).

Unfortunately, blaming the spectators appeared to be the prevailing attitude. The view of the SFA towards public safety and standards of comfort seemed strictly mercenary – at least towards spectators who watched football matches while standing. While the police had made considerable advances in crowd control with radio-vans, traffic and crowd-stewardship and a central control point, the only aim of the football authorities was to cram as many 'spectators' as possible into the existing space.

Mr David S. Brown, a councillor for Glasgow's Provan Ward, revealed that the official estimate of Hampden's capacity was 183,388 – an estimate based on the assumption that the average spectator had a breadth of 18 inches! For all the smug and self-serving claims that limiting crowds at Hampden to 150,000 still left a 'safety margin' of 33,388, the SFA and the civic authorities *were* risking public safety. The councillor's recent experience on the east terracing, where like thousands of others he caught glimpses of the aforesaid international only when the ball was in the air, lent personal authority to his insistence that the ground's estimated capacity was dangerously exaggerated. His complaint was ignored, but he emerges as a visionary compared to officialdom with his assertion that safety and comfort had to be considered as factors in football spectating.

For the most part, Scottish football crowds, once inside the grounds, were well-behaved and co-operative. Outbreaks of violence did occur but appeared confined to the vicious sectarianism promoted by Rangers-Celtic encounters, or from trouble arising out of incidents on the field. Football came first, and hooliganism was secondary – and that genuine Scottish passion and love for the game must be considered the greatest single factor in preventing catastrophes such as in Brussels and Sheffield. One suspects that 'fitba'-mad' Glasgow took a special pride in claiming record attendances for football, and was prepared to overlook the conditions on the overcrowded terracings. The *Glasgow Herald*, while acknowledging football as the national sport, in the same breath described it patronisingly as 'almost the sole inspiration to thought and conversation to so many people in Scotland'. (14 August 1937)

TOP OF THE POPS
Among the most popular recordings of the year 1937 were:

'Over the Rainbow': Judy Garland
'Begin the Beguine': Leslie A. Hutchison
'The Beer-Barrel Polka': Andrews Sisters
'Folks Who Live on the Hill': Bing Crosby
'Hands, Knees, and Boomps-a-Daisy': Joe Loss and Annette Mills
'I Can Give You the Starlight': Mary Ellis

Looking over the newsreels of football matches in the 1930s, and after making allowances for the jerky movements and black-and white film, one is still left with an uncomfortable thought. Those thousands in cloth caps queuing up patiently at the turnstiles and massed on the open terracings would become the people lining up for gas-masks, the soldiers marching on to troop-trains or boats, and would foreshadow the steady streams of homeless refugees plodding along the ruined roads of Europe.

The Scottish Cup final of 1937 would feature two of the most popular and attractive sides in the country, Aberdeen and Celtic, both of whom were neck-and-neck in the race to finish second to Rangers in the Championship (and Aberdeen eventually pipped Celtic). The Glasgow club would be making a remarkable 23rd appearance in the final, and Aberdeen their first. Motherwell in 1931, and Aberdeen in 1937 – the fact that these clubs were making debuts in the final serves only to illustrate more clearly Celtic's magnificent record in the competition.

One week earlier a crowd of 149,547 had assembled to 'see' the Scotland-England international, but few anticipated the final would attract a similar crowd. Perhaps the authorities were deceived by the fact of Aberdeen's geographical remoteness, and newspapers predicted a crowd in the vicinity of 95,000. A police contingent of one-third less than for the international was engaged, and the SFA decided to sell tickets for only the stands and the South Stand enclosure – at a cost of 5/– (25p) for the stand and 2/6d (12^1/2p) for the enclosure.

Aberdeen, after 34 years' existence as a club, were only now making an impact on Scottish football. For years they had been renowned as 'a home team' because of an excellent record at Pittodrie, and the fatigue of the visitors after a long train or coach journey to the north was a contributing factor in that. Conversely, Aberdeen's away record had never been out-standing, and already that season they had suffered League defeats in Glasgow from both Celtic and Rangers.

However, in April 1937, the mood in the Granite City was that of guarded optimism. The enterprise of one retailer illustrated the ambience: he was doing a brisk business in selling scarves and berets in Aberdeen's black-and-gold colours – all sold on the condition that the money would be refunded if the Dons were victorious. Confident in public, the vendor observed cannily: 'If Aberdeen win, then I won't grudge the money; but, if they lose, I'll have the consolation in the fact that I've done good business.'

HOPE SPRINGS ETERNAL

The Aberdeen players had a rousing send-off from the Joint Station last night. Over half an hour before the train for Glasgow was due to depart there was quite a large crowd of enthusiasts around the barrier, but as the time of departure drew near the crowd had swelled so much so that there were over a thousand men and women in the station . . . . Eddie Falloon, the Aberdeen captain, was also cheered to the echo, and before entering the train he was presented with a small black cat as a lucky talisman. It was noticed that when the train drew out of the station, Eddie had the cat standing on the table in his carriage. As the final cheer went up, the captain pointed to the mascot, then waved confidently to the crowd.

(*Aberdeen Press and Journal*: 24 April 1937)

The exodus from Aberdeen started early in the week for some young men, still unemployed, who set out on foot to walk to Glasgow; on the road to Glasgow they were joined later in the week – and passed – by a group of bicyclists wearing berets of black and gold.[4]

Trawler owners, it was rumoured, had instructed their skippers not to land fish in Aberdeen on the day of the final, and the best estimates indicate that more than 15,000 fans travelled to Hampden from Aberdeen. Most left on the 'specials' that ran from the city's Joint Station starting at 4.30 a.m.; others travelled on the convoys of buses estimated as totalling two hundred from all over the north of Scotland heading by road to Glasgow; hundreds of private cars left Aberdeen for the match, some on the Friday afternoon. At the stadium, no doubt, their numbers would be swelled by thousands of former northerners now resident in or near Glasgow.

The supporters – and the more casual camp-followers – were buoyed up with the realisation that Aberdeen, the city as much as the football club, was going to share centre-stage in Scotland's most popular drama. The folk from Aberdeen were displaying the same pawky self-confidence that had motivated a local haulier recently. The London and North Eastern Railway, apparently trying to reduce the competition, had sent him an insultingly brief telegram which read, 'Name price required for your company'. The Aberdonian sent back an equally terse rejoinder, 'State price required for your railway company'.

Most people considered it would be a close match, and the League standings did suggest little difference between the teams:

	P	W	L	D	F	A	PTS
Aberdeen	37	22	7	8	87	43	52
Celtic	37	22	7	8	89	50	52

The results in their League fixtures verified the equality between the sides: Celtic won 3–2 at Parkhead on 3 October, but Aberdeen won the return at Pittodrie on 23 January by 1–0.

Aberdeen might have gained a measure of confidence when considering the different routes the teams had followed to get to Hampden. Aberdeen's march to the final had been relatively uneventful, disposing of Inverness Thistle (6–0) and Third Lanark (4–2) at Pittodrie, edging out Hamilton by 2–1 away from home and defeating Morton 2–0 in the semi-final.

Celtic's progress to Hampden, on the other hand, had not been a stately procession, as they needed replays to get past Stenhousemuir and Motherwell. At Ochilview in the first hurdle Celtic were fortunate to escape with a 1–1 draw after McGrory had given them the lead; Stenhousemuir equalised deservedly and in the closing minutes, amid the fury of a 3,000 crowd, had a penalty claim turned down by the referee. At Parkhead against a Motherwell team that still retained most of their class and elegance, Celtic struggled, and found themselves 2–4 down shortly after the interval. They fought back with typical spirit and, after Delaney was fouled in the box, Lyon took over a captain's responsibility to smash the spot-kick past the keeper. Only nine minutes from the end Buchan equalised by finishing off a solo effort in which he deceived two defenders before hooking the ball past the helpless McArthur.[5]

Celtic had the experience of playing before big crowds, but Aberdeen were not suffering from an inferiority complex. The only advantage conceded to Celtic was a greater snappiness in finishing and the fear that the elusive Jimmy Delaney could instil in the best organised defences.

THE WINGER'S ROLE

An amusing retrospect of how football was played in 1937:

> Every football fan appreciated the need for wingers ('If there weren't wingers, who'd we give the No. 7 and No. 11 shirt to?'). All football pitches had a worn furrow down each wing. This was the result of wingers continually running up and down their own wing, game after game. When the winger reached the end of his furrow, he knew instinctively that if he had the ball it was time to centre it. The defending team made the wingers' job harder by placing a 'full back' at a point near the end of the furrow. Full backs were blessed with bigger boots. Wingers, however, had a trick. As the winger approached the full back, he would dip his left shoulder and then go right. Sometimes, just to crush the full back's ego, the winger would drop his right shoulder and then go left. This trick never failed. Wingers were therefore men of great skill and courage. As such, they were loved wherever they wore a furrow. Sadly, the winger was doomed. Thirty years or so later, the winger's furrow had gone, full backs had drifted to new pastures and the 'dip-left-go-right' trick was a lost art.

> (*Foul Magazine*: November 1972)

Aberdeen's new-found status owed much to their shrewd manager, Pat Travers, an ex-Celt who had forged a redoubtable side by a judicious mixture of recruits and transfers – and in the process transformed the club's financially precarious position. Nobody could consider his outlook as parochial; his team featured an Irishman, a Welshman and a South African. The Irishman was Eddie Falloon, captain and centre half although small at five feet five inches. Signed from Larne Crusaders, he was an exceptional pivot, in Scotland surpassed as a defensive player only by Rangers' Jimmy Simpson. The Welshman was Jackie Beynon, a speedy right winger signed from Doncaster Rovers for a little more than £1,000, Aberdeen's most expensive purchase. The South African Billy Strauss was noted for his dashes along the left touchline, and his finishing was lethal, his goals a major factor in Aberdeen's march to the final.

Celtic too could claim a cosmopolitan status: Joe Kennaway, the keeper, was born in Canada and signed from an American club to replace John Thomson; Willie Lyon, the captain, was signed from Queen's Park but was born on Merseyside.

Unfortunately for Aberdeen, Strauss had to withdraw, an ankle injury received against Morton in the semi-final still bothering him. Aberdeen drew some comfort in that the replacement, Johnny Lang, had made his

Willie Lyon in action against Jimmy Smith of Rangers.

debut the previous season against Celtic and scored twice in a 'roasting' of his immediate opponent in the final, Bobby Hogg.

The northern hordes arriving by the hour at Buchanan Street met with a good-natured reception from the Glaswegians; out for a good time, cheerful and colourful in black-and-gold scarves and rosettes, they traded insults cheerfully with the locals, crowded into the pubs and restaurants, bought souvenirs – seemingly determined to eradicate their city's reputation for thrift within a single day. The visitors were impressed with the efficiency of Glasgow's transportation system, as corporation tramcars and buses carried upwards of 25,000 passengers per hour towards Hampden Park; trains from the Central Station every few minutes carried thousands more. Minute by minute the 'big match' atmosphere was growing . . . but the scenes of chaos outside Hampden Park must have eroded most of the good feeling.

'Half an hour before the start of the match the gates at the north-west and south-west ends of the park were closed. The crowd pressed forward; temporary barricades had to be put up to reinforce the gates. A large section of the locked-out at the north side of Hampden dashed for the south side, and, shortly before the kick-off, crowds were still clamouring for admission, and the gates behind the south stand – which had been closed as a precautionary measure – were forced open. About 500 people scrambled into Hampden before the gates could be shut again.' (*The Bulletin*: 26 April 1937)

The attendance was given eventually as 146,433, but that did nothing to describe the scenes outside the ground with an estimated 20,000 milling around in growing confusion. In words reminiscent of events in Sheffield 52 years later, one onlooker told the *Aberdeen Press and Journal* of the terrifying spectacle in Somerville Drive 'packed with struggling humanity that looked like resolving [dissolving] into a jelly'.

Inside the ground on the packed terracing – where many saw little of the match – more than 100 fainted because of the crowding and had to be treated by the ambulance attendants. It was of little consolation to the victims inside and outside the ground that the SFA secretary announced after the match that future Cup finals would be all-ticket.

SCOTTISH CUP FINAL
24 April 1937
Hampden Park

CELTIC 2	**ABERDEEN 1**
Kennaway	Johnstone
Hogg	Cooper
Morrison	Temple
Geatons	Dunlop
Lyon	Falloon
Paterson	Thomson
Delaney	Beynon
Buchan	McKenzie
McGrory	Armstrong
Crum	Mills
Murphy	Lang

Scorers:
Crum (12)   Armstrong (13)
Buchan (70)
Referee: Mr M. Hutton (Glasgow)

Attendance: 146,433

Both sides were greeted by tremendous ovations when they took the field, Celtic first, and although Falloon won the toss the advantage for Aberdeen was negligible as only a slight breeze moved the corner flags.

Celtic settled almost from the start and pressed Aberdeen back into defence. Most of the danger was coming from Celtic's right, where Delaney

124

FANS!

In his *So This Is Glasgow!* (1938), the journalist Colin Milne – writing under the pseudonym 'Gulliver'– captures the flavour of travelling to an Old Firm match in the late 1930s. It seems a touch sedate, compared to the present.

> We took a bus from George Square shortly after one o'clock. The square was swarming with men, most of them wearing caps, and I was impressed by the orderly way in which they queued up to get into the buses that came along every few seconds. I listened attentively to the conversations going on around me, both in the queue and in the bus; they were unintelligible. Certain names had only to be mentioned to start fierce arguments. Years of football events were unrolled, and players long dead or long retired were severely criticised for shots they had missed in matches twenty or thirty years ago. My friend told me this sort of thing was quite usual, but it seemed strange to me that events so long past should still have the power to excite men almost to a frenzy.

and Buchan showed early signs of being on form; behind them, Chic Geatons was in an attacking frame of mind. Twice he reached the bye-line and crossed dangerous balls into the area. All this activity on the right must have been disconcerting for Temple, at left back for Aberdeen, who had replaced the regular full back halfway through the season; perhaps that was the reason for Mills opting to play a defensive role in midfield.

Aberdeen's opening was edgy; three times in the first ten minutes they gave away free kicks near the penalty box. Twice Lyon came upfield to take them with his short run; twice his shots were beaten away, and chances fell to both McGrory and Murphy but were missed. Conceding a third free kick was fatal in 12 minutes; from Paterson's kick McGrory headed for goal, but the ball was blocked only for Buchan to shoot strongly. Johnstone parried the drive and Crum, nippiest of inside forwards, dashed in for the score. It was a goal born of his quick reflexes, perhaps confirming the rumour in Glasgow that he owed his elusiveness to his frequent escapes from policemen while playing 'street-fitba'' in his native Maryhill. Small and fast, he had become a player almost impossible to mark for 90 minutes.

Celtic's lead lasted for little more than a minute. Aberdeen combined well down the right for Beynon to cross into the goalmouth; his awkward cross was deflected eventually by Lyon past a confused Kennaway, and Armstrong was on the spot to equalise. Armstrong was second only to Strauss in scoring goals for Aberdeen in their Cup run, and he had displayed intelligence in positioning himself for Beynon's cross.

Aberdeen gained in confidence from the goal, and play went from end to end for the rest of the first half. McGrory, although a veteran, was still full

125

Veteran Jimmy McGrory harries the Aberdeen defence.

of running and came close when he chested the ball past Falloon in a thrilling run, only to lose control of the bouncing ball and have Johnstone race off his line to save. Falloon was playing well in the heart of Aberdeen's defence, and had to be alert – as every pivot did – with McGrory chasing everything; he had enjoyed success against Celtic's leader in the past, and continued his relative mastery. Near half-time Aberdeen created a clear-cut chance when Lang, after work by Mills and Armstrong, got away on the left. He raced for goal, but Kennaway came out of his goal to cut down the angle, and the winger shot straight at him.

During the interval – as later – opinions were divided about the calibre of the final. 'Man in the Know' considered it 'one of the best finals ever', but in the same newspaper another correspondent, 'Onlooker' (presumably also pro-Celtic) disagreed, feeling that 'Contrary to the opinions of other critics, I think this final was devoid of brilliant football . . . On the whole the game was mediocre. It dropped far below the standard set for it, because Aberdeen brought south a cartload of "nerves".' (*Glasgow Observer*: 1 May 1937)

A more famous journalist, W. G. Gallacher (better known as 'Waverley'), was still enraptured by his memories of the match a quarter of a century later and described it as 'unrivalled in the sheer delights of football as it can – and should – be played . . . a classical display, skill of high degree, craftsmanship in plenty, almost every move dictated by innate football intelligence. The crowd were entranced at the science, the beauty of it all. Not that it was soft play, such as we sometimes have from the Continentals. There was the strong tackle, the hefty, but always fair, shoulder-charge . . . It was like a contest between two scientific boxers who, masters of the straight left and the right counter, eschewed in fighting, disdained clinching, and depended solely on the application of perfection in the art. Celtic were worthy winners, Aberdeen magnificent in defeat.'

The divergence in opinion about the worth of the match could be explained by the undoubted fact that both teams concentrated on football, and the match from beginning to end was played in a sporting manner. When attacks broke down, it was usually as the result of an interception by a player who had anticipated the next move – and not a faulty pass. The final did disappoint, however, in one major regard; none of the goals was entirely worthy of a Cup final.

The vast crowd, though, found it exciting enough and an incessant roar from the terracings accompanied every thrust by both teams: 'The atmosphere was punctuated with the staccato and broken cries that spoke of a game of see-saw fortune.' (*Glasgow Observer*: 1 May 1937)

In the second half play raged from end to end, and all the indications suggested that the next goal would win the Cup. Buchan was coming on to a strong game for Celtic, and in the opening minutes he beat his marker neatly and shot fiercely for the far corner only to see his shot, described as the best in the entire game, swerve past. Again Aberdeen settled down and

MULTINATIONAL

Joe Kennaway, Celtic's Canadian keeper, had become the first non-Briton to win a Scottish Cup-winner's medal in 1933 when Celtic defeated Motherwell 1–0. He received another medal in 1937, when Celtic beat Aberdeen 2–1. He gained the further distinction of winning 'caps' with three different countries: Canada, the United States and Scotland.

For some unexplained reason Kennaway turned out for the Celtic reserve side on the eve of the Scottish Cup final. He was the goalkeeper of the Alliance side which won 3–0 at Hamilton. The *Scottish Daily Express* of 24 April 1937 in its Cup final 'Special' section commented: 'Such a thing before the final is almost unheard of. If Kennaway had been injured . . .'

Presumably he was fielded in an emergency, probably an injury to the regular Alliance keeper. The match report indicates that he was not troubled much; however, it was an amazing risk!

put Celtic under some pressure for a ten-minute spell: Kennaway saved well from Beynon, Aberdeen's danger-man, and Lang could have done better with two chances within a five-minute spell.[6] All Celtic hearts stopped beating when Mills, virtually anonymous throughout, sent a curling ball from the left touchline that beat Kennaway but rebounded from the crossbar.

Celtic rallied, and during their spell of dominance scored the winning goal 20 minutes from time. A through ball was directed towards McGrory, marked tightly by Falloon; McGrory diverted the ball slightly and into the path of Buchan moving into space. Buchan, described by one critic as 'a master of a lively ball and a soloist par excellence', took possession in full stride and galloped through the middle to drive a low shot from 12 yards into the net off the post. 'The terracing became a sea of green and white; caps and hats winged in a carefree flight through the air. Strangers hugged each other with an affection that made one hope even for a future for the League of Nations.' (*Glasgow Observer*: 1 May 1937)

Willie Buchan nets the winner.

128

The goalscorers, Buchan and Crum, share the cup.

Aberdeen tried gamely to come back from this reverse, but Celtic's forwards were now finding more space and their raids menaced Aberdeen's goal frequently. Even Bobby Hogg scampered upfield to test Johnstone with a shot.

However, in a cup-tie and a goal down, every team can find reserves of stamina and resolve; in the last few minutes Aberdeen threw themselves into attack and exerted great pressure on Celtic's goal. Lyon's strength was invaluable at this stage, but Chic Geatons continued to be the most dominant player on the field; as an attacking right half he had caught the eye in the first half, but now his tackling and covering were outstanding. Aberdeen's last effort was cleared upfield by Lyon, and amid roars of celebration mingled with relief the Celtic players received the congratulations of their opponents, whose captain made a point of shaking hands with the referee.

The essential difference between the sides lay in the quality of the understanding among the half backs and inside forwards – the basis of the traditional Scottish style. Geatons operated in the modern midfield role and was a ball-winner and superb passer, and George Paterson was effectively quiet in subduing his immediate opponent; Willie Buchan and Johnny Crum linked well with the wing halves, and harried the opposing defence by their strong running, audacious dribbling and intelligent passing. Aberdeen were outgunned in this vital area; their wing halves were overworked in defence and unable to help much in attack, and the inside forwards, McKenzie and

Mills, failed to get the famed forward line moving with its customary cohesion, McKenzie lacking his customary forcefulness and Mills concentrating too much on defence.

In the *Daily Express* 'Alan Breck' dismissed talk of the occasion being too much for Aberdeen: 'What was too much for Aberdeen was Celtic.'

The Cup was presented in the pavilion, as was usual then, and Tom White, Celtic's Chairman, in accepting the trophy stated that he would not have been too disappointed in an Aberdeen victory and congratulated the northerners on their splendid effort. Several others made speeches: the Chairman of the SFA, the Chairman of Aberdeen, the Lord Provosts of Glasgow and Aberdeen. The ceremony was civilised, discreet, and private.

Out on the terraces an odd thing was happening: 'And at the close many spectators lingered to have a final look at the gigantic enclosure – evidently regretting that another season had come to an end – before they were shepherded towards the exits by the police.' (*Glasgow Herald*: 26 April 1937)

✳ ✳ ✳

Within a few years the worst fears were realised, and the winds of war would scatter many of the participants in the drama, player and spectator alike, to distant corners of the world. This time, survival – real life and real death – was the name of the game, and the heroes of countless thousands had to adjust to grimmer surroundings and to real tragedy.

On 2 January 1939, when a British attendance record for a League match was established at Ibrox with a crowd of 118,567, Willie Thornton of Rangers and Willie Lyon of Celtic were in opposition; the next time they spoke was in 1944, when they met up with each other on a dusty road in Italy, wearing the same uniform, soldiers in the same army.[7]

Sometimes it was enough just to be alive . . . but many would never return from those distant campaigns. Among the missing would be the luckless Private Keats, a fictional representative of the anonymous figures in the crowd at pre-war epics at Hampden, Ibrox and Celtic Park, and in those sun-bathed Italian hills always dreaming, like a Scottish Walter Mitty, of playing centre forward for Celtic – but now dead, victim of a German attack: 'Poor Keats with half his face missing. "You poor old sod [said the officer], I would have given half my Gran's fields to have you play once for Celtic, with me in front of the stand, eh? With funny hat and rattle." ' (Len Deighton: *Declarations of War*, 1971)

Footnotes

1 Most of the 500 German tourists carried expensive miniature cameras throughout their visit, although no newspaper hinted at any possibility of espionage .

2 One of the notable victims of Nazi persecution was Matthias Sindelar, a member of the Austrian 'Wunderteam' of the 1930s. Betrayed to the Gestapo shortly after

Hitler's annexation of Austria as being part-Jewish, he killed himself in a gas-filled room, according to at least one report.

3 A personal note. In November 1962 one of the authors was driving to Toronto and listening to the radio describe the latest developments in the Cuban Missile Crisis. His companion listened with growing gloom: a recent graduate, he had just started to teach, was saving up for a car . . . but he was more disturbed that, just when Celtic finally seemed to have found a prolific forward line, with successive victories at Airdrie (6–1) and Love Street (7–0), nuclear disaster threatened the world.

4 Before World War One Aberdeen had been nicknamed 'the Wasps'. The colours were changed to red with white shorts in 1939. Thus, in their first three Scottish Cup final appearances against Celtic they wore three different strips: black and gold in 1937, red and white in 1954, and all-red in 1967.

5 Motherwell gained a measure of revenge with a memorable 8–0 thrashing of Celtic in the last match of the season. Celtic suffered from injury in the game, but may have approached the fixture in a cavalier fashion a few days after the final.

6 Sadly, within a week of the final Jackie Beynon travelled to South Africa with his club on tour – and died in hospital there of peritonitis.

7 Both Old Firm players were decorated for gallantry during the war.

IN THE SWING

When in the spring of 1937 a carnival of 'Swing' was held at Randall's Island in New York, with twenty-five bands present. Over 23,000 jitterbugs listened for five hours and forty-five minutes with such uncontrollable enthusiasm that, as a reporters put it in the next morning's *Times*, the police and park-officers had all they could do to protect the players from 'destruction by admiration'. . . A good swing band smashing away at full speed, with the trumpeters and clarinetists rising in turn under the spotlight to embroider the theme with their several furious improvisations and the drummers going into long-drawnout rhythmical frenzies, could reduce its less inhibited auditors to sheer emotional vibrations, punctuated by howls of rapture.

(Frederick Lewis Allan: *Since Yesterday*, 1939)

8

THE LAST HURRAH

THE FLAGPOLE'S SERENADE

O wrap the League flag round me, boys,
On high for all to see;
For it is the emblem that should mark
The Celtic Jubilee.

Tho' countless heroes Time has claimed,
And dimmed the stars that shone,
Their deeds shall never be forgot.
The spirit lingers on.

So, wrap the League flag round me, boys —
Its proper destiny
To crown the last and glorious year
Of half a century.

And when the Exhibition comes,
O Scotia's proud array,
Let football be her greatest art,
And Celts Exhibit 'A'.

(Poem in the Celtic match programme, 5 February 1938)

IT WAS a glittering occasion for Celtic Football Club on the night of 15 June 1938 at the splendid Grosvenor Restaurant in Glasgow. Proudly displayed – and recently polished – the tangible symbols of success stood on handsome sideboards: the Glasgow Exhibition Cup won in 1902, the shield presented by the SFA to honour the feat of six League titles between 1904 and 1910, the Charity Cup gained yet again in 1938 and, perhaps the talking-point of the evening, the Empire Exhibition Trophy won only five days earlier.

Willie Maley: the 'official' portrait (1938).

A sense of pride and satisfaction permeated the room, derived from 50 years' accomplishment; confidence was in the air after the latest triumph and the knowledge that Celtic were the current League champions.

The manager, Willie Maley, associated with the club from its inception, was honoured by being presented with a cheque for 2,500 guineas, representing 50 guineas for each year's service.[1] Maley, visibly affected, had to compose himself before replying, during which time the guests, rising to the occasion, sang *Ole Faithful* in the manager's honour. Replying to these tributes, Willie Maley declared solemnly: 'I thank Almighty God that He has spared me to the age I am [70] . . . I am not a man of riches, but I am thankful that He has given me health to carry on the work that has been allotted me . . . I am the last survivor of that little band that set out heroically to launch the Celtic ship.'

Among the assembled guests were officials of the SFA, and representatives of every other League club; the Lord Provost of the City of Glasgow and members of the council, former players who had been invited to attend, and all current team members were present. If some of the Celtic team did not raise their eyes in disbelief at these outward manifestations of harmony, it would have been surprising in view of recent developments. Any outsider surveying the scene could be forgiven for not recognising that relations between the manager and players were strained, and that the link between manager and directors was frayed.

Willie Maley, in a sympathetic moment, once described sacked managers as 'the despised and the rejected'. He did so in the mid-1930s at a period when the pressures on the manager were different from those that beset present-day incumbents of the position. In that era the manager was not directly associated in the public's mind with the team's fortunes on the field. For example, it would be inconceivable nowadays that even the highly respected Paddy Travers could last for 14 years at Pittodrie without success measured in trophies. In those days the manager, or more accurately the secretary-manager as he was frequently titled, was mostly concerned with the hiring (and firing) of players and general club administration. Tactical insight, the training of players and coaching were not necessarily part of his *curriculum vitae*. It was assumed that, as an ex-player himself, the manager had sufficient expertise to sign players of the required calibre, but his involvement with the recruits afterwards went little beyond disciplinary matters.

The game at that time was viewed more as an entertainment than as a cut-throat business; thus, the player was very much the centre of attention and largely free to express himself creatively on match days. Training and coaching were light years away from today's rigorous and scientific schedules. In common with his peers Maley spent most of his day behind a desk; players largely kept themselves fit with a *laissez faire* series of sprints for speed and laps for stamina. The ex-Celt Matt Lynch described the scene on the odd occasion Maley strolled out of the tunnel for a breath of fresh air: 'You never saw such activity on the track. It was a situation akin to the headmaster-and-pupils type of relationship.'

Remarkably, the players rarely saw a ball during training. Conventional wisdom decreed that, if the players were deprived of the ball during the week, they would be more hungry for it on Saturdays – an outlook and practice to some degree still prevalent at Parkhead a couple of decades later.

The training was nominally in the charge of the famous Jimmy McMenemy, employed in the mid-1930s as a 'coach', although it appears that his role was mainly that of 'geeing up' the players by passing on the fruits of his experience (dispensing practical, largely non-technical, advice). First-team players trained at one end of the ground, and reserves at the other. Years later players would laugh at the recollection that the only coaches they knew were the ones on the trains that took them to away matches!

MISSIONARY

Johnny Madden, the ex-Celt, went to Prague in 1905 to become the first professional coach of a Czech club when he joined Slavia Prague. He was given much of the credit for changing the style of football in Czechoslovakia from 'a technically manneristic soccer into a straight athletic style', and in 1938, aged 73, he was still coaching Slavia. Brought to the ground every day by a club car, he supervised the training while sitting in a wheelchair and brandishing a cabby's whip.

The learning process was based largely on the communication between established players and newcomers on the field during actual matches – a form of on-the-job training. Malcolm MacDonald, regarded by many older Celtic supporters as the purest footballer ever to wear a Celtic jersey – and they persist in that assertion with impressive conviction – recalls how Peter Wilson stressed to him that the game revolved totally around possession and use of the ball. Wilson, a marvellous passer himself, insisted that the obligation of a player who made a careless pass was to regain possession immediately. Other senior players used different forms of motivation: 'Alec Thomson would plead with you and encourage you, while "Peter" McGonagle would exhort you with all sorts of threats,' MacDonald chuckles.

He recalls that Maley rarely dispensed advice, but was liberal with criticism; in dealing with MacDonald's fondness for holding on to the ball, his frequent admonition was 'Cut out all this dribbling!' The young player was not fond of his authoritarian manager, and would travel upstairs on the tramcar to avoid sitting beside Maley downstairs; more often than not, he would stay on the tram for an extra stop to avoid the walk of a hundred yards to Celtic Park with Maley.

Matt Lynch remembers the late 1930s as a time when the only instruction the team received from the manager was 'Go out and win or else!' In fairness he recalls that Maley spoke to him – a relatively young player – at least twice to offer advice in private about opponents. He was advised that one inside forward did not relish vigorous tackling, and that a strong challenge by Lynch would discourage him; he was told that another forward had the habit of following through with his boot after shooting or completing a pass, and that Lynch should be prepared to defend himself. The information, news to Lynch, was accurate and helpful.

Despite the rudimentary training, Celtic sides had developed a distinctive style and managed to retain it down the years despite the many changes in personnel. One of the reasons was the reservoir of young talent on tap to the club through the scouting network headed in the 1930s by a cunning old character named Steve Callaghan. The chief scout had been personally responsible for signing up scores of players, among them John Thomson and Malcolm MacDonald.

The other reason was the character of Willie Maley, who, it was felt, embodied the Celtic tradition. After 40 years in charge at Parkhead he represented the ultimate authority for the players. Few dared to argue with a man who could make or break a career at a club of Celtic's stature; even the greatest players experienced qualms of anxiety as a season drew to an end in case they were not re-signed. The alternative for some would be life on the dole, or a drastic cut in status and wages. Malcolm MacDonald, for example, earned four times as much as his father who was employed at Provan Gas Works. Besides, with the passing of time, Maley tended to regard a difference of opinion as a personal affront and had become increasingly difficult to reason with.

WORKING-CLASS ARISTOCRATS

The average wage for the top players in the late 1930s was £8 a week. It was reckoned that a senior official in the Town Hall or a bank who received similar wages could afford to own his house, run a car and perhaps employ a maid. The famous Rangers goalkeeper, Jerry Dawson, when interviewed by Bob Crampsey, said:

> To lose one's place in the side and receive a free transfer was almost certainly to return to the Labour Exchange. [Despite that fear he considered that he and his team-mates played in the balmy days of football] We had much better tours abroad than now. We went by boat, we had time to see the country, we lived like lords, and the opposition were pushovers. Now it is a very hasty flight and a tough match.
>
> (Bob Crampsey: *The Scottish Footballer,* 1978)

His intimidating build – similar to that of his most illustrious successor, Jock Stein – did much to reinforce his image as a hard, brusque man. He dressed for the part, wearing a grey Homburg hat and heavy black coat almost as badges of authority. There was more than a touch of the old soldier about Willie Maley, whose military bearing and manner may have been inherited from a father who had left his native Ireland in 1847 (in the midst of the Great Famine) to join the British Army as an under-age recruit. Maley's father served with distinction during the Crimean War, and Celtic's manager treasured his father's medals attesting to conduct at the battles of Alma, Inkerman, Sebastopol and Balaclava.

Maley's style of leadership could be described as remote and autocratic, similar to that of a general conducting operations at headquarters, far from the actual front line but with a well established structure of command in place.

At a time when football was played largely 'off the cuff', with players on the field reading the game and making tactical changes for themselves, management of the playing side of a large club such as Celtic consisted of establishing a player's best position – after some experimentation if necessary – and having the patience to allow individual ability and flair to integrate with the framework of the team. The resulting blend was the consequence of players being aware of the team's strengths and weaknesses and making decisions based on that knowledge. Most importantly, Celtic teams and players absorbed the unique, and by now legendary, Celtic spirit. Maley, the last remaining link with the first-ever Celtic team, was responsible for nurturing that mystique and passing it on to his players.

Maley's instincts were those of the ex-pro rather than the technocrat – a mixture of habit, observation, and empirical judgement. He used tried and trusted methods, and his personal authority enabled him to convince his subordinates of their validity

A subscriber to the long-established premise that a good player should be able to play in any position, he had a reputation for tinkering with the make-up of his teams. A recent example was Chic Geatons, signed from Lochgelly Celtic as a full back; Maley saw greater potential in the raw youngster and helped him develop into a constructive, strong-running right half.

Like Stein in a later era he imposed his will in a variety of ways: the harshness of a benevolent despot, the unexpected act of kindness, the tactical use of anger, the fear of dismissal. However, despite personal failings which increased with age, he always allowed his teams to express themselves freely on the field, to the greater glory of Scottish football.

*   *   *

In 1937/38 Celtic had produced yet another formidable team, strong where strength was needed, but noted for its silken touches. Above all, like every truly outstanding side, it was a team greater than the sum of its individual parts. In defence the slightly built and resilient Joe Kennaway in goal had developed an excellent understanding with pivot Willie Lyon, a strong man in the middle. They were assisted by two dependable full backs in Bobby Hogg and John Morrison. Strong, capable, and consistent: the marks of all acceptable defences. Starting at wing half, Celtic could call upon the mixture of power and skill required of great teams: Chic Geatons had blossomed into an exceptional right half, strong in defence and subtle in attack, while George Paterson, stocky and dark-haired, blended skills and intensity admirably.

Up front, Celtic fielded a famous forward line: Delaney, MacDonald, Crum, Divers, and Murphy. More than 50 years later their names are cherished by many Celtic supporters who claim with some justification that it was the best attack ever fielded by the club. Jimmy Delaney was Scotland's right winger, a will-o'-the-wisp attacker and most dangerous in the penalty area; Malcolm MacDonald was an extravagantly gifted, and thoughtful, inside right; Johnny Crum, the successor to McGrory, was not in the spearhead tradition of Scottish centres, but drew opponents out of position with his darting positional play, quicksilver moves and sheer irrepressibility; Johnny Divers was a tall inside left, clever on the ball and a deadly finisher with both foot and head; Frank Murphy, similar to Delaney in his speed and crossing, had the gift for doing the totally unexpected.

Talented individually, they had elevated team-work to a new level. The three inside forwards had established an immediate rapport and under-standing when playing in the reserve side, and perfected it in the first team. The main feature of their play was rapid-fire passing and quick inter-changing that invariably found one of the trio loose in front of goal. Allied to fast-raiding wingers and regular scorers such as Delaney and Murphy, and backed up by the constructive play of Geatons and Paterson, Celtic on the attack was a thrilling spectacle. Malcolm MacDonald summed it up modestly: 'When you brought together the team's various components, they added up to a pretty formidable whole.'

Formidable it had to be to cope with the challenge presented in the Empire Exhibition Cup in 1938, as Celtic strove to cap the official Jubilee Season (for both club and manager) in a fitting fashion by lifting the unique trophy in knock-out competition with Aberdeen, Rangers and Hearts from Scotland, and Brentford, Chelsea, Everton and Sunderland from England.

The tournament, devised to coincide with 'an exposition of the work, life, culture and progress' of the British Empire, quickly became a crowd-pleasing attraction in Glasgow, recognised world-wide as 'a football city'. The Scottish Development Council had initiated the exposition as a shop-window display to encourage new industry to come to Scotland, at a time when the older ones, notably shipbuilding and heavy engineering on the Clyde, were seen as in terminal decline. It was an admirable concept: it displayed Scottish skills and workmanship, it fostered imperial trade, understanding and friendship, and it was hoped by Glasgow's City Fathers that it would do much to counter the sordid image presented in some quarters as typical of the city.[2]

Glasgow, the 'Second City' of an empire which covered one quarter of the earth's surface, made a substantial investment in the enterprise originally conceived in 1936 as an act of faith when Scotland was struggling painfully and slowly out of the Depression. Of the £10 million spent directly or indirectly on the wonderful six-month display, Glasgow itself contributed £1 million, ranging from direct financial contributions to facilities, granting special terms for services such as gas and electricity, establishing a municipal information bureau and upgrading its transport infrastructure. Throughout the period of the Empire Exhibition the city gave up 175 acres of one of its public parks, Bellahouston Park, situated three miles to the south-west of the town-centre. The results were spectacular: 'a world playground of entertainment and instruction . . . An amazing city of "make-belief" has been built with wood, steel, girders, concrete – a city complete with water, gas, electricity, and sewage services adequate for a population of 500,000.' (*The Bulletin*: 3 May 1938)

Among the myriad of pavilions two were devoted exclusively to Scotland, her history and culture in one, and the development of contemporary town-planning, public health and municipal services in the other. The United Kingdom Pavilion promised to have government departments show the sceptics 'what they are doing to make life longer and happier for every man'. A casual stroll down Dominions' Avenue, on one side of the artificial lake, allowed visitors to enter the pavilions of Canada, Australia, New Zealand, South Africa and Eire; on Colonial Avenue, opposite on the other side of the lake, the pavilions of the various colonies and protectorates could be found. One of the most popular spectator-sports was ogling the giraffe-necked Burmese girls. Inevitably, though, for 'fitba'-mad' Glasgow males even the attractions of that sport had to take second place when the competition for the Empire Exhibition Cup started at nearby Ibrox Park on 25 May.

All the matches were scheduled for Ibrox, the nearest stadium to Bellahouston Park, and the football ground served as a giant annex to the Exhibition itself. King George VI and Queen Elizabeth, after being driven round the track in a state-carriage drawn by two white horses, opened the Exhibition there on 3 May before a crowd estimated at little under 100,000. Rallies by Britain's two largest youth movements, the Boys' Brigade and the Boy Scouts, were held at Ibrox later in the month, as was a week-long pageant by Britain's armed forces – as if to assure the public of the country's state of readiness at a time of semi-permanent crisis.

The competition for the trophy that the newspapers were already dubbing 'a British Championship' started with a clash between Celtic and

---

SCOTS WHA HAE

Tommy Walker's goal from a penalty kick in the last minute at Wembley in 1936 prompted the usual celebrations. From a distance of more than 50 years they seem rather quaint and decorous:

> Wembley in the Scotsman's diary takes second place only to Hogmanay. This biennial football business is an institution. Immediately the cheers – or groans – have faded over England's classic amphitheatre, perfervid Scots begin to reckon on ways and means of getting there next time. Win or lose, this trip to the Metropolis is carried out from beginning to end in the carnival spirit – with a dash of other spirits as well. Whether the weather be fine or strong the tartan-bedecked hordes have one aim in common. They are out to enjoy themselves, and they do it in style. London gives them the freedom of the city. They don't, as a rule, abuse the privilege, and from early morn to dewy eve their laughter and good-humoured banter is accepted in the spirit in which it is meant. Londoners on International Day waken to the strains of 'Hielan' Laddie', 'The Highland Wedding', or 'Leaving Glen Urquhart'. From Euston down Tottenham Court Road and on to the Strand and Trafalgar Square there is a continual 'tramp, tramp' to the various places where feeding arrangements have been made in advance. Once satisfied, the many points of interest are covered in an inexhaustible programme culminating in a gigantic yell as the players take the field . . . The scenes on departure form a whirl of gaiety which thousands of Londoners enjoy. There is the inevitable eightsome reel to the skirl of the pipes, and London Scots apply the finishing touch with a loud-throated chorus 'Will ye no' come back again?'
>
> ('Alan Breck': *Book of Scottish Football*, 1937)

Sunderland. A splendid crowd of 53,976 risking threatening weather watched the teams fight out a dour battle with defences well on top. The major surprise was the ferocity of the tackling and the intensity with which the sides approached the match; another surprise was that the visitors improved the longer the match went on, and Celtic were fortunate to survive the extra-time without giving up a goal. Only solid, no-nonsense defensive work by Lyon and immaculate handling by Kennaway kept Celtic level.

In the replay the following night, Sunderland started where they had left off in a tie played in driving rain that reduced the attendance to 20,000; early on Kennaway dived to turn over the bar a magnificent drive from Horatio Carter (Stanley Matthews' frequent partner on England's right wing), then had to save a close-in shot from Burbank. After Sunderland had taken a deserved lead through Saunders, who rounded two Celtic defenders to score in 30 minutes, Celtic started to produce their true form. Eight minutes later Crum equalised, a quick turn and shot surprising the English defence. In the second half Celtic's patented interchanging among the forwards baffled Sunderland's defenders and two goals within the first 15 minutes by Divers ensured a comfortable 3–1 victory. The first came after rapid switching with Crum and MacDonald left him clear ten yards out, and the second after evading an offside trap when he 'chipped' Mapson, stranded in the penalty area. Of concern to Celtic was the injury suffered by Delaney in the first match, although Matt Lynch did well as a replacement on Celtic's right wing in the replay.

Aberdeen struck another blow for Scotland's prestige by hammering Chelsea 4–0 one day later, the pace of the 'Dons' causing such havoc that *The Bulletin* was moved to comment: 'Contrary to usual, it was the Scottish side which proved the faster footballers.' The run was ended abruptly on 30 May when Rangers, the host club, met Everton. Rangers had entered a period of relative decline and only the Glasgow Cup decorated the Ibrox trophy-room: Celtic had won the Championship, East Fife the Cup, and only weeks earlier Celtic had toyed with Rangers in the Charity Cup final en route to a 2–0 win. Another excellent crowd – of 47,682 – watched Everton deal with Rangers' challenge easily, the Englishmen's accurate first-time shooting causing problems for Rangers. Gillick, later a famous Ranger, struck the woodwork for Everton as did Stevenson before Tommy Lawton opened the scoring in 38 minutes. Cunliffe scored another in 59 minutes, and Dawson, Rangers' keeper, was carried off in a collision with his full back, Winning, in a futile attempt to prevent the goal.[3]

Even at this stage of the tournament Everton had emerged as the strongest of the English sides – and, indeed, the only survivors – and were being touted as likely winners. Against Aberdeen in the semi-final they scored through Gillick in ten seconds, and were always the more dangerous side although Aberdeen rallied to lead 2–1 at half-time. Boyes equalised in 51 minutes, and five minutes later Joe Mercer shrugged off several Aberdeen challenges in a long run down the right before crossing accurately for Lawton, a deadly header of the ball, to crash the winning goal past Johnstone.

FIRST CLASS MAIL

A news item from 1938, headed *'Man posts himself as parcel'* :

> An Englishman arrived safely in Amsterdam from London by air parcel post in a properly labelled consignment. He explained that, having failed to catch the passenger plane, he conceived this idea of being in time for a business appointment.

Wizards of the wing – Jimmy Delaney and Frank Murphy.

Celtic faced Hearts in the other semi-final; the Edinburgh side had been lucky to scrape past Brentford in the opening round. Brentford may appear a strange representative of England's First Division, but the Londoners had been consistently placed in the top six since gaining promotion, and Malcolm MacDonald later assessed them as one of the best footballing sides in the competition. Before a crowd of 45,403, Hearts scored in 26 minutes with a volley from Briscoe past Joe Crozier (often Scotland's goalkeeper in the war-time internationals). From then on Brentford pressed continuously to outplay Hearts, and in the dying seconds Gerry McAloon broke through for Brentford to be foiled by Waugh.[4] The Glasgow crowd were victims of mixed emotions – to cheer for Englishmen or for a team from Edinburgh. Predictably, they settled for the underdogs – and the better side – urging on Brentford with a continuous roar of encouragement.

Against Celtic it was an entirely different match; Celtic started off well, but Hearts dominated the proceedings after 20 minutes. An effort by Tommy Walker was disallowed controversially in the first half, and Andy Black, the scorer of Hearts' three goals against Rangers in a recent League match on the same ground, was unlucky. Only exceptional keeping by Kennaway foiled Hearts, and the Edinburgh men were starting to regret a series of missed opportunities when Crum took another half-chance in 65 minutes to allow Celtic to advance. Typically, Crum shot quickly from close range, and Waugh touched but could not hold the shot.

Johnny Crum, a deadly opportunist, slides in to score against Motherwell in 1937 (Jimmy Delaney looks on).

143

It was going to be a popular final, and Celtic, the original favourites, could have no illusions about the task awaiting them against Everton. In the season just ended the Liverpool side had been a disappointment, perhaps as a result of boardroom squabbles, but according to the *Liverpool Echo* of 10 June 1938 the team 'found itself during the competition'.

Tommy Lawton believed that the series of matches in Scotland laid the foundations of Everton's Championship success in 1938/39. He recalls with pleasure the team's stay at Skelmorlie Hydro Hotel for the duration of the tournament and the enjoyment offered by 'the many facilities for steamer runs across to Arran, Dunoon, and the Kyles of Bute; the golf at the neighbouring courses; motor rides through the really magnificent countryside, and the many friends we all made.' After the season's play training was not rigorous, and consisted of five-a-side games played in a light-hearted manner; however, the games lasted for hours, an indication that the players were enjoying themselves and developing further understanding: 'We began to fit in with one another like pieces in a jigsaw.'

Both finalists had a reputation for immaculate football, in attitude as well as skill, and a memorable contest was in prospect for the 82,000 who gathered at Ibrox on a lovely Friday evening, 10 June 1938. One interested spectator was a youthful Kenneth Wolstenholme, later a noted BBC TV sports commentator whose English accent used to irritate thousands of Scots viewers. Along with his brother and two friends he decided:

> to have a shilling's worth of this game, but as we walked down the street towards the ground some Scots heard us talking. When they found out that we were determined to uphold the English by supporting Everton, and that we were heading for a spot behind the goal, they winced and advised us to go with them. It cost two shillings each, but I have always been thankful for that advice. For it was my first taste of the Scottish fervour . . . especially the brand turned on by the Celtic fans. They waved their banners, they waved their flags, and they sang their revolutionary songs and their special war-cry of 'The Dear Little Shamrock'.
>
> (*Sports Special*: 1958)

The Liverpool newspapers expressed some surprise at Everton's reaching the final after an indifferent season. They were not invited originally, and had got a place only through withdrawals, but the *Liverpool Echo* of 8 June was now advertising a 'cheap excursion' to the match from the Exchange Station, the 16/3d (81p) fare including admission to the Exhibition. Any 'Scouser' venturing north could take in some of the entertainment at Bellahouston Park: mannequin parades, dancing to 'Bobby Hind and his Orchestra', cooking demonstrations, fitness displays and a visit to the cinema where 'Travel, News, and Comedy' were continuous from 1.30 p.m. For those Scots unable to attend the final, a radio commentary on the BBC

CLOUD NINE!
Britain's first aerial wedding took place on 14 May 1938 in a Scottish
Airways monoplane circling above the Empire Exhibition site. Nancy
Spencer, a Stirlingshire domestic, married Cecil Ferguson, a Glasgow
engineer.

Regional Service would be delivered by R. E. Kingsley, better known as
'Rex' of the *Sunday Mail*. The Glasgow *Evening Times* announced its plans
to bring out a special edition immediately after the conclusion with a full
match-report by 'Alan Breck'.

EMPIRE EXHIBITION CUP FINAL
10 June 1938
Ibrox Park

CELTIC 1	**EVERTON 0 (a.e.t.)**
Kennaway	Sagar
Hogg	Cook
Morrison	Greenhalgh
Geatons	Mercer
Lyon	Jones
Paterson	Thomson
Delaney	Geldard
MacDonald	Cunliffe
Crum	Lawton
Divers	Stevenson
Murphy	Boyes

Scorer:
Crum (97)
Referee: T. Thompson (Northumberland)

Attendance: 82,000

Everton had become a team of absorbing curiosity to the neutral
spectator, and of more vested interest to the Celtic supporters. Their
formidable squad included internationalists from all four home countries:
Sagar, Mercer, Cunliffe, Lawton, Boyes and Geldard from England; Cook
and Stevenson from Ireland; Jones from Wales; and Gillick from Scotland.
Many of their players were household names: Ted Sagar was England's
keeper, and in a long career fated to be remembered mainly as the victim of
Tommy Walker's penalty goal for Scotland at Wembley in 1936; Tommy
Jones was the prototype of the pivot of the 1930s, authoritative, rugged and
hard as teak; Joe Mercer at right half was determined and strong in the

tackle, disproving the observation of a team-mate that he (Mercer) had spindly legs which 'wouldn't last a postman his morning round' by playing on until he was nearly 40

, by which time he was established as one of footballs most popular players; young Tommy Lawton was on the threshold of becoming the most feared centre in Britain, a sinister presence in the penalty area; 'Torry' Gillick, later to be a star with Rangers, was another menacing figure, an excellent passer and a deadly finisher.

One point had to be cleared up before the final, and that was the choice of referee between P. Craigmyle (Aberdeen) and T. Thompson (Northumberland). The Englishman won by the toss of a coin or by ballot (depending on which paper you read), but all the match reports agreed later that he had done an outstanding job in controlling the match.

The final very quickly became an enthralling contest, the flow of the game first favouring one side and then the other. Some had suggested earlier that the similarity in style might produce a stalemate, but the opening exchanges were bright and promising. Both sides were constructive at wing half and inside forward, and capable of inspired improvisation among the forwards.

The defences were organised capably by two commanding figures – the Welshman, Tommy Jones, for Everton and the Englishman, Willie Lyon, for Celtic. Each had the difficult personal task of marking vastly different centre forwards; Jones had to watch the elusive and diminutive Johnny Crum, while Lyon was confronted with the tall, athletic Tommy Lawton. This latter confrontation was fascinating; it pitted a good centre half at the height of his career against a great centre forward at the start of his. One moment stilled the noise of the Celtic following; Lawton got his head to a corner and his header was so powerful that it cleared the large grass verge and the track behind the goal – a considerable distance in the Ibrox of 1938.

Celtic were encouraged that Delaney could resume his place on the right wing after missing the replay with Sunderland and the semi-final with Hearts; Everton, on the other hand, were without Gillick, out with an injury sustained against Aberdeen, but the strength of their squad could be gauged by considering that his replacement, Geldard, had won a recent 'cap' for England.

The reaction of the crowd told of the events unfolding on the pitch. Every Celtic attack was accompanied by cheering, but it was optimistic and encouraging in tone rather than exultant and triumphant; this Everton defence would not crumble easily. Everton forays were greeted with apprehensive and heart-stopping silence, mingled with murmers of appreciation; this Everton attack was dangerous.

During Celtic's spells of ascendancy the inside forwards interchanged rapidly and shot often; the wingers, Delaney and Murphy, chased every ball and tried to harry the English defence into mistakes . . . but the Everton rearguard was resolute. Everton were equally direct in attack, prompted by the constructive touches of the Irish internationalist Stevenson at inside left and Mercer at right half.

Lyon was marking Lawton closely, but the young centre broke through once, a minute or so before the interval, and only another splendid and daring dive at his feet by Kennaway saved Celtic.

Exhibition Cup Winners. Back row, left to right: Geatons, Hogg, Kennaway, Morrison, Crum and Paterson. Front row: Delaney, MacDonald, Lyon, Divers and Murphy.

Everton had been handicapped by an injury in the opening minutes to Cunliffe who was forced to play on the wing for much of the match.[5] The advantage to Celtic was starting to become apparent, and much of the play was in Everton's half of the field. After 90 minutes the score was still deadlocked 0–0, and so the final went into extra-time.

Celtic were now well on top, and the pressure continued with the crowd urging on the Scots; Sagar, stranded well out of goal, was beaten by one shot but Jones scrambled the ball off the line. But a goal had to come despite the resistance of Everton's rearguard. Divers spotted a gap and flicked the ball into it; the alert Crum had anticipated the move, and his shot from 15 yards was partly saved by Sagar, but he could not prevent the ball from crossing the line. Crum danced away in joy and, before his team-mates could reach him, capered round behind the goal to salute the supporters now ecstatic in the realisation of triumph.

Crum's reaction was unusual in the pre-showbusiness football of 1938;

the captain, Willie Lyon, joined in the celebrations briefly, but could be seen calling a halt and exhorting the others to concentrate.

Everton revealed all the character and skill of a championship team in the remaining 23 minutes, but Celtic, with a sensible emphasis on defence, held on to win.

The trophy, a silver replica of the Exhibition Tower, known as Tait's Tower, after the architect-in-chief of the exhibition, was presented to Willie Lyon by Lord Elgin, the Exhibition's President, on a wooden platform in front of the stand enclosure. The players on both sides received miniatures of the trophy, Celtic as winners receiving silver ones and Everton plate.

*　　*　　*

A few minutes later in the Ibrox dressing-room even as the Celtic players, happy and tired, were unwinding in the communal bath, the manager congratulated them on the achievement – which was little less than the unofficial championship of Britain. He commented in his most 'hard-to-please' manner that the victory had done much to wipe away the sting of a shock defeat in the Scottish Cup a few months earlier, as if the gaining of the League Championship shortly after (and the Charity Cup) had not already redeemed it!

The Cup Presentation.

Increasingly, Maley's preoccupation with money was affecting him adversely; no doubt, as he claimed frequently in the club's handbooks in the inter-war period, an early exit from the Cup meant a financial loss. Money was to be his downfall at Parkhead.

Shortly after the Exhibition final the club captain, Willie Lyon, was appointed by the players to approach the manager about a bonus, promised

---

FREEDOM OF SPEECH

The political turmoil of the period is reflected in this report:

A large motor lorry carrying several May Day speakers had to make a hurried exit out of Glasgow Green under police escort . . . Apparently the Communists among the vast crowd gathered on the recreation ground at Glasgow Green were determined to make things uncomfortable for a meeting run by 'The Workers' Union for Social Justice', which is opposed both to Communism and Fascism. No sooner had the chairman stepped on to the platform than there was a shout by Communist interrupters of 'Arms for Spain!' and 'Run the Fascists to the river!' The shouting became more threatening, and when all effort to hold the meeting seemed hopeless the engine was started up and the vehicle moved slowly through the crowd with the Communists running after it, triumphant at its departure.

(The Bulletin: 2 May 1938)

---

by one director, which had not been paid in full, as only 20 per cent of it had appeared in their pay-packet. Maley stared down his captain and suggested tartly that Lyon should take the matter up with the director who, Maley added, would doubtless pay the balance out of his own pocket.

Little wonder, then, that the players would have mixed feelings at the Jubilee Dinner as the manager was so handsomely rewarded for his services to the club. In fact, the members of the winning team never did get much satisfaction with their grievance, a factor that soured the triumph somewhat and contributed to the lack of morale the following season, a situation which ultimately led to Maley's own removal from office.

For much of the next 18 months Maley himself was embroiled in an undignified dispute with the club over his 'honorarium'. In 1938 Celtic declared a substantial profit of £7,105 on the year's working, and Maley felt that the club could accommodate his request; apparently, the dispute concerned the taxation on the gift, which by 1990 tax standards would have been negligible. However, the directors were becoming frustrated in dealing with a stubborn, and sometimes high-handed, individual, and in employing a 70-year-old manager of institutional status at Parkhead.

It was a time for farewells.

The Exhibition, described by one of its historians (Bob Crampsey), as 'the Last Durbar', was destined to become a farewell to Empire in more senses than one. On 29 October 1938 a remarkable total of 364,000 people braved the rain – common in the city's wettest summer within memory – to visit Bellahouston Park and bid farewell to a festival which had brought a welcome smile to the face of Glasgow. Standing in the rain, watching the

149

fireworks and the floodlit tower, the people seemed to be sensing after the uneasy deal with Hitler at Munich that the lights would be going out again all over Europe.

The British Empire, which Maley's father had served so well, would fray and erode under the strains of wartime and the demands for independence after 1945. Renamed the Commonwealth, and suitably revamped, it could never again summon up the pomp and circumstance of Empire . . .

On 1 February 1940, during the first winter of World War Two, Willie Maley had turned his back on Celtic Park, 'exiled from Paradise' where he had shaped the destiny of one of Britain's most famous clubs, and faced the oncoming black-out of a wartime city; he faced also, bleakly and bitterly, a future without the very core of his existence . . .

Footnotes

1 A guinea, considered a more aristocratic denomination, consisted of one pound and one shilling. Thus, the gift amounted to £2,625.

2 A recent novel, *No Mean City*, had exaggerated the gang-wars, the razor-slashing and the violence; accordingly, Glasgow's reputation had suffered.

3 Rangers' captain, Jimmy Simpson, took over in goal for the rest of the match and did not concede a goal; his young son, Ronnie, watched with approval. Ronnie Simpson, of course, was Celtic's keeper at Lisbon in 1967.

4 Gerry McAloon signed for Celtic shortly after the Second World War, adding some composure to an inept forward line.

5 Substitutes, had they been allowed then, would have been invaluable. Delaney and Carruth were injured against Sunderland but soldiered on limping, Dawson (Rangers) was carried off against Everton, and now Cunliffe (Everton) against Celtic in the final was a 'passenger'. Delaney missed the replay against Sunderland and the semi-final against Hearts; Carruth was out for the rest of the tournament.

9

THE IMPOSSIBLE DREAM

THE CORONATION WALTZ

Said Lizzie to Philip, as they sat down to dine
'I've just had a note from an old friend of mine;
His name is Big Geordie, he's loyal and true,
And his nose is my favourite colour of blue.[1]

'He says that the Rangers are right on their game,
And asks for a trophy to add to their fame.
I'll send up a trophy that the Rangers can win.'
Said Philip to Lizzie, 'Watch the Celts don't step in.'

Said Lizzie to Philip, 'They don't stand a chance.
I'll send up my Gunners to lead them a dance;
With the Celtic defeated the way will be clear
For a cup for the Rangers in my crowning year.'

But oh! What a blow to the boys in the blue,
For the Celts beat the Arsenal and Manchester too,
Beat Hibs in the final and oh! what a scene,
All Hampden was covered in banners of green.

Said Lizzie to Philip, when she heard the news,
'A blow has been struck to my royal true blues.
Oh, tell me, dear Philip, for I want to know,
How to beat Glasgow Celtic and keep them below?'

Said Philip to Lizzie, 'There's only one way,
And that's been no secret for many a day.
To beat Glasgow Celtic you'll have to deport
All the thousands of Fenians who give them support!'

Supporters' Song (Anonymous)

JOCK STEIN was returning to Llanelly with his team-mates from another long away-trip, this time to Hastings on the south coast of England. As the coach made its lumbering way westward to South Wales in the darkness of a cold December night in 1951, Stein had a lot on his mind. For one thing Llanelly were struggling on the field; recently the side had lost 1–6 to Lovell's Athletic (a works' side), while the reserves were losing 2–14 at home to Ebbw Vale. Only a week or so ago a public meeting had been held to discuss the fate of the club that had gambled so much on its future in Southern League football; the local Llanelly paper, The Star, *had described the financial state as 'a losing battle against expenditure'.*

Stein sighed at the prospects, thinking that a return to Scotland would mean at the best a steady job in the pits, and perhaps part-time football for a couple of years more. Later, on his arrival at Llanelly, Jean, his wife, had news, bad news. The house in Hamilton had been burgled again. That was the last straw. A council house in the austerity of post-war Britain was a prized possession, and sensibly the Steins had not given it up when they moved to Wales. Football was too unpredictable an occupation, and would not last for ever . . . but once again the house had been broken into.

Dejected, Stein agreed that the best thing – the most practical thing to do – would be to return to Lanarkshire, and a grimmer future. He thought that he would have to speak to the Llanelly manager, Jack Goldsborough, when he next reported to Stebonheath Park.

Unknown to Stein, his life had started to change – and for the better.

Back in Glasgow, Celtic were experiencing chronic difficulties both in defence and attack. Mediocrity had become a way of life at Parkhead – a dismal change in the fortunes of a once-great club. Jimmy McGrory, the manager, and Jimmy Gribben, a scout, were discussing the recurring injuries and loss of form on the part of Celtic's regular pivots. It seemed obvious to them that an experienced centre half should be signed up cheaply, and fill in for a period; later, if he was the right sort of person, he could help out with the reserves. But who?

Almost as an afterthought, Gribben mentioned the name of Stein, formerly of Albion Rovers and now playing somewhere in Wales; he added the *caveat* that Stein came from Burnbank, a hot-bed of Rangers' fans, and that the player was not exactly Celtic-minded.[2] However, it was agreed to proceed on the understanding that the enquiries should be discreet, and that the fee should be modest. *The Star* reported later that Celtic, possibly sensitive about accusations of parsimony, requested the amount of the transfer fee be kept secret; significantly, the sum (eventually revealed as £1,300) was only £200 less than the amount needed to clear up Llanelly's debts.

When Stein showed up at Llanelly's ground, he was called into the cubicle of an office, and informed that a Scottish club was eager to have him; the last club to enter his mind would have been Celtic. Two journalists

Jock Stein leads out Celtic.

on rival newspapers, John Blair of the *Evening News* and George Aitken of the *Evening Citizen,* were so stunned by a phone-call informing them that Celtic had signed a player from a non-League club that they mutually agreed that one of them would verify this startling announcement. The Celtic manager, Jimmy McGrory, confirmed that Jock Stein had joined the Parkhead club, then added: 'But nobody will believe it!' A few days later, on 8 December 1951, he made his debut for Celtic against St Mirren at Parkhead as a vaguely remembered nobody. That day the Celtic fans saw a solidly-built, 'stopper' centre half, commanding in the air and competent on the ground. They recognised that, despite his lack of pedigree as a player, the newcomer was confident and played with authority, as if assuming that he had a right to be there. One moment in the second half produced a buzz around the terracing, and arguments in 'the Jungle'. An awkward ball, too low to be headed and too high to be kicked, came towards Stein; the pivot made for it immediately, and cleared the ball 30 yards with his knee. Opinion was divided: Was this a mis-kick? Or a deliberate tactic to deal with the situation?

Many people down in Llanelly were not surprised at Jock Stein's confident attitude; they had seen him blossom while in Wales. Indeed, some are convinced that Stein's career started to prosper while in Llanelly, whereas in Scotland it was assumed that the former Albion Rover had returned from obscurity in a football backwater.

Always Stein had seemed fated to be one of those footballers who flit briefly across the sports-pages, doomed to be forgotten. After all, had not his background condemned him to a life in the mines, where, at the age of 16, he joined his own father? It was a grim, hard occupation in the immediate pre-war years when miners still worked underground with ponies, and when pit-head baths were a luxury. Often, coming off his shift at Bothwell Castle pit, black-faced, coated in coaldust, he had to walk home still wearing sodden boots and damp clothing. He spent a dozen years toiling in that depressed environment, long enough to speak from experience when, years later, he could rage about the misuse of the word 'pressure' as applied to football. 'The pit,' he said, 'is a place where phoneys and cheats couldn't survive for long.'

Football, no matter how much he loved the game, could only be considered as another way of making a living – just as it had been when he joined his first senior club as a part-timer during the war years. Playing for humble Albion Rovers at Cliftonhill after a week working in the mines might be considered as an excellent therapy for suppressing an over-heated imagination. At Coatbridge nobody was foolish enough to dream of glory, because football in the late 1940s brought only scant financial reward and no security. In 1950 a moderate player, at the age of 28, married, and with a young daughter, he may have wondered about the distribution of wealth at a time when the most famous players – entertainers supreme who thrilled millions every week – were scandalously underpaid, even during the greatest boom the British game has known.

Tom Finney, Preston North End's marvellous winger, recalls standing in the tunnel at Hampden Park that year with England's centre half, Neil Franklin, and looking out at the gathering crowd. Franklin turned to him in some anger, and said: 'Look at them, Tom. There are 125,000 people here, and they've paid thousands of pounds to watch you, me, and the rest of the lads play a game of football. We get £20 each out of it all. It's all wrong, Tom. It doesn't bear thinking about.'

A few weeks later Franklin became one of half a dozen British players who, to better themselves, would fly out to Bogota in Colombia – a country outwith FIFA jurisdiction, and thus untrammelled by financial regulations.[3] Among the other players was an old adversary of Stein's from Airdrie-Albion Rovers derby matches, Bobby Flavell, then of Hearts.

Perhaps Jock Stein, already noted for a spirit of independence in financial negotiation based on his own estimation of his worth, caught a whiff of the restlessness when a protracted wage dispute with Albion Rovers reached an impasse two months after Franklin's flight to Bogota.[4] Unlike the distinguished English internationalist, he did not have the same range of options; he decided to join the South Wales club Llanelly as a full-timer in July 1950 on a transfer fee of £750. Llanelly's local newspaper, *The Star,* described the purchase as 'John (Jock) Stein, aged 27, six feet and 13 stone'; the report mentioned that Charlton Athletic, a First Division side and recent winners of the FA Cup, had expressed an earlier interest in the Scotsman, but could not agree on a fee with Albion Rovers.

However, for all the average Scottish fan knew about Llanelly, it might

---

BRITAIN AT WORK

The average weekly wage for Britons in 1953 was £7 11/– (£7.55), and the weekly food-bill for a family of four estimated as £4 5/– (£4.25).The distribution of work was as follows:

Manufacturing	8,852,000	
Professional & financial services	3,970,000	
Distributive trades	2,660,000	
Transport & communications	1,723,000	
Building & construction	1,452,000	
Civil service	1,318,000	
Agriculture & fishing	1,107,000	
Mining & quarrying	869,000	
Public utilities	374,000	
Military service	864,000	(Conscript Army)
Unemployed	299,000	

as well have been Timbuctoo. It is not generally known that, within two months of Stein joining them, Llanelly could boast a Scottish contingent of six: Neilly Fleck, an inside forward from Alloa Athletic; Lachie McInnes, a full back from Albion Rovers; Dave Mathie, a centre forward from Motherwell; Bob Jeffrey, a football nomad from Weymouth but formerly of Aberdeen and Exeter City; and Dougie Wallace who had been player-coach at Llanelly since 1949. Wallace was the most distinguished; a wartime internationalist for Scotland, he had earned a Scottish Cup medal with Clyde in 1939 and his role in the signing of the other Scots was crucial.

Llanelly's interest in the transfer market was prompted by their re-election to the Southern League after an absence of 17 years; this accomplishment was intended as a stepping-stone to the Football League. In fact, Llanelly had also applied for admission to the Football League that summer, but did not receive a single vote – a reflection on the demise in the inter-war period of similar-sized clubs such as Merthyr Town and Aberdare Athletic after they had been elected to the League. Llanelly's chairman claimed that his club had never been in a stronger financial position, and indicated that Llanelly and Kettering Town, the successful Southern League applicants, were replacing two clubs who had been admitted to the Football League (Colchester United and Gillingham). He was optimistic that Llanelly would join the latter in the near future, and hinted that football was in the process of rivalling and replacing Rugby Union in popularity in the area.[5]

Needing a stronger team to compete in the Southern League, Jack Goldsborough, the manager, discussed the matter with Dougie Wallace before setting out on his shopping expedition. Wallace's knowledge of Scottish football, and a local partiality for Scots, was a decisive factor. Many fans of Llanelly still remembered fondly the play of Jock Marshall, an outstanding full back who joined the Welsh club in 1923 from Middlesbrough as an internationalist – and for the incredible fee then of £2,000. He became one of the few players in this century to be 'capped' for Scotland when playing with a non-League club. In a curious parallel with the Stein days at Llanelly, Marshall's high wages brought the ambitious Llanelly trouble at an early period of their Football League aspirations, the Welsh FA intimating its concern over the financial liabilities the club had incurred.

Much has been said about Jock Stein's indebtedness to Celtic for giving him an opportunity in 'big-time' football, but the move to Wales may have been more important in his personal development. For one thing, it was his first experience of full-time football; it represented also a substantial increase in wages, and a release from the mines.

The 'romantic' notion is that Stein played out his time in Wales in a mining village against semi-professionals and amateurs on rudimentary pitches surrounded by the industrial slag-heaps of coal-mining valleys. The reality was different. Llanelly (or Llanelli as it is now called) was no backwater. Situated on the eastern seaboard of Carmarthen Bay, Llanelly's growing prosperity over the previous century was based on its location between the coalfields and the sea, and its obvious appeal for industrialists impressed by the availability there of cheap power, abundant water, and excellent rail and road links. The historic dependence on coal and metal – Llanelly was once famed for the manufacture of tinplate – has now been replaced by a more broadly-based economy featuring tourism, automotive products and petro-chemicals.

The reputation of the town and the surrounding area for hospitality is unchanged, however. The town was certainly no social desert in 1950, the 35,000 inhabitants having ready access to five cinemas and three theatres; Jock Stein experienced no difficulty in being made welcome by the locals whose sense of community was little different from that of his native Lanarkshire. [6]

Stein, illustrative of a recurring theme in his career, was soon appointed captain and the club made an excellent start to the 1950/51 season by winning 7–1 against Barry Town; interest in the team was so awakened that 30 busloads of supporters then followed them to Worcester. Stein's impact was immediate, prompting *The Star* to comment: 'Stein followed the Scottish pattern that is sometimes mistaken for slowness. It takes a quick-thinking player to exercise that perfect control and coolness that deceive an opponent.' (26 August 1950)

Gwyn Grant, a contemporary of Stein at Stebonheath Park, is insistent, convincingly so, that Llanelly 'brought out Jock Stein as a personality and a player'. It is little known, for example, that he learned and perfected his famous 'knee-clearance' from watching Dougie Wallace in training there.

The club may have been more obscure than Albion Rovers, who derived at least a vague recognition from the public through the weekly study of football coupons; but the status of Jock Stein had changed to that of 'local hero'. It was not acclaim solely on the basis of popularity. Gwyn Grant recalls that, though Stein was fundamentally a 'stopper', he developed leadership qualities by moving forward for set-pieces and by taking free kicks; he also made himself available in the opposition penalty area at corner kicks, a trait he was to develop most rewardingly with Billy McNeill at Parkhead much later. Indeed, his spectacular header in an epic 5–5 draw with fierce rivals, Merthyr Tydfil (watched by 13,000 in October 1950) helped start Llanelly on a memorable run in the FA Cup that ended with defeat only in a second replay with Bristol Rovers.

The atmosphere for the replay in Merthyr, where Llanelly won by 2–1, tells us much about British football spectators in the 1950s: 'From 2.15p.m. onwards the turnstiles were clicking furiously as black-faced miners and boiler-suited factory-workers direct from their employments mingled with "shoppers" and the regular thousands of supporters hurrying to take up position. The special trains and dozens of motor coaches, supplemented by hundreds of cars, brought in the large Llanelly contingent. Team favours, berets, and scarves were in evidence, and "Sospan Fach" was heard from the Llanelly supporters. Merthyr's fans were strangely subdued. (David Watkins, *Magic Moments of Merthyr AFC*, 1985)

However, Llanelly's drive to build a convincing case for entry to the Football League was soon to founder. That season brought the first glimmerings that the post-war British soccer boom was tapering off; at the end of the 1950/51 season the club had to declare an operational loss of almost £3,000 after 'a shortfall in the anticipated gates'. The committee had budgeted for crowds of 4,000, but reported an average attendance of only 3,600. Wages apart, other costs had been heavy: the running of a reserve team in the Welsh League in preparation for the hoped-for Football League membership, and travelling costs in completing a schedule that called for visits to such distant venues as Hastings, Weymouth, Dartford, Chelmsford, Exeter, Tonbridge, and Torquay. Gravesend, already £1,300 in debt, could not fulfil the fixture at Llanelly in February 1951 and were fined a guinea by the League, which also ordered them to pay Llanelly for the expenses of advertising the match.

The upshot was that Llanelly were again rejected in their bid for Football League membership, and at the end of 1950/51 only Wallace and Stein were retained as full-time professionals. The enthusiasm generated a year earlier with entry into the Southern League, and the prospects of Football League fixtures, had evaporated. Instead, questions were asked about the 'amateur-ish' running of the club: why did Llanelly's professionals on the books in 1950/51 earn an average weekly wage of £15 10/- (£15.50) when the maximum in the Football League was only £12? Why did Llanelly employ only 14 professionals at a weekly total wage of £220 when Merthyr Tydfil, the Southern League champions, paid out £200 weekly for 27 professionals?

In addition, the club's committee claimed that, for some obscure and unconvincing reason, no record had been kept of the 1950 AGM; many felt that this 'oversight' served as an excuse to forget a promise made at the meeting to change the constitution, and form a limited liability company – a move believed feasible only if the club was free of debts. A letter to *The Star*, anonymous and thus unpublished, insinuated that some supporters entertained the suspicion that the committee members had no wish to invite a close scrutiny of the ledgers that would preface the formation of such a company . In a match programme in November 1951 the club threatened to take legal action against anyone spreading rumours about the club's future and the conduct of its management.

Inevitably, such undercurrents already had affected the players. Lachie McInnes apparently refused to take the field for the second half of a match against Bath City. His captain, Jock Stein, was bitterly disappointed to learn that a bid in January 1951 by a Football League side (thought to be the famous Wolverhampton Wanderers) fell through because Llanelly considered the amount was too low. A growing frustration may have been a factor in his being ordered off that month in a match against the Southern League leaders, Merthyr Tydfil, when a 'free-for-all' broke out near the end, the derby match degenerating into 'an exhibition of flying fists and petty fouls'. For his indiscretion Stein was fined £2 and suspended for 28 days, a harsh sentence in the view of *The Star* which pointed out that, technically, he would not be able to draw wages for that period.

And so, an undistinguished career seemed to be petering out in obscurity . . .

*   *   *

In truth, Jock Stein, in transferring from Llanelly to Celtic, had moved only to a more elevated plane of mediocrity. Celtic's ordinariness in the early 1950s is revealed in interesting ways by the comments of opponents who played many matches against them.

Archie Baird, an Aberdeen inside forward after the war, has no outstanding memories of Celtic as opponents, but recalls in his autobiography *(Family of Four, 1989)* 'the formidable array of talent' in the powerful Rangers sides of the period and 'the artistry' of Hibernian's 'Famous Five', considered by many to be the finest forward line in Scottish football history.

Alfie Boyd, Dundee's captain and a most cultured left half, made another interesting observation in October 1952: 'Against Hibs you take the field with barely suppressed excitement coursing through the team, and this "lift" lasts throughout the game, so that you find yourself getting to the ball from positions which normally appear hopeless.' Like Baird he made no mention of Celtic.

Hibernian were *the* talking-point of Scottish football.

The first time the 'Famous Five' appeared as a unit was in April, 1949, and since then they had proved capable of shredding any defence with a devastating blend of power and skill, culminating in artistry. In September, 1952 Hibernian routed Manchester United, the current English champions, and scored seven goals in the process, although critics (mainly in the west of Scotland) could carp that it was in a testimonial match.

Still, it must be considered a major achievement to have deprived those intimidating Rangers teams of three Championships in the first post-war decade. In contrast to the limited appeal of Rangers with their 'Iron Curtain' outlook, Hibs' brand of football was so attractive that they had become a magnet for the attention of 'neutrals'.

Their rise to eminence was no accident. During the war years they had used such guest-players as Matt Busby, and his influence had lingered on in the emergence of young players. Because of frequent tours in Europe,

Hibernian became Scotland's best-known team in foreign parts; thus, it could not have been a surprise that in the mid-50s the Edinburgh club became Scotland's first representatives in the inaugural (and invitational) European Cup, in which they reached the semi-final. Their travels to entertain crowds in Norway, Denmark, Sweden, Germany, Austria, Czechoslovakia, and Belgium were paying dividends on the field, the team's style being described by Ben Wilson of the *Sunday Empire News* in 1952 as 'a blend of true Scottish ball manipulation, Continental speed and precision, and hard shooting'. In comparison, Celtic's sole experience of the Continent during the same period was a 'friendly' in Rome against Lazio in 1950.

Without a doubt, Hibs and Rangers were considered the Scottish teams most likely to best the English challenges for the Coronation Cup. The trophy was devised by the football authorities as part of the wider celebrations for 1953, when the Coronation festivities could be regarded as an excuse to hold a party after long years of austerity and, as the so-called dawning of a 'new' Elizabethan Age, intended as a symbol of national regeneration for a Britain that needed reassurance of its continuing greaness. The rationing system, introduced as a wartime measure in 1940, was just coming to an end. Tea was 'de-rationed' in 1952, followed by sugar and sweets in 1953. The process was completed by the ending of controls on butter, meat, cheese, margarine and cooking fats.

One writer highlighted the need for such relief: 'Austerity was Britain's peculiar reward for surviving World War Two unbeaten at the cost of selling her foreign assets and taking on a crippling load of debt to the United States.' Britain's pretensions to remaining a world power incurred enormous outlay in the early 1950s, when a conscript army was still needed to meet overseas commitments including 'the nursing' of Germany by troops while that country was 'rewarded' for being beaten in war by 'an economic miracle financed mainly by American aid'. (Peter Lewis, *The 50s*, 1978)

It was readily acknowledged that Celtic were participating in 1953 only by virtue of a glittering record in similar tournaments in the past . . . and because their huge support, with good reason called 'the Faithful', would guarantee at least one substantial 'gate' to the exchequers of the various charities designated to benefit.[7] One irony did not escape the attention of some supporters: in the recent past Celtic FC had been suspected of still harbouring Republican sympathies by continuing to fly the Eire flag at their ground – a stance that had recently brought the club into an over-inflated dispute with the SFA and its President, Harry Swan of Hibernian. And now Celtic were about to take part in a tourney arranged to celebrate the crowning of a new monarch.

After virtually abdicating from serious football during the war years, Celtic made little impact on Scottish football for a decade after it. *The* great rivalry – at least, in football terms – was that between Rangers and

---

SECOND CLASS

On Friday 16 May 1953 Dr John MacCormick, a champion of Scottish independence, told the Court of Session that the Queen, shortly to be crowned as 'Queen Elizabeth the Second', had no right to that title, since:

> There is only one reason why Her Majesty is to be titled Elizabeth the Second. That is because there was an Elizabeth of England. If we in Scotland are to accept Elizabeth the Second, then by implication we would be accepting England as overlords of Scotland . . . The implication of the use of the numeral is that the Kingdom of Great Britain is, as it is so often supposed to be, the continuance of the Kingdom of England.

His argument was dismissed as incompetent and irrelevant.

Hibernian, two clubs that had striven to maintain high standards during the war. However, in 1951 Celtic managed to land the Scottish Cup, defeating Motherwell yet again by 1–0 in the final; they followed up that triumph with winning the St Mungo Cup, devised to celebrate the Festival of Britain. The 'double' was a breakthrough, but Celtic did not have the professionalism to build on it. A major problem lay in the delegation of authority at Parkhead where the Board, or more accurately the Chairman, was exercising an unwarranted control in football matters. Bob Kelly underlined this intrusion by turning up at the ground virtually every morning to make himself available for direct access by players with personal problems that might be affecting their play.

The nominal manager was Jimmy McGrory, the greatest ever Celt in the opinion of many, who throughout his managerial career at Parkhead was invariably pleasant and modest, polite and unassuming – a gentleman. 'Gentlemen' rarely make successful managers of football clubs, and so Celtic continued in a pattern of mediocrity that had characterised the club since the dismissal of Willie Maley back in 1940.

McGrory's shyness and gentleness was so ingrained that the players were astonished when he entered the dressing-room after a 1–1 draw with Third Lanark in the 1953 Charity Cup at Parkhead; the players were happy at advancing to the final, having won on the toss of the coin, but McGrory, for once, was furious: 'You fellows should think shame of yourselves wearing that jersey!' he said, quietly emphatic, and then walked out.

In the stunned hush of the dressing-room at least one player approved whole-heartedly of his manager's outburst; in the 1952/53 season Jock Stein had been appointed team captain, and was slowly exerting his influence. Bertie Peacock, at the time a struggling inside left, recalls: 'In my opinion, Jock was the man who introduced tactics to Scottish football. They were unknown before he came to Parkhead. When he was appointed

161

captain, everybody was told exactly what he wanted them to do. A lot of people might have resented that, but they knew Jock was a players' man and he won their respect, as well as their obedience.'

It is a measure of the respect Stein commanded that talented players and famous personalities such as Bobby Evans, Charlie Tully, John McPhail and Bobby Collins could take orders, eventually, from an unglamorous newcomer. Simply, he had impressed his team-mates as someone who knew the game and who was obsessively interested in how it should be played. Any interest in planning and tactics was rare at Celtic Park in the post-war era, when British teams still relied on the natural ability and instinct of the players to decide the outcome of matches. At Parkhead, Stein was already operating by proxy one of the managerial duties that McGrory should have been exercising.

At the end of his first season as captain his leadership qualities were going to be tested in the Coronation Cup, when the opposition would be Rangers, Hibernian and Aberdeen from Scotland, and Arsenal, Manchester United, Newcastle United, and Tottenham Hotspur from England. Some newspapers hinted at the possibility of humiliating defeat.

Celtic had struggled through yet another disappointing season: ending up in the middle of the League table, being summarily dismissed 2–0 by Rangers at Ibrox in the quarter-final of the Scottish Cup and eliminated by the toss of a coin against Queen's Park in a Glasgow Cup replay.

However, the directors were belatedly becoming aware that the team needed strengthening before the Coronation Cup. Their subsequent dealings in the transfer market brought mixed results. Celtic approached Morton for their internationalist goalkeeper, Jimmy Cowan, offering £4,000, an amount the Greenock club dismissed as laughable – a month later Cowan was transferred to Sunderland for double Celtic's bid.

They were more successful in landing a centre forward, one who had wanted to play for Celtic for more than a decade; Neil Mochan, a former team-mate of Cowan at Greenock, had struggled for two years to adjust to the quick-tackling and faster pace of English football, and Celtic's offer of £8,000 to Middlesbrough was acceptable.

Mochan made his debut against Queen's Park in the Charity Cup final the day after signing, and scored twice in a 3–1 victory, quietly adjusting to his new side's pattern of play; his goals were scrambled efforts, but one fierce shot from Mochan that flew inches over the bar had the terracings buzzing. The speedy directness of the centre forward and his willingness to shoot on sight, qualities remembered with mixed feelings from his Morton days, seemed capable of solving a chronic problem at Parkhead – a situation that had existed, one might argue, since the departure of Johnny Crum.

Celtic's regular keeper, John Bonnar, bought in 1949 as a replacement for Willie Miller and himself replaced by a series of short-lived pretenders, raised a laugh when he boarded the coach going to Hampden for that

---

WHERE DO WE PLAY?

Neil Mochan won two cup medals for Celtic without having ever played for
the club at Celtic Park. Signed for Celtic from Middlesbrough on a Friday, he
played against Queen's Park at Hampden Park in the Charity Cup final; his
next three matches were also played at Hampden Park in the Coronation Cup
– against Arsenal, Manchester United and Hibernian.

Charity Cup final. He started to look around for his latest rival: 'Where's
Jimmy Cowan?' he quipped.

Among the interested spectators at the match were the Arsenal players,
Celtic's opponents in the first round of the Coronation Cup, but the
Londoners were singularly unimpressed with Celtic's performance and left
Hampden brimming with confidence – they could limber up against this lot,
and then enjoy their golf-outing before the next round . . .

CORONATION CUP FINAL
20 May 1953
Hampden Park

CELTIC 2	**HIBERNIAN 0**
Bonnar	Younger
Haughney	Govan
Rollo	Paterson
Evans	Buchanan
Stein	Howie
McPhail	Combe
Collins	Smith
Walsh	Johnstone
Mochan	Reilly
Peacock	Turnbull
Fernie	Ormond

Scorers:
Mochan (28)
Walsh (87)
Referee: H. Phillips (Motherwell)

Attendance: 117,060

A sportswriter of the period once dismissed the Celtic supporters' enduring
optimism in these words: 'Celtic supporters? If Celtic get two corners in a
row, they're happy roaring their heads off and enjoying themselves.' What
would he have thought watching the terracings fill up before the Coronation
Cup final – and seeing that same Celtic support still exulting in the unlikely
conquests of Arsenal and Manchester United?

The mood was one of jubilation; nobody on the King's Park terracing entertained the possibility of defeat – even against Hibernian on top form. And yet ten days ago only the most rabid fan would have considered that Celtic should have been competing in the tournament.

Against Arsenal on 11 May Celtic had started slowly but, after Evans took the game by the scruff of the neck, the whole team responded magnificently. The Celtic support reacted with noisy disbelief, and kept up a constant roar of encouragement; players out of touch for weeks started to string together a few passes, and Bobby Collins scored directly from a corner on the right after 24 minutes. Most of the 59,000 crowd expected the English champions to respond but Celtic continued to exert pressure; indeed, they came on to a game in the second half that had veteran supporters reaching far back to recall a similar performance. Cool goal-keeping by Swindin kept Arsenal in the game, including a save at the feet of Alec Rollo – and this was in a time when full backs were conditioned not to cross the half way line.

Celtic's victory was assured by a splendid display from their half backs: Evans, Stein and McPhail. Bobby Evans could be considered the best wing half in Britain, and nobody played with greater spirit and enthusiasm for Celtic for so long with such little reward; against Arsenal his colleagues for the first time played up to his standard, and he revelled in the occasion. John McPhail, never fully fit after 1951, had been moved back to left half, and was playing reasonably well there until the Coronation Cup; then his natural skill, allied to cool professionalism, came to the fore again. Jock Stein exuded confidence at the heart of defence, even against the dangerous Cliff Holton, who had averaged a goal a game during the previous season.

One Celtic supporter described the feeling of watching this match: 'It was like finding a five-pound note in an old jacket pocket. You don't ask any questions; you just accept it.'

In the semi-final Celtic faced Manchester United at Hampden before a crowd of 73,466, and again responded to the mood of their spectators. It was a triumph for speed and directness in attack, and determination and concentration in defence. United tried to play a close-passing game that foundered on Evans' superb anticipation and Stein's forceful interventions. Once again Stein was faced with a formidable opponent in Jack Rowley, a veteran but free-scoring leader; Rowley was a centre forward in the traditional mould, hard, direct and uncompromising in the pursuit of goals. Stein decided to meet strength with strength: W. M. Gall of the *Scottish Daily Mail* accused Celtic's pivot of 'being a bit hard at the outset on Saturday on Rowley, who never quite recovered from a leg injury and latterly went to outside left'. (18 May 1953) Two splendid goals – a shot from the edge of the box by Peacock in the first half, and an exciting breakaway by Mochan from midfield to slip the ball past Crompton – gave Celtic a narrow 2–1 win .

Hibernian had reached the final much less surprisingly, defeating Tottenham Hotspur in a replay, with Reilly getting one of his famous late goals to oust the Londoners. While Celtic were scraping past Manchester United at Hampden, Hibernian were toying with Newcastle United at Ibrox. Ronnie Simpson and a resolute Newcastle defence were helpless against the raids of Hibs' forwards. Two goals by Eddie Turnbull, and one each from Lawrie Reilly and Bobby Johnstone, ensured a 4–0 rout of the Englishmen.

Celtic's hopes were dented before the final with the realisation that Charlie Tully would be unable to play. This was a blow, because the Irishman had performed exceptionally against both Arsenal and Manchester United, and he had made both Celtic goals in the semi-final before pulling a muscle in the closing minutes. After much deliberation his chosen replacement was Willie Fernie, a highly skilled player but still regarded as too selfish on the ball.

One other thought, however, encouraged Celtic. For all their undoubted excellence and flair, Hibernian had not enjoyed much success in cup competitions, their last trophy won being the wartime Southern League Cup in 1943. Still, Hibernian would start as favourites, a testimony to their prowess and the conviction among the bookies that lightning was unlikely to strike three times in the same place. Andrew Wallace felt that, if Hibs scored first, 'Celts will be swamped by the high brand of skill which riddled the Newcastle United defence on Saturday.' (*Scottish Daily Mail*: 20 May 1953)

The largest crowd for the tournament flocked to Hampden to see the final; the attendance was later announced as 117,060 but another 10,000 were estimated to be locked out when the gates were closed. The King's Park end of Hampden had been filling up for more than an hour before the kick-off, and was dangerously overcrowded; attempts to distribute the crowd more equitably were unsuccessful, and so the authorities decided to stop further admission. Before the match the newspapers had guessed that the attendance would be close to 80,000, but the prospect of a Celtic appearance in the final, the appeal of Hibernian, and a pleasant sunny evening resulted in the late surge of interest.

The weather was a factor in making the final a memorable encounter; it had rained in Glasgow for part of the day but the clouds cleared about five o'clock. There was no wind and the pitch was yielding, a relief for the players after the fiery surface of the previous matches.

Celtic stormed into attack from the opening kick-off, and put Hibernian's defence – sometimes considered the Achilles' heel of the Edinburgh side – under immediate pressure. Fernie was racing past the veteran Jock Govan at will and creating havoc down the left with his runs; twice in the first ten minutes Younger was forced to dive bravely at his feet to save a goal. Mochan and Collins were equally direct, and threatened Hibs' goal repeatedly. Overworked, Hibernian had to concede corner after corner – and

Jock Stein keeps Charlie Tully on track.

behind that goal the Celtic support was at its noisiest and most encouraging.

A goal finally came in 28 minutes, at a time when Hibernian appeared to have weathered the storm. Stein cleared – a routine clearance but directed at Fernie; the winger, seeing defenders converging on him, flicked the ball into Mochan's path. The latter raced out of the centre-circle, apparently intent on dribbling towards the penalty area. Throughout his career, however, Mochan was a believer in doing the unexpected. He decided to shoot with his right foot, supposedly the weaker one, from close to 30 yards. The ball swept high into the net at the keeper's right-hand corner, as Younger threw himself vainly towards it. Neil Mochan in subsequent years was to score memorable goals for Celtic but he never hit a ball harder. The Celtic support went wild with delight, and the tumult lasted for several minutes; after the din had started to lapse into mere bedlam, the cheers broke out again spontaneously in tribute to the shot. The goal, of course, has entered the Celtic mythology. So unexpected and so powerful was the shot that estimates of the distance vary considerably.

Shortly after the final, the Hibs players were preparing for an international tournament in Brazil; Tommy Younger mentioned in training that he had managed to get a finger-tip to the ball. His team-mate, Mick Gallacher, a keen Celtic supporter and Eire internationalist, interrupted him: 'If you had, you would have broken your f****** hand!'

Celtic's efforts to break down the Hibs defence continued to the interval, but Younger and his hard-pressed defenders held out: '. . . and the one-goal lead with which they [Celtic] crossed over did no justice to the threats and alarms they were responsible for in the vicinity of Younger's charge . . . As usual Celtic got everything in effort and artistry from Evans, the most consistent and effective wing half in the game. Mochan has given the Parkhead attack an alert, penetrative quality, and the others have responded to his mascot inspiration.' (*Edinburgh Evening News*: 21 May 1953)

One minute before the interval the Celtic supporters were chilled into momentary silence when Gordon Smith, taking a long pass from Combe, sped past Rollo to cross a perfect ball: Reilly headed strongly for goal from ten yards, but Bonnar dived to his right to save at the post. After 44 minutes this first indication of the potential danger in Hibs' forwards was an unwelcome foretaste of the second half – a half considered the most enthralling in Celtic's history, but perhaps the longest and most tense ever endured by its supporters.

Within seconds of the restart Hibernian were on the offensive. And when the Hibs of that era attacked it was an exhilarating sight, as Archie Buchanan and Bobby Combe threw caution to the wind, augmenting that magnificent forward line in attempts to break the Celtic defence.

Smith, Johnstone, Reilly, Turnbull and Ormond: a quintet that adorned the football scene in the post-war seasons, names that could be rhymed off by every schoolboy in the country.

Gordon Smith, nicknamed 'the Gay Gordon' in the relatively innocent 1950s, was a pleasure to watch on the right wing; graceful and deadly, a scorer with head and foot, and an exceptional crosser of the ball, he could change the pattern of any match with his buccaneering forays. His partner, Bobby Johnstone, could react with lightning speed and was sharp within the six-yard box, able to distribute the ball so well that, after his transfer to Manchester City, one English fan described him memorably: 'That Johnstone! He could pass the ball with his arse.'

At centre, Lawrie Reilly was the quintessential striker; he was the epitome of alertness, skilled with head and feet, and never gave defences a moment to relax. He had earned a new nickname – 'Last-Minute Reilly' – after his late goals against England at Wembley, and against Tottenham Hotspur at Ibrox.

Eddie Turnbull at inside left was considered the least naturally talented member of the line, but he more than made up for that with a prodigious work-rate. He challenged for every ball, helped out in defence, provided a steady supply for the other forwards, and was recognised as the dead-ball expert. Willie Ormond at outside left could be ignored only at peril; slightly built and with a deceptive swerve, he was goal-hungry. Quietly courageous, he came back from two broken legs in his career.

Immensely gifted, individually talented but with complementary skills, the five combined with a deadly artistry; the football they provided delighted many in the grim, austere Britain of the early 1950s.

As the minutes crawled past, it seemed impossible that any side could have withstood the Hibernian onslaught, but that night Celtic's defence included some outstanding performers and a goalkeeper, often maligned, who on the night of 20 May 1953 was positively inspired.

John Bonnar, considered too small to be a dominating keeper, produced in that second half arguably the best display ever given by a Celtic goal-keeper. The intelligent Smith, aware of Bonnar's frequent problems with high crosses, sent over a stream of cunningly-flighted balls – only to see Bonnar clutch them cleanly, punch them away when being challenged, or scrape them to momentary safety with his fingertips. The inside forwards, Reilly and Johnstone, usually so deadly from close range, had to shake their heads in disbelief as Bonnar saved their headers in spectacular style – in Reilly's case, the keeper had to twist in mid-air to deflect the ball over the bar. Turnbull drove a fierce shot round the 'wall' but Bonnar dived to parry the shot, and went down at Turnbull's feet to block the rebound. Time after time the Celtic supporters behind the goal roared approval of his heroics.

He was not alone in his resistance: Haughney and Rollo, not always the steadiest of full backs, defended tenaciously against Ormond and Smith; Stein, an inspiring and reassuring figure in the middle, refused to allow Reilly any room to manoeuvre; McPhail, although often in danger of being over-run, never broke under the pressure and continued to use the ball well

John Bonnar.

– indeed, on the one occasion when Bonnar was beaten, McPhail headed a hook-shot from Johnstone off the line. And Bobby Evans played at his incomparable best. In a career studded with magnificent performances, he never played a better game.

Hibernian continued to attack in waves, and Celtic continued to hold out. With four minutes left another magnificent save by Bonnar foiled Hibernian once again: 'His [Turnbull's] lob was perfectly flighted. Johnstone rose, and with a turn of the head, sent the ball speeding for goal. It carried the stamp of the equaliser until, in the last split-second, up shot Bonnar's hand to divert the ball over the bar. Johnstone – unluckiest of all Hibernian forwards – could be excused for throwing up his arms in despair; and, as the players sorted themselves out for the flag kick, his disappointment did not prevent him from sportingly patting the goalkeeper on the back.' (*Edinburgh Evening News*: 21 May 1953)

Jimmy Walsh nets the second goal.

The corner kick was cleared by Evans as far as Fernie, back helping out in defence, who released Bobby Collins; the diminutive Celt raced up the wing, gaining seconds of relief for the defence, and beat Paterson neatly. He slipped the ball across to Walsh and the redhead shot past Younger, but the ball was scrambled off the line by Howie only as far as Walsh, who smashed it into the net. Hibs rallied yet again, and Reilly's shot was turned on to the base of the post by Bonnar; seconds later the whistle went, and Bonnar was hugged by his team-mates. The Hibernian players joined in the congratulations, but must have been dismayed; indeed, one of their team later described it as his 'greatest disappointment in football'. Willie Ormond's feelings were graphic: that Celtic team were 'a puir bloody lot' and he still bitterly regretted the fact that his side 'couldna get one by that bugger Bonnar in 1953'. (Interview with David Potter in *The Celt*, August 1984)

The Coronation Cup.

At the close of the match the Coronation Cup was presented to Stein by Lord McGowan, an honorary president of the SFA. The trophy, a solid-silver cup standing 22 inches high surmounted by the representation of a footballer, and with a silver-gilt profile of the Queen on one side, was not paraded for the crowd to admire.

Both teams were ushered into the pavilion, each player clutching a solid-silver replica of the trophy. Despite the roars – that turned to slow hand-clapping – of the crowd, most of whom stayed in their places for 15 minutes, the teams were ordered to remain inside.

Thousands waited outside the Hampden grandstand later, hoping to get a glimpse of the players and the trophy; Jimmy McGrory made a brief appearance at the doorway, but could not produce a sight of the Cup for the throng. Because the match had been carried on BBC Radio, the news had spread around Glasgow like bushfire; whole families gathered to celebrate in the streets of Celtic strongholds such as the Gorbals, and thousands cheered the Celtic bus making its way to a victory banquet in the city centre.

Throughout it all, seated on top of the bus surrounded by happy team-mates, Jock Stein clutched the trophy as if for dear life, with the dazed expression of one who has realised all his ambitions.

Reviewing the year, an English sports writer dubbed 1953 'the year of the veterans', but he was not thinking of Jock Stein and the fairy-tale transformation in his career. Indeed it is highly unlikely that he had ever heard of the player, and he could never have imagined that one of the most significant chapters in British football was now under way.

The writer's interest lay in two legendary sporting figures whose careers had culminated in spectacular fashion.

At Wembley, hard-bitten reporters broke down in the press-box, while thousands on the terracings (or watching on television) wept with joy as Stanley Matthews sparked a late fightback by Blackpool and won – finally – the FA Cup-winner's medal he had long cherished. The whole country celebrated with Matthews, at the age of 38 the most renowned football player in the world.

A month later at Epsom the ageing jockey, Gordon Richards, preparing to retire and recently knighted for his contribution to racing, won his first Derby at the 28th attempt; he took his mount, Pinza, to the front, two furlongs from home, and held off the Queen's horse, Aureole, to win amid frenzied cheering

Between these two momentous sporting events, an unfashionable journeyman player, at the age of 30, seemed to have scaled his own personal Everest in the same year that the famous mountain had been conquered at last. He may have thought that football could have little more to offer him. If so, for once, he was totally wrong . . .

THIRSTING AFTER KNOWLEDGE
Supporters had a variety of drinking establishments close to Celtic Park in which to toast the Coronation Cup triumph. In 1953 there were 66 public houses in the Gallowgate, a two-mile stretch between Glasgow Cross and Parkhead Cross – literally a pub on every corner. By 1990, due to re-development, the number had dwindled to 20.

Footnotes

1 The reference is almost certainly to George Young, Rangers' captain, although some 'literary' critics see in it a reference to George Graham, the SFA secretary and a man considered by the supporters (and Board) as being unsympathetic to Celtic.

2 Alex Hosie's obituary of Jock Stein in *The Scottish Sportsbook: 1986–87* mentions that 'in this traditional Rangers' country [Burnbank]' Stein's association with Celtic made the words 'turncoat' and 'traitor' almost complimentary beside the more colourful comments: 'The opinion of Jock's ability as a player when he signed for the Parkhead club nose-dived so quickly it would have made an outsider wonder how the hell the Big Man ever had enough sense to get his boots on the right feet . . . When Stein took the Parkhead [managerial] job, it did not, as expected, cause a scandal in his native Burnbank. It was treated in the same way folk would react to a no-good son who had expeditiously vanished. They washed their hands of the whole affair.' However, Hosie adds that, 'when he almost lost his life in a car-crash, the whole town held its breath. That was the sort of grudging esteem in which he was held. A lot of people disagreed with his choice of employer, but by Christ he was still a Burnbank man and a good yin at that!' Stein became, in the 1950s, the middle man in one of the most famous half-back lines in Celtic's history. Intriguingly, the *Glasgow Herald* writer Jack McLean stated in the 5 September 1990 issue of the newspaper that Evans, Stein and Peacock was a formation known as The Three Brothers, "due to the fact that they were all, rather surprisingly, Freemasons".'

3 Bogota did not prove to be an Eldorado for British players, who soon returned home. However, the monetary grievances were still valid enough nearly a decade later for Charlie Tully to voice in his autobiography: 'The men who are cheered and lauded on that glamorous football field are probably in as much of a financial struggle as anyone eles.' (*Passed To You*, 1958)

4 Scottish clubs at that time exercised quasi-feudal rights over players. When a player signed on, he had to be prepared to stay with the same club throughout his career if required. A player refusing to re-sign could be kept idle – and without wages – for years, and unable to sign for any other club. For example, Johnny Whigham, Morton's full back, rejected the terms offered him at the end of 1951-52; the club declined to improve them, and Whigham was forced to sit out the following season without kicking a ball.

5 Not too fanciful. Many Welsh rugby clubs came out of the war badly in material

terms; for example, Llanelly RFC's committee had recently debated whether the club could afford hospitality for visiting sides.

6 *The Star* of 9 December 1950 reported that Stein partnered his team-mate Lachie McInnes for The Hatchers, a local snooker club, in a match against rivals Gorseinon in the West Wales Snooker League.

7 The profits from the tournament were to be distributed thus: 50 per cent to charity (the King George Memorial Fund, the National Playing Fields Association and the Central Council of Physical recreation) and 25 per cent to each of the two clubs. At first, the players were receive £10 per match – but that sum was revised upwards after protests and the threat of a strike.

10

PERFECT, JUST PERFECT!

*HAMPDEN IN THE SUN**

Oh, Hampden in the sun
Celtic 7, Rangers 1;
That was the score when it came time-up.
The Timalloys had won the Cup.
[This first verse is also the chorus]

I see Tully running down the line;
He slips the ball past Valentine.
It's nodded down by 'Teazy Weazy',
And Sammy Wilson makes it look so easy

Chorus

I see Mochan beating Shearer;
The League Cup is coming nearer.
He slams in an impossible shot.
The Rangers team has had their lot.

Chorus

Over comes a very high ball;
Up goes McPhail above them all.
The ball and Billy's head have met.
A lovely sight, the ball is in the net.

Chorus

Young Sam Wilson has them rocked,
But unluckily his shot was blocked.
Then Big Bill with a lovely lob
Makes it look such an easy job.

Chorus

Now here is Mochan on the ball;
He runs around poor Ian McColl.
Wee George Niven takes a daring dive
But Smiler Mochan makes it Number Five.

Chorus

Down the middle runs Billy McPhail
With big John Valentine on his tail.
With a shot along the ground
The Cup's at Parkhead safe and sound.

Chorus

Here comes Fernie, cool and slick;
He ambles up to take the kick.
He hits it hard and low past Niven.
The Tims are in their seventh heaven.

Chorus

*The tune was that of Harry Belafonte's calypso 'Island in the Sun'. 'Teazy Weazy' was a reference to Billy McPhail, at that time the owner of a hairdressing salon, and who bore a resemblance to a TV hairdresser of that nickname.

SOME FOOTBALL matches just refuse to fall into any sort of pattern. That was certainly the case on 12 October 1957 when 20,000 watched in growing irritation as Celtic and Raith Rovers played out a boring 1–1 draw at Parkhead. It had proved most frustrating for the supporters in view of Celtic's bright start to the League campaign: a 1–0 win at Brockville against Falkirk, and a 3–2 victory at Ibrox over Rangers.

Andrew Wallace, in the *Scottish Daily Mail* two days later, scoffed at the possibility that this was 'the great new Celtic, having their best opening to a season in years . . . Who is kidding whom? It was the same old Celtic, jerky and in need of forwards with ideas.' His counterpart at the *Scottish Daily*

Bobby Collins – the 'wee barra'.

Express, John McKenzie, agreed, mentioning in a litany of complaints the following: that Bertie Peacock had played his worst game for years; that Bobby Collins, normally the spark-plug in attack, had been out of touch; that the youthful right back, John Donnelly, had been sloppy in his clearances; and that Raith Rovers' goal was scored following a 'comical' mix-up between Bobby Evans and Dick Beattie.

It could not have been a good omen for the match one week later – the League Cup final against Rangers, the first time the Old Firm had met at that stage in the competition.

Even worse was to follow in training a couple of days later. The Celtic players, exuberant and noisy, were still trooping into the dressing-room in ones and twos before the seriousness of the situation dawned on them. Flushed with anger, Bobby Evans and Charlie Tully glared at each other, face to face and with fists clenched; inevitably, one pushed the other, and instantly both players were grappling; punches were thrown and in the ensuing confusion both team-mates slipped to the floor. Within seconds other players rushed to separate the two internationalists and keep them apart as the pair continued to trade insults across the room . . . Later, when some order had been restored, one player attempted the role of peacemaker: 'It's a good job you two make your money from fitba', and no' the fightin'.' The tense silence from the combatants indicated his singular lack of success.[1]

In recent seasons Celtic had not been altogether successful on the field. Unable to develop consistency in the League, Celtic appeared unconcerned with their reputation as 'merely a cup side'. After beating Aberdeen by 2–1 in the 1954 Scottish Cup, Celtic had lost in successive finals to Clyde and Hearts – when eccentric team selections had been a contributory, if not the major, factor in the defeats. In 1956, however, after a decade's striving, Celtic at last won the League Cup by beating Partick Thistle 3–0 in a replay, but without much distinction.

Since Jock Stein's retirement because of an ankle injury, Celtic's League form had been miserable . . . and the answer was not too far to seek. Success in the League, the bread-and-butter of football, depends on consistent performances. For all the club's abundance of talent, Celtic could not develop that sort of steadiness because of a cavalier approach to the sport that had become a handicap in the more competitive post-war era. Robert Dunnett attempted to describe their outlook: 'Celtic's admirable formula for the most challenging circumstances of football, or of life, is "We attack!" It has become an instinct . . . Honest fans, analysing the thrill of football, will go far before finding a better definition of their feelings than that delicious mixture of fear and admiration which Celtic inspire as the green-and-white jerseys take the field.' (*Picture Post*: 12 March 1955)

That perceptive journalist, Hugh McIlvanney, later characterised Celtic's football outlook as having 'sufficient Positive Thinking to unnerve Norman

Vincent Peale'. Unknowingly, he was echoing the assertion 50 years earlier of 'Man in the Know' that, without the Parkhead side, Scottish football would have been 'rather tame and commonplace, lacking personality and distinction, and rendered unattractive by the absence of the famous combative spirit which the mere name "Celtic" seems to stir up wherever they go.' (*Glasgow Observer*: 25 June 1927)

Few clubs in world football could match Celtic's faithful adherence to the tradition of open, skilful, attacking play, at the calculated risk of exposing their own defence. The concentration on the mechanics of defence by modern coaches is simple to explain: it is practical, and it is easier to teach. A solid and organised defence can help win games, when allied to possession play . . . but the consequences for the spectators can be deplorable. The true follower of the sport has to describe a slavish devotion to defence as 'stultifying' or 'soporific'. Results are important, specially at the higher levels of the sport, organisation, at any level, is admirable . . . but a concentration on defence takes much of the excitement and adventure out of the game.

The dilemma for Celtic fans is best illustrated in recalling the Cup-Winners' Cup match at Parkhead in 1989 between Celtic and Partizan Belgrade, won 5–4 by the home side – a match thrilling in intensity, unbearable in tension, but ultimately frustrating in its outcome (away goal qualification for the outplayed visitors).

Celtic's insistence on positive football goes back to the earliest days of the club, when the primary purpose was to raise money by providing entertainment. The *Scottish Umpire* of 2 October 1888 gave early testament to the infant club's emphasis on 'attractive, free-flowing football' by enthusing over the way 'the entire team played a magnificent passing game now seldom witnessed', a verdict endorsed in the same issue by a report on proceedings at Glasgow's Eastern Court. Seven tramway conductors had been hauled before the magistrates on charges of having overcrowded their cars on a Saturday. All pleaded 'guilty', but in extenuation claimed that 'it was an utter impossibility to keep the crowds, who were thronging to the Celtic's park, at a respectable distance'. Training methods in Britain then emphasised the need to increase strength and stamina through skipping, walking, sprinting, dumb-bells, Indian clubs, punching bags etc. One entry in the 1893 minute-book, however, suggested a more enlightened approach at Parkhead; it recorded a decision allowing the players to use the ball on Tuesdays 'provided they do their usual training on Thursdays'. The provision of steak pie and toast after training was an added incentive to these sessions.

The results were apparent almost immediately, as Celtic teams soon became recognised as experts in combined play and in keeping the ball on the ground; it was claimed rather fancifully that the only practice the players got in heading was in rising for balls punted by opponents on

Saturdays! A tradition of studied passing developed at Celtic Park and was to be sustained by a consciously groomed succession of skilled players: from Johnny Campbell through Jimmy McMenemy, from Alec Thomson, Malcolm MacDonald, Pat Crerand down to Paul McStay – all stamped with the ability to judge their passes, long or short, to an inch.

One of the men mentioned, Malcolm MacDonald, views those who wear the Celtic jersey as 'caretakers of a heritage', an assertion he underlines by recalling a visit to Celtic Park in the 1950s when he was manager of Kilmarnock. After the tousy match he was startled to hear the shout of 'Callum', as he had been known in his youth in Glasgow's Garngad. He turned to find himself being rebuked, more in sorrow than in anger, for his team's physical approach by a Celtic fan standing in the enclosure that fronted the Parkhead stand. He remembers the words clearly: 'You didn't learn to play like that here!'

FAITHFUL TO THE END

James Scott, recalling the death of Willie Maley in 1958, paid tribute to the unique relationship Celtic have enjoyed with their supporters. He told how, after the announcement at the Supporters' Association Rally of the former manager's illness, a group of Celtic followers waited outside Maley's home in the pouring rain:

> They wanted to find out how he was, but did not go to his door because they felt they would be intruding. They patiently waited until a reporter came out to tell them the news. [In this incident, the writer felt, the loyalty, understanding and bond between Celtic F.C. and their supporters was crystalised.]
>
> (*Charles Buchan's Football Monthly*, March 1961)

Ideally, Celtic's emphasis on pure football required genuinely skilled players, imbued with a philosophy of the game. At times, most notably just after World War Two, even the basic skills were not there, but Celtic persisted in their outlook, often at the expense of results. Bob Kelly believed most passionately that the team should play in 'the true Celtic way' and never lost his conviction that Celtic could win the way back to 'its rightful position in Scottish football by our own culture, that of sheer football'.

Often, however, the club was doomed to disappointment. The individual talents of some outstanding players, allied to the whole-hearted efforts of the others, could not achieve consistent success for Celtic. The League Cup final of 1956/57 against injury-hit Partick Thistle illustrated the problem most clearly: a feckless attack that included Willie Fernie, the finest ball-player in the country but on the day notably wayward and unproductive, exasperated the fans with a fitful, unco-ordinated performance. Only 31,126 bothered to turn up for the midweek replay to see Celtic win the League Cup for the first time – and end a hoodoo in the competition.

Bob Kelly had great faith in the club's ideals of clean play, sporting conduct, and attacking football. Faith alone was not enough; what the supporters, and the players, needed was a sign that unadulterated football could prevail under any circumstances . . .

✳   ✳   ✳

Celtic's opponents, Rangers, had not distinguished themselves in winning by 3–1 at Love Street against St Mirren the week before the 1957 final. The reporter from *The Bulletin* deplored the emphasis on the power-play by both teams, but singled out Rangers wing halfs, Ian McColl and Harold Davis, for an inclination to use force rather than skill.

Rangers, however, were perpetuating their own tradition. In Scotland football remains a winter sport, played often in miserable weather and on treacherous surfaces; it becomes, then, a physical sport, demanding fitness, and power. For Rangers the emphasis would continue to be on strength and determination rather than subtlety.[2]

To be fair to the Ibrox club, theirs was an approach prevalent throughout much of Britain during the 1950s. Sports fans crowded round television sets to watch Wolverhampton Wanderers take on a series of distinguished Continental sides, among them Honved and Spartak, at Molineux. Those floodlit matches were thrilling confrontations – clashes between strength and skill, between artistry and power . . . and Wolverhampton, representing Britain, defeated the best of the Continent deservedly and in epic manner.

However, even in the middle of an English winter, the groundsmen at Molineux had been given orders to soak the pitch for hours at a time prior to certain matches, when deemed necessary. Invariably, the heavy, muddy surface did much to nullify the superior skills and artistry of the Europeans.

In an interview in October 1957, just before the League Cup final, Gordon Smith of Hibernian, most elegant and skilled of Scottish wingers, testified to the effects of the 'power-game' in Scotland by pointing to his legs and bruised ankles. He bemoaned the fact that he had rarely seen the traditional Scottish game, exemplified by the skills of the 'Wembley Wizards' of 1928, and wondered if the recent visit of the wonderful Hungarians had done anything to wean Scottish football away from the all-too-prevalent 'get stuck in!' outlook.

Hungary had inflicted the first European defeat on England at Wembley by 6–3 in 1953, and followed that up by thrashing England 7–1 in the return in Budapest. They had also fulfilled an engagement against Scotland at Hampden Park in December 1954, winning 4–2; some Scots took a perverse pleasure in the defeat, consoling themselves with the thought of doing better than England, applauding the vigorous tackling and physical approach of the home side.

NO COMMENT

The opening of the commercial TV channel STV in 1957 was considered to be another nail in the coffin of the cinema. More than 8,000 British cinemas closed between 1954 and the end of the decade; many of the buildings are now used as bingo halls. The growth in popularity of bingo was not a universally welcomed development. One historian of Glasgow certainly disapproved:

> Presumably the public that supported the bingo halls – a strange phenomenon of the late 1950s – were drawn from the less intelligent members of society, particularly women.
>
> (C.A. Oakley: *The Second City*, 3rd edition, 1975)

The parochial attitude of the more conservative players was best illustrated by George Brown; once a distinguished half back for Rangers, Brown, in 1957 a director at Ibrox and a Scottish selector, had a few years earlier derided Continental football as 'a circus' and its players as 'robots' and 'football freaks'. Brown would have derived satisfaction only two days before the League Cup final in reading of how 'the non-stop, lion-hearted' Wolves, widely viewed as a carbon-copy of Rangers, defeated Real Madrid on a heavy Molineux pitch, where the guile and cleverness of Real, orchestrated by di Stefano and Kopa, was negated.

Rangers were no longer the wholly dominant team in Scotland, although their massive support and financial resources ensured the continuance of success on and off the field. Rangers' traditionally dour rule over Scottish football would soon be challenged by the likes of Hearts. The Edinburgh club had added the power of Dave Mackay and the strength of John Cumming to complement the undoubted skills of Alex Young and Jimmy Wardhaugh, and were ready to mount consistent challenges for the League Championship.

Rangers' feared 'Iron Curtain' had been eroded by age, retirement and suspension: Woodburn was suspended *sine die* in 1954 after a series of violent indiscretions on the field, and the others had retired or moved on, except for Ian McColl, still retaining his place at right half. The most difficult position to fill was that of George Young whose massive physique and calming imperturbility, allied to scrupulously clean play at the heart of defence, was bound to be missed. Rangers signed up the tall, solidly-built John Valentine of Queen's Park to succeed Young, and the ex-amateur looked to have a glittering career ahead of him at Ibrox. However, in his ten matches as Rangers' pivot Valentine had shown some hints of nervousness, and his shakiness in the recent Old Firm clash at Ibrox, won 3–2 by Celtic, had caused anxiety.

One observer of the Scottish scene remarked that, while both Old Firm clubs would always be considered the top people in the domestic game, Rangers would be the very top people; Celtic, on the other hand, had slipped: 'once football kings as mighty as Rangers, holding an equal share of the spoils of soccer battle, they are no longer in the ranks of royalty, taking, as it were, the position of football arch-dukes of Scotland.'

In the days before the 1957 League Cup final the Celtic support, generally considered to be anti-Establishment in nature, might have drawn some consolation from the coverage of a bad week for royalty. In an American magazine (*Saturday Evening Post*) the irreverent Malcolm Muggeridge had cocked a snook at the British monarchy, comparing it to a long-running soap-opera and questioning its relevance to the 20th century. He remarked that, before they could walk, Prince Charles and Princess Anne had mastered 'that characteristic gesture of royalty, the flapping of a hand in acknowledgment of applause'. So great was the ensuing uproar in the British newspapers that Muggeridge's scheduled appearance on *Panorama* to defend his views was cancelled on the personal instructions of the Director-General of the BBC.

SCOTTISH LEAGUE CUP FINAL
Hampden Park
19 October 1957

CELTIC 7	**RANGERS 1**
Beattie	Niven
Donnelly	Shearer
Fallon	Caldow
Fernie	McColl
Evans	Valentine
Peacock	Davis
Tully	Scott
Collins	Simpson
McPhail	Murray
Wilson	Baird
Mochan	Hubbard

Scorers:
Wilson (23)   Simpson (58)
Mochan (44, 75)
McPhail (53, 68, 80)
Fernie (90)
Referee: J. A. Mowat (Burnside)

Attendance: 82,293

NOODLES OF FUN

The most famous April Fool joke of them all was played in 1957 by the BBC's *Panorama* programme. That most authoritative presenter Richard Dimbleby – who had been the anchor-man at the Coronation, and the wedding of Princess Grace in Monaco – was filmed beside harvesters in Switzerland filling their baskets with 'the produce of spaghetti trees'. The BBC switchboard was inundated by callers anxious to know where they could buy spaghetti plants!

Rangers, despite that defeat at Ibrox by Celtic, had been installed as slight favourites. They might be uncharacteristically vulnerable in defence, but their forwards, it was felt, would have the advantage through their directness. Alex Scott, on the right, had speed and control; Johnny Hubbard, on the left, was a tricky winger and an exceptional crosser of the ball. Rangers' inside trio – Billy Simpson, Max Murray and Sammy Baird – were more powerful than their Celtic counterparts and, if the final became a physical contest, this would be an advantage. Celtic's worst scenario involved Rangers' wingers, Scott and Hubbard, achieving a mastery over their full backs; Donnelly was still inexperienced, while Scott might be too fast for Fallon.

On the other hand, Celtic's wingers – Charlie Tully, now on the right and Neil Mochan on the left – were viewed as an enigmatic pair. Tully was clearly a veteran, lightning-fast in thought but slow in movement. His *forte* now lay in intelligent distribution, and he could still beat his opponent with swerves and dummies, but questions had to be asked about his ability to last the whole match.

Two idols of the 1950s, George Young of Rangers and Charlie Tully.

Neil Mochan's career at Parkhead continued to puzzle many football men. Signed in time for the Coronation Cup in 1953, he ended up as the team's leading scorer the following season when Celtic won the 'double'. However, despite his proven ability to score from either centre forward or outside left, he seemed to be out of favour at the start of the 1957/58 season. Already, in preference to him at outside left, Celtic had tried Eric Smith, Charlie Tully, and a promising youngster, Bertie Auld; the reluctance to restore Mochan to the position astonished and angered those supporters with whom he had remained a great favourite. A rumour kept circulating in Glasgow that some misdemeanour on his part had offended the puritanical streak in the chairman, Bob Kelly – ensuring his frequent banishment to the reserves.

Other clubs had expressed an interest in Mochan's availability, noting that he had spent eight of the 12 matches prior to the final in the reserves. Willie Thornton, the famous ex-Rangers forward and now Dundee's manager, made an enquiry and expressed surprise that Mochan was not a first-team regular. In the days before the final the latter was linked with Crewe Alexandria, perennial strugglers in England's Third Division North; however, Mochan refused to complain and waited patiently for a re-call.

Celtic's three inside forwards were considered more 'dainty' than Rangers', although Bobby Collins could be a tough little man when required to be. Doubts continued to exist about Billy McPhail's fitness; he was making a return to the side after three weeks' absence due to an ankle injury sustained in training. Despite his two crucial goals against Partick Thistle in Celtic's 3–0 victory in the League Cup replay the previous season, McPhail seemed more likely to be remembered for an injury-proneness that had dogged his career since he joined Queen's Park in the mid-1940s.

He had been given the opportunity to play for Celtic as a professional in 1947 – thus joining his brother at Parkhead – but the less wealthy Clyde offered better financial terms. He was unlucky when injury ruled him out of Clyde's side to play Celtic in the 1955 Scottish Cup final and deprived him of a winner's medal. Transfer-listed by Clyde in 1956, he managed to persuade a sceptical Bob Kelly that he could do a job for Celtic despite a chronic knee-condition; Kelly insisted that he be examined by the club's trainer, Alec Dowdalls, who reported back to the chairman – accurately, as it turned out – that Celtic might get two years' service out of him. The extent of the gamble was best illustrated by the comment of one journalist: 'It's just as well McPhail's good in the air – for with his legs he wants to stay up as long as he can.' His skill with the head was undeniable, and it was reckoned that in contests for a 50-50 ball in the air McPhail could win an impressive nine times out of ten. He could head powerfully for goal when required, but he had developed the technique of heading down to the feet of his inside forwards and allowing them a chance of a shot at goal. His favourite target in 1957 was Sammy Wilson, who had joined Celtic in the close-season on a free-transfer from St Mirren and made his debut at right half against East Fife in the League Cup. When neither Eric Smith nor Jim Sharkey took the opportunity to establish himself at inside left at the start of the season, Wilson was drafted into the forward line as an experiment.Wilson and McPhail quickly established a rapport and soon were scoring goals regularly; but would the unlikely combination – described affectionately by terracing wits as 'the crock and the cast-off' – be able to produce results against Rangers in the super-charged atmosphere of a Hampden final?

FEET FIRST

In these days of sponsored kits and boots it may be worth recalling that little more than 30 years ago the boots of all Celtic players were repaired in a small shoemaker's shop in Whitevale Street, close to Celtic Park. The business was run by the Diamond family – Frank Sr. and Jr. – who had been taking care of the footwear of famous Celts since before World War One, an era when the Celtic boots were conveyed to the shop in a spring cart drawn by a horse on loan from Dalbeth Cemetery. The same horse, incidentally, was used to pull the roller on the Parkhead pitch. Such was the skill of the elder Diamond that the great Jimmy McMenemy's 'swirl' (a quick change in direction calculated to send opponents the wrong way) was said to be the result of a special stud on the outside of the sole to ensure a firm grip on the turf. Bobby Collins, a shoemaker to trade before joining Celtic, did not repair his own boots, but was happy to leave them in such capable hands. As far back as the Diamonds could remember – from the days of Jimmy Quinn through to Bobby Evans – little boys had invaded the shop asking to touch their idols' boots.

The weather co-operated on the match-day, and Hampden presented a stirring spectacle as the teams trotted on to the pitch. Gair Henderson described it thus: 'From a sky of Mediterranean blue the sun splashed down on turf green as an emerald, but there were other colours on parade.' (*Evening Times*: 19 October 1957) He amplified his comments two days later in the same paper, deploring the conduct of both sets of supporters, as usual segregated and brandishing their 'colours' – orange and blue at one end of Hampden, Eire tricolours at the other – in a display of 'phoney patriotism'.

The experts considered that the heavy pitch, a consequence of rain on the Thursday and Friday, had to favour Rangers, the stronger side physically, but Bertie Peacock won the toss and chose to take first-half advantage of the wind by setting Rangers to defend the goal at the 'Celtic' (King's Park) end of the ground.

Celtic started off and controlled the early minutes; their football was sprightly and bright, laced with elegance. The attacks were being prompted by the wing halfs, Fernie and Peacock, both of whom had started off their career as inside forwards; they had never abandoned the constructive approach, and soon Baird and Simpson were struggling to hold back their own markers. Unfortunately, this superiority was not translated into goals, to the growing anxiety of the supporters. Bobby Collins' fierce drive hit a post with Niven beaten and, a few minutes later, Tully was desperately unlucky when he drifted past several bewildered defenders to lob a cross-shot that baffled Niven, but struck the inside of one post, rebounded across the face of the goal, then went behind for a goal kick.

At last, after 23 minutes of sustained attacking, Celtic scored; Billy McPhail beat Valentine in the air and headed the ball back and down to Sammy Wilson who volleyed the ball into the net from 12 yards. Only three minutes later, after Rangers had conceded another free kick, Collins drove the ball from 30 yards, leaving the smallish George Niven stranded, but the shot crashed against the crossbar. At that stage some pessimists among the Celtic support were muttering that a one-goal advantage after such domination was a meagre reward.

However, in the last minute of the first half the score-line reflected more accurately the reality of the situation. Once more McPhail and Wilson combined neatly, and the centre forward chipped the ball intelligently, and in his most languid manner, down the left wing for Mochan, who gathered the ball without fuss, sped past both Shearer and McColl, then cut in to blast the ball past Niven in his patented manner from the narrowest of angles. That was the decisive blow for Rangers; had they held Celtic to one goal at half-time, they might have regrouped in the second half with the wind behind them, and posed a real threat to Celtic.

Throughout the interval the Celtic end celebrated noisily, rejoicing in the mastery their team had established over Rangers. Most would have settled for that two-goal margin to be retained to the end and probably expected Rangers to come more into the match. If so, they had failed to notice that Celtic players were winning the individual jousts and duels in every area of the field; in this eventually most one-sided of all Old Firm encounters Celtic had established an overwhelming psychological advantage.

Charlie Tully, slower than in his younger days but infinitely more cunning, was at his trickiest, dribbling deceptively and passing astutely; his immediate opponent, young Eric Caldow, as always, played fairly – and was 'roasted' as a result.

Neil Mochan was being marked by Bobby Shearer, nicknamed 'Captain Cutlass' by his team-mates and glorying in a reputation for toughness. In the League game at Ibrox his robust challenges, fluctuating on the margins of legality, had disconcerted Tully; Mochan, however, appeared to relish the physical exchanges. After one fierce tackle by the Ranger, Celtic's stocky winger delivered a shoulder-charge that sent Shearer head over heels. Poor Shearer had met his match, in skill and physique . . . and Mochan was creating havoc down the left, drawing McColl out of position to help cope with the danger.

In the middle another duel was being decided in Celtic's favour. Billy McPhail was winning every ball in the air despite being marked closely by Valentine, and had now started to hold the ball before dribbling past his increasingly flustered opponent. Strangely, prior to this match, Valentine had generally come out on top in his past jousts with McPhail. Celtic's centre takes up the story: 'It was a funny thing, for I knew that I had the beating of him, but somehow or other, he scarcely gave me a kick of the ball.' In fact, so impressed was McPhail by Valentine when he first spotted him during National Service days at Fort George in the Highlands that he had recommended him to Queen's Park; McPhail considered that Valentine was equally skilled in three positions – centre half, centre forward, and goalkeeper.

In midfield Celtic's domination had been total. Willie Fernie, Bertie Peacock and Bobby Collins were combining well and, being on the smallish side, concentrating exclusively on the ball, rightly ignoring the frustrated attempts of their more muscular opponents – Baird, Simpson and Davis – to reduce the match to a physical contest. In defence Bobby Evans was immaculate in his relatively new role as centre half, his anticipation so razor sharp that he made Rangers' infrequent raids look more haphazard than they were. Sean Fallon, that most rugged of full backs, resumed his mastery over Alex Scott whom he had appeared to intimidate for a spell early in his career.

Despite that list of exceptional performances, the most outstanding player on the field was Celtic's Willie Fernie. Ostensibly, as right half, his primary task should have been to mark the dangerous Sammy Baird, but the defender's penchant for attack forced Baird to move back and employ crude, often illegal, attempts to stop Fernie. Time after time Fernie would attract the ball and stride forward into attack, leaving Baird and the equally hard Davis floundering in his wake. He was the true architect of Celtic's victory, described in the match report of the *Glasgow Herald* as 'this wonderful player . . . who suffers the crude, unfair attempts to stop him without a thought of retaliation.'

Fernie, to a lesser degree than Mochan, had at times been dropped from Celtic's team as a consequence of valid criticism of his holding on to the ball too long. At one period in the early 1950s it appeared that this apparently ingrained habit might force him to leave Celtic Park. Jimmy McGrory received a telephone call from Scot Symon, then manager of East Fife, who had noticed Fernie's absence from the first team. Symon had always been interested in him, attempting to recruit him for East Fife when the player was with Kinglassie Juniors in 1949. In answer to Symon's

Willie Fernie, artist supreme.

inquiry about the youngster, Celtic's manager informed him that Fernie still figured in the Parkhead club's plans. Had McGrory left his office to watch the practice matches, he might have seen his whole squad trying to get the ball away from Fernie – and failing.

However, it is fascinating to consider that Scot Symon, a great admirer of Fernie, almost certainly would have obtained the quiet Fifer for Rangers after he became manager at Ibrox in 1954; if Fernie had gone to Methil, and become available later at a price, his religion (Protestantism) would not have acted as a deterrent to Rangers.

The prospects of a Rangers comeback in the second half were dimmed with the sight of Murray switching to the left wing with a noticeable limp; any sympathy for Rangers' centre was diluted with the awareness that he had injured himself in tackling Evans – and had been penalised for it by the referee, Jack Mowat. Rather than settling into a semi-defensive game Celtic continued to swarm into attack, as Rangers' defence became more and more disorientated.

In 53 minutes McPhail settled the outcome, if not the margin of victory, with a neat header past Niven from a perfect cross by Bobby Collins; the goal was scored in an almost casual manner, a fact that may have disconcerted Rangers' defenders unduly. Still, Rangers' hopes were raised when Simpson dived to net a spectacular header from a McColl cross. Those among the Celtic support inclined to play down Rangers' goal – and willing to rub salt into wounds – pointed out later that the goal came when Evans was off the field and receiving treatment from Celtic's trainer.

It was the last moment of consolation for the Ibrox side and their supporters. From then till the relief of the final whistle, Celtic raised their game and toyed with their greatest rivals, who became more ragged as the minutes passed. For Celtic supporters the joy was complete as the mastery on the field was translated into goals.

After 68 minutes McPhail collected a loose ball in the penalty area and rammed it into the roof of Rangers' net for Celtic's fourth. That is the image that remains indelibly in the mind: Niven and Shearer sprawled helplessly on the ground, Valentine unable to intervene, McColl in the distance with an agonised expression – and McPhail, unmarked in front of goal, leaning back as he watches his rising shot bulge the net.

In 75 minutes Celtic advanced down the right, and the ball eventually reached Wilson, who swept it out to Mochan on his left; once more the hardest shot in Scottish football lashed the ball into the far corner. Rangers' defence was in total disarray as Celtic concentrated on combined football. The ball was swept from player to player as Rangers struggled to get a touch. In 80 minutes McPhail completed his hat-trick with an individual goal. Beattie punted the ball downfield towards the centre circle, where once more McPhail beat Valentine in the air; both players stumbled upon landing but McPhail recovered first to race away with Valentine in pursuit.

Billy McPhail turns away after netting Celtic's fourth goal.

He ran 40 yards, advancing upon the undecided Niven before tucking the ball past him.

In the midst of all this Celtic pressure, and the chaos in front of him, George Niven had an exceptional match in goal; his saves prevented the

A perfect end to a perfect day – Fernie's penalty.

score from reaching double figures and the only goal for which he could be faulted in any way was Mochan's just on half-time, scored from a near-impossible angle.

POWER STRUGGLE

In 1957 the Scottish League and the SFA were locked in a jurisdictional struggle over the involvement of Hearts, Hibernian and Partick Thistle in an Anglo-Scottish floodlight League. The Scottish clubs were threatened with expulsion from the Scottish League if they took any further part in the mid-week tourney against Manchester City, Tottenham Hotspur and Newcastle United. The rule cited was that no outside competition could take place without League sanction, and the Scottish League claimed the competition 'would financially injure other League members'. Although the SFA had sanctioned the competition, the venture disintegrated after the League threat. Clearly, parochial jealousies sabotaged the idea before it took off.

Immediately after the sixth goal, the crowd-trouble that had been threatening for ten minutes or so erupted at the Rangers end of Hampden. Fighting and bottle-throwing broke out among the thinning crowds at the Mount Florida end; hundreds of youngsters fled to the safety of the track, as the violence was contained by two hundred policemen who rushed to the trouble-spots. Seventeen spectators were injured, and 11 arrested; modest numbers, perhaps, by the standards of modern times but vastly disappointing to the authorities, who had noted a marked improvement in behaviour at this fixture throughout the mid-50s. The newspapers praised the prompt and stern handling by the police of a situation in which 'the innocent fled over the retaining wall to escape the insane fury of the guilty'.

On the pitch Rangers' agony continued, and some Ibrox defenders appeared so confused that it seemed possible that one of them would score for Celtic. For all their desperation, however, that did not happen, but in the last minute McPhail, who had once again eluded Valentine, was pulled down in the box by Shearer. To the delight of the Celtic support, still massed on the other terracing, still singing every song in the repertoire, the most accomplished player on view, Fernie – a man who had never missed a spot-kick in competitive football – stepped forward to take the penalty. Four quick steps and one crisp shot later, the ball was nestling again in the corner of Rangers' net.

At last – but still too soon for Celtic fans – the whistle went and the most one-sided match in the history of Old Firm matches had ended, to be celebrated in song, poetry and folk-memory for decades.[3]

Seventh heaven indeed.

POSTSCRIPTS

John Valentine never played another match for Rangers, dropped after only 11 competitive games in a Rangers jersey. Nearly a year later he joined St. Johnstone of the Second Division. This ruthless streak in the Ibrox club was to be echoed a dozen years later, when Alex Ferguson suffered an identical fate after failing to mark Billy McNeill at a corner kick in the first minutes of the 1969 Scottish Cup final, when McNeill's header opened the scoring in a 4–0 rout.

* * *

On the way to the club's favourite restaurant to celebrate the victory with other members of the Celtic party, Bob Kelly had a kind thought. He arranged for a car to be sent to Hamilton, to the home of Jock Stein, where the former Celtic captain was recuperating after yet another operation on his ankle. Stein had listened to the match on the radio.

* * *

The injured pride of Rangers and their supporters was apparent, although the *Rangers' Supporters' Association Annual* (1958) congratulated Celtic graciously on proving that 'the true art of football will triumph in face of all opposition'.

Perhaps more reflective of the grass-roots support is the recollection of Cliff Hanley, then on the staff of the *Daily Record*: 'I knew a sports writer who was fairly pro-Rangers (what I mean is that he got his eyes dyed blue for his birthday), and the great 'Gers were beaten seven to one by some obscure set of upstarts. I actually tried to josh him about it, and he strode past me with unseeing eyes and blood squirting out of his ears. And that was a month after the game.' (Ian Archer and Trevor Royle: *We'll Support You Evermore*, 1976)

* * *

Shortly after 8.30 that evening keen observers might have noticed a strange sight in the heavens; it was the world's first artificial satellite, *Sputnik I*, on its umpteenth orbit of the planet. A Glaswegian, brooding over the result and inspired perhaps by the same spirit as Robert Burns, tried to emulate the Bard:

Twinkle, twinkle little Sputnik;
You are sure a dirty tricknik.
Up above the world so high,
Making zig-zags in the sky.

RHAPSODY IN GREEN

How the hell can people sleep,
When all night you go 'Beep – beep – beep'.
Telling all the Tims in Heaven,
Rangers one, and Celtic seven?

* * *

Before the League Cup final Celtic had considered fielding a young outside
left called Bertie Auld, but opted in the end for Neil Mochan. Auld, of
course, went on to become a key member of the Lisbon Lions. Apart from
his skill on the field, Bertie could have earned a living as a stand-up
comedian. One of his favourite party-pieces is said to be the following:

During a particularly bad spell of adverse publicity for the Old Firm,
both clubs made efforts to improve their image, to show that they could get
on off the field.

Two Rangers players, along with two Celts, were invited to a Quiz Night -
at a Celtic supporters' function. As guests, Rangers were given the chance
to earn some points first: 'Question One – what was the first British team to
win the European Cup?' Two points to Rangers, who were allowed to
continue: 'Question Two – what Scottish team won nine Leagues in a row?'
Another two points for Rangers, but some consternation from the Ibrox
players. One of them clears his throat, and interrupts: 'These questions,
Jimmy. Do you not think they're a wee bit slanted?'

The quizmaster looks at him in some surprise, but thinks it over in the
new-found atmosphere of harmony: 'Aye, right. Ah, here's one for you. Who
scored Rangers' goal when Celtic won 7–1?'

Footnotes

1 Evans and Tully, despite many years at Parkhead, had never been close.
Essentially it stemmed from a difference in temperament. Tully always retained an
impulsive Irish streak and was sharp in mind and tongue: Evans always gave the
impression of a dour, hardworking Scot, reticent to a fault.

The reason for the latest misunderstanding appeared to be a column, ironically
ghost-written for Tully, in an evening newspaper; the article criticised a recent
Scottish performance against Ireland, to which Evans took exception.

2 Rangers' philosophy is illustrated by a Willie Waddell quote on the Ibrox
mystique which surrounded the club until Jock Stein's reign at Parkhead undermined it: 'The atmosphere of Ibrox, the attitude of everyone connected with the
club, made you feel that it was your duty to shatter all opposition, to prove that there
was only one Rangers.' (from a chapter by Hugh McIlvanney in *Soccer: The Great*
Ones, 1968)

3 The memory lingers on. Tommy Burns, an ardent Celt born within a stone's throw
of Celtic Park, shuddered in a TV interview in recollection of his anguish during a
1–5 thrashing by Rangers at Ibrox in August 1988 as the realisation started to dawn
on the player that Rangers might match (or surpass) the margin of the famous victory.

In 1986 one of the authors mentioned this final to an acquaintance whom he considered only mildly interested in Celtic; to his astonishment the other launched into a verbatim and enthusiastic rendition of the match report from the *Glasgow Herald* that he had committed to memory.

A PENNY SAVED

In 1957 it was revealed that the billionaire, J. Paul Getty, was probably the richest man in the world. Getty later became notorious because of his installation of a coin-operated telephone for the use of guests at his country house.

11

FREE AT LAST!

THAT'S THE TEAM FOR ME

Aye, it's Celtic, Celtic, that's the team for me!
Celtic, Celtic , on to victory.
They're the finest team in Scotland,
I'm sure you will agree,
They'll never give up till they've won the Cup
And the Scottish Football League.

There's Fallon, Young and Gemmell,
Who proudly wear the green;
There's Clark, McNeill, and Kennedy –
The best there's ever been.
Jim Johnstone, Murdoch, Chalmers,
John Divers, and John Hughes –
And sixty thousand Celtic fans
Who proudly sing the news:

Aye, it's Celtic, Celtic . . .

(Supporters' song, 1964-65)

FOOTBALL WOULD be the poorer without its romance. The idea that an individual (or a team) may have a date with destiny is an inviting one, as this account of the dramatic, closing stages of the 1965 Scottish Cup final illustrates: 'He came flying upfield like a tornado. Almost at once opponents spotted a new danger to their defence. They tried to stop him long before he reached the penalty area. They might as well have tried to stop a runaway jet. He knew what he was doing and he knew he was fated to score. And so did most of the 108,800 spectators at Hampden. And so did his opponents. *And he did.*'

A sixth sense must have gripped the Celtic support *en masse* on the eve

Billy McNeill heads the winner against Dunfermline, 1965 Scottish Cup Final.

of that final against Dunfermline Athletic, for the bookies had to take note of a last-minute change in the betting, a sudden surge in the money pouring in on Celtic to take the Cup. Naturally, the odds changed, as an accurate barometer, to reflect this phenomenon and the eternal optimism of Celtic supporters. The fact that, eventually, Celtic would start the match as slight favourites seemed a classic case of the heart ruling the head, because most bookmakers would have bet on Dunfermline.

John MacKenzie underlined the doubts about Celtic when he tipped the Fifers to take the Cup to the Kingdom for the second time in four years: '*If* John Hughes strikes his most profitable game. *If* Steve Chalmers can blaze the way to goal. *If* Bertie Auld can control the flow of the game. *If* the defence makes no vital mistakes . . .' (*Scottish Daily Express*: 24 April 1965)

Publicly, at least, little self-doubt existed in the town of Dunfermline, where the Town Council publicised its intention to hire the same open-top, double-decker bus which had borne the triumphant Dunfermline side to the Chambers in 1961. The local newspaper, the *Dunfermline Press*, equally confident of victory, asserted that the side of 1965 was not the Cinderella outfit of 1961 but 'a classy team, with star players blending into an efficient machine that has beaten the best in Scotland this season and won fame in Continental arenas. From goal to outside left, each Athletic player bears at the least complete comparison with his opposite number, and in several positions they have a distinct edge in ability and experience. Better still, Celtic's team-work is not on a par with Dunfermline's, nor is their tactical knowledge . . . And in the Athletic's dugout is a manager who has proved himself every bit as good as his rival in preparing his team for the big occasion.'[1]

The confidence in Dunfermline was entirely justified.

The turnabout in Dunfermline's football fortunes came with the appointment of Jock Stein as manager in 1960. Stein's first task was to lead the revival that helped Dunfermline escape relegation; after that, came the rebuilding. Within a season Dunfermline Athletic had won the Scottish Cup by beating Celtic in a replayed final, and later emerged as legitimate challengers for the League Championship.

In 1961, after the upset victory over Celtic – the first Scottish Cup triumph in the club's 76 years – the euphoric chairman, David Thomson, spoke at the celebrations: 'We are now in the top-class division. We intend to remain at the top. We are now on a par with the greatest clubs in the world, and we are going to make sure we have the facilities to meet teams like Real Madrid and Barcelona in Dunfermline.'

Certainly the ground was soon vastly improved, and a splendid new stand constructed, financed in part by shrewd trading in the transfer market and fine runs in the club's European ventures. Despite the improvements, few Continental teams welcomed a visit to East End Park. Between 1961 and 1970 Dunfermline played 20 European matches at home, and lost only one; their 'scalps' included Olympiakos of Greece (4–0), VFB Stuttgart of Germany (1–0), Orgryte of Sweden (4–2), Boldklub of Denmark (5–0), Dynamo Zagreb of Yugoslavia (4–2), Bordeaux of France (4–0), Anderlecht of Belgium (3–2), West Bromwich Albion (1–0) and Everton of England (2–0), Valencia (6–2), Real Zaragosa (1–0), and Atletico Bilbao of Spain (1–0) . . . Some of those clubs boasted a impressive pedigree, and had made an impact in the various European competitions at one time or another.

Approaching the final in April 1965 Dunfermline could derive satisfaction from the standings in the League table that showed them to be decidedly superior to Celtic. At the season's end the top half of the table was as follows:

	P	W	D	L	F– A	PTS
Kilmarnock	34	22	6	6	62–33	50
Hearts	34	22	6	6	90–49	50
Dunfermline	34	22	5	7	83–36	49
Hibernian	34	21	4	9	75–47	46
Rangers	34	18	8	8	78–35	44
Dundee	34	15	10	9	86–63	40
Clyde	34	17	6	11	64–58	40
Celtic	34	16	5	13	76–57	37

It was the best team in Dunfermline's history: assembled by Jock Stein, sustained and improved by Willie Cunningham. Little known to the general public, however, a personal feud was simmering between the two managers – a feud that apparently led to a reserve game, scheduled just before the

Scottish Cup final, being postponed in order to avoid the chance of a face-to-face confrontation. Dunfermline's Irish-born manager would not deny this in an interview with Brian Meek of the *Scottish Daily Express*. In that interview Cunningham expressed his admiration of the man who had first brought him to Dunfermline (and secured his appointment as coach, and later manager), but admitted that a clash in personality had developed over time. No doubt Cunningham – as any manager would – resented the fact that, walking in the footsteps of Jock Stein, he was assumed to be following to the letter some master-plan of his predecessor.

Cunningham was at pains to insist that everything achieved at Dunfermline by Jock Stein had been surpassed at East End Park that season: 'To be told that you are only succeeding because someone else has built up the side for you hits where it hurts most.' What gnawed at Cunningham was the understandable fear that Dunfermline, despite the overall improvement, might end up with nothing – except praise.

To bolster the confidence of his squad he made conscious efforts to play down the legend of Jock Stein: 'You can have all the ideas in the world, but if you haven't the players you still won't succeed.' He tried to land a few blows in the psychological warfare before the final: 'When Dunfermline were playing their defensive type of game until last season, the team was being subdued.'[2] He tried to dismiss the lingering fears of some Dunfermline players that Stein had a dossier on them: 'The players also know Jock Stein. We will bring the Cup back to Dunfermline on Saturday night!' Despite his efforts it could be seen that he was allowing Jock Stein's formidable presence to get under his skin.

It would have been surprising if the Dunfermline players had not been pondering what their former manager might have up his sleeve this time. Certainly they might not have cared to listen to Bob Shearer, the Hamilton Academical groundsman – and the father of Bobby Shearer, Rangers' captain. The elder Shearer, a former neighbour and great admirer of the Stein, would regale visitors with his recollection of the Stein master-stroke that helped defeat Celtic in the 1961 final. Stein used his friendship with Shearer to arrange a practice-session at Douglas Park on the day of the replay. There he put his men through a brisk workout in the afternoon, rehearsing a series of moves that kept their minds concentrated on the task ahead at Hampden that evening.

Cunningham did have one immediate problem to solve because Dunfermline, chasing for a Championship flag along with Hearts and Kilmarnock, had dropped a vital point in a home match against lowly St Johnstone in a 1–1 draw. It was a disappointing performance highlighted by three chances missed by the side's leading scorer, Alex Ferguson. The young striker had lost form at a vital time, and had been criticised earlier in the local press for an unsatisfactory performance in a narrow 2–1 win over Third Lanark. Against St Johnstone he remained out of touch, and his late equaliser did little to make up for the point lost. The side had abandoned its studied style of play, opting for all-out attack that left them exposed at the rear; repeatedly, the forwards had fallen into St Johnstone's offside-trap.

Questions were being asked about Dunfermline's line-up, and speculation was widespread in the Kingdom, and elsewhere. It could not have been doing the fraying nerves much good as Cunningham decided to delay his team selection until the hour before the match.

* * *

Stein had seized the initiative by giving his players the Monday off, and then took the squad for a three-day break at Largs away from the hordes of well-wishers, friends seeking tickets, requests for interviews and the interruptions that plague teams preparing for a Cup final.

The captains, McNeill and McLean, lead out their men for the final.

Stein knew that only one question could be uppermost in the players' minds. Shortly after arriving at the hotel he called a meeting and announced his team for the Saturday. He revealed some of the thinking behind the selection of the 11 men chosen; he told the group that he did not want players brooding over their chances of being picked, he sympathised with those for whom he could not find a place.

The move was welcomed by the whole squad as relieving the tension, and as an indication of the manager's confidence in the outcome – and in himself. The practice of the chairman picking the sides over lunch on the day of the final were gone.

In the recent past, reportedly, Celtic's 'preparations' for a Cup final consisted of discussion of 'variations in free kicks and throw-ins'; now, Stein presented a detailed evaluation of the opposition's strengths and weaknesses to the players. Always a pragmatist, Stein's philosophy contained a central belief – that tactics might not guarantee victory, but would bring the best chance of success. So, he briefed his players in such a fashion as to leave no doubt in any mind about what was expected individually: he detailed John Clark to mark the Dunfermline playmaker, Alec Smith; he instructed Charlie Gallagher to drop back alongside Bobby Murdoch in midfield; and he advised the full backs, Ian Young and Tommy Gemmell to play wide to keep close contact with Edwards and Sinclair.

Harold Wilson, when Prime Minister, stated once that a week was a long time in politics; in football, the week before a Cup final can be interminable. As the players prepared for the match, some may have thought back to the warning contained in the previous week's club programme, following a 2–6 thrashing from Falkirk: 'It will not make pleasant reading – it is not intended to do so. Our own staff of players have had their chance, and there can be no justified complaint if we seek to strengthen our team. And that is going to be done, irrespective of what happens within the next week or two.' (17 April 1965) Stein may have been concentrating on the Scottish Cup final, but his restless mind was already starting to look ahead. The players were getting the message that the future would be planned and systematic – professional at last.

The statement in the programme was more than a declaration of intent; it was a reminder of the high standards the new manager demanded, and it hinted at the crucial importance of the forthcoming final for Celtic, and Stein.

The manager was well aware of his reputation as the saviour of doomed clubs; defeat at Hampden would tarnish that image and make later success more difficult to attain. Celtic had to win this match because, as Brian Meek stated in his profile of Stein, '. . . the Celtic trophy cupboard has been bare for so long even the frenzied faithful have threatened to dwindle. He [Stein] has to win because, if he doesn't, Celtic will once more be excluded from the rich pasture lands of Europe. And, if that happens, the importance of

Celtic in Scottish football will be equal to St Johnstone, or Falkirk, or Partick Thistle.' (*Scottish Daily Express*: 23 April 1965)

Celtic, because of the fans' collective frustration at a maddening inconsistency, had been suffering financially. Before Stein's arrival a protracted slump in form in early January had caused substantially reduced 'gates'; even after his arrival, the home attendances had averaged only 15,000 in March and April of 1965.

I BELONG TO GLASGOW

In 1965 Drumchapel, one of the city's three largest housing estates, was described as 'a teenage jungle' where gangs of youths roved the streets reportedly dressed in military-style uniforms. The 40,000 residents, while living in decent housing, lacked the amenities of a community: cinemas, dance-halls, shops, youth-centres, swimming-pools. One resident, stuck in the estate, complained: 'I might as well be sitting in an igloo in Greenland.'

The root of Celtic's problem had lain in the organisation of the club in a period of rebuilding so prolonged that one critic termed it 'permanent transition'. The side that won the League Cup in 1957 by beating Rangers 7–1 featured veteran players in vital positions; when injury, retirement and transfers affected the staff, the directors embarked on 'a youth policy' so haphazard that the supporters' unrealistic expectations were dashed repeatedly. In January 1965 Jimmy McGrory admitted that his charges lacked the mental hardness that 'other Celtic teams always carried. This is not something you can develop easily. The players must find this themselves.'

The meteoric rise and fall of young John Hughes serves as an indication of the traumatic early 1960s. Immediately promoted to the first team on the strength of two splendid goals in the pre-season public trial (a feature of the Scottish game until abandoned a few years later), Hughes made a winning debut at centre forward by scoring in a 2–0 win against Third Lanark. The hyperbole of the newspapers did not help the newcomer: '. . . the power and pace of a teenager . . . the poise and purpose of a veteran.' Only a week later the normally reserved 'Waverley' was captivated when he saw Hughes 'roast' the more experienced Doug Baillie of Rangers during Celtic's first outright victory at Ibrox in three years: '. . . a youngster in the great Celtic tradition . . . a powerfully-built boy, but as light on his feet as a soft-shoe dancer. His ball-control at times was masterly, and produced a deceptive drag in the dribble that puzzled and tormented those who went into the tackle.' (*Daily Record*: 22 August 1960)

Such praise in the newspapers, and adulation from a support desperate for success, would have had an adverse effect on any player . . . but, at the time, John Hughes was only 17, and expected to fill the centre-forward role with the same distinction as his famous predecessors: Quinn, McGrory, Crum, McPhail . . . The teenager, still learning his trade as a player, should have been nurtured and brought along more slowly; in essence, John Hughes was asked to learn his job in public each week, watched by thousands of spectators with an emotional investment in Celtic.

Halfway through the next season his life was being made a misery as total strangers taunted him in the streets about being a member of 'the worst forward line in Britain'. The more impatient supporters could not understand the 'failure' of this youth, then only 18, to impose his great physical strength on any opposition. Hughes can still recall a miserable day at Stirling when Celtic missed chance after chance and ended up losing 0–1. He skidded over the goal-line in a vain, diving attempt to connect with a cross. Lying there, winded by his effort, he heard Celtic 'fans' close up behind the goal hurling a torrent of abuse at him; stoically, he got to his knees, glanced over at the section of 'supporters' and, to his disbelief, he saw prominent among them a 'friend' from Coatbridge for whom he frequently got match tickets!

Black comedy of this sort always seemed to intrude in that era. A frequent contributor was the young goalkeeper, Frank Haffey – often brilliant, sometimes shaky, and never consistent. In November 1962, for example, Haffey played splendidly against Rangers in a Glasgow Cup-tie played in mid-week at a fog-bound Parkhead; near the end he blocked a first-timer at point-blank range from Wilson with a daring instinctive dive. His save, one in a series, enabled Celtic to survive into extra-time when a goal two minutes from the end by Bobby Murdoch won the tie for Celtic.

A few days later Celtic, still in contention for the League title, took the field at Parkhead to the tumultuous acclaim of a 40,000 crowd. The Celtic 'choir' had barely struck up the first rendition of 'Sean South of Garryowen', when Partick Thistle's Hogan tried a speculative grounder from 35 yards; Haffey 'semi-dived and semi-knelt' to deal with the effort, and to his mortification the ball squirmed under his body with barely enough momentum to trickle over the line. A disorientated Celtic went on to lose 0–2 amid a chorus of boos and catcalls from the bitterly disappointed crowd.

Haffey was fated to be involved in the drama of a Scottish Cup final replay against Rangers. On 4 May 1963 once more he played superlatively against the Ibrox side before a crowd of 129,527 at a windswept, rainy Hampden; time after time his confident handling had rescued Celtic in a 1–1 draw. However, in the replay, he looked decidedly uneasy against the skilful raids of a rejuvenated Rangers, and could be blamed for the loss of two goals in a 0–3 defeat that turned into a public humiliation in the last 30 minutes while Rangers toyed with their outclassed opponents.

Apart from mistakes by Haffey, other factors influenced the outcome of that replay. In the morning the newspapers announced the Celtic forward line as: Murdoch, Craig, Hughes, Divers and Chalmers. The fans on the terracing were still arguing before the kick-off about the exclusion of Jimmy Johnstone and Frank Brogan, both of whom had troubled Rangers in the first match. Johnstone, in fact, had perplexed Rangers' defence to such an extent that he had threatened to run riot if he were provided with a supply of passes. Speculation on the relative worth of the new forward combination was cut short by the roar that greeted the appearance of the teams in the tunnel, and the announcement, barely heard, of further changes in Celtic's lineup. Jimmy McGrory's post-match statement, defending the recast line of Craig, Murdoch, Divers, Chalmers and Hughes, served only to confirm the belief that the club's guardians had more expertise in bingo-calling than tactical insight: 'We selected a team, had a late conference before the match and then decided it could be bettered by making positional switches.' (*Daily Record*: 17 May 1963)

The reference to 'we' was disingenuous because the first and last word in team matters lay with the chairman, Bob Kelly. Celtic's selection of players for important Scottish Cup matches had become a laughing-stock among football men, who described them as 'bizarre' or 'eccentric'; later, Jock Stein described the chairman's permutations charitably as 'romantic'. The result in 1963 was that Rangers' task became infinitely easier: Provan did not have to deal with the unpredictable moves of Jimmy Johnstone, who had proved himself in the first match; McKinnon felt relief at not having to oppose Hughes who had always troubled him when chosen at centre . . . Celtic's 39th combination of forwards that season could not put together a single constructive move in the replay, managing only three direct shots at Ritchie in the Rangers goal.

Many thousands of Celtic fans among the crowd of 120,263 deserted the terracing as Rangers enjoyed the last 30 minutes by passing the ball around and not allowing a totally dispirited Celtic side to get a touch. Some of the

---

WHAT'S UP, DOC?

The Chelsea manager, Tommy Docherty, caused a sensation in 1965 by sending home eight of his players for breaking an 11 p.m. curfew at their Blackpool hotel on the eve of an important match at Burnley. The night-porter at the Cliffs Hotel reported: 'Mr Docherty went to the bedrooms of all the players. Several were missing. He waited in the residents' lounge. The players came in, in pretty high spirits. Then I saw him hand them train-tickets for London.' Chelsea's makeshift side lost 2–6 at Burnley – and went on to lose out in the championship race to Manchester United. Ironically, prominent among the disgraced players were two who would make a name for themselves as managers two decades later – Terry Venables and George Graham.

fans may have noticed in the papers the accounts of the launching of a new space capsule from Cape Canaveral named *Faith 7*; if they had been super-stitious enough to take it as an omen, they were doomed to disappointment yet again. Doomed, too, to a cruel summer of enduring workplace jokes about 'Billy McNeill and the Easybeats' in mocking imitation of the current craze for Mersey pop-groups.

The newspapers expressed a genuine concern for Celtic's plight and for the effects of a weak Celtic upon the Scottish game. Jack Harkness, an opponent of Jimmy McGrory on the field but a long-time friend off it, wrote in the *Sunday Post*: 'Celtic in a Scottish Cup final replay. Half an hour still left for play. Then suddenly this mass exit from the Celtic end of the ground. A demonstration of resentment proclaiming to the world that "the faithful" had lost faith in their team. A demonstration which cannot be lost on those whose responsibility it is to run Celtic.' (19 May 1963)

Worse was to follow early in the 1963/64 season. Twice Rangers defeated Celtic easily in August, winning both sectional matches in the League Cup by a similar 3–0 margin. Orchestrating Rangers' triumphs was the arrogant Jim Baxter, who imposed his will over Celtic's impressionable youngsters with his confident, assured skills. Later, in his memoirs, he confirmed his contempt by describing Celtic as 'just another team'.

Hints of frustration appeared in the club programme following the defeat at Parkhead on the opening day of the season: the captain, Billy McNeill, was rebuked for gifting Rangers the opening goal with 'a very stupid pass-back'. The anonymous comment bore the unmistakeable *imprimatur* of the chairman, from whom a resolute Billy McNeill extracted an apology.

A week later, against Queen of the South, Celtic scraped a 1–1 draw when the forwards missed chances, and became more and more fankled the longer the match wore on. Booing, whistling and slow-handclapping were directed at the hapless players from the 19,000 crowd, but more pointedly at the Directors' Box. After the match an assembly of 2,000 formed 'a threatening ring' around the main door of the stadium chanting, 'We want Kelly! We want Kelly!', clearly unaware that the chairman, who had arranged to be in Dumfries that afternoon, had not attended the game. Police formed a protective cordon separating the angry, excited crowd from the club offices before pushing the demonstrators back slowly towards London Road.

A prominent Glasgow solicitor and lifetime supporter, James F. Reilly, added more fuel to the fire, claiming that the Board's inefficiency could be illustrated best by comparing the share prices of the Old Firm. He pointed out that the club's £1 shares were currently valued for estate purposes at 30/- a share (£1.50) each, while those of Rangers were changing hands on the open market at £13.15/- (£13.75) each. He emphasised the need for change in a set-up that had produced 'ten years in which we have seen little more than an accumulation of raw youngsters quite unsuited for the job of carrying on the great playing traditions of the Celtic club.' (*Weekly News*: 17 August 1963) He called for the directors to transform the club into a public company, and to allow for new directors by putting shares on the open market – a situation not possible under a constitution which gave (and in 1990 still gives) the Board the right to veto share transfers.

The only respite from domestic travails was an unexpected run in the Cup Winners' Cup, the entry to which being courtesy of the 0–3 defeat by Rangers in the Scottish Cup. Celtic thrashed Basle (Switzerland) home and away by 5–0 and 5–1 scores, got past Dinamo Zagreb (Yugoslavia) by a 4–2 aggregate, and won both legs against Slovan Bratislava (Czechoslovakia) by 1–0 margins . . . before a naïve performance in Budapest against MTK (Hungary) in the semi-final threw away a three-goal advantage from the first leg.

Malcolm Munro's preview of the quarter-final away clash in Bratislava was blunt about the consequences of failure in both the short and long term: 'Defeat would mean a steep falling-off in interest among the fans. Unless Celtic retain an interest in either (or both) the Cup and the League, and the financial rewards thereof, economics could force them to sell such valuable properties as Billy McNeill.' (*Evening Citizen*: 3 March 1964)

A solo goal by John Hughes five minutes from the end gave the young Celtic side a repeat victory over the Czechs. However, it was a return to reality a few days later at Ibrox; the Rangers players lined up before the start to applaud Celtic on to the field, and then proceeded to run them off it. Two goals, one a minute before half-time and the other a minute after it, confirmed Rangers' supremacy in Scotland. For Celtic supporters it marked a continuation of the misery; for the fifth time in five matches that season Rangers defeated their old rivals.

Strictly speaking, Celtic's repeated failures against Rangers were not solely the result of a deficiency in skill; Celtic were suffering from a neurosis, a nervous disorder that afflicted them in vital situations. It was a recurring crisis in confidence, and the longer the period of failure continued, the greater the pressure on the side. They had become conditioned to fail at the vital stage.

In September 1964 Celtic appeared to have ended the jinx with a deserved 3–1 League win over Rangers in a downpour at Parkhead. The sports writers, after years of reporting false dawns, were convinced the revival was real, praising 'the best Celtic side in years, perfectly balanced, tight and commanding in defence and with one of the most devastating attacks in the country'. With ease the team swept through to the League Cup final where they were due to meet an out-of-form Rangers. And once more Celtic failed to break through in an important match, losing 1–2 at Hampden Park on 24 October after dominating the early stages before a crowd of 91,423.

At Ibrox on Ne'erday 1965 Celtic continued the chronicle of failure against Rangers losing 0–1, when a frustrated Jimmy Johnstone was ordered off for retaliation, and Bobby Murdoch blasted a penalty in the 85th minute both high and wide.

The Scottish League president, William Terris, had recently made an unprecedented plea for more competition for Rangers. He clearly had Celtic in mind when he asserted that clubs could enhance their existing resources by concentrating on getting more out of their players, both in terms of preparation and performance.

Hugh Taylor, in the *Daily Record*, perceived the roots of Celtic's crisis in the club's stubborn refusal to modernise its structure and approach:

> Like the Parkhead fans, I'm tired of hearing about Celtic's potential, Celtic's bad luck, Celtic's missed chances . . . All right, I agree that bouncy Celtic, non-stop Celtic, fiery Celtic can be an exciting, even exhilarating team. But to me they're Bing [Crosby] singing 'Please', a wall-of-death showground rider, a flip in a Tiger Moth, a pleasant and often exciting echo from the past . . . It's my sincere belief that, until Celtic stop kidding themselves that only British-style football will bring honours, they will go on struggling. Celtic must go back to the kind of football that made them great, speed it up, and evolve a modern defensive system.
>
> (18 January 1965)

Celtic supporters were quick to respond to the *Record*'s request for feedback; most letters advocated a more ambitious transfer policy, a few recommended that Celtic make efforts to secure the services of Jock Stein, then guiding Hibernian to an increasingly likely League and Scottish Cup double. If Stein could do that at Easter Road, having come close with even thinner resources at East End Park, what could he do at Celtic Park?

In reply to the frequent criticism in the press – and, let it be noted, that the tone and content appears informed, reasonable and constructive – Jimmy McGrory suggested that the remedy lay in acquiring an experienced inside forward to act as a calming influence on the younger players, and started the negotiations that led to Bertie Auld returning to Celtic Park. The longest serving player, full back Jim Kennedy, admitted that the anxiety stifling the side was caused by the players fretting about the elusive breakthrough, but he stressed the difficulty of winning a major trophy with a young side lacking in experience.

At the end of January 1965 came the bombshell that transformed Scottish football.

To the vast delight of the supporters Jock Stein was appointed as Celtic's manager; any lingering doubts among the directors about Stein's acceptance by the support because he was not a Catholic were revealed as out-of-date.

However, the initial euphoria had subsided a little as the time approached for the final; Stein had chosen to use the weeks before the final to examine all his players in match-conditions before making up his mind about them. Some of the results were disquieting: a home-defeat by St Johnstone (0–1), another loss at Parkhead to Hibernian (2–4), a thrashing at Brockville by Falkirk (2–6), and only a week before the Hampden clash, yet another defeat at home, by Partick Thistle (1–2) . . . And Dunfermline's recently established pedigree made them opponents worthy of the highest respect.

SCOTTISH CUP FINAL
24 April 1965
Hampden Park

CELTIC 3	**DUNFERMLINE ATHLETIC 2**
Fallon	Herriot
Young	W. Callaghan
Gemmell	Lunn
Murdoch	Thomson
McNeill	McLean
Clark	T. Callaghan
Chalmers	Edwards
Gallagher	Smith
Hughes	McLaughlin
Lennox	Melrose
Auld	Sinclair

Scorers:
Auld (31, 51)   Melrose (15)
McNeill (81)   McLaughlin (44)
Referee: H. Phillips (Wishaw)

Attendance: 108,806

FAME

The phenomenon of the Beatles continued in 1965 with the Liverpool group dominating the pop-charts as a result of successive hit singles: 'Ticket to Ride', 'Help!' and 'Day Tripper/We Can Work It Out!'. When John, Paul, George and Ringo were awarded the MBE in the Birthday Honours' List, several previous recipients returned their medals to Buckingham Palace as a protest; one irate gentleman was upset at 'the honouring of moral degenerates'.

Hampden was a spectacular sight, its huge bowl rimmed with a vast crowd. The Dunfermline fans soaked up the atmosphere, secure in the knowledge that they were supporting a side no longer considered country bumpkins, a different story from 1961. Ian Jack recalled his first visit to Glasgow for the latter final when he got the afternoon off school to see Dunfermline make history in the evening; the special train 'crept into Glasgow through smoking steel mills' to disgorge its passengers at a sub-urban station near Hampden, where the Dunfermline fans mingled with 'Glaswegians of the old-fashioned sort, men who had come from their work with green-and-white mufflers over their vests and screwtops in their jacket pockets. Like Glaswegians of the old-fashioned sort, they believed that Scotland beyond Glasgow consisted solely of ploughmen who went home to their bothies and scraped fiddles of an evening. "Hey, son, did you mind an' milk the coos before you came?" ' (*The Observer*: 6 March 1988)

In contrast to the heavy rain of the 1961 replay, sunshine bathed the stadium, although a freshening wind threatened to affect play on the fast turf.

McNeill won the toss and gave Dunfermline the task of defending the goal at the King's Park end: Jim Herriot trotted downfield to face a gusty breeze, the sun in his eyes, and behind him the thousands of Celtic supporters desperate for success.[3]

Celtic attacked from the start, but Dunfermline remained cool in clearing the danger. John Hughes caused early anxiety among Dunfermline's defenders with his awkward but forceful thrusts; every time he gathered the ball the Celtic following roared in anticipation, and his thundering runs kept Jim McLean and the heart of Dunfermline's rearguard fully occupied.

It was vintage Scottish football: hard, fast, non-stop action. As those critics who had picked Dunfermline to win had predicted, the Fifers were deadly in the counterpunch: 'In brilliant style in 15 minutes Dunfermline made a chance and took it. McNeill had been injured and after he received attention, a throw-in by Thomson came to Willie Callaghan, who squared the ball into Celts' goal area. Fallon rushed out but could only push the ball away; Sinclair lobbed it back in, and Melrose, on the turn, hooked the ball into the net with Fallon still out of position.' (*The Dunfermline Press*: 1 May 1965)

Celtic were stung by this unexpected reverse; they continued to attack in waves, and Dunfermline's resistance was becoming shakier. Tommy Gemmell, only recently aware of the possibilities of the attacking full back, managed to get as far as the bye-line and saw his fierce shot cannon off Herriot's legs; Ian Young broke through on the right and crossed for Auld but he was crowded out. It came as no surprise when Celtic equalised on the half-hour mark, but the goal itself was an astonishing one.

Charlie Gallagher, a fine and precise striker of the ball, picked up a pass and decided to shoot for goal: his drive deceived Herriot and crashed against the crossbar, rising high in the air. Auld was first to realise the possibilities, and rushed into the goalmouth before the ball started its descent; amazingly, the ball dropped virtually straight down, and Auld reaped the rewards of anticipation and courage by forcing it over the line despite challenges from the rugged defenders.

Bertie Auld opens Celtic's account.

Dunfermline wilted after that goal, and it appeared certain that Celtic would go on to score more. However, just before half-time the complexion of the match changed yet again. Ian Young halted a Sinclair run with a foul 25 yards out; the Celtic defensive 'wall' formed, but crafty Harry Melrose rolled the ball a couple of yards to his right where McLaughlin crashed a ferocious drive past the diving Fallon. With that one shot McLaughlin looked to have justified his manager's preference for him over Ferguson.

Celtic, players and supporters alike, slumped in despair. Two good goals for Dunfermline, but undeserved on the run of play; no team, it was said, had ever come back from being behind twice in a Scottish Cup final. No wonder the Dunfermline players celebrated on the field.[4]

The Celtic players trooped into the dressing-room clearly disappointed:

NO PLACE LIKE HOME

Bertie Auld might well have set some sort of record when he rejoined Celtic in January 1965 from Birmingham City. Celtic's manager, Jimmy McGrory, signed him on four times: Auld was a provisional signing when with Maryhill Harp, and joined Celtic as a professional in March 1955; after a six-month period on loan to Dumbarton, he re-signed in April 1957, and finally returned to Celtic from the Midlands in 1965.

Dunfermline's organised defence had coped with their all-out attack, and had expended little physical effort in creating two goals, and would have the advantage of a freshening wind in the second half. Stein realised that his task would be to restore morale after the loss of a goal so near half-time, and his manner and words were reassuring: Celtic would get the result they wanted if they carried on as before. It would mean minor adjustments, greater determination, and plugging away. Not heroics, but hard work . . .

Dunfermline, with wind advantage, may have been in two minds about how to approach the second half; they knew Celtic would make immediate efforts to get an equaliser, that Celtic would come out in the traditional Parkhead show of spirit. Containment, especially in the first ten minutes of the second half, would be required . . .

Auld, rarely viewed as a regular goalscorer, accepted that his role was a leadership one and displayed notable resolve and cunning. Fittingly, he got Celtic an early equaliser: he sent Lennox away down the left with a deft pass, then sprinted into the box to take the return in his stride, look up and send Herriot partly the wrong way as he cracked a low shot into the net. And to think that both players appeared to be heading for Falkirk earlier that season![5]

Now Dunfermline had to revise any plan of holding Celtic; both teams had everything to play for, as the play switched from end to end. Urged on by their support, Celtic came close when Chalmers raced clear on the right, only to see his low cross-shot pass in front of the goal and slip narrowly past the far post; Sinclair responded with a fine run down the left, and Edwards' effort to beat Fallon with a finely-judged lob was thwarted by the keeper at full stretch.

Eighteen minutes into the second half every Celtic heart stood still as a move involving Melrose, McLaughlin and Sinclair split the defence for Smith's shot to be blocked; the ball broke to Sinclair whose fierce drive was scrambled off the line by Clark, the ball drifting upwards on to the crossbar and rolling down the net over the goal while some Dunfermline players appealed half-heartedly for a penalty.

A minute later Fallon had to deal with another strong shot from McLaughlin. The Celtic supporters cheered the keeper, and continued with a roar of encouragement as the side attempted to weather the spell of Dunfermline pressure.

Jack Harkness wrote: 'As time wore on and these 22 players had already given everything they had, there was still never one single moment when you felt that either side was ready to settle for a draw. Especially Celtic. Where they got their fantastic stamina, I just don't know. I am quite sure, in fact, it was their non-stop play that had as much to do with flummoxing Dunfermline as anything. You felt inwardly that things out on that field were building themselves up for a dramatic climax.' (*Sunday Post*: 25 April 1965)

Nine minutes from the end Lennox embarked on another stamina-draining run down he left, obeying Stein's prior instructions to tire defenders by running wide. Cut off by a Dunfermline player, Lennox settled for a corner.

Gallagher took his time in preparing the ball, looking twice into the area; Billy McNeill hovered round the centre circle about 50 yards from goal. Beside him, watchful and wary, stood Alex Smith, his shadow throughout the afternoon at set-pieces. McNeill may have sensed it was now or never: 'I knew Charlie Gallagher wouldn't attempt to send over a hanging cross which would give the Fifers a chance to get the ball away. When I started my run from about 30 yards, I knew it was going to be a hard cross, and I took off the moment he bent over the kick. My eye was on one thing only – Charlie Gallagher's cross – and it never left the ball until I connected.'

Alex Smith relaxed momentarily at McNeill's original hesitation. The same thought might have crossed the two players' minds: the score was 2–2 and only nine minutes remained, a clearance from Dunfermline's penalty area could leave Celtic exposed for a breakaway. McNeill arrived in the box in a rush, almost knocking over Bobby Lennox in his determination to be first to the ball; the cross was struck crisply and angled away from the goal, perfectly placed out of the reach of the goalkeeper.

The photograph showed it all: McNeill rising above everybody, Lennox brushed aside, Herriot's despairing stretch into the space behind McNeill, Dunfermline's backs on the line, helpless as the ball rages into the net. The camera-angle shows McNeill above the others in the goalmouth and gives the odd impression of him rising above the distant terracing of the King's Park end of Hampden – Caesar bestriding the world like a Colossus!

McNeill had scored his first goal in two and a half years; his goals were so infrequent up to then that a friend of his wife listening to the radio commentary burst into tears, thinking it was an 'own goal'!

For a second Hampden was stilled, stunned with the shock of decision, and then the terracings erupted into a frantic joy: 'The sunshine is rent for the remaining nine minutes with the roar of a 100,000 voices. But it is not the Hampden Roar. It is charged with deeply felt, personal emotions. It is choked with the wonderful relief that ends years of frustration. The players dance and hug and kiss. The stand – to a man – is on its feet. But men in scarves and bunnets have tears in their eyes, eyes that have faithfully watched and waited for a decade for such a miracle as this. Infants, as well as banners, are hurled in the air. Gruff, undemonstrative men embrace and kiss their startled sons.' (*Scottish Daily Express*: 26 April 1965)

From then till the end the prevailing tone in the continuous waves of sound pouring down from the terracings changed by the minute – from exultation, to triumph, to encouragement, back to exultation, but always the motif of anxiety present in the undertow, and finally joyful impatience. Bobby Murdoch recalls the closing nine minutes as interminable. The

---

THIRSTY WORK

After the League Cup final between Celtic and Rangers, watched by a record 107,609 on 23 October 1965, the Hampden groundsmen cleared the terracings of an estimated 50,000 empty cans (bottles were not counted). Doubtless, the staff would drink to the fact that it is now illegal to carry such objects into Scottish football grounds.

---

thought running through his mind as the play continued to surge back and forth was 'Is it never going to end?' Still a youngster, he had already known the disappointment of losing in two major finals – the Scottish Cup of 1963 and the League Cup of 1964.

At last Hugh Phillips blew the final whistle; in a passionate, hard-fought Cup-tie he had only awarded 20 free kicks, a tribute to his control as much as to the conduct of both sides.

The scenes of jubilation on the terracings defied description. One veteran reporter sat back in the press-box, and watched for a few minutes; 'Well, it's about time surely? They'll be happy the night.' Could he ever have imagined the party would go on and on for another decade?

Congratulations and celebrations – the winner.

213

The party started that night, the Celtic team-bus having to edge its way through streets filled with dancing, singing, delirious fans. Outside the Central Hotel, where the players and officials celebrated with champagne, supporters shouted and cheered for hours until the Cup was held out of the windows for all to see. The sense of relief was such that one overjoyed player was heard to say: 'It's like we've been let out of prison.' Indeed, it was exactly like that, and *nothing* could contain this Celtic side now.

Footnotes

1 Dunfermline Athletic have always been nicknamed 'the Pars'. The word is often construed as a shortened form of 'Paralytic', a scornful parody of 'Athletic'.

2 A valid point. At Dunfermline and at Hibernian a recurring criticism was Stein's reliance on a strong defence at the expense of attack.

3 The goalkeeper's name might ring a non-football bell. The author of a famous autobiographical series on the life of a Yorkshire vet saw Herriot play in a televised game, and adopted the keepers's name for his books.

4 The film of the match shows a young Tommy Callaghan dancing with joy. After he joined Celtic years later, the sight of his celebrations always raised merriment among Celtic players whenever the film was shown.

5 Jock Stein stated some years after his return to Parkhead that a deal was in the pipeline to take Lennox to Falkirk (before Stein came back), and Falkirk had actually made a bid for Auld, then with Birmingham City, before the player returned to Celtic. Falkirk's chairman, James Doak, had gone to watch Auld play against West Ham in London but, sitting in the same stand, Celtic's coach, Sean Fallon, was on the same mission.

THE AMERICAN DREAM

In April 1965 the death of Owen Madden occurred in Hot Springs, Arkansas, where he was described as 'a respected member of the Chamber of Commerce, and generous to local charities'. A notorious gangster, and 'a street-brawling product of New York's "Hell's Kitchen" ', Madden, nicknamed 'Clay Pigeon' because of frequent gunshot wounds, had emigrated to the USA at the age of 11 from Leeds. At the peak of his career during Prohibition he was operating a brewery which turned out 300,000 barrels of beer daily. At the time of his death Madden lived next door to the local chief-of-police.

12

ALL IS CHANGED, CHANGED UTTERLY

WE SHALL NOT BE MOVED

We shall not, we shall not be moved;
We shall not, we shall not be moved –
Not by the Hearts, the Hibs, or the Rangers.
We shall not be moved . . .

We shall not, we shall not be moved etc.

(Supporters' song, 1966-67)

[The authors make no apology for selecting the 1967 Scottish Cup final to illustrate their theme. The European Cup final, played later that season, has been covered so exhaustively as to defy further originality; besides, that game is the subject of One Afternoon In Lisbon *by Kevin McCarra and Pat Woods, a 1988 publication. It is worth noting that Bobby Lennox has said that, apart from the European Cup final, the 1967 Scottish Cup final was the Lisbon Lions' finest hour.]*

'MY GREATEST accomplishment in football?' Jock Stein pondered for a moment, and rubbed his cheek thoughtfully. 'It would be keeping Jimmy Johnstone in football for five more years than I thought possible.'

He smiled broadly at his own answer – no doubt thinking of some of the scrapes his talented, troubled winger had been through, playing for Celtic or Scotland. It was clear that he had a lot of affection for the tiny redhead; he could never consider him as rebellious, nor as wicked. 'Jimmy Johnstone? He's not a bad boy, but whenever there's trouble . . .'

Jock Stein had much the same feeling for the whole Celtic support. The men on the terracing, the punters, sensed that Celtic's manager liked them, cared for them, and felt responsible for their welfare. The sincerity showed when he spoke of the supporters as 'the salt of the earth', and equally when he was angry or disappointed at their lapses in behaviour.

Perhaps one of Jock Stein's major accomplishments was in transforming the tarnished image of Celtic supporters. Shortly before he returned to Parkhead as manager in 1965 the reputation of Celtic supporters was at its lowest, reflecting the sheer frustration of enduring a maddeningly unsuccessful period. One supporter wrote in some anguish to the sports editor of the *Scottish Daily Mail*: 'Anywhere in Britain the name of Celtic is synonymous with bottle-throwing and trouble. On the Continent they just don't know who or what you're talking about if you mention the club while discussing football.' (17 May 1963) The letter was written by a 30-year-old fan, a J. McGarrity, who despaired of ever seeing Celtic FC regain its eminence in Scottish football.

Sadly, his blunt assessment of Celtic's image was depressingly accurate; the accumulation of evidence indicating the frequent misbehaviour of Celtic supporters makes sorry reading:

April 1961: In the closing minutes of the replay of the 1961 Scottish Cup final, as lowly Dunfermline moved two goals ahead of Celtic, fighting broke out and bottles were hurled from the terracing in an ugly mood of resentment and, frankly, intimidation . . .

September 1961: Drunken supporters attempted to overturn an ambulance vehicle tending injured spectators after a wall had collapsed at Ibrox Park. The ambulance was painted blue . . .

November 1961: During and after an afternoon League match lost by Celtic 1–2 at Dens Park, fights and scuffles broke out. One report stated that as late as 11 p.m. at least 60 supporters' buses were still parked along Riverside Drive 'with men and girls weaving about the road'. Police arrested 47 fans, and 30 people had to be treated at hospitals after a day that left Dundee 'a dazed and bewildered city'. (*Sunday Post*: 5 November 1961)

February 1962: During an upset defeat at Stirling 'cowardly mobsters' lobbed more than a hundred bottles and beer-cans on to the pitch, hitting a linesman, several press photographers, and fellow fans at the front of the terracing . . .

March 1962: As outsiders St Mirren played out time to maintain a comfortable three-goal lead, Celtic 'fans', frustrated at events and hopeful of causing the match to be abandoned, poured on to the Ibrox pitch in hundreds. The referee called a halt, and some St Mirren players were jostled and pummelled as they struggled to reach the safety of the pavilion; police managed to clear the field after a delay of 20 minutes. When the Scottish Cup semi-final was resumed, Celtic did manage to score one goal, but the Parkhead directors, to their credit, had already conceded the match to St Mirren . . .

The club did make efforts after each outburst of hooliganism to disassociate itself from the guilty: the directors condemned 'the quite outrageous conduct of those who claimed to be our "followers" '. The Celtic Supporters Association in its 1962/63 handbook echoed the condemnation, urging the genuine fans: '. . . to eradicate the already erroneous conception that "Celtic supporter" and "hooligan" are synonymous'. The concern was genuine, but the appeals were being unheard because neither the Association nor the Board carried much weight nor clout with the average supporter – and certainly not with the hooligan element.

The atmosphere at many Celtic matches was being poisoned by the undercurrents of tension caused by years of failure. At least one Celtic player, who preferred to remain anonymous, intimated to the newspapers his personal distaste for playing in 'an atmosphere of senseless hatred and violence'; Ian Ure, Dundee's international centre half, alleged that visiting players were often scared to venture near the 'Jungle', the vast corrugated-iron shelter at Celtic Park which housed 10,000 of the club's more fanatical supporters.[1]

Celtic could well argue that every great club does attract an unsavoury element within its support; unfortunately, however, by the early 1960s the club had lost its claim to greatness within the game, as Mr McGarrity indicated in his letter.

Celtic's minimal involvement in Europe had not gained the club much attention nor glory. On the Continent, the club and its teams were ignored as unworthy of attention – except when hooliganism or vandalism on an epic scale drew unfavourable publicity.

In 1950 Celtic played a bruising 'friendly' in Rome, a scoreless draw in which John McPhail and Lazio's pivot were ordered off. To judge by the words written about the tour, the real highlight was meeting the Pope at St Peter's in a semi-private audience.

At last, in 1962, Celtic qualified for an official UEFA competition but were ousted at the first hurdle in the Inter-Cities Fairs Cup by the holders, Valencia; Valencia won handily 4–2 in Spain, and held Celtic to a 2–2 draw at Parkhead. The newspapers praised Celtic's 'decent' result, but it should be noted that in the next round Valencia lost by 2–6 to Dunfermline under Jock Stein at East End Park.

Pat Crerand could tell at first hand of Celtic's reputation in Europe, when the club decided to take part in the ill-fated Anglo-French Friendship Cup – an inferior and financially disastrous substitute for the real stuff of European competition. Celtic were drawn to meet Sedan in the first round, and travelled to the French mining town in the first week of August 1960. To the chagrin of the Celtic officials and players, the locals had never heard of the world-famous Glasgow Celtic. Adding insult to injury, it took until three hours before the kick-off before a Sedan official, who could not speak English, turned up to greet the Scottish club which had been virtually ignored for two days. James Sanderson, the *Scottish Daily Express* reporter, spotted among the meagre (3,000) crowd only one Celtic fan; Sanderson commented that the fan's sole contribution to the match was his repeated cry: 'Oh, no, Celtic! No, no!'

On the field Celtic's performance, even making allowances for the fact that the Scottish season had not yet started, was pitiful; 'a butcher-baker-taxi-driver' French team of part-timers who scored their goals within the space of six minutes finished up winners by 3–0. At Celtic Park in the second leg the result showed some improvement – a 3–3 draw, that meant elimination by an aggregate of 3–6.

Prior to Jock Stein's appointment Celtic's experience in European competition remained pretty thin and unsuccessful, apart from the extended run in the 1964 Cup-Winners' Cup that ended in a shambles in Budapest. The reputation of the supporters, the inconsistency of the team, the current image of the club: that was what Stein had to alter. It has been said of him that 'no man knew more about the Celtic tradition on the one hand and the revitalisation of jaded hopes on the other.'

The new manager had to attack the challenge on several fronts simultaneously. Nobody could compare his initial message with Lincoln's 'Gettysburg Address', nor Henry V's speech before Agincourt, but it was a masterly statement of policy – one worthy of inclusion in any textbook on management. He wrote in the club programme:

> I have a most important job to do at Celtic Park, to help in restoring this great club to the forefront of football. I don't think I'm speaking out of turn when I say that with the co-operation of everyone at Parkhead – players, officials, supporters – this job can be well done. I am lucky to be starting again with Celtic when the club is getting results consistently, the atmosphere is good, and the supporters are in buoyant mood. Seeds have been sown and I hope to help them grow into powerful plants.
>
> One isolated major success, one flash of glory is not what I am aiming at. If it is in my power, Celtic are going to get consistent success that will take them into competition with the very best in Britain and Europe. The supporters deserve no less . . .
>
> I must make this point quite clear. I did not become Celtic's manager until after the directors and myself had come to an amicable agreement as to my position. I have been handed the reins of management, and I alone have to do the driving. For the playing side, team picking, tactics, coaching and scouting I take full responsibility. I have been given great scope. The Board agreed that Celtic have to march with the times, and I have been guaranteed expression of my ideas of what Celtic have to do to win the major honours of the game, and at the same time to entertain the supporters and the public.
>
> Let's not expect miracles, but may all of us in the non-distant future be sharing in great Celtic success.

(13 March 1965)

Stein's personal recipe for success stressed the basic ingredient of hard work. Glib references to Stein's 'magic wand' only serve to obscure the

Jock Stein, looking forward to reviving Celtic.

long hours and tireless dedication needed to refashion Celtic into an all-conquering outfit. A newspaper once printed a truncated schedule of Stein's daily routine:

7.45 a.m.: Wakes up, washes, dresses; 'a spartan breakfast, and a glance through the papers' . . .

8.30 a.m.: Leaves home for drive to Celtic Park.

8.45 a.m.: Arrives at ground, chats with secretary; sorts out mail, and attends to matters requiring attention; makes phone-calls; examines state of pitch . . .

9.30 a.m.: Meets with training staff, discusses routine for the day at practice ground . . .

10.00 a.m.: Supervises training-session at Barrowfield.

12.15 p.m.: Light snack, or business lunch; back to Celtic Park to deal with administrative matters; correspondence, phones, interviews . . .

2.00 p.m.: Chats to players, dispenses advice to those who have come back for extra training, exercises, or treatment . . .

3.15 p.m.: Plans for next opponents, or future matches; reads papers and football magazines, phone-calls; travels frequently: 'I often nip down the motorway to Manchester or Liverpool.'

4.45 p.m.: If there is no match to see, or function to attend, prepares to leave for home.

5.00 p.m.: Has tea with Jean, his wife, and George, his son.

7.00 p.m.: Four nights a week he is out: supporters' functions, charity events, etc.

Such a taxing schedule may seem commonplace for managers today, but Stein's regimen was vastly different from the more leisurely approach adopted by his contemporaries and predecessors such as Willie Maley who could take a tram-car ride to Parkhead to fulfil the relatively undemanding duties of 'a nine-to-five' job. Most 'managers' were little more than 'glorified secretaries' with some knowledge of football gained by playing the game. Jock Stein, almost single-handedly, changed that concept. Tom Reid, Partick Thistle's chairman, was only half-joking in 1969 when he told Stein: 'We were all doing fine, scratching a living and keeping our heads above water, until you came along and spoiled it all.'

Stein, tireless and inventive, was displaying a dynamism rare in contemporary Scottish life by blowing away the cobwebs of its professional football, perhaps the most durable and conservative of native exports. Celtic's new manager caught the vibrant mood and spirit of the mid-1960s – that sense of endless possibilities and the realisation that the traditional ways were no longer viable. The cult of the amateur and privilege died hard in the 1960s, a period marked by an outpouring of learned articles and editorials deploring the calibre of managers engaged in tackling the twin features of the 'British disease': shoddy economic performance, and abysmal industrial relations. The accusation was made frequently that management was so remote that those in charge of many companies had only the vaguest idea of how the firms' products were conceived, developed, manufactured and sold. Fairfield's, the Clyde shipbuilding-yard, was spotlighted as one organisation whose decline stemmed from unimaginative, inefficient control and lack of foresight; the government was forced to intervene in January 1966 to rescue the firm from the hands of people who, said one observer, thought 'critical-path analysis was a Greek shipowner'.

HE SAID IT

After the value of the pound was cut by almost 15 per cent to $2.40 late in 1967, Prime Minister Harold Wilson claimed: 'This does not mean that the pound in your pocket has been devalued . . .'

Jock Stein may not have recognised the term either, but within him commonsense had become elevated to an intellectual force.

No manager ever did more in forging positive links between the team and the supporters, and Stein accomplished it through personal magnetism and managerial skills. Week after week he hammered home the message that the supporters had an important part to play in the Celtic revival.

He had an early opportunity to make his views known. In a pre-season 'friendly' at Sunderland, where Celtic thrashed the Wearsiders by 5–0, some supporters disgraced the club's name. One letter-writer to the recently established *Celtic View* – itself an admirable innovation – described himself as 'sick and utterly ashamed' of 'guttersnipes in green-and-white favours with their drunken, swaggering, obscene songs, and filthy manners'. In the same issue (18 August 1965) the manager made a point of laying the groundwork for his whole approach to hooliganism: 'If success is going to breed what we have seen recently, there can be no good future for Celtic. I appeal to all who love the club to try and make the club proud of its entire support.'

His emphasis was always on the positive rather than the condemnatory; he stressed time after time in the club newspaper that the supporters were as much the ambassadors of the club as the players on the pitch. At the many supporters' gatherings he was invited to attend, when asked to speak, he invariably returned to that theme: he, Jock Stein, would see to the performance and discipline of the players . . . but only the supporters themselves could improve their own image.

His work was paying off – and Stein was astute enough to give credit when it was due. After the League Cup final against Rangers – a lousy match spoiled by five bookings and in which two penalties were awarded to

The crowds roll back to Celtic Park – the enthusiasm of this toddler in running on the pitch has to be restrained (October 1966).

Celtic – he praised the conduct of the support unstintingly: 'The team are fighting for the club with real old-time spirit. Their determination can bring them great rewards and restore old-time glories to Celtic Park. I feel with the continued wonderful support the new Celtic need fear no one.' (*Celtic View*: 27 October 1965)

His praise was prompted by the fact that at the end of the match the Celtic players' attempt to hold a lap of honour was aborted by a field invasion from hundreds of Rangers supporters. The Celtic fans, despite the provocation, stayed on the terracing and allowed the police to clear the pitch.

A week later in the same paper, after a 6–1 victory over Stirling Albion, he again praised the growing maturity of the support: 'I was pleased with the way our team played even in the period in which they were baulked of scoring. The instructions were that the opponents were to be kept moving and working, and the team carried them out. I was pleased with the supporters' behaviour during the spell of no scoring. They did not hurl criticism at the team, obviously believing that Celtic would get the goals all right in the end.' (*Celtic View*: 3 November 1965)

That mutual trust helped inspire Celtic to their first League flag since 1954, and was enough to withstand the double disappointment in the Scottish Cup and the European Cup-Winners' Cup at the season's end.

At Hampden Park, when Rangers beat Celtic 1–0 in the Scottish Cup final replay, the setback was rightly dismissed as 'one of those things' rather than the resumption of the old order. At Liverpool it was different. In the last minute of a fiercely contested European tie, Lennox broke away to collect a header from McBride and score for Celtic; the goal would have been enough to see Celtic through to the final on the away-goals rule, but the referee, visibly swayed by the home-ground atmosphere throughout, disallowed it for offside – and later admitted it was 'a wrong decision'. The bottles hurled in rage were generally considered as a reaction, 'unjustifiable but understandable', to events on the field, and not the product of mindless hooliganism.

The gist of the manager's end-of-season report was a belief that significant progress was being made in encouraging a support worthy of a great club. Stein thanked the thousands of faithful followers who had been 'patient and understanding', he paid tribute to the vast majority who had followed the club's wishes with regard to conduct. He added, 'Those who haven't I don't consider supporters at all.'

A sequel to the bitter defeat at Anfield revealed another facet of Jock Stein's style – his 'carrot-and-stick' approach to the media. Enraged on learning that a Scottish journalist, an old acquaintance of Bill Shankly, had congratulated the Liverpool boss on the win, Stein's reaction to this 'unpatriotic' behaviour was apparently a sight to behold, frightening in its intensity.[2]

About the same period a BBC sports executive in Glasgow was startled to find himself the victim of a familiar Lanarkshire rasp down the telephone line. Anticipating a response from Stein in the wake of recent coverage of Celtic, he had given strict instructions to his receptionist that he was 'out' when Mr Stein called. Stein tumbled quickly to the ploy to keep him at bay, and disguised his voice and telephone identity to make his views sharply known to the shocked executive.

Stein could not be described as subscribing wholly to the well-known Parkhead obsession with media bias against the club, but he was sensitive to any unfair criticism. Suspicious about aspects of the BBC's long-time coverage of Celtic's matches, he was incensed by the radio commentator who attributed Celtic's four-goal drubbing of Rangers in the 1969 Scottish Cup final solely to defensive errors. He was never reluctant to voice his displeasure to its reporters or top brass; frequently, he referred to its sport editor, Peter Thomson, with barbed wit, as 'Blue Peter'.

If writers and broadcasters had to think twice before voicing criticism of the club, its players, or supporters, the same journalists often ended up in Stein's debt for his availability, his ready-made quotes – and his astute habit of saving up a titbit for reporters struggling to meet a deadline on a dull day.

Besides, Scottish journalists were getting used to receiving unaccustomed requests from abroad for comments or articles about the emerging force in European football, and they basked unashamedly in the opportunity.

Jock Stein's manipulation of the press stood out in sharp contrast to the maladroitness of his principal adversary, Rangers' manager Scot Symon. The reserved Symon always remained on cool terms with the reporters, and rarely sought to curry their favour. On one occasion, put on the defensive by a journalist's casual use of the expression 'your fans', he answered: 'Rangers Football Club has fans; I don't.'

SEEING IS BELIEVING
Colour TV was introduced to Britain finally in July, 1967 – nearly 15 years after its first appearance in the United States. The initial transmissions were on the BBC2 channel, which inaugurated the new service with a telecast of the Wimbledon tennis championships. That year proved to be the last of the 'amateur' Wimbledons.

In 1967, with Celtic FC emerging as a major European force, foreign journalists flocked to Parkhead to study this new phenomenon. Accustomed to high-flown technical expositions by Continental coaches, they were struck by Stein's ability to cut through the verbosity and reduce his job to its essentials. The correspondent of Berlin's *Neues Deutschland* was apparently bowled over by the sheer simplicity of the Scottish manager's recipe for success: 'My players must be made to believe that they are the best footballers in the world.' (19 June 1967) Bobby Murdoch would agree: 'Jock Stein was forever reminding us that if we played to our best, then nobody could live with us. You know, if you keep hearing that and take it in, then you start to believe it. Maybe he borrowed it all from Muhammed Ali who used to shout about being "the greatest", but it was a shrewd piece of psychology all the same, because it added a touch of arrogance that all great sides need.'

One of the sport's oldest truisms states that teams find it harder to remain at the top than to fight their way up. Thus, Stein's true greatness as a leader has to be founded on the unique relationship he enjoyed with his players –

and that talent was expressed often in continuing to motivate his players when complacency might have crept in.

The Scottish Cup final in April, 1967 normally would have been anticipated as a great occasion for Celtic but, in the midst of so many other and greater accomplishments, it was in danger of becoming just another game. In football that assumption is often the prelude to disaster. And Jock Stein, better than most, was well aware of the danger.

He made special efforts to appear relaxed and confident. In the unusual circumstances of that season, when all the prizes were within reach, he remained available at all times to his players. In the past two years he had won the respect and trust of his squad, as Billy McNeill underlined at the time:

> He has never been a god to the players, an unapproachable master. He is completely down-to-earth, always available and he has an easy way of talking to a player, a boss who is quietly telling him what has to be done, but still talking on level terms. Each man is an individual with his own personality, his own likes and dislikes, his own ideas of what he can do . . . and each player is treated exactly that way. If things go wrong, and we can all have bad games, you don't need to go to him. He comes to you, and it is usually just a quiet suggestion. It is a case of 'Try this, Billy. It can't hurt, and it might help.' . . . The talk-ins, the assessment of the opposition, doesn't just happen before the big ones. We get it for them all, and how it helps! There must be other men who know as much as he does, but it is how he applies it all that counts.

Jock Stein may have done much to help Celtic win the Scottish Cup in 1965 against his former club, Dunfermline, but that one success was no guarantee of lasting effectiveness. Winning the Cup can be due to a combination of factors unrelated to skill or method: the luck of the draw, the bounce of the ball, the surge of adrenaline . . .

Even after the victory against Dunfermline in April 1965 a healthy scepticism regarding miracle-workers still persisted among the playing-staff at Celtic Park. Added to that was the unvarying disposition among football players to 'suss out' managers. Within a season any lingering disbelief in the manager's capabilities had been dispelled.

Stein made it a matter of pride to be involved in the training sessions; he was a track-suit manager, mingling with his players, involved in the drills and the practice-matches. Joe McBride, his first signing at Parkhead from Motherwell, recalls the stimulating variety of those sessions: 'I used to wake up in the morning and look forward to it all, jumping into the car and heading for Barrowfield with the same expectations as going to play in a vital Cup-tie.'

Some claim that Jock Stein's total acceptance by the players came as a result of Celtic's victory in the League Cup final over Rangers on 23

October 1965 when the team avenged an earlier League defeat at Ibrox. That latter disappointment had suggested to many that Rangers would continue their domination of Scottish football, as evidenced by the embarrassing gap in League titles then of Rangers' 34 to Celtic's 20. *Goal*, a new Scottish football magazine, ran a banner headline that read 'No Surrender!', as if to proclaim Rangers' resolution to counter the much-vaunted revival at Celtic Park. Stein had still to combat a defeatist attitude among his players; Celtic may have won the Cup, but they had not beaten Rangers when it mattered, and doubts remained about the mental toughness of the side.

Stein took dramatic steps to overcome that attitude. Only a few minutes after the Celtic players made their way into the dressing-room at Ibrox after a splendid 4–0 win over Hibernian in the replay of the League Cup semi-final, Stein stormed his way into the room. He looked angry – eyes hard, cheeks red; the chatter and laughing died down quickly. The players, who had every reason to be satisfied with their performance as individuals as well as a team, tried to avoid the manager's eyes; Stein looked at them long and hard, fists clenched and demanded: 'Do you *want* to win on Saturday?'[3]

The players were shaken by the manager's intensity, and nodded agreement. Only five days later Celtic were due to meet Rangers in the final – a repeat of the same meeting a year earlier when Rangers, out-of-form, had raised their game to edge out a youthful Celtic side. Stein wanted his players to concentrate on the next – and vitally important – task, to prepare emotionally as well as physically. How successful his motivation proved!

Within a few minutes of the start of that final Celtic's right back Ian Young sent Rangers' winger, Willie Johnston, crashing with a ferocious tackle. For the rest of the match Celtic laced their undoubted skill with an unexpected level of commitment that may have offended purists, but which gave Rangers the clear message that the days of them intimidating Celtic sides were over. Stein always insisted that, once the players crossed the touchline, he was powerless to affect the outcome. But the manager knew very well that their collective state of mind went a long way to determining the result – especially in an Old Firm clash.

A few days later Celtic went to Dundee and eked out a narrow 2–1 win – and on the way back to Glasgow the players could reflect on the situation: Celtic had won the League Cup and Rangers had lost it; Rangers still led in the League but Celtic were now in close contention . . . Three months later, when Rangers visited Celtic Park for the return League fixture, a confident Celtic side thrashed them 5–1, a result that contributed hugely to Celtic's winning the title for the first time since 1954.

Within two years of Stein's arrival Celtic had taken a quantum leap: the players had reached that stage of development where they possessed the on-field maturity to adapt intelligently to circumstances; they could employ their superb physical fitness as a means to an end. The manager, most pragmatic of football men, provided the ideal formation into which the individuals dove-tailed as if pre-designed for the roles. The whole team moved now, said one observer, with a precision which 'combined the old tradition of elegance with a new-found power'. Previously, an air of excitement had characterised Celtic's play; now the aura of invincibility permeated the side.

The team had become the centre of European attention as the club advanced to the semi-final of the Champions Cup, the stage at which every other British challenge had died. Speculation was growing that it might be possible for this squad to garner every trophy possible: the League Cup had been retained by beating Rangers 1–0 at Hampden in October 1966; the Glasgow Cup, only starting its decline into insignificance, had been won in November with a 4–0 rout of Partick Thistle.

What remained? In the League Celtic retained a lead over Rangers, but still had to face a visit to Ibrox for a postponed match, in the Scottish Cup only Aberdeen stood between Celtic and glory, in Europe Celtic were preparing to fly to Prague and hold on to a two-goal advantage from the first leg of the semi-final . . .

Whenever Celtic played, it seemed impossible for them to lose: Craig and Gemmell were adventurous, over-lapping full backs; Murdoch and Auld, heirs to a tradition of constructive play, dominating the midfield with skill, strength and vision; Johnstone had emerged as 'a wild card', capable of upsetting the plans of any defence, Lennox was a swashbuckling raider, speedy and brave, Wallace had been bought as if in anticipation of McBride's later knee-operation . . . Could a universal plan be unfolding at Parkhead?

And yet a nagging, persistent doubt lingered in the minds of even the most ardent supporters as the 1966/67 season entered its final weeks. Football is so riddled with superstition that the seeds of doubt can undermine even the grandest of designs. Suppose Aberdeen, the opponents in the Scottish Cup final, were to inflict an unexpected reverse on Celtic, thus removing the first brick in the edifice of their self-belief? Would the design collapse like a house of cards? Would the dream of completing a clean sweep, so confidently asserted in the pubs, fade away with further losses? After all, a younger Celtic side had faced virtually the same challenge a season earlier and had fallen at two of the last three hurdles.

Prague was the scene for a crucial engagement in Celtic's unprecedented

Celtic manager Jimmy McGrory welcomes Bertie Auld back to Parkhead,
January 1965.

thrust for the 'clean sweep', a campaign that would end in football immortality or anti-climax. Celtic lined up against Dukla in a defensive formation, and stuck rigidly to it throughout the match; only Chalmers remained up front, and his brave running and chasing kept the Czechs occupied. The match was played in the smallish Juliska Stadium on a bitterly cold afternoon, but Celtic's mood afterwards was euphoric. Any fears that the

228

tiring trip to Czechoslovakia and the tension of the semi-final would affect Celtic's performance four days later were dismissed by Bobby Murdoch: 'It was a magic feeling, knowing that we had made the European Cup final.'

He went on to say that Celtic were at such a pitch of fitness, even at that late stage of the season, that he felt fit enough to have played in the Scottish Cup final on the Thursday, only two days after that tension-fraught encounter in Prague. Apart from Chalmers, the drain on Celtic had been on the nerves rather than the legs; Celtic's normal all-running, all-attacking style had been vastly overhauled by Stein for this one match.

On the return to Glasgow Stein embarked on a preparation for Aberdeen with a programme of 'masterly inactivity'. The Celtic party slipped down to Seamill on the Clyde coast; a long-lie-in was followed by swimming and golf. On the Friday the team returned to Barrowfield for a light training session under the watchful eyes of Stein, his assistant Sean Fallon, trainer Neilly Mochan, and physio Bob Rooney – all ex-footballers who recognised the need to keep the members of the squad merely 'ticking over'.

SCOTTISH CUP FINAL
29 April 1967
Hampden Park

CELTIC 2	**ABERDEEN 0**
Simpson	Clark
Craig	Whyte
Gemmell	Shewan
Murdoch	Munro
McNeill	McMillan
Clark	Petersen
Johnstone	Wilson
Wallace	Smith
Chalmers	Storrie
Auld	Melrose
Lennox	Johnston

Scorers:
Wallace (42, 49)
Referee: W. Syme (Glasgow)

Attendance: 127,117

Though Aberdeen had to be viewed as the outsiders. the northern team were bound to provide a real test of Celtic's mettle. For one thing, in both League matches against Celtic they had avoided defeat: a 1–1 draw at Pittodrie on Christmas Eve and 0–0 at Parkhead on 19 April. As that scoreless draw at

Parkhead had been Aberdeen's last game before the final, it was felt they would be better rested than Celtic, although Bobby Murdoch stated that Celtic's result in Prague had removed the weight of a European Cup semi-final from their shoulders, and Stein had pointedly reminded the players that the Lisbon final would not be played until 25 May, almost a month away.

Stein was confident about winning the Cup because he had noted the differing reactions of both sets of players after the match at Parkhead: his own team were annoyed with themselves, and were preparing mentally to lift their game 'by at least 500 per cent'. Aberdeen, on the other hand, had come to Celtic Park determined not to lose, had played a very defensive game – and appeared overjoyed at the result.

Those who played against Aberdeen during that season might smile ruefully at the thought of the Dons having a 'soft spot'; Aberdeen were considered 'a hard team' and had accumulated the significant number of 17 bookings that season, way above the average for the domestic game in 1967. Their approach was a physical one, and they had won few friends at Dens Park in the semi-final against Dundee United by kicking the ball anywhere out of danger when holding grimly on to a precarious 1–0 lead.

Aberdeen appeared to have taken on the image projected by the manager, Eddie Turnbull – one of the famous forward line fielded by Hibs in the 1950s. As a player he always gave the impression of energy and hard work, as if compensating for a slight lack of sheer natural talent. In a 1950 League match against Celtic at Easter Road he scored four goals against Celtic, three of them from the penalty spot; walking off the pitch at the end to the applause of the stand, he still remained grim-faced and intense.

He took over at Pittodrie about the same time as Stein at Parkhead, and like other Scottish managers he suffered in comparison with Stein. In a brusque, no-nonsense approach to his task he cleared out half the playing staff at Aberdeen within six weeks by dishing out free transfers. As a highly capable, hard-driving manager, he continued to project an austere image, befitting his wartime service on the grim Arctic convoys with the Royal Navy; his players at Pittodrie joked among themselves, with a misplaced sense of geography, that he was the only man in naval history to have attacked a shark!

Rangers, seeing in him a man stamped in their own mould, had approached him in 1966 with a view to bringing him in as assistant to Scot Symon in an attempt to keep pace with the standards being set by the new Celtic. But Turnbull gained a higher level of esteem at Pittodrie by turning down the offer. Now, as Aberdeen prepared for the final, Turnbull tried to raise morale among his men by stating in interviews: 'We are their [Celtic's] equals in team strength, team work, in any position and in individual skill. We have played them twice this season, and they have yet to beat us. In 180 minutes they scored only one goal against us.'

His comments were true – at least about Aberdeen's defensive qualities – but Turnbull made no reference to the fact that Aberdeen had scored only once against Celtic that season, and in the last match had rarely looked like scoring. Aberdeen lacked firepower, and their League average of a goal a game less than Celtic was a contributory factor in finishing up a distant 16 points adrift of Celtic. Critics and supporters of both sides viewed with scepticism Turnbull's assertion that his side would play differently at Hampden, but some analysts detected a slight advantage for Aberdeen in the fact that Aberdeen had played ten fewer matches than Celtic.

Before the match Aberdeen projected a confident image by choosing the up-market Gleneagles Hotel as their base for the final to give the impression they were used to travelling in the highest company. A positive outlook was displayed by the loading of celebratory champagne on to their bus as it was about to leave Pittodrie for Gleneagles.

Turnbull was fighting a battle of another sort as he led the preparations; for the past three weeks he had been suffering from a virus complaint that caused him to lose 19 pounds. Despite his discomfort, he dealt manfully with all the managerial responsibilities in the days leading up to the match while he struggled privately to regain his health.

Unfortunately, on the Saturday, Turnbull was forced to remain behind at Gleneagles as his squad drove off to Hampden without him. Confined to bed, he could only endure the radio commentary helplessly as Aberdeen tried to put into practice his plans for Celtic. His misfortune was a psychological boost for Stein, who had a healthy respect for Turnbull's knowledge of the game and his astuteness.

The extent of the influence Turnbull may have exerted from the bench at Hampden remains debatable. So ingrained were Celtic's good habits, and so precise their mechanism, that they often seemed to be on auto-pilot.

Within a few minutes of the start the 127,117 crowd realised that Aberdeen were playing the tie as they did most away matches – a hard, physical professionalism in defence and the occasional sortie into attack, reportedly the game-plan laid down by the absent manager.

In Celtic's 60th match of the season, however, Jock Stein had devised something different for Aberdeen – a method of breaking down their defensive shell. Stein had observed a gap on the Dons left flank that could be exploited: Aberdeen deployed Petersen in a twin centre-half role along-side McMillan, and tended to play Melrose deep in the midfield, leaving a fair amount of space in which opponents could operate.[4] Stein's nimble mind had worked out a strategy that involved Steve Chalmers and Jimmy Johnstone running at the Aberdeen defence from that 'vacant' area, and planned to sow confusion by playing Johnstone on the inside, rather than on his regular beat on the right wing, which would be occupied by Chalmers, the regular centre forward.

This switch confounded Aberdeen, whose left back, Shewan, was faced with an ongoing dilemma of which opponent to mark. Should he follow Johnstone wherever he went, as he had been geared up to do? Or should he stick to his own position and mark Chalmers, who was operating mainly as an orthodox right winger? It was a conundrum never fully solved as an Aberdeen newspaper had to admit: 'The Pittodrie defence which has ticked over smoothly all season was never entirely at ease against this new-look Celtic forward formation.' (*The Press and Journal*: 1 May 1967)

After the rough treatment meted out to Steve Chalmers in Prague, Stein had given some thought to resting him for the final; fortunately, Chalmers was ready to play, and his tireless, intelligent running on the wing stretched the Aberdeen defence and saved him from the physical buffeting of playing down the crowded middle.

Aberdeen did not have the flexibility to adapt to Celtic's subtle change in tactics. Their over-methodical system of play, their stringing together of an elaborate series of 'safe' passes, lacked the cutting-edge of Celtic's more purposeful, direct approach.

Both goals came from swift, incisive and simple manoeuvres that caught Aberdeen off-guard, their defence being turned by cut-backs from near the bye-line.

Only three minutes before half-time Celtic gained another corner kick; in the first half, although faced with a stiff breeze, they dominated the proceedings. Lennox assessed the situation, and saw the impressive figure of Billy McNeill striding downfield for the setpiece; as if using the latter as a decoy, he decided to pass short to Auld, who deftly returned the pass. Lennox weaved his way to the bye-line, his speed carrying him past a defender, before squaring the ball across the goalmouth where the stocky striker, Wallace, lurking on the edge of the six-yard box, sidefooted the ball into the net at the near post.

A mere four minutes into the second half Wallace settled the outcome of the match with a second goal. Johnstone was sent scampering down the right to collect a pass almost on the bye-line, but he still had enough time and control to chip the ball back across the area where Wallace had positioned himself 'like a man waiting for a bus'. Completely unmarked, Wallace took his time, and smashed the ball past Clark from ten yards .

Astonishingly, after the second goal the match burst into life, and

Aberdeen started to attack with neat, constructive play. Ronnie Simpson, playing at the ground where he made his debut back in 1945, had to make a spectacular save from Jim Storrie. A few minutes later he foiled Wilson's attempt to slip the ball past him; the Aberdeen fans groaned at the effort, because it had looked easier to 'chip' the veteran keeper as he left his line. One was left with the feeling, however, that Celtic would have responded with another goal had Aberdeen scored – enough to preserve the two-goal cushion.

Celtic rode out the minor storm, and ended up playing possession football to deflate their opponents totally. The sportswriter Hugh Taylor summed up Celtic's 'breathtaking performance' as follows:

> If economy, as they say, is the basis of all style, Celtic must be the most stylish side of the century. They do just what they have to do. Sometimes it may not seem to be much, but what they do is always brilliant.
>
> Confidence, belief in themselves and their colleagues, and faith in the tactics of manager Jock Stein enveloped Celtic like a suit of impregnable, shining armour. They reminded one of a champion boxer at the peak of his prowess, carefully conserving energy, breaking out only when there's a glimpse of a chance – but always taking care to be well on top of an opponent.
>
> (Scottish Football Book No. 13, 1967)

Much has been written about Celtic's attacking style in their greatest of all years, somewhat to the detriment of the sheer, all-round professionalism of a side that could deliver under all sorts of conditions: in the freezing cold of Prague, in the sun and wind of Hampden, in the mud and rain of Ibrox, and in the blazing sun of Lisbon . . .

Pat Crerand, analysing the remarkable success of his former club, remains emphatic that the 'attacking team' label applied to Celtic was nonsensical: 'You can only attack when you have the ball, and for the rest of the time you are as much a defensive team as anyone else. What people really mean when they speak about "attacking teams" is that they attack much better than anybody else. The speed of the Celtic attacks created tremendous excitement for the fans and made them forget that Celtic had a better-than-average defence.'

However, the supporters at Hampden were too busy savouring the latest triumph of the Stein era to bother overmuch about the genesis of it all. For at least 20 minutes, after the final whistle they waved their banners, and thundered excerpts from an extensive choral repertoire; they chanted their demands for a lap of honour from their favourites – but that last crowning touch was denied them because of the ban still in operation since the Rangers fans invasion after the 1965 League Cup final.

Still, one could get used to the winning habit . . .

Jimmy Johnstone, Tommy Gemmell, Bob Rooney and Neil Mochan join in the celebrations.

POSTSCRIPT

The transformation in Celtic's fortunes and image was gloriously completed in May when Celtic won the Holy Grail of club football, the European Cup. A few short years earlier the club and its supporters had been the object of contempt and neglect; now, as a banner waved at the King's Park end of Hampden had announced, if a little prematurely, Celtic were 'Kings of Europe'. Coming back from Lisbon, the motorcades of Celtic fans were greeted with cheers and applause by Frenchmen, and in the capital the supporters returning by train were congratulated on the team's performance by the normally indifferent Parisians, many of whom had witnessed the Lisbon final on TV.

One wonders what they thought about it all in Sedan?

* * *

Six years earlier the MP for Thurrock (Essex), after a particularly bad outbreak of hooliganism by Celtic supporters, had called for 'the voluntary liquidation of Celtic FC' in order to end their followers' 'riotous behaviour'. Had he read his *Hansard* in April 1967, that honourable member, Hugh Delargy, might have seen this motion:

That this House congratulates the Glasgow Celtic Football Club on reaching the final of the European Champions Cup and wishes them success in the next stage, and would deplore any attempt by the air-charter companies or travel agencies to exploit the occasion by charging excessive fares in conveying the supporters to the final in Lisbon.

The signatories were five Glasgow Labour MPs: Richard Buchanan (Springburn), James Bennett (Bridgeton), Maurice Miller (Kelvingrove), Alice Cullen (Gorbals) and William Small (Scotstoun).

* * *

The happiest sequel was the comment of the Chief of Police in Lisbon: 'The wonderful Celtic fans can come back any time.'

Footnotes

1 Unfortunately, it has proved impossible to discover the origin of the nickname, the use of which became more common in the 1940s. Regardless of the origin, the expression certainly conveys a sense of the atmosphere frequently found in that part of the ground.

2 Stein himself had congratulated Shankly with the briefest of handshakes in the tunnel; he said only one word, 'Referees!' Shankly nodded sagely, and went in to welcome his own players.

3 The words have been amended slightly; according to one player, they were more emphatic and colourful.

4 When Melrose played for Dunfermline in 1961, Stein had deployed him in a similar deep-lying role in order to contain the threat posed by Willie Fernie. He had also played against Celtic in the 1965 final, opening the scoring for Dunfermline.

13

ENGLAND EXPECTS

TO JIMMY JOHNSTONE

Wee juking, jiving, jinking Jimmy,
What endless joys yer antics gie me;
Ye twist and shuffle, shake and shimmy
Wi' feline grace.
Defenders sprachle oot behin' ye
A' ower the place.

O laddie wi' the twinkling feet,
Ye mak' defenders girn and greet;
Ye waltz aroon, through rain and sleet
Or sunshine bricht.
I sit and squirm here on my seat
Wi' sheer delicht.

Wee teasing, tantalising chiel,
O shades o' Morton, James, and Steel:
Wi' rasping shot and cute back heel
Or deadly flicks.
For like trump cairds in ony deal
Ye' er fu' o' tricks

In fitba' books ye'll write yer name,
Wee weaving wizard o' the game;
Yer photo in the Hall o' Fame
Will surely hing.
And Celtic fans will make the claim
Ye're soccer's king.

(Poem by Henry McCracken of Drummore, Galloway, 1970)

AMONG THE thousands lining the fairways of the famous Royal Lytham and St Anne's links in July 1969, few paid much attention to the two burly figures engrossed in the closing stages of the Open Championship. The galleries were carried away in the excitement of urging on a British player, the Englishman Tony Jacklin, in his quest to become the first native player to win the Open since Max Faulkner back in 1951.

It was an international field that threatened to thwart the attempt: the formidable American challenge was led by Palmer, Nicklaus and Trevino, the cool, left-handed Bob Charles from New Zealand remained in contention. But, in a thrilling, emotional finish, Jacklin held on to win. Watching

The inimitable 'Jinky'.

intently, caught up in the drama of one of sport's great moments, were two of Britain's most celebrated football managers, Jock Stein of Celtic and Don Revie of Leeds United. Over the years the two had become close friends, united in rivalry and football knowledge, and Stein was in Lancashire as a guest of Revie, himself a keen golfer.

Observing the euphoria of the ultra-patriotic crowd around the 18th green and affected by the mood, Stein turned to Revie: 'Wouldn't it be great if our two teams were to meet in the final of the European Cup next year?' Revie nodded in emphatic agreement, thinking of the emotional appeal of

Scotland's champions matched against England's in the climax of the greatest of all European tournaments.

To the undisguised and bitter disappointment of everybody in football, the draw for the semi-finals pitted their teams against each other at that stage, both having emerged as the best in the field in the opinion of most European critics.

As if to confirm the reputation of the Football League as Europe's toughest, Leeds had swept magnificently and imperiously through the three previous rounds, winning every match home and away, scoring 24 goals and giving up none against Lyn Oslo (10–0, 6–0), Ferencvaros (3–0, 3–0) and Standard Liege (1–0, 1–0).

Celtic, seasoned campaigners in Europe, had advanced with rather slightly less authority beating Basle (2–0, 0–0), Benfica (3–0, 0–3) and Fiorentina (3–0, 0–1). In fact, against the Portuguese champions Celtic won only through the toss of the coin after extra time in Lisbon.[1]

FAIR-WEATHER FAN

The *Yorkshire Post* showed a photograph of a Celtic supporter being turned away from the turnstile at Elland Road. The police searched fans entering the ground, and asked the man to deposit his bottle of whisky in the box provided; after taking a minute or so of sober reflection, he left still clutching both whisky and ticket for the match.

Within hours of the draw Leeds United's office was being inundated with requests for tickets: the telephone pleas came from voices with Scottish accents; the next day's mail brought hundreds of applications from Scotland accompanied by money orders and 'open' cheques. The Yorkshire club had decided to double the prices charged for their quarter-final tie against Standard Liege, but that had no effect on the Scots. Leeds eventually made available to Celtic 6,000 tickets, but it was becoming clear that many thousands more Scots from all over Britain would be in attendance.

The home supporters expressed unhappiness with the increase in prices; one letter in the 'football edition' of the *Yorkshire Evening Post* complained about the raise, and the writer added he would attend the tie reluctantly as ' . . . Celtic would be very lucky to be in the top half of our Division 1'.

English sportswriters such as Alan Smith shared his opinion: 'Less important matters were being sorted out . . . Celtic became champions of Scotland, and Cambridge won the Boat Race. Celtic have now won their extremely domestic title five times in a row, which merely establishes them as the biggest fish in surely the smallest pond ever dug. At least the boredom of the Boat Race is easily avoided. But Celtic fans force their opinions on you as chirpily as they toss their empty beer bottles. They obstinately refuse to recognise that England regards their rantings with only tolerant smiles. Now they play Leeds in the European Cup and they had best look out . . . Revie's lads are not due to lose again until next Pancake Saturday.' (*The People*: 29 March 1970)

The newspapers, of course, were concerned with profit, and whipping up hysteria was guaranteed to increase sales. So, even more than usual, the heady brew of nationalism crept into the columns of the sports pages. However, the consensus did reflect the fact that Leeds would be favourites to prevail over the two legs. Even that fervent ex-Celt Pat Crerand, who had often played for Manchester United against Leeds, expressed doubts: 'Celtic will never have played a harder European tie than this one. I would love to see them winning, but it will be very, very close.' Other Scots who had played against Leeds were pessimistic: 'I feel Leeds just have the edge, but if Celtic could get a draw down there they would have a real chance at Hampden.' (John Greig, Rangers) . . . 'I would very much like to see Celtic going through, but I'm afraid I would give Leeds a slight edge.' (Frank Beattie, Kilmarnock) . . . 'It's difficult to pick out any particular Leeds danger man . . . they have so many. They are one of the most professional teams I have ever come across.' (Pat Stanton, Hibernian) . . .

To their great credit both managers, aware of the historical significance of the clash, avoided controversy, and carried out their responsibilities with dignity during the weeks before, during, and after the two legs. For the first time the reigning League Champions in England and Scotland would be meeting in an official match in a European competition. Newspapers dubbed it 'The Battle of Britain', but the two managers, Stein and Revie, refused to add oil to the flames by belittling the other's team. On their part the decision was based on mutual respect and liking.

Don Revie, so frequently criticised in his early seasons at Leeds for the hardness of his side, immediately set out to praise the enthusiasm of the Celtic fans. He made a particular point of recalling 'the wonderful reception when we played them in Scotland', and reminded the journalists that he had married a Scots girl. However, always the consummate professional, he did add blandly that in both recent friendlies Leeds remained undefeated: a 2–1 win at Hampden in 1968, and a 1–1 draw at Celtic Park in 1969.

He made a point of being at the railway station to welcome Jock Stein and the Celtic party. At the last press conference before the match he assessed Celtic: 'As far as I am concerned, Celtic are as great as any of the great teams from Europe we have played in the past five seasons . . . Even away from home they have the ability to come at their opponents, and this is what makes them a great, great side. As far as weaknesses are concerned, I don't know if they have any. We have watched them three times, and we haven't found any yet.'

At the Cairn Hotel, Celtic's headquarters for the first leg, Jock Stein praised Leeds United, but refused to give up the psychological advantage:

Friendly rivals, Stein and Revie.

'Normally, everyone expects us to win our European games. This time we feel a lot of people, including our friends, expect us to lose. Just let me say we are not worried, and we are as well prepared as we could possibly be.' Asked to comment on Revie's claim that Leeds could match the glories of Real Madrid, Stein refused to be drawn into discussion, and contented himself by saying that they (Leeds) were not as good as the manager said they were. To his own players in private Stein made it plain that he wanted very much to be victorious in both legs, although outwardly he remained guarded in his comments.

Billy Bremner, Leeds' inspirational captain, had expressed delight at the draw. Bremner had matured into a magnificent midfield player, having channelled his energy and determination into more creative outlets. A self-confessed Celtic fan, he stated in his weekly column that the fanatical Celtic support was worth two goals of a start. He asked for the elland Road fans to 'Come on! Give us all you've got!' (*Yorkshire Evening Post*: 28 March 1970)[2]

Apprehension had gripped Yorkshire in anticipation of the invasion from Scotland. Some of it was understandable. English newspapers recalled the bottle-throwing at Liverpool in 1966 when Celtic were knocked out of the Cup-Winners' Cup after the referee disallowed a goal by Lennox in the last minute. Leeds itself had even more immediate memories of another

240

Scottish occasion: Rangers had visited Leeds in the UEFA Cup after a 0–0 draw in Glasgow and, when the match slipped away from the Scots in a 0–2 defeat, fights, bottle-throwing, and field-invasions had marred the match. Mr John Mays, landlord of The Hope and Anchor in Call Lane, spoke for many in the city: 'When Rangers fans came to Leeds two years ago, they ordered beer which they didn't pay for. And then they broke into the cellar, and smashed open cases of whisky.' He added *apropos* of Celtic's visit: 'We will be closed all day.'

A dozen other public houses within walking distance of the football ground decided to remain closed, as did most of the others within the city centre. Back in Glasgow, James Anderson, convenor of the Corporation Police Committee, criticised the precautions: '[It's] a slander against Glasgow and the Celtic supporters.' He might have derived slight comfort from Mrs Mary Myers, who defended her decision to keep the Prince of Wales Hotel open: 'It's like a Wild West film – everyone boarding up their houses when the "baddies" come to town. I am sure they won't smash the place up; they won't have time to get drunk.'

The first priority of Celtic supporters was to get tickets for the match: the official allocation of 6,000 had been snapped up within hours, but other briefs were circulating in the Glasgow pubs at inflated prices. According to a Leeds newspaper: 'It became apparent that a large-scale ticket-touting operation was in being when, earlier this week, telephone calls to offices in Glasgow known to employ Roman Catholics . . . offered £2.10/- [£2.50] stand seats for £7.' Fortunately the hundreds of tickets bought that way were valid: 'Yesterday a Glasgow detective paid £5 for a £2 ticket in the Central Station area of the city, and rushed it to Celtic Park to check if it was genuine. A CID spokesman said last night: "We were satisfied that the tickets on sale in Glasgow were not forgeries. If people want to buy tickets at high prices, there is nothing we can do – no matter where they come from." ' (*Yorkshire Post*: 1 April 1970)

Celtic, despite a magnificent record in the European Cup and a monopoly of the honours in Scotland, did not start the match as favourites. According to Tony Queen, a Glasgow bookmaker – and a close friend of Jock Stein – the odds for the first leg were as follows:

Leeds United:	4–6
Celtic:	4–1
Draw:	5–2

The odds indicated the enormity of Celtic's task in England, and recognised the talent inherent in Leeds United. For one thing virtually every member of the Leeds team was an internationalist: Sprake of Wales, Giles of Eire, Gray, Lorimer, and Bremner of Scotland, Cooper, Reaney, Charlton, Hunter, and Jones of England. The other two regular members of the squad

(Clarke and Madeley) were to be honoured for England soon afterwards.

Secondly, Leeds United were considered the most 'professional' side in England, and the word was not intended in its most complimentary sense.

In clawing their way out of the Second Division, Leeds had practised a relentless and cynical professionalism in which physical intimidation bordered on brutality. They continued with the same policy until they had established themselves in the First Division, a point underlined by the journalist David Miller in a 1978 profile of Don Revie: 'This reputation was substantiated when the FA disclosed that Leeds had the worst disciplinary record, at all levels, of any club. Yet, it was not merely that Leeds were "dirty"; they employed every ruse in the book such as time-wasting, feigning injury, and carefully studied tactics to undermine the referee, with two or more players applying incessant verbal pressure, with every decision disputed.'

Characteristically, Leeds gloried in their notoriety. In 1964 at Goodison against Everton the referee had to take both teams from the field to cool things down. During the match two players had collided and the Everton man was carried off on a stretcher while the Leeds player, Willie Bell, struggled to get to his feet. His trainer, Les Cocker, sensing the wrath of the home crowd, advised Bell to stay down, and called for another stretcher. The ambulance men on the sidelines shouted back: 'Get your own f****** stretcher!'. Leeds players and officials delighted in retelling the story.

In 1973, a week before the FA Cup final between Leeds and Sunderland, a journalist in the *Sunday Telegraph* criticised Leeds in considerable detail for their methods; he received a solicitor's letter written on behalf of Johnny Giles about the comments. Within a week the newspaper had five managers of First Division clubs willing to testify in open court that the comments were fair.

In the long run Leeds United were unfortunate in that they never did shed the image that clung to them, because Revie and his players did make a conscious and successful effort to mend their ways. On the eve of the 1968 friendly in Glasgow against Celtic at Hampden, Don Revie took great pains to point out the merits of the new Leeds, and throughout the match his side played fluidly and imaginatively to beat Celtic 2–1 – although Gemmell did score Celtic's goal from a penalty, awarded after Hunter had felled Johnstone in the box.

That most perceptive of journalists, Danny Blanchflower, gave them credit for reforming:

> I still see a certain brutality in the Leeds team, but it is not so much as I used to see there . . . but what may be more important to the game is its own great democratic character. All kinds can fairly compete within the structure of its rules. That means the strong are entitled to a fair deal as well as the skilful and beautiful. The strong are entitled to combat the skilful with their strength

as long as it is fair. Where you draw the line between 'strong' and 'dirty' is difficult to define . . . In their early days the present Leeds team were too aggressive to my mind. Their strength and brutality rather than their individual and collective skill caught my attention . . . Now I see something different when I watch Leeds . . . It [skill] has blossomed with their experience and, because time has taught them to devote more of their energy in that direction, they now devote less in the other direction . . . They are the most efficient and effective team in the land, but no team can escape its own past . . . and such a team wins little affection outside its own walls . . . but they are entitled to our respect.

(*Sunday Express*: 1 March 1970)

Perhaps the odds reflected even more the persistent reality of a Scottish inferiority complex, disguised most predictably under an aggressive nationalism. Celtic had already won the European Cup, and were a name heard in all corners of the football world; Leeds' history, until recently, had been an undistinguished one, more often than not a struggle for survival. But Leeds were accepted on both sides of Hadrian's Wall as justifiable favourites because they were an English side, a logic which does not surprise observers such as William Paul:

The English have always been arrogant buggers, confident of their own role in the scheme of things and equally confident that everybody else should be subservient to them. Such a world view originates from a medieval land that was fertile enough readily to feed its people, breeding self-confidence, and leaving its leaders free to indulge a taste for exploitation and adventure. It also derives from a more modern role as a leading world power that once controlled one-seventh of the land area of the globe. Conversely, we Scots spring from poor-quality soil where the need to ensure the next day's meal was paramount, breeding uncertainty; and wanderlust was inspired by a longing to make life not so nasty, not so brutish, and not so short.

(*Scotland on Sunday*: 17 September 1989)

One aspect that the media picked up was the duel between the managers. Stein, at 47, was five years older than Revie and his reputation had been firmly established, but many considered that Revie would be the manager of the 1970s.

Like the Scot he came from a humble background, and he never did escape the insecurities caused by harsh economic times. He was born in Middlesbrough, considered the hardest of North-East towns, and lived in a two-bedroom house near Ayresome Park. His father, a joiner, was frequently laid off and unemployed, and his mother died when he was 12. Like most poor youngsters he left school as soon as possible, at 14, to become an apprentice bricklayer.

In 1944, at the age of 16, he joined Leicester City, and started a distinguished career as a player. After a spell at Hull City he was transferred to Manchester City where he gained a reputation as a thoughtful centre forward; having seen the Hungarians thrash England twice, he devised a tactic new to English sides, instantly dubbed 'the Revie Plan'. He based it on the role played by Hidegkuti, who tended to play behind the other Magyar forwards, spreading the play around but joining into attack with devastating suddenness. With Manchester City he participated in two Wembley Cup finals, and played on the winning side in 1956. Later moves took him to Sunderland, and eventually to Leeds as a player in 1959; within six weeks, as a result of near-unanimous endorsement by the players, he was elected captain, replacing Wilbur Cush, the Irish internationalist, whose game had suffered under the strain. Leeds continued to be threatened with relegation to the Third Division but, after being appointed manager in March 1961, Revie transformed the club.

One of his first moves was to change the strip. Leeds United had worn blue and gold throughout most of its history; Revie decided that a change in image was required and chose the famous all-white of Real Madrid. Considered a hopeless romantic, he was criticised in Yorkshire for insisting that Leeds United travel first-class – with good hotels, transportation facilities and playing gear. But he persevered, and the club was slowly turned around. The slide to the Third Division was arrested, but it took three years to get promoted out of the Second Division with a team based on 'players of character' – to use a euphemistic phrase. It took longer to win some tangible trophies, but the progress had been methodical and consistent.

At last came the psychological breakthrough, a win in the League Cup against Arsenal in 1968. That triumph, gained by unadventurous tactics in a grimly professional display, earned few friends, but Leeds, freed from the shackles of relative failure, went on to win the Championship in 1969 with a more talented squad, a formidable side which created a new First Division points record in losing only two out of 42 matches. By 1970 his side looked even more impressive as it pursued an incredible treble: the European Cup, the League Championship, and the FA Cup. Leeds deserved to be considered a great side, and they were, but: 'They were often feared, but seldom loved. And as they became more admirable, quite brilliant indeed as their rough edges gave way to elegant frills in the early 70s, it irked Revie and his players that the commentators never gave full credit. These people are often accused of having short memories; in this case, they never forgot.' (*The Independent*: 27 May 1989)

Don Revie was a paradoxical figure; a track-suited manager, he participated in the training of his players and he appeared, with his burly frame, wind-swept hair and massive jaw, the epitome of Yorkshire solidity and grit; indeed, he seemed to embody down-to-earth Leeds itself, 'a city of commerce, spun from the textile mills and carved from the coal mines'. But he also conveyed a sense of anxiety, especially on the most important of occasions. His compulsive attention to detail at those times could backfire; for example, his assistants prepared a 30-page dossier on Celtic. Preparation is admirable in managers, but such obsessive worrying could transfer itself stealthily to the players. His Welsh keeper, Gary Sprake, once described Revie as 'utterly brilliant but knotted with fear'.

Don Revie had become a prisoner of his own childhood, exhibiting an outlook hardened by his experiences as a young player. His later obsession with financial self-sufficiency constitutes clear evidence of a deprived childhood, and incidents in his playing career must have brought home to him the uncertainties of a football career.

In 1949 Revie scored twice for Leicester City in an FA Cup semi-final against Portsmouth in an upset 3–1 victory, but he was forced to pull out of the final because of a persistent nose-bleed. The bleeding was so bad that Revie had to be hospitalised to stop the haemorrhaging.

In 1955 Revie was the highly-acclaimed leader of Manchester City's new-look forwards in the FA Cup final against Newcastle United, but an injury to City full back Meadows forced the defender to limp off, and ten-man Manchester went down to defeat.

In 1956 Revie had been replaced in Manchester City's side, but had a premonition that he would still play at Wembley. He continued to train diligently in the weeks before the final against Birmingham City, and on the actual day another player had to withdraw because of an outbreak of boils.

Those three Cup finals disrupted by injury or illness served to reinforce the element of luck in football. And Revie could look upon his appointment as manager of Leeds United as a matter of chance. Nearing the end of his playing career at Leeds, he considered applying for the vacant managerial post at Third Division club Bournemouth; he asked the club chairman, Harry Reynolds, to provide a reference. Reynolds, while writing out the letter, soon came to the conclusion that Revie might be the man to revive Leeds United. And the opportunity was offered to Revie.

He was one of the new breed of managers: a track-suit manager, a thoughtful coach, and motivator. Despite his success and later fame the self-doubts remained. His methods of coping with the stress of management were two-fold: sheer hard work and reliance on ritual.

The rituals bordered on the superstitious. The most infamous was his blue suit that he regarded as 'lucky' and, therefore, had to be worn on every possible occasion. Another ritual was the time of arrival at the ground. Revie wanted his side to arrive at away grounds exactly 50 minutes before the kick-off. Once, on the way to Liverpool, the coach driver fell behind schedule because of a newly implemented one-way system that involved a detour; the Leeds party arrived 40 minutes before the start – a delay of only ten minutes – but Revie spoke sharply to the driver in private: 'You should have known that the streets had been changed. It's your job to know, and I expect you to know.' Habit, ritual or superstition?

The other component involved sheer hard work and attention to detail, but the preparation for important matches became so obsessive that his underlying tension inevitably communicated itself to the players. Some men, most noticeably Sprake, were put under unfair pressure. Shortly before a relatively 'safe' Cup-tie against Fourth Division side Colchester United in 1971, Revie spoke to his keeper, warning him not to repeat errors that he had made recently. Curiously error-prone when playing in 'televised' matches, the Welsh internationalist was haunted by his manager's warning, and the keeper's uneasiness contributed to the loss of two goals in Leeds' shock 2–3 defeat.[3] Planning, professionalism or obsession?

Whatever the cause, and despite a magnificent record of accomplishment, Leeds United never did attain the heights expected of them under Don Revie: twice champions, but five times in second place; once FA Cup winners, but losers in another three finals; UEFA Cup winners twice, but losers in three other European finals. A team fated to receive qualified praise, muted acclaim . . .

EUROPEAN CUP SEMI-FINAL			*EUROPEAN CUP SEMI-FINAL*	
1 April 1970			15 April 1970	
Elland Road			Hampden Park	
LEEDS UNITED 0	**CELTIC 1**		**CELTIC 2**	**LEEDS UNITED 1**
Sprake	Williams		Williams	Sprake (Harvey)
Reaney	Hay		Hay	Madeley
Cooper	Gemmell		Gemmell	Cooper
Bremner (Bates)	Murdoch		Murdoch	Bremner
Charlton	McNeill		McNeill	Charlton
Madeley	Brogan		Brogan	Hunter
Lorimer	Johnstone		Johnstone	Lorimer
Clarke	Connelly (Hughes)		Connelly	Clarke
Jones	Wallace		Hughes	Jones
Giles	Lennox		Auld	Giles
Gray	Auld		Lennox	Gray

Scorers:

Connelly (1) | Hughes (47) Bremner (14)
Murdoch (52)

Referee: M. Kitabdjian (France) | *Referee:* G. Schulenburg
(West Germany)

Attendance: 45,505 | *Attendance:* 136,505

THE REEL WORLD
Veteran performer John Wayne at last won an Oscar for 'Best Actor' in the
western *True Grit* on 7 April 1970.

Celtic secured the Scottish Championship at Tynecastle with a 0–0 draw
against a ten-man Hearts side on 28 March; their display was unconvincing,
although only Jim Cruickshank deprived Celtic of an outright win by saving
a Gemmell penalty kick. Three days earlier Celtic had failed to clinch the
flag at Parkhead when losing 1–2 to a determined Aberdeen side, one
preparing to meet Celtic again in the Scottish Cup final on 11 April. Celtic's
performances seemed casual, apparently distracted from the immediate
task.

Clearly, Leeds had made a very conscious decision about their Championship prospects. Behind in their fixtures due to extended runs in the
European Cup and the FA Cup, they were trailing a young, skilful Everton
side in the race, and Revie opted to concentrate on the cups. Only two days
before the first leg of the European Cup semi-final Leeds fielded their
reserve side against Derby County in the Championship, and Revie claimed
the decision was 'on medical advice'. Certainly Leeds did have a backlog
of fixtures to clear up, although Alan Hardaker, the Secretary of the
Football League, was to state later that he had presented Leeds with a
variety of convenient dates to rearrange the fixtures, but that Leeds had
rejected them all.

Both clubs had been preoccupied with the semi-final, and were tending
to regard the League fixtures as a distraction, a draining away of the energy.
Leeds deserved sympathy for the pile-up at the start of April . . . but it
should be noted that the first leg at Elland Road constituted the 57th match
of the season for Celtic, and the 58th for Leeds United.

Stein had given thought to the selection of Harrogate as Celtic's base,
and the atmosphere at the hotel was as the manager wished – quiet,
convenient and with no distractions.

Holding court in the lounge after midnight, seemingly relaxed and
passing the time of day with everyone, but mostly with the press corps from
Scotland, he said: 'I have never seen Don Revie look so strained. They have
watched us often recently and we haven't played two games the same.
We've been good and bad and indifferent . . . It will be a matter of our
flexibility against their predictability. A manager can't do it all. Sure, you
rehearse set-pieces, but eventually the players on the field have to
improvise and use their own intelligence. They have to sort it out for
themselves . . . The players are in the right mood, and in good shape. I can
leave the rest to them.'[4]

One local paper was impressed with the homespun deportment of the squad: 'The Celtic players had a quiet start to their big day – walking about the Cairn Hotel in their stockings. They had turned in early after the journey from Glasgow and a quick training session at the ICI sports ground at Harrogate, and came down for a late breakfast in their emerald-green tracksuits. But they carried their football boots, which they left outside the dining-room. A few wore slippers, but the majority were content to pad around silently in their green-and-white ringed stockings.' (*Yorkshire Evening Post*: 1 April 1970)

Revie chose to take his squad to the bracing air of Ilkley, and Billy Bremner conceded that the Leeds coaching staff had arranged for a two-hour tactical talk on the afternoon of the match.

On the day of the match the siege of Leeds took place: 'The barbarian horde flooded down from the North. Ten thousand Celts – or at least they were supporters of Glasgow Celtic – invaded Leeds. They came by train, car, bus and plane. The city shivered. Nothing had happened quite like it in Yorkshire since the Roman legions left York. Public houses closed. Windows were boarded up. Policemen walked hand-in-hand. Horses stalked the streets.' (*Yorkshire Post*: 2 April 1970)

All police leave in Leeds was cancelled; constables, some with dogs, were on patrol every hundred yards. Security was tight, as the trainloads from Glasgow found out at the Leeds City station where more than 2,500 Celtic fans were directed to a fleet of buses ready outside the side entrance. The buses whisked the fans immediately and directly to the Elland Road ground.[5]

The atmosphere at Elland Road was charged with electricity: Celtic supporters waiting outside the ground gave Leeds, and Billy Bremner in particular, a rousing reception when their coach arrived, but roared out a welcome when the Celtic bus pulled up a few minutes later. Inside the ground the attendance constituted Leeds' largest of the season, but it was not a full house. Ticket touts still tried to sell off briefs right up to the kick-off; despite the shortfall in the crowd, Celtic's support was massive, estimated at 13,000, drawn from all parts of Britain.

SADDLED WITH GUILT

James O'Donnell (39) of Methil, Fife, was fined £10 for being drunk and disorderly at the Leeds-Celtic match. The prosecutor stated: 'An officer was on duty on a horse controlling crowds outside the ground when O'Donnell came up to him shouting and waving his arms. He was told to go away, but made several attempts to jump on the back of the police horse. As a result, he was arrested.' Asked if he had anything to say, O'Donnell replied: 'In the condition I was in, I would not have been able to jump on to the horse.'

The teams took the field together to a deafening reception, but the noise

Celtic get off to a flyer. George Connelly (No 8) sees his shot diverted past Sprake.

was coming from those draped in green and white. A minor dispute had taken place before the teams left the dressing rooms; the referee objected rightly to the similarity in stockings, and Celtic were ordered to change. Stein thought that he and Revie had decided that Leeds would switch, but Revie disagreed; the Leeds manager offered Celtic an intriguing choice – a set of orange stockings, or blue. Because of Leeds' reputation for sharp practice, it was assumed that the choice was a deliberate attempt to upset Celtic. Stein dismissed the notion, smiling broadly at the dilemma – and chose orange. Bobby Murdoch agrees: 'The Celtic team at that time had great belief in itself, so we just shrugged off that business with the stockings that Revie tried on.'

In any case, the manager was more concerned to get his players in exactly the right frame of mind just as they left the dressing-room, reminding them of Leeds' reputation for hurting opponents. No need for rough stuff, he stressed, but 'just let them know you're here!'

The pitch was bare but drying out after the ravages of a wet spring and heavy use. Celtic seized control from the opening. A series of passes ended in a high, bouncing ball through the middle for Wallace which was misjudged by Madeley; the ball found George Connelly open at the edge of the penalty area; Connelly may have figured in Leeds' thick dossier as a defender, but he had advanced into a dangerous position; he shot for goal, and Sprake moved to his right to attempt a save, but the ball was deflected by Cooper and found the corner of the net at the post. Celtic, playing away from home against the favourites for the European Cup, had seized the initiative and were one up after 40 seconds. Only a handful of players on the field had touched the ball.

The dramatic emergence of George Connelly in the Leeds penalty area had to spread doubt among the home team; everything they had been told suggested that Connelly would be played as a sweeper and yet . . .

For most of the first half Celtic kept Leeds off-balance: Revie had mentioned that a two-goal lead would be needed for the visit to Glasgow, and Leeds were shaken badly by the loss of the vital goal. Terry Cooper, England's full back and noted for his surges down the left wing, had been expected to add another point of danger for Celtic's defence. But Cooper was otherwise engaged. Stein and other perceptive Scots, including Pat Crerand, felt that Cooper, who had started out as a winger, was less comfortable defending; he gave Jimmy Johnstone his instructions – hold the ball, use the wing, take on the back. As Stein confided to a friend before the match: 'They say this Cooper is a great attacking full back, but he's never had this tricky wee dwarf running at him for 90 minutes.'

Johnstone had one of his greatest nights. Marked by a sporting back who played him cleanly, Johnstone was unstoppable. Within minutes the other Celtic players sensed that the redhead was 'on', and so they plied him with the ball. Johnstone came back deep to pick up passes, swept past defenders inside and outside, cut back, cut in, raced down the wing, and passed the ball intelligently to players moving into position – it was 'Jinking' Jimmy Johnstone at his incredible best. The dour Yorkshire crowd watched in amazement as Johnstone went through his whole repertoire; the visiting supporters revelled in the sight of the wee Scot prancing round burly, bewildered Englishmen.

Again Bobby Murdoch makes an accurate observation about the team's followers: 'The Celtic support matters a great deal, especially when you're far from home, and it gave us a great boost to see – and hear – so many of them at Elland Road. You just knew that somehow or other they would get their hands on thousands more [tickets], because they are absolutely daft about Celtic.'

Leeds had no answer; playing in a League where wingers who held the ball could be considered an endangered species, nobody in their defence could fathom out a way to halt him fairly. To their great credit most attempts to stop him were fair, if hard. The *Yorkshire Evening Post* had to sympathise with the baffled defenders: 'I doubt if Elland Road has ever seen such feinting, swerving and sidestepping inside a square yard. It must have been horrible to see such an individual genius on such form in control, and so fleet into the open spaces.' (2 April 1970)

Revie had warned his team that Celtic would be prepared to shoot on sight: Johnstone added another element of worry for Leeds by his gift for the unexpected, when in six minutes he drifted past three men on the edge of the box and shot for goal, but Sprake saved well; Murdoch in his attacking phase strode forward, but his hard shot scraped over the bar; Lennox drove a first-time shot just wide of the post after yet another Celtic corner.

Leeds did not come into the match until the second half, but found

Celtic's rearguard in dominant form: McNeill won every ball in the air, and the longer the match went on, the speculative, high ball into the penalty area appeared Leeds' only tactic. Hay and Gemmell had attempted the occasional overlap in the first half, but opted for strict defence in the second. All three were in resolute form, a mood best expressed by Gemmell, usually so affable, who berated Williams at length for dropping a high cross into the goalmouth. The battle was won in midfield where Murdoch, Auld and Connelly were immense whether defending or attacking; Leeds could not find a way past them, and had to be alert in dealing with their switches to attack. Alongside McNeill the nippy Jim Brogan had established himself as a top-class defender, being the first player to break through into the side to replace one of the famous Lisbon Lions (John Clark).

Leeds did have one spell of comparative domination early in the second half, and Clarke's close-range shot rebounded from Williams' knees for their first corner. Within a three-minute spell Leeds, now backed up by the roar from their support, came close more than once to scoring: Lorimer unwisely decided to pass instead of shooting; Gemmell later cleared from Jones as the striker tried to gather a ball; and Williams dived bravely at Clarke's feet.

At that stage it was cut-and-thrust, but Leeds were still sorely perplexed as to how to deal with Celtic's front runners. It remained a problem they never fully solved, as Johnstone and the dangerous Lennox were still full of running.

In 68 minutes Bremner crashed to the ground going for a high ball in the penalty area, and received prolonged treatment; he resumed briefly, but was led from the field a few minutes later, obviously dazed. Shortly afterwards Leeds came closest to an equaliser when a right-foot shot from Gray hit the crossbar, but Leeds, outplayed in midfield, were being more and more reduced to playing the long, high ball and Celtic were under no great pressure.

An odd incident occurred as the match entered the closing stages: Williams, Celtic's keeper, cleared the ball upfield and went down on his knees calling for the trainer. Stein held back Neil Mochan and gestured to the goalkeeper to get up and continue to play. The message was clear:

AFTER-SHOCKS

Celtic fan, G. P. Condron of Los Gatos, California, was in a state of trauma after reading in his local paper the score of the first leg at Elland Road. The result read as follows: Leeds United (England) 9, Celtic (Scotland) 1. He recovered later after a friend phoned from San Francisco with the correct score.

Celtic did not need to indulge in time-wasting, and he would not allow it. Indeed, with ten minutes left Stein replaced the goalscoring midfielder, Connelly, with John Hughes to keep the home defenders more occupied. A minute earlier Johnstone had waltzed around three over-stretched defenders to set up a chance for Wallace, and Sprake, Leeds' best player on the night, effected a splendid save while on his knees.

At last the whistle went, and the celebrations started among the Scots. Jock Stein expressed satisfaction: 'It was a magnificent victory, but I always say it is only half-time at this stage. I was delighted with the football our boys played. Now we have got to plan for Hampden.' Revie congratulated the winners, and smiled gamely: 'Celtic played very well. They are a great side. It makes it very hard for us at Hampden, but nothing is impossible in football.'

Billy Bremner, assisted from the field with concussion, wandered into the noisy Celtic dressing-room to congratulate his fellow Scots in a sporting gesture; the noise and hubbub died down momentarily as the Celtic players noticed his dizziness and pallor, and the Leeds captain was led gently away. Shaken, too, the English football writers, so confident of Leeds' victory before the event and who, to their credit, marvelled the next day at the sheer effrontery of the Glasgow side. Celtic headed north to be met with a totally spontaneous and jubilant welcome. All day long individuals had bombarded the switchboard of Glasgow's Central Station with calls asking when the team was coming home. As the train pulled in early that evening, a 5,000-strong crowd, massed ten-deep behind specially erected crush barriers, burst into song. When Jock Stein led the Celtic party down the platform the station erupted into a tremendous roar, and its cavernous structure echoed and re-echoed the chorus of 'We are the champions!' and 'We want Stein! We want Stein!'

Other passengers on the train, many from outwith Scotland, gaped in astonishment and bewilderment at the tumultuous scenes, during which the victorious players would have been engulfed by their supporters but for the intervention of railway staff and police to clear a pathway out of the station.

* * *

For several seconds Jock Stein's customary air of brisk confidence deserted him and the cares of being a football manager showed on his face; on the Hampden pitch the Leeds United players were rushing towards Billy Bremner to hail his extraordinary equaliser in only 14 minutes of the second leg, and the Scot stood with arms upraised in triumph. Bremner, after picking up a pass from Giles, his partner in midfield, advanced to chance a shot from more than 30 yards. The ball was well struck, and Williams' difficulty was compounded by a vicious swerve that helped the ball end high up in Celtic's net.

The European Cup semi-final was level once again; Leeds United's goal had wiped out fully Celtic's advantage of the 'away' goal scored by George Connelly. Seventy-six minutes remained – and the possibility of extra-time loomed, and the thought of a third and decisive game on the ground of Sheffield Wednesday entered some minds.

For the first time that evening Hampden Park was quietened; and only the cheers of the 3,000 or so Leeds fans resounded hollowly across the vast bowl.

Stein looked anxiously at Celtic's rearguard, not so much in blame at the loss of the goal. Another fear was gnawing at the Celtic manager's mind; Celtic's captain, Billy McNeill, was playing with a badly damaged ankle, and had been receiving treatment from Bob Rooney since the end of the Scottish Cup final against Aberdeen four days earlier. The ankle had been strapped, but Stein was checking his captain's movements every minute.

Hampden Park presented a magnificent spectacle. Crammed into the vast terracing and stands were 136,505 spectators, and the noise – apart from the brief silence after Bremner's goal – had poured down in waves of sound, frightening in its intensity. Everybody who could pass as a Celtic supporter was present, as were many other Scots, drawn to Hampden by the promise of a great football occasion.

FAIR COMMENT?

On the same night that Celtic won 1–0 in Leeds, Everton clinched the First Division title by beating West Bromwich Albion 2–0 at Goodison.

> Everton's manager, Mr Harry Catterick, claimed his team's triumph as 'a breakthrough for free expression'. He added: 'We do not play assassins in our side. Nor do we try to take key players out of a game. We have always believed in playing attractive football and this has been a wonderful team effort.
>
> 'I am not prepared to look ahead even as far as the European Cup, because there are teams who have won that competition who could not live in the English League. We have won 28 games this season, which is a record for the toughest competition in the world, and that is enough for me at the moment.'
>
> (*Yorkshire Post*: 2 April 1970)

Bobby Murdoch still marvels at the feeling: 'The atmosphere at Hampden was just unbelievable. It was so electric that you could have reached out and touched it! To have 136,000 packed into a ground like that was fantastic, especially since we'll never see the likes of it again.'

The only group who did not show up in force was the Leeds United supporters; Celtic fans heard with disbelief that Leeds had returned half their allocation of 6,000 tickets to Celtic Park, and this windfall of 3,000 was snapped up within two hours. When rumours spread through Glasgow that the one special train from Leeds would contain Englishmen with spare tickets the Central Station was jammed with hopeful Celtic followers. Some tickets did change hands, and it was reported that 'touts' were selling others at three or four times the nominal value.

The so-called 'Classic Slopes' may have been a spectacular sight, but the reality was more frightening; hundreds of fans had to struggle out of the densely packed terracings without ever having seen the pitch, and terrified children were passed overhead so that they could leave the ground in safety. No evidence, however, exists to substantiate the rumour that many spectators had gained access via a gate which had been forcibly opened.

One other lingering doubt had taken root in pessimistic minds; on the Saturday Celtic had lost to Aberdeen by 1–3 in the Scottish Cup final and their display had been ragged in execution as well as in discipline – although it has to be admitted that some of referee Bobby Davidson's decisions bordered on the mystifying. On the same day on a heavily sanded Wembley pitch Leeds United had returned to sparkling form in the FA Cup final although held by Chelsea to a 2–2 draw after extra-time.

Both sides had to make changes from the first leg. For Celtic, McNeill had passed his fitness-test shortly before the kick-off, unlike Willie Wallace, a sturdy striker and physical presence, who was forced out after a late and secret test of a sprained tendon. Stein, with his gift of total recall, remembered John Hughes roasting Jackie Charlton in a League International five years previously, and replaced Wallace with the massive forward. Leeds had suffered a body-blow in the loss of Paul Reaney at full back, sidelined with a broken leg suffered in a League match but, as with all well-organised teams, the changes were minimal. Madeley, a valuable all-purpose player, moved to right back, and the ferocious Hunter was recalled to help cope with Jimmy Johnstone.

Reared as he was in his 'Celtic-daft' boyhood on that club's folklore, particularly its fabled qualities in adversity, Billy Bremner found his exultation all too soon turning to unease, as if he sensed the calm before the storm. Twenty years on, the unfolding drama remains etched in the memory of the Leeds captain, who confesses to having been disconcerted by the funereal atmosphere which enveloped Hampden after his goal and suddenly enabled the redhead to make himself heard as he urged on his colleagues. The sheer unreality of it all was unique in his wide experience of European competition, but Bremner ruefully testifies to its deceptiveness: 'The crowd didn't stay silent for long, did it? . . .' Indeed, its encouragement of Celtic seemed to intensify as the battle raged on for the control of the vital midfield where three Scots and an Irishman contested every ball. For Leeds Billy Bremner had started the match with his irrepressible enthusiasm, and his partner, the diminutive but rock-hard Johnny Giles, was creating more space than at Elland Road. Celtic's pair, Murdoch and Auld, had to assert their authority to deal with the threat, and gradually the tide turned in Celtic's favour.

The pressure began to build up on Leeds' goal: again Jock Stein in the training sessions and team-talks at Seamill had stressed the importance of Jimmy Johnstone's role, and the wee man again responded in style. Over-simplified the opinion may be, but Jack Charlton still maintains that Jimmy Johnstone was the difference between the teams over the two matches.

John Hughes (hidden) nets the equaliser at Hampden.

Johnstone disrupted the whole left side of Leeds' team, and nobody could get to grips with the problems he posed. Films of the match show Johnstone gathering the ball, and a closer examination reveals the screen filling up with United players, drawn out of position by the threat; too often for their comfort they lined up only to be bewildered in a variety of ways by the swerving, scuttling Johnstone.

At half-time Leeds still held the one-goal lead, but had been sorely pressed to hold out. One characteristic of Stein's team was the astute use of pace and physical fitness as a tactical weapon; resistance to a Celtic bombardment constituted a drain physically and emotionally.

At the start of the second half Celtic raised their game to another level . . . and Leeds United crumbled beneath the onslaught amid the bedlam raised by 136,505 fans giving voice to the greatest Hampden Roar of all.

Hay overlapped frequently on the right and, because of the confusion that Johnstone was creating, the full back had space and freedom. He won a corner and, taking it himself, dropped it back to Auld, loitering with intent; the wily midfield player whipped over a short, curling cross to the near post where Hughes with a brave header glanced the ball into the net.

The second half was but two minutes old, and the Glasgow skies were rent with joyous uproar. Straight from the resumption Celtic gained control of the ball, and Leeds were reeling as the Scottish side moved in for the kill. Sprake dived gallantly to save at Hughes' feet, but was hurt in the collision. As he received treatment, the substitute, David Harvey, warmed up on the sideline; within a minute he knew he was to play, as Revie signalled for him to take his place in Leeds' goalmouth. It was a European debut to test the strongest nerves: Hampden Park with 136,505 spectators baying and roaring in anticipation, the Scottish champions in full cry for victory and already one goal up on aggregate, a defence stretched to the limit in trying to contain one of the most feared forward lines in the world.

If it was the script for comic-book heroics, poor David Harvey – later to play for Scotland – did not fit the part; his first touch of the ball was to pick it out of the back of the net.

He could not be blamed for the loss of the goal; once again Johnstone drew defenders like a magnet before releasing the ball for Bobby Murdoch to come thundering through the right side of the penalty box to crash a shot into the net.

CROWD PULLERS

One newspaper estimated that more than 2,500,000 spectators had watched Celtic's 61 matches from a friendly against St Etienne of France on 30 July 1969 to the Leeds match at Hampden on 15 April 1970. The paper's unofficial attendance aggregate was tabulated as follows:

Scottish League	(33 matches)	1,000,000
League Cup	(11)	440,000
Scottish Cup	(5)	342,000
European Cup	(8)	608,000
'Friendlies'	(4)	126,000

All around Hampden the celebrations began; the noise was unbearable. The sound bore the tone of triumph, loud and defiant; in it could be heard the slightest hint of relief. Leeds United may have been the enemy, but the Celtic supporters had a wary respect for them. Bremner's goal – in retrospect – added the challenge of equality to the drama, and the spectators were rejoicing in the catharsis. The crowd, the largest ever to watch a European Cup-tie, sensed instinctively that the issue had been decided; it was all over bar the shouting, and the singing. A choir more than a hundred-thousand strong went through every song in the repertoire, as the match continued with Celtic now in full control and playing with confidence and flair.

At the end of this epic tie Celtic went on a victory lap of honour in a stadium that had become 'a Niagara of noise'. As Jimmy Johnstone, overcome with emotion, wiped away tears of joy, an ecstatic Jock Stein firmly resisted the attempts of his players to hoist him up on their shoulders to share their triumph. While the players basked in the thunderous acclaim of the legions on the terracing, Jock Stein sought out the unsung Bob Rooney whose patient treatment of Billy McNeill's injury by the old-fashioned remedy of hot and cold compresses had made possible the captain's presence on the field, where his aerial command would prove vital. He told the physio: 'You did as much as any man on the pitch to earn us this victory.' Later, in the hubbub of the dressing-room, Stein's outward calm deserted him. 'I'm knocked out . . . I'm knocked out. I'm so proud of everyone,' he repeated several times. He then had to withdraw to a small room, just to wind down.

Revie was gracious in defeat: he praised the performance of Celtic as a team, he commended the referees, he marvelled at the enthusiasm of the Celtic support, he summed up Jimmy Johnstone's performance, 'Even better than George Best!' He made no further excuses about his side's exhausting schedule, but inwardly he must have felt sick at the ruins of Leeds' season. He added: 'Celtic were great at Elland Road, but were out of this world – and I mean that – before their own fans.'

Leeds United must have been the greatest side to have won nothing in the season they reached their peak. They contrived new ways to lose: they conceded the League to Everton by opting not to challenge for it in the last weeks of the campaign; they lost unluckily to the energy of a workmanlike Chelsea in the replay of the FA Cup final; in the European Cup they were fated to confront a Celtic side and club at its greatest and were, in the end, outclassed.

The Scottish press trumpeted Celtic's double triumph; for the native champions to defeat, and deservedly, the champions of England, home and away, was a notable feat. One could read into the results a justification for the national character:

> Whatever the rewards of such specific ploys, however, any success Celtic have against the leading clubs of England may have more to do with a difference in philosophy than a difference in technique.
>
> Many people in English football have come to have an obsessive respect for the safe and the sensible. In conversations with players or managers, you hear much about the need to learn good habits on the field, about being professional, not putting yourself in trouble, and so on. All this is entirely admirable – and, indeed, essential up to a point.

But too much emphasis on the puritanical virtues of industry and economy can build inhibitions in footballers. Some of them begin to suspect their own flair, to think that sweat is a more worthy contribution than inspiration.

Men who could readily accomplish the remarkable find themselves settling for the mediocre. Celtic never make that mistake. They are a disciplined side, but they have never lost their enthusiasm for the outrageously skilful . . .

(The Observer: 5 April 1970)

Bobby Murdoch sets the seal on a great Celtic night with his winner:
Jimmy Johnstone looks on.

Jock Stein was more than satisfied, as Hugh McIlvanney records:

. . . little needed to be said on the Thursday. As the players stood around talking idly, savouring the implications of the previous night, Stein contented himself with quick smiles and handshakes in response to the repeated congratulations. It was only when we were behind the closed door of an inner room that he allowed his feelings to show. When he turned away from the door, his great bulk suddenly shook with laughter. He looked like a man making a commercial for happiness. 'What about that, then?' he said. 'What did you think of that? It wasn't bad, was it? Eh?'

(The Observer: 19 April 1970)

The last details needed to make Stein feel completely proud were the reports filtering in from around the country and letters arriving at Celtic Park praising the conduct of the fans. One such letter was printed in the *Celtic View* of 15 April: ' . . . They conducted themselves like perfect gentlemen. My pub was open to them at the full hours allowed and I did not have one instant of concern. They were happy and cheerful at all times, and even thanked me for the hospitality they received. All I can say is thank you to all your supporters. My door will be open any time you visit Leeds, which I hope will not be too long. Also good luck to your great team.' (T. Freeth, Yorkshire Hussar Hotel, Eastgate, Leeds)

Celtic FC never stood in higher public esteem . . .

POSTSCRIPT

It is sad to record that two of the central figures in one of the most dramatic football confrontations in British football died relatively young.

In September 1985 Jock Stein died of a heart-attack, a few weeks before his 63rd birthday, while acting in his capacity as Scotland's manager in the vital World Cup-tie in Wales, where he had once played in the relative obscurity of non-League football.

In May 1989 Don Revie succumbed to Motor Neurone Disease – shortly before his 62nd birthday after a vain fight against the muscle-wasting condition that left him confined to a wheelchair in an Edinburgh nursing-home with scarcely enough strength to speak or lift a cup of tea. With his Scottish wife, Elsie, he had retired to Kinross, Fife, to enjoy his beloved golf, but the onset of the crippling disease prevented his playing.

Unlike his rival, whose funeral service was attended by every major figure in British football, Revie was ignored by football's establishment – partly as a consequence of his quitting the post as England's manager in 1977 to coach the United Arab Emirates.

However, his Leeds players were well represented at the funeral of 'a players' manager'.

DISSENTING VOICES

Four students, two of them girls, were shot dead by National Guard soldiers at Kent State University in Ohio on 4 May 1970. The Guard shot into a crowd of anti-war demonstrators, injuring and wounding 11 on the third day of violent rioting at a university hitherto not noted for political activity.

President Nixon, while deploring the deaths, stated: 'When dissent turns to violence, it invites tragedy.' The president's recent decision to send American troops into Cambodia sparked off the most recent round of student demonstrations.

Footnotes

1 This was the last time the method of tossing a coin to settle the outcome was used. In the semi-final, had the score been level after both legs, 30 minutes' extra-time would be played; away goals would have counted as double only up to 180 minutes. A play-off had been arranged provisionally between Celtic and Leeds at Sheffield Wednesday's ground, Hillsborough, as Revie had won the toss for the choice of venue.

2 Bremner had been considered by Celtic in the early 1960s but the Scottish club felt that £30,000 was too much to pay. Rumours spread around Glasgow that one of the reasons was Bremner's combative style of play, of which Bob Kelly did not fully approve.

3 In one match at Liverpool's ground, Sprake accidentally threw the ball into his own net, reportedly prompting the announcer to play the record 'Careless Hands' at half-time.

4 In fact, Stein had made deliberate changes to baffle the watching Leeds spies. For two of Celtic's last three League matches before the Elland Road tie Craig replaced Hay at right back, while in the Hearts match reserves Callaghan, Quinn and Macari replaced Johnstone, Auld and Connelly upfront or in midfield. Connelly replaced McNeill at centre half for the Hearts match.

5 The modern football fan may find the descriptions depressingly familiar, but in 1970 the precautions were considered extraordinary. For the record, 13 people were arrested inside and around the ground during the game, and a spokesman for the police stated: 'This is about normal for one of United's home games.'

14

A DIXIE MELODY

THE CELTS

. . . Renowned is Hampden's Old Brigade,
With proud striped flag unfurled;
And hardy lads, my Renton,
The Champions of the World.
But these and more in combat fierce,
That stirred the soul to see,
Before the might of jackets green
Were forced to bend the knee.

The Warriors fight in red and white,
The Rangers love the blue;
Dumbarton bold sport black and gold;
Hearts to maroon are true.
But not from Wick to Solway tide
A match you'll find, I ween,
For the dazzling combination
Of the wearers of the green.

Extract from poem in the *Glasgow Observer,* 5 June 1897
[Hampden's Old Brigade is Queen's Park, the Warriors were Third
Lanark and Renton were self-proclaimed 'champions of the world'
when they defeated the English cup-winners in 1888.]

ALTHOUGH THE early matches in 1971/72 indicated that Celtic would
continue to dominate Scottish football, Jock Stein was giving a lot of
thought to changes in personnel. The results had been acceptable, spec-
tacularly so – a 9–1 trouncing of Clyde, and three victories (2–0, 3–0, and
3–2) over Rangers, all at Ibrox; but Stein sensed that it was time for change
because the young team he inherited in 1965, and developed, had passed its
peak and some of his players now lacked the incentive of 'hunger'. With a

finely developed sense of tact, he delayed implementing the changes until an era had ended at Parkhead .

Sir Robert Kelly was dying after a gallant fight against cancer. Stein had a great deal of respect and affection for the former chairman, once so autocratic and still influential even as the club's president, and he sensed that too many changes would upset Bob Kelly, a man of undoubted conservatism.

Stein had been manager for more than six years – incredibly successful years – but he continued to be careful about offending Kelly's demanding standards. All managers have to tread that thin line when dealing with club chairmen, and Stein was well versed in the game's politics.

The hitherto unpublished case of Jim Craig's dropping illustrates the situation perfectly. In 1966 Craig was ordered off in the away-leg of a European tie against Dynamo Kiev; Kelly was furious at the full back's dismissal, and expressed himself so forcefully about it that Stein thought it prudent to omit Craig from the line-up against Hearts in the forthcoming League match. The manager switched Billy McNeill to right back, where he had played for both Celtic and Scotland, and played the competent, dependable John Cushley at centre half. The consequences were mixed: Celtic lost 2–3 to a ten-man Hearts, but Hearts' centre forward, Willie Wallace, so roasted Cushley that Stein's resolve to sign him for Celtic was hardened. Later, Wallace was to become one of the key players in Celtic's greatest era.

The chairman had been appeased, 'punishment' meted out, and the manager's authority remained unquestioned. Jock Stein never ceded the hard-won right of Celtic's manager to full control in playing matters, but he remained conscious of Kelly's residual authority and exacting standards of discipline.

It did not require a long memory to recall the banishment of Bertie Auld to Birmingham after the young Celt's conduct on the field was causing trouble with referees; only after Auld could be considered 'a reformed character', did Kelly relent and approve his recall from the Midlands. Similarly, Pat Crerand had been transferred to Manchester United after a scuffle in the Ibrox dressing-room with Sean Fallon; all the negotiations, the details of the transfer, were worked out between Kelly and Matt Busby, with neither the manager nor the player being consulted until the deal was virtually closed.

Accordingly, it was not until after Sir Robert Kelly's death in September 1971 that Stein started to implement the changes that would alter Celtic radically.

The timing and extent of his dealings certainly suggest that. Of the famous 11 who played at Lisbon, Ronnie Simpson was the first to depart, after a recurring shoulder injury; Bertie Auld had been granted a free transfer to join Hibernian in May 1971, and John Clark went to Morton in

June. One other hero of Lisbon, Steve Chalmers, was allowed to join Clark at Greenock early in September. This erosion of the squad would be considered normal, given the duration of an average-length career in football.

However, the speed of change quickened shortly after the president's death. On 19 October Willie Wallace and John Hughes were allowed to leave for London to join Crystal Palace for a combined fee of £50,000; Tommy Gemmell, the scorer of European Cup final goals at both Lisbon and Milan, went south to Nottingham Forest for £35,000 in December 1971. In January 1972 David Cattenach, a useful and long-time utility-player, went to Falkirk; in the following month John Fallon, so often Celtic's back-up keeper, moved to Motherwell.

The young Kenny Dalglish takes on Hibs.

With the transfers of his redoubtable veterans Jock Stein was obviously clearing house, although he claimed, rather disingenuously, that he would never want to see such fine servants playing in reserve-team football. However, one player of that era commented later that the manager had a policy of transferring players far enough away that they could not inflict any damage to Celtic on the field.

Among Celtic supporters, renowned for their sentimentality, the feeling might have been that Stein was too premature in unloading Wallace and Hughes . . . because only four days later Celtic suffered the club's most embarrassing defeat of the Stein years.

On 23 October 1971 Celtic met Partick Thistle in the final of the League Cup, and incredulous newsrooms the length and breadth of Britain checked and rechecked the half-time score that read: Thistle 4, Celtic 0. Celtic did rally in the second half but, faced by a brilliant young keeper in Allan Rough, they could score only one goal through Kenny Dalglish. During half-time at Ibrox some hundreds of spectators left Rangers' match with Motherwell to head towards Hampden to witness for themselves the humiliation of Celtic. At the end of the biggest upset for years, Stein congratulated the manager and players of Partick Thistle, and put up a brave front in public; in private he was furious, refusing to accept the absence of the injured Billy McNeill as an excuse.

Stein moved quickly to effect damage-control. Within a few days he had purchased goalkeeper Dennis Connaghan from St Mirren for £20,000; clearly Evan Williams had been nominated as a scapegoat for the collective failure.[1]

An even greater shock was in store for the football world when, on 31 October – little more than a month after Sir Robert Kelly's death – Jock Stein signed John 'Dixie' Deans, Motherwell's striker, for £17,500.

Deans had become a controversial figure because of his apparently incurable tendency to get into trouble; in a six-year senior career he had been ordered off six times, and had accumulated 17 weeks in suspensions for indiscretions which included a run-in with Jimmy Johnstone at Parkhead in December 1966.[2] Indeed, Deans came to Celtic Park in the middle of serving a lengthy six-week suspension after being sent off while playing against Stoke City at Fir Park in a Texaco Cup-tie. Deans' plea – that, in attempting to tackle one opponent on the greasy surface, he accidentally slid into ex-Ranger Billy Stevenson – fell on deaf ears. Leaving the SFA headquarters after hearing the severity of his punishment, Deans was quoted as 'feeling sick and shattered'.

Admittedly, his offences were never vicious, and usually retaliatory. His problems on the field may have stemmed from the frustration of having to play at Motherwell, a club which he had been eager to leave for some time. Imagine his feelings upon hearing from the Motherwell chairman years later that in 1968 Rangers had swithered about signing Deans or Colin Stein of Hibs; in the chairman's words 'it was a toss-up'.

A move to Rangers would have delighted Deans, whose Renfrewshire background made him well-disposed towards the Ibrox club; in fact, on the day he joined Motherwell back in 1965 he was wearing a Rangers 'bunnet' at the Linwood engineering works where he was employed as a labourer.

Even the manner of his joining Celtic contained a bizarre note. A journalist, and long-time friend of Jock Stein, hinted at Celtic's interest by drawing Deans' attention to the Carfin Grotto (situated close to Motherwell) as they were passing it, and commenting in Delphic tones: 'Miracles can happen'.

Stein, ever the pragmatist, had been interested in Deans for more than a year, after seeing the stocky Motherwell striker thoroughly embarrass the much-vaunted Tottenham Hotspur centre half, Mike England, in a dramatic Texaco Cup victory at Fir Park. Despite his lack of height at five feet seven inches and an unathletic appearance, Deans could out-jump the tallest of opponents, and pursued goals with considerable enthusiasm. Some of Stein's own players at Parkhead had told him that Celtic needed the tall centre forward then in vogue in order to exploit high balls into the penalty area; Stein could see the argument, but still opted for the Deans' 'model'.

Motherwell's supporters were outraged, and they suggested that Stein had committed grand larceny yet again. The transfer-fee came to a modest £17,500, and constituted a bargain similar to that six years earlier when Celtic signed Joe McBride, Deans' predecessor at Motherwell. No doubt Jock Stein cunningly raised the matter of the player's poor disciplinary record as a lever in the negotiations, and pointed out the undeniable fact that the player was presently under suspension.

Predictably, the reaction from Celtic supporters was mixed; many felt concerned that the new player might present too many problems for Celtic with a record 'as long as your arm', as one fan put it.

Another respected football man – the ex-referee and chief scout for Aberdeen, Bobby Calder – was overheard to say that the late chairman, Bob Kelly, would have been turning in his grave. Calder had been a close friend of Kelly's for years in a relationship unharmed – and perhaps enhanced – by the fact that he had turned down Kelly's overtures for him to switch allegiance from the 'Dons'.

THE BEST YOU CAN BE

The Reverend Michael Dunn of Rochester took as his theme for the Sunday sermon the wayward behaviour in the early 1970s of George Best, Manchester United's talented forward. Noting that Best had been dropped from the side to face Wolves because he had missed training during the week, the vicar reflected: 'He was reckoned to be unfit for the match, and so not allowed to take part. It is that rigour and discipline I want us to copy. Far too often we come to Sunday worship spiritually untrained.'

However, the *New York Times'* headline was decidedly ambiguous – 'Britain's Swinging Soccer Star Banished to Tea and Crumpets'. The motto of the newspaper reads 'All the news that's fit to print'.

Deans' reputation as a trouble-maker did not concern Stein unduly; he had no doubts about his ability to deal with any player, as the new Celt found out quickly enough. Upon arrival at Parkhead, Deans was given the news that he had to undergo a rigorous training schedule of both morning and afternoon sessions, designed to bring him up to the manager's idea of acceptable fitness.

His treatment was not universally harsh. At half-time in an early game for Celtic the striker sat slumped in the dressing-room, head down after missing some chances. Stein spoke to the whole team briefly, making minor adjustments, then moved over to Deans. The manager's tone was brusque but encouraging; the advice was to lift his head, and not to dwell on the past: 'Look, they know that you're a threat; so, let them do the worrying. You'll score all right; they just don't know when!'

Dixie Deans settled in quickly at Celtic Park and soon was scoring goals regularly, a factor which, allied to an extrovert personality, endeared him to the Celtic support.

The extent of his popularity was to be tested in the semi-final of the European Cup, played at Parkhead against Inter Milan in April 1972. Celtic had survived the trip to San Siro and escaped with a scoreless draw; for the return-leg Inter were openly apprehensive, and concentrated exclusively on defence for the full 90 minutes and the extra 30. The tie was going to be decided on penalty kicks . . . and Dixie Deans, who had come on as a substitute, missed the first one, scooping the ball over the crossbar. Parkhead slumped into apprehensive silence, as Deans trudged back to the centre-circle – a walk that he described as 'lasting two hours'. All the other penalties were converted, and Milan advanced to the final having side-lined Celtic before 75,000 at their own ground. A crestfallen Deans slipped out of Parkhead, unnoticed by the throng of exultant Italian fans waiting to greet their heroes.

The striker's anguish could not have been eased by the photographs in the newspapers showing him covering his face with his hands, and by re-runs on television showing the miss. Even the cartoonists got into the act; one depiction in the *Daily Record* had American astronauts, who had just landed on the moon, calling Houston: '*Apollo 16* to Ground Control. Tell Dixie we've found the ball!'

On Friday the astute Jock Stein called his full-time staff together to raise morale. He made the point of reminding the players that responsibility for Celtic's success or failure had to be collective, and not individual: Stein pointed out that the choice of penalty-takers was his [Stein's], and that nobody could be blamed for a miss under such stressful conditions. He pointed out that yet another challenge soon faced them – the Scottish Cup final – where they would have the opportunity to complete 'the double'.

On the Saturday, Deans was reminded that he had been fully accepted (and forgiven) by a critical brotherhood. When Celtic emerged from the tunnel to play Motherwell, the crowd gave Deans a tremendous welcome and, in his own words, provided 'an unforgettable boost'.[3] To the delight of the crowd Celtic were awarded a penalty in the first half and, smilingly, Deans fended off the good-natured chants from the terracings to take it; he left it for Bobby Murdoch to convert in a 5–2 win.

*　*　*

A startled audience attending a Scottish League dinner listened in growing

266

discomfort as Desmond White, Celtic's chairman since the death of Sir Robert Kelly the previous year, spoke at length about his concern for the future of British football.

It was a bleak picture. White offered no simple solutions, but suggested that immediate and positive steps had to be taken to inject the necessary vitality and dynamism into the sport.

Unfortunately, the audience, the representatives of the member clubs of the Scottish League, was prepared only to listen and not act, and Desmond White was neither the speaker nor the visionary to rouse them from their self-satisfied torpor. He never projected a positive image; tall, awkward-looking in appearance, highly idiosyncratic in his interests, he was respected but not readily liked. He remained a 'loner' within the circles of football administrators, despite his intelligence and qualifications.

He droned on, quoting from Gibbons' *Decline and Fall of the Roman Empire* – that classic, and usually unread, account of decay and final collapse. By profession Desmond White was an accountant, and one journalist felt he best exemplified the sarcastic definition of an accountant as 'an economist without the charisma'.

Football, he declared, was starting to lose that hold on the imagination of the working-man which had brought about 'the fantastic rise of the game in this country until, in the halcyon days of the late 30s and 40s, it was a giant among dwarfs in the world of sport'. He illustrated the public's insatiable appetite for football in that era by citing some attendance figures from November 1948: close to 56,000 at Parkhead to see Celtic play newly-promoted East Fife; 40,000 at Love Street to watch St Mirren against Rangers; and 12,000 spectators attracted by the prospect of Petershill versus Annbank in an early round of the Scottish Junior Cup.

In his most pedantic tones he outlined the reasons for the sport's popularity and subsequent decline:

> Certainly there was competition from the cinema, but Saturday afternoons were usually given over to the children's matinee. Certainly the working-man gambled, but as cash-betting was illegal there was no betting shop, and his business had to be conducted furtively at the street corner. Again, the era of the family car was in its infancy if, indeed, it had begun at all. Today the position has altered radically. Like Rome, we have enemies at our gates. Some of these enemies we have practically embraced unto ourselves. The betting man has his luxury haunts where the blower system and television give live coverage of racing. The motor car has become an adjunct of the working man. Television, after having practically destroyed the cinema industry, has deliberately set up sports programmes at the same time and in direct opposition to the main sport of the people – football.[4]

As an analysis of the game's declining appeal, White's speech was more in the nature of a well-bred polemic than a fully-developed argument.

Television had performed a notable public service in alerting Scottish football to the extent of its lagging behind foreign standards, most vividly with the telecast of the humiliation in the 1954 World Cup, when shocked Scots saw the national team routed 0–7 by Uruguay. TV viewers, as well as the enraptured multitudes on the Hampden terracings, were left to wonder what the average football spectator had been watching each Saturday as they were left spellbound by the dazzling exhibition of Real Madrid and Eintracht Frankfurt in the 1960 European Cup final. And had not the same medium brought the speaker's own club admiration and instant fame throughout Europe by its coverage of the 1967 final at Lisbon?

Some of his other observations betrayed an essentially middle-class attitude. His characterisation of betting-shops as 'luxury haunts' flattered their more prosaically utilitarian decor and accommodation – described more bitingly by one critic as 'as inviting as a urinal'. In a later section of his speech he expressed scorn for the growing support for all-seated stadia as an ideal: 'Would, for example, the thousands who occupy the Kop in Liverpool turn out in equal numbers if they had the luxury of a stand seat? I doubt it!'

His words were uttered with the certitude of a man who never stood on the terracing, nor loitered in a betting-shop no matter how luxurious. They revealed unwittingly the gaps in awareness caused by the vast social gulf that existed between the game's administrators and the average fan.

Writing about the Taylor Report and its recommendations on safety at football grounds, prompted by the Hillsborough Stadium Disaster in 1989, Doug Baillie, a former player and now a journalist, criticised the antediluvian 'thinking' of most British clubs since the war:

> Club directors wouldn't consider standing to watch a game – or do without a tipple in the warm boardroom afterwards. While the life-blood of their clubs – the fans – drip off rain-soaked terracings and disappear into the night without complaint. Clubs could get away with that when football was one of the few entertainments a working man could afford. Not now. Would you stand in a cinema while rain seeped under your shirt collar, your shoes were fit only for the dustbin afterwards, and some nutter was giving you aggro throughout? Neither would I? And football clubs had better believe it, before it's too late!
>
> *(Sunday Post*: 4 February 1990)

The number of disasters at football grounds in recent years, when combined with the increase in hooliganism, has had one beneficial result; at last the government has become involved in the sport to ensure that minimum standards of safety apply for spectators. If the matter were left entirely to the clubs, little change could be discerned in most grounds around the country. In 1971 John Rafferty, the respected sports correspondent of the *Scotsman,* was scathing in his denunciation of the way in which the stadia reflected the lethargy of the clubs in the first post-1945

'THE DEAR, GREEN PLACE . . .'

The new Glasgow became a subject for emotional debate in the early 1970s, as houses, shops, office buildings, works, warehouses and districts were razed to make way for motorways. Malcolm Munro, better known as a football writer, lamented the passing of the old city:

> For thousands life will pass by. We on the ground won't see the Jones'car because they'll be going round and round looking for openings to take them to the suburbs; without the wee shops people lose touch with one another. Old Mrs Harkins used to hold the people of Seamore Street – 'Did you know Mrs White is ill?' or, 'Young Mary Tillie is expecting, . . . fancy, and her just married.'
>
> *(Evening Times: 25 April 1969)*

The same concerns were expressed in the words of the fictional John Gallagher on his return to Glasgow, where he glimpsed through the cab windows

> the re-planned and re-built Glasgow of underpasses and flyovers and feed-in lines and motorway signs, a concrete rabbit warren where once there had been a black, rectangular city of monster tenements, a grimy, battered bar on each windswept corner. Now it was Detroit on the Clyde. He didn't like it. But he had to shrug for he hadn't liked the old Glasgow much either. To be sentimental for the old Glasgow was like weeping tears for long-remembered humiliations.

(Gordon Williams/Terry Venables: *They Used To Play On Grass*, 1971)

decade: 'Scottish clubs had big supports, costs were low, and unsophisticated spectators wanted no more than a step to stand on to raise their eyes above the heads in front of them. In those days Scottish football fell asleep, and only brief flashes of consciousness have shown since.'

Football administrators failed to anticipate, and react to, the social changes affecting post-war Britain, and eventually paid – and continue to pay – the price for their dereliction. Three years before Desmond White's address the club's newspaper printed a peevish and lengthy article by 'a Celtic follower of long standing' which, in effect, questioned the customer's fundamental right to exercise his freedom of choice. The writer condemned the club's followers' alleged preference for glamour matches over the regular fixtures, suggesting that they were being 'fed a too-rich diet of champagne soccer with silver cups'. He contrasted unfavourably Celtic's home attendances with those of Manchester United, Liverpool and Chelsea who, he claimed, enjoyed 'regular full houses'. He did not mention that Celtic's average was a highly respectable 37,000, nor that the Football League had an infinitely more glamorous appeal with its level of competitiveness. Even the Manchester United of Denis Law, Bobby Charlton, and Georgie Best would not have filled Old Trafford for a visit by the likes of Arbroath, who, it must be said, would have struggled in the English Third Division.

As the Scottish game entered the 1970s it could be seen as an industry in decline: the sport lacked credibility at an administrative level, appeal on the field, and comfort in the grounds. John Rafferty's fear was that, unless the required changes were made, Scottish football would degenerate into the semi-professional level of Northern Ireland. He could draw no comfort from the lack of any real attempt to streamline and modernise in the wake of the recommendations of the Chester Report on British football issued in 1968. Among other things the report revealed the unpalatable truth that Scottish football had 'lost' 2,500,000 spectators or customers in the previous decade; the report suggested that 'if Celtic and Rangers ever decide to throw in their lot with a British or European League, the general future of the Scottish game would be very bleak indeed'.

Most club directors were more interested in living in the past than in planning for the future, and so the most notable reaction was the umbrage taken at the identification of the Old Firm's indispensable contribution to the financial health of Scottish football. In fact, that stark – if unwelcome – truth was being underlined in red by the plight of some famous names as attendances at Scottish matches plummetted by some 30 per cent in the 1972-74 period.

Two jokes of the period had an uncomfortable ring of truth. It was said that someone planning to attend a match at Cliftonhill Park, the home of perennial strugglers Albion Rovers, phoned the ground to determine the kick-off time and was asked 'What time can you get here?' Another jester claimed that the scarcity of break-ins at Scottish grounds was due to players out-numbering spectators! Jock Stein found it no laughing matter, and his forthright observation in 1971 that 'It is difficult to stay in an unhealthy house without catching some of the disease' seemed to echo John Rafferty's concern that, unless drastic remedies were found, only Celtic and Rangers would remain as full-time clubs in the mid-1980s.

Stein did not have to look very far for the evidence. Celtic's close neighbours Clyde, twice winners of the Scottish Cup as recently as the 1950s but badly hit by the 1960s redevelopment which affected the once heavily-populated Oatlands, Hutchesontown, and Gorbals districts adjacent to their Shawfield ground, were 'dying a slow death', in their chairman's words, as they strove unsuccessfully to avoid relegation in 1971/72, watched now by a pitiful remnant of their former support. Steps were considered to stop the rot: a proposed merger with Hamilton Academical foundered, and abortive plans were even drawn up to move Clyde to the 'new town' of East Kilbride.

Even the two teams who had provided the most credible challenge to

Rangers and Celtic in the 1960s were counting the cost of competing with the Old Firm in the changed economic climate. Sadly, Dunfermline Athletic, Scottish Cup winners in 1961 and 1968, and European Cup-Winners' Cup semi-finalists in 1969, were relegated in 1972 alongside Clyde, both victims of financial crises as well as decline on the field of play. A club of similar stature, Kilmarnock, who had won the championship in 1965 – on the same day that Billy McNeill's header beat Dunfermline at Hampden – was phasing out its full-timers and relying on players who came to Rugby Park to train only three nights a week. Walter McCrae, the manager, had to admit: 'As a club we don't believe that Scottish football can survive in its present shape.'

The decline of the two clubs, so often described as 'sturdy provincials', mirrored the erosion of the Scottish game's credibility in terms of public interest and competitiveness. Even Celtic were not immune from the decay. In 1968/69 the visits of Dunfermline and Kilmarnock had attracted crowds of 43,500 and 40,000 to see the teams that finished third and fourth in the League. In 1971/72, when both these clubs were struggling; for the identical fixtures the crowds were 25,000 and 28,000 – a discouraging drop of over 30,000 paying customers.

Scottish football was in the middle of a crisis, and it would take the introduction of the Premier League in 1975 to start the turnaround. The advent of that new League format heralded at least a greater degree of competition into the weekly schedule. Jock Stein frequently asserted that League reconstruction was an attempt to break up Celtic's monopoly of the championship. His statement was made without rancour or paranoia and one sensed that, from a competitive viewpoint, he approved of the streamlining.

The subsequent introduction of the scheme to allow home clubs to keep their 'gates', and the guarantee of two extra visits a season from Rangers and Celtic, would serve to motivate provincial clubs such as Aberdeen and Dundee United to mount successful challenges to the Glasgow giants, and to prepare for forays into Europe. The most ambitious and far-sighted club of all, Rangers, would eventually see the opportunity to expand; the result was the new Ibrox Stadium which constituted an investment in the future of football in Scotland.

But, above all, the crucial element in the game's credibility and apparent fight for survival had to be the activity on the pitch. To hold on to its customers in the early 1970s, never mind bring back the lost generation of spectators, it was essential that, in an uncertain period when Scottish football seemed rudderless at the top, the leading lights underline their commitment to entertain by positive, attractive football. The Scottish Cup final of 1972, fortunately, would match the country's finest exponents of that philosophy: Celtic, renowned the world over for their buccaneering style, and Hibernian, traditionally linked with exciting, and often elegant, football but a team which had now added a touch of steel to its make-up as evidenced by its semi-final conquest of a Rangers side which went on to win the European Cup-Winners' Cup that season.

SCOTTISH CUP FINAL
6 May 1972
Hampden Park

CELTIC 6	**HIBERNIAN 1**
Williams	Herriot
Craig	Brownlie
Brogan	Schaedler
Murdoch	Stanton
McNeill	Black
Connelly	Blackley
Johnstone	Edwards
Deans	Hazel
Macari	Gordon
Dalglish	O'Rourke
Callaghan	Duncan (Auld)

Scorers:
McNeill (2)   Gordon (12)
Deans (23, 54, 74)
Macari (83, 87)
Referee: A. MacKenzie (Larbert)

Attendance: 106,102

Celtic's preparations for the 1972 final were refreshingly old-fashioned with a few days on the bracing Ayrshire coast, where one of Stein's ploys was to take his squad walking over the sand dunes.[5] During such a stroll on the Friday he found a convenient hollow. There he held a team-talk and started to discuss the tactics which he felt sure would beat Hibernian the

---

FEVER PITCH

Dr Neil Phillips, the honorary medical officer of the FA, illustrated graphically the pressures of modern football when he spoke in 1972: 'I have noticed the change in top players over the past few years – a sort of disenchantment with the game, a lack of sparkle. One finds oneself looking around a dressing-room more like an officer looking at his men in the trenches in the First World War. Which ones will crack when the shelling starts, and which will still have the nerve left to go over the top?'

---

next day. He declined to reveal his lineup there and then, but he did make one announcement; since the party included only one recognised right back, Jim Craig would play, and he added that this appearance would be Craig's last for the club before leaving for South Africa.

McNeill rocks Hibs with the opener.

It was a radical departure from the method he had employed for the 1965 final against Dunfermline Athletic, but it represented the manager's caginess and his knowledge of his squad; his 1972 players might be on edge, but they would not allow that to affect them on the day of the match.

Dixie Deans, despite his goalscoring, felt that Stein would prefer Bobby Lennox as his main striker for the match, but he kept Billy McNeill, his room-mate, awake till the early hours by speculating about the chances of appearing in his first ever major final. Only after the party arrived at Hampden Park did Deans learn of his selection.[6]

The coach had drawn up at a stadium that was starting to reflect much of what was wrong with the Scottish game in the early 1970s. One of the few administrators to give real thought to the situation was Desmond White, who had recently formulated a plan to halt Hampden Park's further decay into decrepitude and restore the ground to its past glories. As a former Queen's Park goalkeeper in the 1930s, White may have had a sentimental attachment to the ground and its past. He felt that £300,000 would be required for the repairs and reconstruction, and he proposed that the finance be obtained in the following manner: £40,000 each from the SFA and the Scottish League, £20,000 each from Celtic's and Rangers' development pools, a matching grant from the Conservative government of Ted Heath, and the balance to be raised from the proceeds of a gala match – Great Britain versus the Rest. He recommended that Queen's Park play their fixtures at Lesser Hampden, while retaining ownership of Hampden.

Rentals from the use of Britain's largest stadium for Cup finals and internationals (and advertising revenues from such occasions) could be paid into a special account with a view to Hampden Park being established as the national stadium, run by a select committee from Queen's Park, the League, and the SFA. A share of this money would be apportioned to Queen's Park to meet the club's running costs, and thus gradually pay off the existing debts.

The views of the Celtic chairman were admirable, but his plans were already obsolete. His plan, admirably thorough in its thinking, was logical but no longer reasonable. Changes in society, springing from greater affluence in the game's traditional constituency, would soon be reflected in the thinking of football followers who increasingly preferred to stay away from all but the most attractive fixtures rather than put up with the antiquated conditions on the terracing.

Also, however outmoded his concept, it was not to be given serious consideration because it was still too advanced to overcome the inertia and indifference endemic in football's administration. Perhaps the legislators were fooled by the gritty grandeur that Hampden could present on a big occasion when a huge crowd assembled on its terracings.

That was the image conveyed on 6 May 1972: only a few clouds threatened to interfere with the sunshine of the spring day, and two of the most famous names in Scottish football took the field to fight it out for the Cup. Both sides had been in impressive form, Celtic having won a record seventh Championship in a row and Hibernian ending in a respectable fourth place.

Scottish sportswriters hoped for an exciting and skilful match to act as a counterblast to the media attention being devoted to the Wembley final on the same afternoon between Arsenal and Leeds United. It may have been the Centenary Cup final in England, but Hugh Taylor of the *Daily Record* was incensed that 'every time you tune in on your radio, you listen to

---

ENOUGH SAID

Alastair Dewar, a freelance BBC sports reporter, prefaced his account of Celtic's League match at Tynecastle on 29 April 1972 with this comment: 'It gives me great pleasure to repeat the result – Hearts 4, Celtic 1.'

The BBC switchboard in Glasgow lit up with incoming calls from protesting Celtic fans. A friend was quoted as saying, 'Alastair's not a Hearts supporter as far as I know. I think he was just pleased to see an Edinburgh team beating a Glasgow one.' The *Celtic View* was less charitable in its interpretation: 'Suffice to say that the attitude – "We don't care who wins as long as Celtic lose" – does not surprise anyone at Celtic Park.' (10 May 1972)

"Ar's'nal, we love you!" or "Leeds United for ever!", but not one mention of what can be the most exciting Scottish Cup final for a decade.' Taylor's complaint was justified because, while the English sides were more noted for the functional approach, both Celtic and Hibernian enjoyed a reputation for open, attacking football – and a classic final was anticipated.

Celtic had been established as favourites at evens (with Hibs at 5/2), mainly as a result of two narrow wins in the League and in strict accordance to the flow of Glasgow money being placed on them. However, a pre-match *Daily Record* poll of players from every other First Division club resulted in a split of 8–8. Jock Stein expected a closely-fought match, and was fully prepared for a replay.

Hibs' new manager, Eddie Turnbull, had transformed the side in his first season from a talented but disorganised outfit into a team respected and feared throughout Scotland. Hibernian had gained a place in the final by beating Rangers 2–0 in a replay – a result that earned professional plaudits for the Edinburgh club because the manner of the victory was significant. It appeared that Hibs had used much of the first match probing for weaknesses in Rangers' makeup, and a great deal of the second game in exploiting those weaknesses.

Turnbull hated losing as much as Stein did and, like Stein, he had found himself back at the club where he had played for much of his career. He had returned to Edinburgh at the request of Hibs' chairman, Tom Hart, a wealthy builder, after having spent seven productive seasons in Aberdeen. He reacted sharply to accusations that he was too hard on his players: 'Success brings money and recognition. It's far better to be recognised as a winner in Princes Street than have to skulk out of people's way. Losers don't interest anybody!'

Turnbull had a personal score to settle with Jock Stein: in 1967 Celtic won easily by 2–0 against Aberdeen while the indisposed Turnbull remained behind in the Gleneagles Hotel, helpless to do anything; in 1970, however, a young Aberdeen side defeated Celtic by 3–1 in the final. This would be both a grudge-match and the 'rubber'. Hibernian's manager could be brusque and abrasive. He felt compelled to exercise his authority at times: before the 1970 final, for example, he locked the Aberdeen directors out of the dressing-room, and only two weeks earlier, after Aberdeen had shocked Celtic by winning 2–1 in the League at Parkhead, he had marched up to Stein, not to commiserate but to inform him:'And we'll do the same to you at Hampden!'

Stein maintained a wary respect for this obsessive man described by Hibs captain, Pat Stanton, as 'a superb reader of the game and tactically sound, with an enviable awareness of the practicalities of football'.

Some newspapers had pointed out an interesting phenomenon. During Stein's reign at Parkhead, Celtic had never won the Cup in successive seasons, and in that period had not won the trophy in an 'even' year. Under

Stein, Celtic had won the Scottish Cup in 1965, 1967, 1969 and 1971; in 1966 Celtic lost in a replayed final to Rangers, in 1968 they had lost to Dunfermline at Parkhead, and in 1970 they had been upset by Aberdeen in the final.

It could scarcely be considered a 'hoodoo' but it represented the slightest shadow, the touch of uneasiness in the minds of the supporters as they set out for Hampden; as an insurance many took along with them the latest talisman, an inflatable three-foot mascot in Celtic's strip. Perhaps Hibs had the greater jinx to overcome, for it had been 70 years since they won the Scottish Cup (by defeating Celtic 1–0 in a match played at Parkhead).

Amid the roars of the 106,102 crowd anticipating an exciting match, Celtic set Hibs an immediate problem; Jimmy Johnstone, once again given a roving commission by Jock Stein, lined up at outside left. In fact, a foul on Johnstone by Hazel on the left led directly to Celtic scoring in two minutes; Callaghan took the kick from 25 yards out, but his cross seemed inconclusive, too high for Deans and too low for McNeill's head. Hibs' covering, however, was slack, and when McNeill, behind the defenders, found the ball dropping conveniently at his feet, he sidefooted it into the net.

A great start for Celtic, but a disaster for Hibernian! The Edinburgh men needed some time to settle and find the game that had destroyed Rangers in the semi-final; they were not going to obtain that luxury.

Urged on by their huge support, happy and relaxed now that Celtic had the lead, the Cup-holders swept into attack, and Hibs were put under some pressure. It appeared certain that another goal would be scored shortly; it was, but Hibs scored it.

Neat passing out of defence found Blackley in midfield; he spotted the speedy Duncan on the left, ready to burst into space. Duncan, regarded beforehand as one danger to Celtic's hopes, raced down the wing and fired over a menacing low ball; Williams and a defender could not cope with it decisively, and Gordon managed to get a foot to it for the equaliser.

After 12 minutes of a wide-open match the teams were level again, but it soon became evident that in midfield Celtic were starting to dominate. Bobby Murdoch, back to full strength, spread the play around with immaculate precision; Tommy Callaghan, given the task of marking Stanton, was also managing to release some excellent first-time passes; a young Kenny Dalglish, if somewhat unobtrusive in such distinguished company, was playing with typical intelligence. A few years earlier, as a raw recruit (in his own words, 'a wee fat No. 4'), he had had no illusions about the task he faced in making the first team at a period when Celtic had a squad of formidable quality and depth; now he had blossomed into an established first-team player of such versatility that terracing arguments were already raging as to his best position – a midfielder or a striker? Soon, when Dalglish was being hailed in the mid-70s as an all-time Celtic 'great', Jock Stein would add his authoritative contribution to the debate by observing:

276

'Don't bother about numbers – just give Kenny a jersey and he'll play well anywhere.'

Heading for glory – Dixie Deans nets his first.

One Celtic forward in particular was starting to enjoy himself. Overjoyed at being picked for the side, Dixie Deans exuded confidence – especially after winning the early aerial challenges against taller opponents. Every now and then he would verbally remind the opposing defenders that he was bound to score. In 23 minutes he did.

Once more Johnstone was fouled, this time out on the right. Even as Murdoch trotted up to place the ball for the kick, Deans was signalling. Murdoch assessed the situation, and flighted a perfectly judged cross into the area where Deans, on the move, rose above everybody to score a spectacular goal to restore Celtic's lead.

Hibs had to be in some confusion, with two goals given up from set-pieces. Previously, it had been felt that Gordon would be posing problems for Celtic's defence in the air but, disconcertingly, this squat and chunky striker, Dixie Deans, was winning everything in the air for Celtic.

At half-time Celtic deserved their 2–1 lead in an exhilarating and absorbing contest, one full of 'grand moments with both teams attacking and showing us how enjoyable a Cup final can be'. (*Sunday Mail*: 7 May 1972) Despite the two fouls on Johnstone, neither of them vicious, which led to Celtic's goals, the match was being played in a sporting and hugely entertaining fashion, providing a welcome counterblast to critics who saw the Scottish game as being in terminal decline. Jock Stein, for one, was not surprised. In a pre-match interview he pointed out that both clubs had already qualified to play in Europe the following season and thus one source of tension had been removed. And, he added, the fact that it was not yet another Old Firm clash lightened the atmosphere considerably.

Hibs came out for the second half determined to get back on level terms quickly; that might have been a fatal miscalculation, since nobody could attack this Celtic team with impunity. Impatience proved to be Hibs' undoing.

In 54 minutes Deans scored the goal that will forever be associated with him. Macari released a long cross-field ball from the right which appeared to be aimed for Deans, who was already heading for the penalty area on the scent of a goal. Brownlie, trying to cut out the danger, misdirected his attempted clearance into the path of the onrushing Deans, who controlled the ball near the bye-line after the Hibs keeper, Herriot, unsuccessfully challenged him for it. Deans then rounded Brownlie, who had run back towards the goal in a frantic attempt to redeem his error, but the striker now found himself unable to get a clear shot on target from the tight angle close to the bye-line. Showing great aplomb and intelligence by forsaking the hopeful pass across the goalmouth, Deans evaded another challenge by the goalkeeper and, in doing so, created a more advantageous position for himself under pressure. He saw his chance to shoot for goal . . . and seconds

Dixie takes the long way round for his second.

later he was celebrating with a spontaneous somersault as his team-mates rushed up to congratulate him on a truly remarkable goal. Deans later admitted that he was aware of the crowd behind the goal urging him to shoot almost as soon as he got the ball, and that the whole manouevre seemed to take an eternity, but he is rightly insistent that the persistence of Herriot and Brownlie forced his circuitous route.

After the obligatory uproar to celebrate the goal the Celtic supporters roared out Deans' name for several minutes – and all the misery of his penalty miss only 18 days previously was forgotten.

Hibs should have buckled at this stage, but they did not; in fact, they started to look even more dangerous, and the Celtic support remained anxious. They would have to admit to some relief at the sight of Arthur Duncan being carried off after a clash of heads in the 62nd minute . . . but the replacement for the speedy winger was the wily Bertie Auld.

Within minutes Auld demonstrated that he could still impose a measure of control over a game by intelligent distribution; nobody felt this remarkable final was over.

But, after 74 minutes' play, the outcome was decided: Callaghan, playing a superb match in midfield, sent Deans away yet again with a clever pass. The striker, 'on a roll', had sensed that he would score another goal; he pounced on the pass, and shot it past the helpless Herriot for a hat-trick – the first such feat since the immortal Jimmy Quinn's back in 1904.

The celebrations began in earnest on the King's Park terracing, where as always the Celtic following was massed. At the other end of the ground, unfortunately, an outbreak of fighting and can-throwing (followed by a short-lived invasion of the space behind the goal) took place. Apparently, once over-crowding at the Celtic end became obvious, the police had allowed thousands of Celtic supporters to watch the final from the Mount Florida terracing. With both teams favouring green-and-white colours it was difficult to tell the followers apart – until the goals!

That remained the only blemish in a wonderful day's entertainment.

Celtic were now rampant, and Hibernian had little more resistance to offer. Macari, a noted poacher, scored a spectacular counter in 83 minutes, ending up a move begun by a free kick from Connelly; the ball was touched on by Dalglish to Jim Craig, and the right back, up with his forwards, swept the ball over for young Macari to blast past Herriot.

Four minutes later Celtic scored again. Once more Craig had advanced down the right – perhaps keen to end a fine career with a goal in a Scottish Cup final – and his cross was played back past the keeper by Connelly, nominally the sweeper. Again Macari was perfectly placed to finish the move.

Celtic had won the Cup by a score of 6–1, a feat that matched Renton's scoring in the 1888 final – and against a competent, disciplined side that had given up only one goal in reaching Hampden.

Celtic's dazzling exhibition – and Hibernian's gallant fight – had brought a ray of sunshine to a sport which was gradually being brutalised by expediency and a naked will to win. Only three weeks later the same ground would be turned into a battlefield when the Scotland-England international, once regarded as the showpiece of the British game, degenerated into a disgraceful affair '. . . a cluttered midfield, and anyone trying to hold the ball ruthlessly chopped down'.

Oh, yes. That much-trumpeted FA Cup final at Wembley? For all the publicity, the ballyhoo, and the marvellous pageantry beforehand, it evolved into a grim war of attrition with violence always close to the surface, and the single-minded pursuit of victory at any cost predominating.

For all its economic woes and structural faults, Scottish football, as personified by Celtic and Hibernian, still had a lot to offer. In particular, Celtic once more had lived up to the title of the brightest and best entertainers in British football – only this time the merry tune was led by surely the unlikeliest Pied Piper of them all.

UNAUTHORISED VERSION

Early in 1972 the American author Clifford Irving was forced to admit he had faked the autobiography of the reclusive multi-millionaire, Howard Hughes. Supposedly based on interviews with the mysterious Hughes, the 'autobiography' was revealed as a fraud when the subject let it be known that he had never heard of Irving. The author was clearly banking on Hughes maintaining total silence and continuing his practice of shunning the outside world from his Las Vegas hotel.

Footnotes

1 Stein's record with goalkeepers would produce mixed reviews. Apart from Ronnie Simpson, who was signed from Hibs by Jimmy McGrory, he did not enjoy much success until signing the latterly luckless Ally Hunter from Kilmarnock. During the 1971/72 season, for example, he obtained Gordon Marshall on a free transfer from Hibernian, Denis Connaghan from St Mirren, and Lief Neilsen formerly of Morton; in the same season he transferred Marshall to Aberdeen for £1,000, and John Fallon to Motherwell. The goalkeeping job was shared between Williams and Connaghan, with Marshall making one appearance in major competition.

2 Ironically, Willie Wallace made his debut for Celtic that day in a 4–2 win. Deans became the recognised successor to Wallace after his transfer.

3 Deans, the one-time Rangers supporter, is insistent that the Celtic fans are the best in the world – and cites his forgiveness after the penalty miss as only one example of their spirit. Interviewed by one of the authors after attending a function in a Glasgow hotel in January 1990 for the benefit of a young Celt, Steve Murray, whose career had been ended with a serious injury, Deans confessed that he had been 'staggered once again' by the generosity of Celtic supporters.

4 If the media were affecting football attendances, the fees charged them for covering the matches could not be construed as an endorsement of the commercial acumen of the football authorities. Even from the viewpoint of 1990, and making due allowance for inflation, one would have to agree with Desmond White's

dismissal of them as 'ludicrously low'. According to a *Celtic View* article of 20 December 1972 the rates were as follows:

League Cup final	£75
League matches (2nd half)	£50
European Cup ties	£25

5 Joe McBride recalls a similar situation while preparing for the European Cup-tie against St Etienne at Parkhead in 1968. Stein made a point of talking with McBride on such a stroll; he asked McBride, in and out of the team after his knee operation in 1967, how he felt about playing, and the striker's response was: 'I'm bursting to play!' Stein chose McBride for the match that Celtic entered two goals down, and McBride played well, scoring the last, and decisive, goal in the 87th minute.

6 One would have thought that, because of Deans' goalscoring record he would have been an automatic choice. For interest, here is the complete record of Deans' appearances and goals against Hibernian during his Celtic career:

29 January 1972	League	Celtic 2, Hibs 1 (1 goal)
6 May 1972	Sc. Cup	Celtic 6, Hibs 1 (3)
23 December 1972	League	Celtic 1, Hibs 1
28 April 1973	League	Hibs 0, Celtic 3 (2)
20 October 1973	League	Celtic 1, Hibs 1 (substitute)
23 February 1974	League	Hibs 2, Celtic 4 (2)
19 October 1974	League	Celtic 5, Hibs 0 (3)
26 October 1974	League	Celtic 6, Hibs 3 (3)
22 February 1975	League	Hibs 2, Celtic I
25 January 1975	Sc. Cup	Hibs 0, Celtic 2 (1)
10 December 1975	League	Celtic 1, Hibs 1 (1)
20 December 1975	League	Hibs 1, Celtic 3 (1)
28 February 1976	League	Celtic 4, Hibs 0 (1)
21 April 1976	League	Hibs 2, Celtic 0

Thus, in 13 full matches against Hibernian, Dixie Deans scored 18 goals.

15

IT'S STILL THE SAME OLD STORY

MIDDLE MAN

'You,' I said, 'are the first I've met
That aren't sporting a gay rosette
To show which side'll win the Cup.
I do not hear you shouting, "Up!
Up the one, or up the other!"'

'No,' he replied, 'I wouldny bother:
For they're a couple, they're a pair,
An' which yin wins Ah dinny care!
Whichever fit they kick wi', mate
Ah'm telling you, baith teams is great!'

'Hooray!' said I as I patted his back
(Up with the standard of the play,
Up with the better team on the day):
'You have the quality most of us lack,
You see the game as a work of art,
You cheer the artists that take part:
For you, with vision connoisseury,
It isn't a contest, a rammy, a boory!'

'Naw,' he said, with a rueful grin,
'It's jist that Ah'm handicapped – colour-blin'!'

'Scoticus'
This poem appeared in the *Evening Times*, 26 April 1969, on the day
of the 'Old Firm' Scottish Cup final.

AT THE END of his performance in a Glasgow theatre in May, 1963 the
late Sammy Davis Jr. received an enthusiastic standing ovation from the

audience. Afterwards, at a press conference, the entertainer spoke eloquently and passionately about the Civil Rights campaign being waged in the American south. The reporters were attentive, responsive and sympathetic to his comments, nodding in agreement as Davis, black and Jewish, made his points.

Apparently, not one of the listeners deemed it ironic that, only a few miles from the theatre that same evening, Scotland's own form of apartheid had been put into effect, as usual, for a football match – the replay of the Scottish Cup final between Rangers and Celtic.

As the rival fans queued up for admission to their totally segregated ends of Hampden Park, one young mounted policeman, struggling to bring some order to the increasing congestion at the turnstiles at the Rangers end, shouted to the milling thousands that they might gain a quicker entry at the other end of the ground. The responses were predictably unprintable, and a

Only the winners smile after an Old Firm clash. Roy Aitken, George McCluskey and Murdo MacLeod celebrate their title-winning goals in 1979.

nearby reporter jested to a companion: 'I can't see that one ever becoming Chief Constable!'

For the past century, however, the frequent clashes of the Old Firm have been no laughing matter.

As early as 1894, only six years after the two clubs first met in an amicable fashion, *Scottish Sport* headlined its report of 25 September on the League match at Parkhead, won 5–3 by Celtic, as 'The Parkhead Passion Play'. The encounter was watched by 20,000 who had established a new record for gate-receipts of £500 for a Scottish League game. The intense rivalry between the Glasgow clubs was already evolving, spurred on by the formation of the Scottish League in 1890 and the inevitable legalisation of payment for players in 1893.

The editorial in the newspaper deplored 'an element of coarse ill-nature infused into the play, which was altogether reprehensible. It is surely very much below form to find two such prominent clubs, two of the leading clubs in the country – who have hitherto been on at least apparently good terms – all at once, and without any very insurmountable excuse, supplying the Philistines with food for effectual scoffing.'

The newspaper went on to note that Celtic were so desperate to win – and prevent Rangers from gaining their first ever League victory at Celtic Park – that the players 'trained last week for the first time this season'. The reporter was critical of the intimidating atmosphere in which the match was played: 'The very devil was in it, and one team was as bad as the other . . . not so much real roughness as there was temper and, unfortunately, the crowd roared a passionate chorus to it . . . The second half was begun with "a mothers' meeting" in the middle of the centre circle. Referee Baillie (St Bernard's, Edinburgh) got the whole 22 players together – not one was allowed to escape – and delivered to them a brief homily.'

As if to foreshadow a multitude of similar complaints by both clubs after these fixtures down through the years, it was reported that Rangers were most unhappy with the officiating, feeling that their offences were mainly retaliatory in nature. In an even more sombre vein the newspaper also noted that 'a member of the Lambhill Brake-Club, which sports light-blue colours, got his head seriously cut with a stone on the way from Parkhead on Saturday. There is definitely a danger in this fanatical partisanship with its driving to matches with unfurled flags, partisan cries etc.'

Scottish Sport's conclusion, since then so often repeated in the media – 'The continuance could be advantageously curtailed' – has been revealed as wishful thinking, since the nature of this rivalry between the clubs, the teams and the supporters is unparalleled in the world of sport; nearly a century later, in 1989, one writer deplored the atmosphere at Old Firm matches as 'a psychic wall of hatred so tangible that it bounces off the chest'.

Some might claim that the animosity existing between Barcelona and

Real Madrid in Spanish football is the closest analogy – a mutual loathing and distrust, a nationalism fostered in part by the legacy of the Civil War in which the Catalans fought hardest against Francoism.

Others would suggest that the on-going rivalry between the Toronto Maple Leafs and the Montreal Canadiens – an ice-hockey manifestation of the schism in Canadian society between English and French Canada – reveals similar passions and intensity. But, even when the two great hockey clubs used to meet as often as 14 times in a regular season, the rivalry never became as bitter, as vicious as in the Old Firm clashes.[1]

Only in Glasgow does the factional conflict take on the aspect of a *jihad* or 'holy war', imported in part from Ireland. Yet, Glasgow was not unique with respect to the socio-religious tensions arising from waves of Irish immigration which have generated, fuelled, and sustained the Old Firm strife.

Industrial Lancashire, too, absorbed a flood of ill-educated peasantry in the 19th century, driven from Ireland by a cruel combination of poverty and famine. With only raw muscle power to offer, they became the navvies, the dockers, the iron-workers, and unskilled labourers of Victorian Britain. Regarded by the English (and Scots) as semi-barbarians, the exiles' sense of alienation and injustice was vivid and enduring.

In Manchester and Liverpool the rivalry between the local teams was compounded by religious differences. Folk-memory has it that in the 1920s and 1930s the fans of Everton (believed to be 'the Catholic club') and those of Liverpool (believed to be 'the Protestant club') clashed at times in the streets outside Goodison and Anfield. As late as 1970 Michael Kennedy, a native Mancunian, asserted that the rival fans of City and United regarded each other 'with at the best, scorn, and, at the worst, bitter and bigoted hatred, because religion enters into it – United being the Catholics' team and City the rest.' (*Portrait of Manchester*) Religious troubles had broken out periodically on Merseyside in the first decade of the century, when Liverpool was a metropolis with a quasi-official policy of 'segregating people geographically along strictly religious lines'. For example, in 1909, it was claimed that more than 3,000 Catholics had been forced to vacate one district because of Protestant 'harassment'. Until the 1950s the city was still characterised by Catholic and Protestant districts but, fortunately, in the past three decades Liverpool has become determined to bury a sectarian legacy already being undermined in the post-war years by the twin strands of urban redevelopment and the remorseless tide of secularism. The momentum of social change has made it difficult for critics to attach religious labels to any of the clubs in Manchester and Liverpool today.

The frequent assertions of John Smith, when chairman of Liverpool, that the city is united by football and not divided by it, were underlined most graphically and poignantly by the intermingling of Everton and Liverpool supporters at their first derby match shortly after the Hillsborough tragedy in 1989. Later in the season the Merseyside rivals met again, this time in the FA Cup final at Wembley; fans from Liverpool, bonded more solidly together by tragedy, travelled south on the same trains and in the same compartments. On the same day in Glasgow, Rangers and Celtic faced each other in the Scottish Cup final; police had worked out the routes for supporters' buses to make sure that the fans could not get at each other.

And yet the exact same opportunity for some form of conciliation between the two sets of fans had arisen in the final of the Scottish Cup in May 1971, in the wake of a similar disaster at Ibrox Park when spectators were crushed to death at the conclusion of a match: 'sixty-six men and boys suffocated in the struggling hell of a jammed stairway at Ibrox Park on New Year's Day 1971 – 66 out of the 80,000 who had come to see the Old Firm do battle, mere martyrs to the old drama.' (Gordon Williams/Terry Venables: *They Used To Play On Grass*, 1973)

BLESSED MARGARET OF GRANTHAM?
Margaret Thatcher became Britain's first woman Prime Minister in May 1979. As she stood on the threshold of 10 Downing Street she solemnly intoned thoughts attributed to St Francis of Assisi: 'Where there is discord, may we bring harmony . . . Where there is despair, may we bring hope.'

Many people in Glasgow did make efforts to reach out and try to bridge the decades of misunderstanding and intolerance, but sadly, and perhaps inevitably, it was a moment missed. Within months the same old tension and hatred was manifesting itself at Rangers-Celtic matches. Indeed, the rival supporters in Glasgow, including many fans of both clubs whose behaviour is otherwise exemplary, seem to take some perverse satisfaction in the continuing situation as they shrug off the bigotry and bitterness that pervades every Old Firm meeting.

Terry Houston, the *Evening Times* (Glasgow) columnist, despaired of the communal hysteria which surrounded the transfer of ex-Celt Maurice Johnston to Rangers:

We in Scotland (and particularly the West) are a most monstrously bigoted society. We walk, at least in public, a daily tightrope of tolerance and it takes but little to dislodge us from our perch. The very fact that Johnston's signing is being given media coverage commensurate with a Royal wedding is shrill testimony to how great a grip bigotry has upon the country. Let's talk turkey here. Bigotry is not just the province of the uneducated, or the working class. It is just as prevalent within the supposedly better educated middle class, whether they be white collar workers or bosses. The 'bears' on the terracings of Parkhead and Ibrox simply express their views more candidly and forthrightly than the rest. The system of religious apartheid practised in education (and upheld by law) in this country has played, and continues to play, a large part in sustaining its existence. Society has bent the rules to accommodate it and contain its simmering presence within acceptable boundaries. Far from fomenting religious animosity, in my opinion, the Rangers-Celtic clashes probably act as a kind of sick, safety valve. If there were no Old Firm matches those tensions might erupt in more serious fashion elsewhere. By limiting it to a ritual which, every so often during the football season half paralyses the city and makes it a slightly less safe place to be in because of inflamed passions, the authorities can by and large cope with it.

(12 July 1989)

To illustrate the permanence of the division in Glasgow one might consider the visit of Curtis Sliwa, the self-styled 'Archangel' of the Guardian Angels which had originated in New York as a disciplined vigilante-group to combat crime on the subways. Hoping to set up similar anti-crime patrols in Glasgow, he was shocked, when he visited the city in March 1989, by the refusal of youths in the tough housing estates to join youngsters of a different religion in the patrols. 'The Protestant-Catholic issue is worse here than our black-white problem in the States,' he concluded.

Nobody should be fooled by the perfunctory interchange of pleasantries and platitudes between the officials and players of both clubs, a product of their symbiotic relationship. The politeness only serves to mask the deep-seated animosity that still festers, a tension that surfaces frequently enough to be identified as a recurring pattern of hatred.

One such manifestation of the mutual suspicion might well have spurred Celtic to the winning of their 31st championship. A sense of injustice can act as a powerful incentive, if channelled properly.

In late March 1979 Scottish football was emerging slowly from the ravages of a harsh winter which had played havoc with the fixture list. At that stage, for example, Celtic were three matches behind in their schedule, and were hopeful of catching up in the immediate future because the side had run into better form. Rangers, on the other hand, had been forced by bad weather to play a European Cup-tie at Ibrox against FC Cologne on Thursday 22 March, instead of the previous day.

On the Saturday Celtic and Rangers were due to meet in the League, and Rangers, chasing after another 'treble', could not have relished the prospect of such a demanding, important fixture only two days after a draining European match.

Because Ibrox was undergoing massive renovations, the Old Firm game was fixed for Hampden Park. On Friday, 23 March the referee inspected the pitch at 1 p.m. and pronounced it as 'playable'; shortly afterwards, however, Frank Campbell, the secretary of Queen's Park, announced that the Rangers-Celtic match would be postponed because the terracings remained 'snowbound and dangerous'.

Celtic were angered and suspicious, feeling that the decision to postpone the fixture had not been made solely by Queen's Park. Clearly, they chose to disbelieve the assertion made by Willie Waddell, Rangers' general manager, that 'the decision was Queen's Park's alone as the licence-holders of the ground; Rangers as the renters for the occasion had no say in the matter.'

Celtic's chairman, Desmond White, had visited Hampden Park four hours after the announcement that the match would be postponed, and discovered that the situation had improved with a change in the weather; he later informed Celtic supporters through the club newspaper that 'the warm sun had done the work of 50 to 100 men, and 90 per cent of the playing pitch was clear of snow. The Hampden approaches, stairways, and terracings were almost completely clear of snow, and the little that remained could have been eliminated by the spreading of salt.'

Furthermore, he had volunteered the services of a snow-removal squad to render the terracings totally safe within a few hours; the offer, however, was declined by Queen's Park. A grim-faced Desmond White concluded that 'if Rangers *had* wanted the match on, it would have gone on.' What must have irked White on a personal level was the fact that he had been a Queen's Park goalkeeper in the 1930s and, as Celtic's chairman, he was largely responsible for gifting the amateur club £10,000 in 1971 to help restore Hampden as 'the national stadium'.

The *Celtic View*, always quick to scent an element of injustice, raised the matter again:

> . . . and if Rangers had triumphed against Cologne on Thursday would not the necessary work have been done at the Queen's Park ground to ensure that the Old Firm game went ahead as scheduled? In failing to apply one fraction of the time and effort that was devoted to Ibrox Stadium last week, Rangers showed scant regard for the people who are supposed to be the lifeblood of football – the spectators. The swiftness with which they organised a Glasgow Cup-tie with Partick Thistle [at Ibrox on 24 March, the scheduled date for the Old Firm match] indicated that they wanted continuity of games – so, why not at Hampden?
>
> (28 March 1979)

In the same issue, the comments of George Delaney, an official of the Celtic Supporters Association, reflected the feelings of a delegates' meeting a few days before: '. . . the general opinion that it is time that every team had the same treatment, and [that] membership in secret societies has no place in sport.' He echoed the delegates' condemnation of 'this sort of action where one club can manipulate the running of the Scottish Football League to suit their own ends.'[2]

Reduced to its simplest terms, on the eve of a critical match, one that would have an important bearing on the outcome of the Championship, the situation was one in which both rivals wanted to derive the maximum advantage. Rangers would welcome some respite from their commitments in the major competitions, complicated and extended by lengthy runs in the European, Scottish, and League Cups as they were, and would not have relished the prospect of a dent to morale in the wake of an Old Firm defeat which followed so closely on an exit from the European Cup. Celtic, behind in their fixtures because of the weather, would have been jumping at the chance to play a Rangers side potentially demoralised after the loss to Cologne.

The suspicions of all connected with Celtic, an organisation often accused of collective paranoia, could not have been allayed had they read the *Rangers News*. In it, an article praised the Ibrox ground-staff for its 'army exercise' in clearing the pitch of snow in time to allow the European tie against Cologne to proceed. However, sharp eyes noted the following sentence: '. . . after the 90 minutes were up, the ground-staff had to get down to the task of clearing the stadium of tons of rubbish, and have it spick and span for Saturday's Glasgow Cup-tie [against Partick Thistle].'

It was, of course, not until the Friday afternoon – *the day after the Cologne match* – that the Old Firm fixture was postponed officially, and it could have been only at that stage Rangers might prepare and announce alternative plans. Waddell explained lamely that, with the weather putting the Celtic match in jeopardy, Rangers were 'thinking ahead' – an excuse that angry Celtic officials were unwilling to accept, dismissing it as laughable.

At that relatively late time in the season the Premier League had an unfamiliar look about it: Dundee United, emerging as legitimate if unlikely contenders, had led the table for months; Rangers, lurking in third place behind St Mirren but with games in hand of the top two, were favourites for the title; Celtic, five matches in arrears of Dundee United, languished in sixth place behind Aberdeen and Morton:

	Played	Points
Dundee United	25	31
St Mirren	24	29
Rangers	23	28
Aberdeen	24	24
Morton	25	24
Celtic	20	23

One month later, on 21 April, the situation had come into clearer focus. On that day Celtic had fought back to earn a hard-won point against Aberdeen at Pittodrie, and Rangers had triumphed 2–1 over Dundee United at Tannadice. The top of the table looked like this:

	Played	Points
Dundee United	32	41
Rangers	28	35
Celtic	28	34

On 28 April Dundee United's gallant challenge ended at Parkhead when second-half goals from Johnny Doyle and Andy Lynch (from the penalty spot) gave Celtic both points. Still, both United and Aberdeen had served clear notice that the breakthrough of the 'New Firm' could not be delayed much longer . . .

As always, Rangers would present the biggest barrier to Celtic's rising hopes of another title. In the previous season the Ibrox club under Jock Wallace had managed to gain the elusive 'treble' of the Championship, the Scottish Cup, and the League Cup. Having retained the League Cup, and having marched through to another Scottish Cup final against Hibernian, Rangers' expectations of completing another treble were high.

SNAKES ALIVE!

Peter Snyman, a South African, established a new world record in May 1979 by living in a glass cage with 24 deadly snakes, including adders and cobras, for a period of 36 days. He had prepared for his stay by training in yoga for the previous 18 months.

When the Old Firm match so contentiously postponed from 24 March was played finally at Hampden on 5 May, the result was anti-climactic; Rangers won 1–0 over an inept Celtic team. It was a highly satisfactory result for Rangers, giving them a vital one-point advantage over Celtic in the run-in for the Championship. Almost as important perhaps was the confident, emphatic manner in which their victory was gained, much more easily than the score suggested.

In the previous close season momentous changes had taken place at Parkhead and at Ibrox. The two men who, in their capacity as managers appeared to symbolise the clubs, had left; neither Jock Stein at Parkhead nor Jock Wallace at Ibrox would be in charge of their teams, both having departed controversially in the summer of 1978.

Supporters of both clubs were disturbed at the manner of their going. Stein had always stated that he felt a manager should not linger on after the age of 55, and after a disastrous last season at Celtic Park he was prepared to leave. The club offered him a new role as a member of the Board, but the offer was never taken up amid rumours of discord.

Relentlessly hard-driving and a disciplinarian, Wallace had guided Rangers to a highly commendable treble, all the more praiseworthy because his side was not a vintage Rangers. However, for reasons that have never been fully explained, he tendered his resignation and left to take over at Leicester.

Celtic had replaced Stein with Billy McNeill, and that appeared a logical and positive step, because he had gained valuable experience as manager of Aberdeen. Rangers, on the other hand, appointed John Greig as their new manager, and he was faced with the daunting prospect of having to manage the club instead of leading the team on the field.

John Greig deserved credit for his attempts to change Rangers' image as a 'rummle-'em-up' side. His outlook came as a surprise to many who considered Greig the player as the embodiment of Rangers' traditional dourness and determination. Thus, almost a decade before Graeme Souness' arrival at Ibrox, a Rangers' manager had realised the need to rid the club of its obsession with what one writer described as 'the big blooter, the big kick, the cavalry charges' if Rangers were to make any lasting impression in Europe. And how successful was Greig's insistence on the patient build-up from the back, and on the controlled soccer in midfield to which the Ibrox trademark of resilience could be allied!

It has become too easily forgotten how Rangers sent a shudder through the rest of Europe by eliminating two of the hottest favourites for the European Cup, Juventus and PSV Eindhoven, on their march to the 1979 quarter-finals. Such was Rangers' self-belief that they came from behind twice in Eindhoven (after a 0–0 draw at Ibrox) to win 3–2, although two of their players were less than 100 per cent fit. The winning goal came from the type of build up more readily associated with the Continentals: a quick break from defence with McLean astutely holding the ball long enough for Russell to sprint into an open space; Russell controlled McLean's cunningly weighted pass, before beating the advancing keeper with commendable coolness. The bemused Eindhoven coach, still in a state of shock, had to admit later that Rangers had been a revelation, 'because they played imaginative and stylish football, the likes of which I didn't expect from a British side'.

However, Rangers became arguably another casualty of the most severe winter in decades which put Scottish football in cold storage for most of January and February. One postponement after another, some felt, had taken the vital edge off an Ibrox squad that was in a state of euphoria before the New Year; their supporters had started to entertain realistic hopes that Rangers might be able to emulate Celtic's memorable sweep in 1967. The return leg of the quarter-final of the European Cup against Cologne had to be postponed from the Wednesday in the return, to allow the Ibrox pitch to be rendered playable. Rangers started that second leg down only 0–1 from the chilly Mungersdorfer Stadium where defensive heroics kept their

*Celtic manager Billy McNeill, player Andy Lynch and assistant manager
John Clark have cause for happiness.*

interest alive; on the Thursday Rangers played in their now customary disciplined fashion, but could not break down the German defence. Hugh Taylor noticed that Rangers played in 'a too-slow, too-dull method', and his verdict was that the Ibrox men 'failed at the vital time to find their form, their belief in themselves'.

And thus, despite all the prestige that the earlier accomplishments had brought Scotland, the new-look Rangers were suddenly reduced to the task of defending the previous season's treble won by an industrious, undistinguished side. The struggle would be magnified by the pile-up in fixtures that beset the club as a result of the weather and of its successful involvement in four major competitions (the European Cup, the League Cup, the Scottish Cup, and the Championship).

Nine days after their exit from Europe Rangers regrouped to win a postponed League Cup final with a goal scored in a prolonged injury-time period after Aberdeen's Doug Rougvie had been ordered off in controversial circumstances.

Time was not on Rangers' side in the Scottish Cup, however, as Hibernian pushed them into a third match in a final that would evolve into a monumental bore.

THE LIFE OF BRIAN

Trevor Francis, the Birmingham City striker, became Britain's £1 million footballer when he joined Nottingham Forest in February 1979. His new manager, the inimitable Brian Clough, soon had his new signing brewing the tea and sweeping out the dressing-rooms at the City Ground! The investment had an early pay-off when Francis' goal against Malmo won the European Cup for Forest. Clough was an admirer of Jock Stein whom he described as 'the manager of the century'; Stein praised the Forest manager for his football 'cleanliness, clear thinking, and 11-man collectivism'.

Rangers had to be concerned about the pressure that Celtic continued to exert in a bid for the Championship. While the Ibrox men had struggled at the start of the season to come to grips with the new style laid down by the manager, Celtic and Dundee United made the early running. Later Rangers adjusted and enjoyed a strong middle period, as Celtic faltered, but such were the fluctuations in the Premier League that even in February only five points had separated the top eight clubs.

At the beginning of March the title seemed wide open, but after Celtic's victory over Dundee United at Parkhead, the race for the Championship had resolved into the perennial struggle between Rangers and Celtic. The outcome of the two upcoming clashes between the Old Firm was considered the crucial factor in deciding the Championship. Rangers' victory in the first of those matches on 5 May was so comprehensive, despite the narrow score-line, that the sportswriters' acceptance of them as champions-elect seemed incontestable.

However, Celtic's manager, Billy McNeill, both as player and observer of his illustrious predecessor, Jock Stein, knew better than most the pressures that can build up on a side hoping to win everything. And, unlike his rival, John Greig, he did have managerial experience; after a short spell with Clyde, he had been invited to become Aberdeen's manager in 1977, subsequently coming tantalisingly close to the Scottish League and Scottish Cup 'double' in the following season before the siren call to Parkhead.

Though McNeill and Greig had been appointed to their respective Old Firm managerial posts at virtually the same time, the latter had taken over a battle-hardened side which had won the 'treble' in his last season as captain. McNeill was faced with the task of rebuilding Celtic after the debacle of Stein's last season in charge. McNeill was depressed initially by the legacy of mediocrity that tarnished the end of Jock Stein's reign. He set out to rebuild the side, both in personnel and mental attitude. He bought astutely: winger Davie Provan came from Kilmarnock and midfielder Murdo MacLeod from Dumbarton. He attempted to motivate the players with, on his own admission, 'badgering and hammering', until eventually Celtic started to emerge as unexpected title-contenders. After winning only seven out of 18 matches in the first half of the League season, Celtic had emerged from their enforced winter-break looking fresh and eager, boosted by a trip to Portugal where the manager detected signs of a resurrection of that 'togetherness' and 'family atmosphere' which had underpinned Celtic's long run of success.

After the Hampden loss to Rangers that appeared to have settled the Championship, Celtic managed to produce three consecutive victories within seven days. Although the wins were unconvincing in execution, no one could question Celtic's stamina and fitness at a crucial stage in the season. McNeill had restored character and fighting spirit, as witnessed by those results: at Firhill after giving up a goal in only three minutes Celtic fought back to eke out a 2–1 win at Ibrox against St Mirren a strong second-half performance assured a 2–0 victory and against Hearts at Park-head a single goal by Conroy, again in the second half, was enough for both points.

Thirteen victories in 17 League matches in the second half of the season had brought Celtic to the brink of the Championship, and the stage was set for a thrilling finale to the club's season with the Old Firm clash at Celtic Park in a fixture postponed from 6 January. Celtic's revival would be tested in the most trying of circumstances because Celtic had to win in order to gain the League flag; Rangers, with games in hand, could afford to give up one point in a drawn match.

Roy Aitken (hidden by goalkeeper McCloy) revives Celtic's hopes.

SCOTTISH PREMIER LEAGUE
CHAMPIONSHIP
21 May 1979
Celtic Park

CELTIC 4	**RANGERS 2**
Latchford	McCloy
McGrain	Jardine
Lynch	Dawson
Aitken	Johnstone
McAdam	Jackson
Edvaldsson	A. MacDonald
Provan	McLean (Miller)
Conroy (Lennox)	Russell
McCluskey	Parlane
MacLeod	Smith
Doyle	Cooper

Scorers:

Aitken (67)	MacDonald (9)
McCluskey (75)	Russell (76)
Jackson o.g. (83)	
MacLeod (90)	

Referee: E. Pringle (Edinburgh)

Attendance: 52,000

The atmosphere was crackling with tension, broken by the roar of welcome for the teams' entry on to the field. Later, the attendance was given as a shade more than 52,000, but the terracings appeared packed, and the din from both ends of the ground was frightening in its intensity . . . and within seconds of the kick-off it became clear that the match would develop into one in which players would gain standing ovations for winning throw-ins.

Rangers, in the more favoured position, immediately tried to impose order on the match, but their early attempts to pass the ball back and forth were hampered by Celtic's harrying and chasing.

Celtic soon assumed control and the Ibrox defence had to be alert and organised; Celtic's first attacks broke on a solid back four, and the match settled into a cut-and-thrust affair. Skill, allied to speed and power, marked the first ten minutes. However, Rangers opened the scoring with a simple goal in nine minutes, in their first real raid. They broke from midfield, finding Davie Cooper free on the left; Cooper, a relative youngster but a skilled ball-player, dribbled neatly round two Celtic defenders before crossing for Alex MacDonald to hit past Latchford. This was a body-blow to Celtic's hopes, as they had needed the stimulus of the first goal. The

Rangers end celebrated at length, willing their side to hold on to that lead, and for a few minutes it seemed that the Ibrox men had settled down to their fine form of mid-season as they slotted back into well-drilled defence and used the ball intelligently and confidently.

Skill . . . control . . . method: managers can preach and coach their players *ad infinitum* but, in the pressure-cooker of an Old Firm match, nerves take over sooner or later. Celtic stormed into attack, and dominated play until the interval, but could not break down Rangers' defensive barrier. Roy Aitken came closest with a powerful header that crashed against the junction of bar and post with Rangers' giant keeper, Peter McCloy, hopelessly beaten.

At half-time the terracings were still buzzing with the excitement of a fast-paced 45 minutes of non-stop football. Rangers surely considered themselves in a strong position, needing a draw and holding a one-goal lead. In retrospect that apparent advantage may not have been in their best interests. From the restart Rangers appeared more concerned with containment; in an Old Firm match, giving your opponents the high ground can be dangerous.

Only ten minutes into the second half, with Celtic exerting frenzied pressure on Rangers' goal, came a dramatic moment. Alex MacDonald was fouled and lay on the ground; Celtic's Doyle, apparently incensed at what he considered play-acting, aimed a kick at the prone figure; the referee, Mr Pringle from Edinburgh, promptly sent him off amid contrasting reactions from both ends of the ground. Johnny Doyle, a most popular Celt, downcast and distraught, had to leave the battlefield with his side already a goal down; little did he know that his sending-off would turn the match around, and ensure his place in Parkhead mythology.

The reporters in the press box sat back momentarily; surely Celtic, after this second blow, would have to settle for second best. The great danger now would be an outbreak of fouling, petty or otherwise, with personal scores being settled.

That was not what happened . . .

Celtic continued to storm into attack despite the handicap and two players dominated. Murdo MacLeod, a terrier in midfield who seemed to win every ball, harried and forced opponents into mistakes; a young Roy Aitken covered every inch of Parkhead, as he made dangerous forays down the wing or brave dashes through the middle.

Young Roy Aitken. Throughout the first half he had played well in an attacking midfield role; now he had become an elemental force. Challenging for every ball, storming up the wing, or urging on his older colleagues, he imposed himself upon the most physical, most stressful, most demanding of football matches. If Aitken had never kicked another ball for the club, his display that night guaranteed him a Celtic immortality.

Essentially the motivation of the men in the hoops was a team one, a pride in the jersey. The defence was solid, requiring little help from the midfield; Tom McAdam, a vastly under-rated central defender, and the Icelandic international, Johannes Edvaldsson, had bottled up Rangers' strike force of Gordon Smith and Derek Parlane from the kick-off. Danny McGrain and Andy Lynch were able to attack down the wings and put greater pressure on a Rangers defence that had coped – if barely – with everything thrown at it so far.

The roar from the Celtic fans was frightening in its intensity, acting as a spur to the short-handed Celtic side; on the field, it appeared as if Celtic had the advantage of an extra player as the men in green and white reached for an extra effort. The equaliser came in 67 minutes, turned into the net after a goalmouth scramble in which the ball broke to Aitken conveniently placed in front of goal. The exultation on the terracings defied description, but a draw was of no use to Celtic, and the onslaught continued amid bedlam in the ground.

With 15 minutes left to play Celtic took the lead, after Aitken's fierce drive had been blocked only by a desperate intervention; the ball broke to George McCluskey, who hooked the ball superbly into the net past McCloy. Even as the Celtic fans were celebrating, Rangers managed to get a grip on their feelings, and to their immense credit forced themselves back into the match.

Celtic massed into defence to deal with the threat, and gave up a corner which was taken by Cooper. The ball found its way to Bobby Russell, and the Rangers midfielder gathered the ball, manouevred to gain position, and finally shot for goal. His raging shot threaded a path through a crowd of players to find the net, and Rangers were back in the match, after having contributed so little to it, apart from courage and desperate defence. The Celtic supporters were thunderstruck by the goal, scarcely a sound from their terracing and the 'Jungle'; gloomy voices muttered darkly of 'another moral victory'.

Celtic attacked yet again, and another fine header from Roy Aitken was saved splendidly by McCloy, to the relieved cheers of the Ibrox supporters. The desperate roars from the Celtic fans resumed in full voice, and the bombardment of Rangers' goal was taken up once more, and Rangers lived dangerously yet again. With only seven minutes to play, Celtic took the lead for the second time, and it was a tragedy for Colin Jackson, a defensive hero for Rangers throughout the match. McCluskey was revelling in the atmosphere, and his clever play had disrupted Rangers' defenders repeatedly; he crossed from the right, and McCloy did well to block the spinning ball, but the ball rebounded awkwardly against the luckless Jackson and from him into the net, chased there by Roy Aitken.

By now, as the titanic contest entered the closing minutes, pandemonium was reigning in every corner of the ground. Astonishingly, Celtic continued to press forward. The men on the Celtic bench – Billy McNeill, his assistant

John Clark, and trainer Neil Mochan, all removed a little from the drama – shouted and screamed at the team on the pitch to control the play, imploring it to slow things down, to waste time. But their words went unheard, or ignored, in the turmoil.

Rangers, outplayed and outfought, could not summon up any reserves of stamina to mount another challenge; Celtic, ten-man Celtic, in the most draining of all matches, continued to attack in wave after wave. In the last minute Murdo MacLeod, an energetic youngster like Aitken who had covered every blade of grass on the pitch, broke through from midfield; he was beseeched by colleagues, by fans, and by his mentors on the bench to kick the ball anywhere out of touch in order to use up the last precious seconds. MacLeod, however, bored on with only one idea in mind; from almost 20 yards he drove a tremendous ball into the net, high up at the 'postage stamp' corner.

Would you believe it? Andy Lynch and Murdo MacLeod can.

Seconds later the whistle went to signal the end of the match, but it almost went unheard amid scenes and a din unmatched since the great nights in Europe a decade earlier. Players flopped to the turf, utterly drained in defeat and in joy; some tottered towards opponents to mumble congratulations or consolation. One Celtic player has described any Old Firm clash after which players could trot off the field as a failure: 'You shouldn't be able to raise another gallop; you should just have enough strength to crawl off.'

This was one of those nights.

Within a few minutes, youth and spirit revived, the Celtic players, a happy, exuberant group shouting and singing with joy went over to salute their fans – bounding with delight, and struggling to come to terms with the magnitude of their achievement.

Another victory over Rangers, but one gained with only ten men in the final 35 minutes; a triumph against all the odds in coming back to score four goals when short-handed. A night of passion, and pride, a triumph for inspiration. A night in which Celtic won the Championship, out of reach for so many months. A night to celebrate.[3]

Even Hugh Taylor, whose sympathies more often lay with Rangers, was carried away by the emotion of the occasion when reviewing it:

> The game will be talked about, relived for all time, for it was the most legendary Old Firm match of all . . . but statistics alone will never be able to tell the tale of 90 minutes of football, passion and courage, the likes of which none of the crowd, so hoarse at the end, had ever seen . . . For Celtic came off the ropes not once, not twice, but three times . . . The endless courage, dynamic determination, and resolute reserves of stamina were displayed in glorious technicolour. No words can convey the colour, the drama, the triumph and tragedy of the match . . . But it was probably the best match, in terms of excitement, of the century.
>
> (Hugh Taylor: *Scottish Football Annual*, 1979)

Of all time, many Celtic fans claim . . .

POSTSCRIPT

The Govan Brighton [Street] Celtic Supporters' Club was travelling back to Govan, still celebrating noisily, when the members realised that the Rangers team bus was directly in front of them. Approaching the roundabout close to Ibrox Stadium, the Rangers party became aware that they were being followed; they must have suspected an ulterior motive because their bus deliberately circled the roundabout twice in order to elude their 'pursuers'. 'We just waved to them and went off on our own lap of honour,' recalls one member of the supporters' club committee.

It was an apt metaphor for the runaround the Light Blues had been given in the last 30 minutes of the match.

* * *

Billy McNeill would describe the match later as 'a fairy tale', but for John

Greig it heralded grimmer days ahead. The Ibrox manager's policy of playing skilled, controlled football was a bold and imaginative step; it was highly successful that season, bringing Rangers the League Cup and the Scottish Cup, besides a second-place finish in the Championship, and an excellent run in the European Cup. Perhaps it was not enough for Ibrox ambitions, because Greig struggled from then on, so much so that it would take eight years for Rangers to land the Championship, by which time Greig had departed. The turning-point in the match – the moment when Johnny Doyle was ordered off – blighted John Greig's career as a manager, because his Rangers were destined to play second fiddle to a rejuvenated Celtic, and to the emerging Aberdeen and Dundee United, for the better part of a decade.

*　　*　　*

An STV 'strike' meant disappointment to the thousands of Celtic fans thus deprived of television highlights of the League decider at Parkhead. The supporters had left Parkhead eventually, delirious with delight and heading for the nearest pub with a television set.

DIVIDED THEY FALL

The result of the referendum in March 1979, called to determine the question of Scottish devolution, effectively killed the idea for a decade. In the voting for establishing a mini-parliament in Edinburgh 33 per cent voted in favour of an assembly, 31 per cent against, and 36 per cent did not vote. The proposal thus failed to meet the 40 per cent eligibility test established by the British Parliament.

Footnotes

1 Hockey has such a mystic hold on the Canadian psyche that it transcends nationalism. Les Canadiens have always been an entertaining, colourful team and they have fans in every English-speaking part of the country, where they are frequently referred to as 'the Flying Frenchmen'. The Maple Leafs, a less flamboyant club, have only a limited appeal in Quebec.

2 The condemnations were not entirely fair. Queen's Park would have been liable for any injuries on the terracing attributable to the underfoot conditions.

3 Murdo MacLeod, the scorer of the last goal, went on to be a most popular player at Parkhead; later, after his transfer to Borussia Dortmund, he returned to play against Celtic in the UEFA Cup in 1987. He was greeted with waves of generous applause.

16

CHAMPAGNE CHARLIE

CHAMPAGNE CHARLIE

For Champagne Charlie is my name,
Champagne Charlie is my game,
Good for any game at night, my boys,
Good for any game at night, my boys.

For Champagne Charlie is my game,
Good for any game at night, my boys,
Who'll come and join me in a spree?

George Leybourne

(This is an extract from a Victorian music-hall song.[1])

CHARLIE NICHOLAS can still do it! Now in his late 20s, Nicholas can produce flashes of skill that take the breath away. Examine these matches he played recently in an Aberdeen jersey; four quite different moments stick in the mind, to be replayed in conversations and in the memory.

September 1989: In a torridly-contested Aberdeen-Celtic League match at Pittodrie the marking was close, the tackling keen. Nicholas picked up a pass just over the halfway line, controlled it deftly, gaining an extra split-second. Then he flighted a long pass, at least 40 yards in length, curving the ball gracefully past Celtic defender Chris Morris for Aberdeen's left back, embarking on an overlap, to take in his stride. A moment of greatness, the sum of a few seconds' activity, but beyond the capability of most players.

October 1989: At Hampden Park in the Skol League Cup final Rangers' defence, hard as always, presented resolute opposition for any forward within the box. In a packed goalmouth, Nicholas found himself with his back to Rangers' goal, and being challenged vigorously. He continued to shield the ball, attracting more defenders towards him; at the last possible second – just when it appeared he might be playing for a penalty – he

Charlie Nicholas in action, 1982.

prodded the ball back to Mason, who cracked it past Chris Woods for the winning goal. The ability to create a chance for others, a sense of vision even in the changing kaleidoscope of the six-yard box . . .

December 1989: In a Premier League match against Hearts at Pittodrie Nicholas gathered a loose ball on the edge of the box, and headed left to avoid the congestion of the middle. The ball was bouncing awkwardly, and the Hearts' defenders held back, expecting that Nicholas would lose control. The Aberdeen striker, using those moments to tame the ball and create space in the area, moved on; casually, he swerved past one defender, and as the others belatedly converged upon him he swept the ball past Henry Smith to find the net low at the post . . . That talent for decisive, unhurried action, the confidence to act on his own . . .

February 1990: Another Aberdeen-Celtic match was evolving into a keenly contested affair. Bobby Mimms, Aberdeen's English keeper, looked downfield and decided to clear with a long ball; his kick cleared the half-way line by 20 yards, and was headed on by Gillhaus. The ball, deflected towards Nicholas, still had not touched the ground . . . and the striker volleyed it in mid-air from the edge of the penalty area past a helpless Pat Bonner. The gift for the totally unexpected . . .

Yes, Charlie Nicholas can still produce . . . and one should not be too surprised.

Although he is still not a veteran in chronological terms, most followers of football are united in considering that the best days of his career are behind him. Some insist, in an Irish expression, that 'his best days were never played at all'. These are the people who feel passionately that the young Nicholas should never have been allowed to leave Celtic Park in 1983, that Nicholas represented the sort of player around whom teams are built, and that a player who wanted to play for Celtic should have continued to do so. These people see his move to Arsenal – and London – not so much as a betrayal but as a personal tragedy for the most gifted young player of his time.

His subsequent return to Aberdeen came as a surprise, and some detected the hints that a career, once so promising, was winding down; Nicholas has proved them wrong, and his performances – or, more accurately, in the tradition of strikers, his moments – are etched in the collective memory.

That haunting refrain from the Corries' 'Flower of Scotland'– 'When will we see your like again?' – sums up the sense of loss that many feel in assessing the career of Charlie Nicholas. It also serves as an epitaph of sorts for the great nights of European football at Celtic Park in the late 1960s, when Celtic could take on the most illustrious names in football and consistently triumph.

It is no mere exercise in nostalgia to assert that only rarely in the past two decades has the atmosphere for the European ties at Parkhead been marked by that tingle of pleasurable anticipation that characterised such events in more halcyon days. How can a younger generation of Celtic supporters, accustomed to years of indifferent performances and to a sense of forboding about home European ties, ever realise the might and majesty, the fear and pride that Celtic generated when Jock Stein was in his managerial prime?

Who can ever forget the impatient counting-down of the weeks, days, and then hours – starting with the announcement of the draw and culminating at the moment of kick-off at Celtic Park? The collective ritual of the Sunday morning ticket sales, with massive queues snaking out of the Kerrydale Street concourse in front of the stand and down into the main thoroughfare of London Road . . . match-night itself, when the floodlights – dominating the skyline of the East End like cathedral steeples – drew the faithful in their thousands, glowing like beacons for the multitudes wending their way to Parkhead . . . the bedlam of cheerful, excited chatter, interspersed with speculation, the outpourings of song – patriotic, sentimental, nationalistic, doggerel – as the most enthusiastic support in the world ran through the most extensive choral repertoire in football . . . the increasingly frequent glances at watches as the minutes ticked away, until a full-throated roar from 'The Jungle', opposite the players' tunnel, heralded the emergence of the ball-boys and the match-officials, all followed by the sight of both teams taking the field side-by-side to an eruption of noise and acclaim from every side of the vast arena?

*Tommy Gemmell's penalty sparks the revival against St Etienne at
Parkhead in 1968.*

In 1968 a skilled St Etienne team found the atmosphere, and a fired-up
Celtic side, all too much for them; their captain's impressions of the frenzy
that greeted the French visitors remained vividly in his memory when he
wrote his autobiography 15 years later. Robert Herbin was still bewildered:
'A fanatical support, tanked up with beer, behaved like the Ancient Roman
spectators in the arena, looking for a fight to the death. They sang, roared,
jumped up and down, and hurled abuse. It was most intimidating.' As in
Roman times, the lions usually won.

The above excerpt suggests that nobody could ever confuse the people
on the terracings at Parkhead with those found in the members' enclosure at
Ascot, but the passion and self-belief that motivated the Celtic side and
enveloped the Celtic following drove the club to heights never before
dreamed of.

None of the great teams in Europe relished a trip to Celtic Park.

The visit of Liverpool in April 1966, as representatives of a vibrant city
which gloried in the fame and success of its pop-groups and the deeds of
the football team that Shankly built, caused a mammoth road-jam, the result
of a huge build-up in London Road and the Gallowgate as thousands,
walking to the match and encroaching on the roads, slowed traffic to a
crawl. Once inside the ground, the crowd of 80,000, mostly wedged into the
terracings, had to endure the frustrations of a series of missed chances as
Celtic carved out openings against the champions-elect of England. Liver-

pool paid Celtic the ultimate compliment by 'stringing a red-shirted barrier of muscle' across the park and trying to hold on for a draw; their defence was breached only once, in the 50th minute, when Bobby Murdoch hooked the ball back from the bye-line into the path of Chalmers, who back-heeled the ball cheekily for the speedy Lennox to sweep past Lawrence.[2]

Celtic's European reputation was only burgeoning then, and the power of Liverpool, allied to some good fortune, prevailed in the return leg, but in the following season Celtic reached the pinnacle of club football by winning the European Cup – after their nerve held in the most dramatic night ever seen at Parkhead. The epic quarter-final against Vojvodina was decided only by Billy McNeill's storybook header *47* seconds from time. After 'tidal wave of joy' swept around and around the stadium, after the post-match acclamation from the terracings, the fans – 70,000 of them – finally went off into the night still delirious with excitement and relief.

By the time Celtic met Vojvodina's compatriots, Red Star Belgrade, two seasons later, the Scottish side had become a mature and highly professional outfit, one which forced the Yugoslav newspaper *Sport* to describe Celtic's 5–1 demolition of Red Star at Parkhead as the work of 'a truly great side – in a different class'. In that match a technically proficient side of excellent ball-players, 'method men' expert at fast switches from defence to attack, had Celtic struggling for spells in the first half; but Jimmy Johnstone, in one of those moods where he could beat half a team in one run, destroyed the visitors in the second half, encouraged and fed by a conveyor-belt of superb passes from the incomparable Bobby Murdoch, so often a star on the European nights. It was reported from the Yugoslav capital that the city was in mourning: 'Groups of people could be seen reading the papers in the streets; they looked shocked and some of them refused to believe that the scoreline was right.'

Celtic's name rang around Europe more and more after such exhilarating nights, and even a defeat – virtually unthinkable – was to become invested by the conquerors with a status worthy of ultimate victory in the competition.

When AC Milan punished one error by Celtic's defence in ruthlessly clinical fashion at Parkhead, and held on to win by that single goal in March 1969 to qualify for the Champions' Cup semi-final, their supporters back home celebrated wildly, 'touring the city in cars with horns blowing full blast; the cheering, toasting and flag-waving went on until the small hours.' After a tie previewed as 'the final before the final', *Il Giorno* described the win simply as 'a miracle', while *La Stampa* recalled that 'no one had believed in a victory'. With a fine sense of irony the *Corriere dello Sport* hailed the victors as 'the Milan Lions', and their manager admitted cheerfully that he had been anticipating a 0–4 thrashing.

The excitement, the sheer glamour, of those occasions so eclipsed the events in the domestic season that, even after Celtic had pushed aside the disappointment of the AC Milan reverse to win the 'treble' in Scotland, it could not compensate fully for the aching void felt by the supporters. They felt that the failure to reach – and win – another European Cup final meant 'a bad season' for the club! Perhaps the expectations raised were unrealistic, but the prestige conferred on Celtic – and, by extension, on their followers – justified amply the emotional roller-coaster of European competition; undeniable, too, was the psychological boost to be derived from competing successfully at the highest level in club football.

Jock Stein was totally aware of the contribution made by the supporters on the nights of those triumphs, frequently referring to the thousands on the terracing as 'Celtic's 12th man'. After one match he put it all into perspective: 'They were singing here at six o'clock and they are still singing outside. I like to think that these people who roared us on to the last will waken up that bit happier tomorrow before they go to work.'

It was just like that. Almost 80,000 thought that life might not be so bad after all on a morning after Celtic had notched up a stunning 3–0 victory over one of the legendary names in the tournament, five-times finalists Benfica, led by 'the Black Panther', Eusebio, the scorer of 37 goals in 38 European Cup matches.

David Lacey, the estimable correspondent of the *Guardian*, recalled the dramatic opening at Celtic Park in November 1969: 'For an hour before the start Paradise had echoed to its songs of praise, and the main talking-point of the day was the future of Tommy Gemmell, who had been off form and was not seeing eye-to-eye with the club. Within two minutes of the start Celtic were awarded a free kick a yard from the penalty area. Auld and two colleagues stood over the ball like Macbeth's witches; a tap sideways, a firmer, longer square pass and there was Gemmell thundering in on the opposite side to score with a glorious shot into the top far corner. [Someone in the press box timed it at 76 seconds!] Gemmell raced 80 yards back up the touchline, saluting the ecstatic crowd. In one delicious moment all his problems had been solved . . . or so it seemed at the time.'

The whole 90 minutes were played at such a fever-pitch of excitement, sustained by a barrage of cheering and singing, that the concentration of even such an experienced official as Italy's Lo Bello lapsed; the referee disallowed a goal for a 'foul' on a Benfica defender by a Celtic forward whom he was unable to identify at the post-match press conference.

The devilment and wizardry of Bertie Auld, restored to the side for the occasion after a lengthy absence through injury, conjured up a memorable Parkhead finale to the greatest epoch in Celtic's history. Against Fiorentina, the Italian champions, he bamboozled his opponents in a breathtaking display of leadership: on the half hour he struck a low, crisp 20-yarder through the defensive wall with power, accuracy and such confidence that he was holding up his hand in triumph before the ball had crossed the line; only five minutes after the interval his cunning cross had an Italian defender so disorientated that he nudged the ball past his own keeper; and in the very last minute Auld put a personal seal on a magnificent individual (and team) performance by crossing with pin-point accuracy for Hood to head back across goal where Wallace was lurking to nod home.

On that bitterly cold night in March 1970 a capacity crowd of 80,000 had relished the opportunity to bask in the reflected glory of another famous victory. In the view of John Rafferty, the correspondent for the *Scotsman*, they were making a fetish of their support: 'Every pass from Bertie Auld was received rapturously, every overlap of Tommy Gemmell and David Hay cheered as if it were the finish of the Derby.' There have been few, if any, cases of a top Italian club being scared of meeting a British side before a ball was kicked, but the reputation of Celtic and their fanatical support had affected the Fiorentina party to an extent which could not be hidden from both the Italian and the Scottish press. The Fiorentina coach, Bruno Pesaola, had seen his pre-match fear of 'the Glasgow inferno' justified, while La *Gazzetta dello Sport* was in awe of the Scottish side's 'cyclonic fury' and the *Corriere della Sera* marvelled at the 'Celtic dynamo [which] swept aside . . . Fiorentina's attempt to get Celtic caught up in a midfield spider's web'.

So accustomed had Celtic supporters become to such performances that it took Jock Stein to place the magnitude of the latest triumph into perspective by observing that, despite the massive resources of the Italians, a Scottish side had humiliated them. After speaking of the Italians' 'million-lire transfer-fees, their £60,000 a year coaches, and a football fanaticism which is almost a religion'. Stein added, 'It was not just a good night for Celtic, it was a wonderful advert for our football.' The controlled football of Celtic in the return leg earned them another piece of history – the first British side to oust an Italian one on aggregate from the Champions Cup.

Ironically, it was one of those expensive coaches, the most famous of them all, and Jock Stein's adversary at Lisbon, Helenio Herrera, who foreshadowed Celtic's decline in Europe even at the very height of their ambition to regain the Champions Cup, at a time when their stature in world football was never higher. On the morning of Celtic's spectacular triumph over Leeds United at Hampden Park in 1970, Herrera, then with AS Roma, interjected a cautionary note, based on an extensive dossier on the Continent's top sides: 'Watch out for Feyenoord . . .'

That sad night in Milan marked a true watershed in Celtic's history – and in Stein's career. The defeat by Feyenoord had been so numbing, so unexpected that the nightmare haunted a Celtic fan who had followed them all over Europe; several times on the early-morning train back to his lakeside hotel he woke up shivering: 'Each time San Siro seemed only a bad dream, then the harsh reality took over.'

Jock Stein tried to put a brave face on it all by asserting that 'If we can take the victories, we must also take the defeats – and there is always tomorrow.'

However, in the 1970s Celtic never did get over the trauma of Milan. The panache and flair, the thrust and conviction, which had been their hallmark in the preceding five seasons was to be displayed only spasmodically. Celtic, who had jousted gloriously with giants, now fought grimly with pygmies.

After watching their ineffectual attempts to pierce the defence of the amateurs of Rosenborg Trondheim in September 1972, one writer had to comment: 'This wasn't the intelligent, explosive Celtic of European Cup legend . . . a desperate, frustrated Celtic.'

BANNER HEADLINES?

Seen at the World Cup finals held in Spain, 1982 printed out on placards:

'COMMUNISM Vs ALCOHOLISM.' At the USSR–Scotland match at Malaga.

'DON'T WORRY, LADS. ALLY MACLEOD'S IN BLACK-POOL!' At the Brazil–Scotland match in Seville.

A year later another writer was dismayed at Celtic's lack of sophistication as they failed to score at Parkhead against Vejle, dismissed as a team of schoolteachers, but one which earned the accolade of 'a gallant band of amateurs.' The Jutlanders refused to be drawn into a slogging match with Celtic, whose main tactic was to try to run their opponents off their feet.

Admittedly, Celtic reached the semi-final of the European Cup in 1972 and 1974, but only by the good fortune of the draw – in which they consistently avoided the big guns. This factor tended to conceal for a while the club's shortcomings at the highest level, most notably the tactical failure of excessive caution abroad when the new realities of European competition underlined the value of an away goal – a lesson learned by Rangers *en route* to their Cup-Winners' Cup triumph in 1972 in Barcelona. Significantly, Celtic failed to score in all four semi-final ties of the European Cup in 1972 and 1974 – although Atletico Madrid's cynical savagery at Parkhead might be offered in partial mitigation in one instance.

The predictability in Celtic's style was exploited by Olympiakos of Greece to the full at Parkhead in 1974 when they took the sting out of the home team's 'hash-bash, 100 mile-per-hour stuff' by absorbing all Celtic's guileless pressure – and then set Celtic a hopeless task in Athens by scoring on the break.

When Desmond White, the club's chairman, had asserted in 1971 that Celtic's goal was to repeat the triumph of Lisbon, many hoped it was true; his statements took on an increasingly hollow ring as it became clear that the club was set on retrenchment rather than advancement throughout the later 1970s. Celtic, it appeared, would be content to do well in Scotland, and did not want to be measured against the elite of Europe.

Inevitably under such circumstances, players such as David Hay and Kenny Dalglish, the young men who should have formed the nucleus of another top-class side, were allowed to depart. Even more disquietingly, as David Lacey of the *Guardian* observed, '. . . [it was] sad to see Celtic signing Fulham reserves so soon after selling Dalglish to Liverpool.'[3]

Although the writing had been on the wall for some time, it took the transfer of Dalglish to signal the extent of the drain in quality; a mere three months later, while Liverpool were advancing into the next round, all Celtic's shortcomings were being exposed in Salzburg by SWW Innsbruck on a night that Jock Stein described as his worst experience as Celtic's manager. Allan Herron's column was headlined: 'Now Nobody Fears Celtic' and he went on to say that 'the way they gave the ball away during the first 45 minutes [when three goals were conceded] was nothing short of criminal.' (*Sunday Mail*: 6 November 1977)

Jock Stein, disillusioned by it all – and already perceived by some at Parkhead as a spent force after a recent brush with mortality – brooded that 'it's going to be a long way back form this'.

Who could have thought that in the following season – little more than a decade after the greatest moment in the club's history – Celtic would be taking part, with little distinction, in a competition strictly for the selling-platers' after failing to qualify for Europe? Surely the Anglo-Scottish Cup was no place for Celtic!

Some degree of respectability was salvaged in a run to the quarter-final of the European Cup in 1980, but the horrendous struggle to get past the totally under-rated Irishmen from Dundalk *en route* was forgotten conveniently. To date (1990) that remains the last occasion in which the once-proud Celtic have reached the last eight in any European competition . . .

. . . And yet, in the autumn of 1982, with the memory of Lisbon fast receding and youngsters wondering if they had been brought up on a fairy-tale, the vision was revived.

All the dreams were suddenly within the realm of possibility as the supporters rejoiced in the appearance of a new star. The exciting skills and personality of 20-year-old Charlie Nicholas were instantly recognised, and he had served notice of an enormous potential when he first burst on the scene in 1980/81, netting 28 goals in that first season as a regular. He became the focus of national attention after stealing the show when Celtic became the first Scottish club to win the UK networked *Daily Express* National Five-a-Side Competition in London.

Shortly afterwards, he was made aware of the fragility of a career in football; going for a 50-50 ball in a reserve match at a wintry Cappie-low, Morton's ground, in January 1982 Nicholas suffered the most traumatic injury possible for a football player – a broken leg. For four long months he exercised and trained with weights, striving patiently to rebuild wasted muscles and to recover his strength.

Previously considered a young playboy, Nicholas revealed considerable mental toughness in his bid to regain full fitness. His lifestyle off the field might have induced apoplexy in the likes of Jock Stein, but his current manager, Billy McNeill, conceded readily that only the precocious young-ster's resilience and cockiness had enabled the player to overcome the horrendous setback to his career. Still Nicholas would chafe at his manager's concern with his social life, complaining: 'He seems to have spies every-where'. McNeill, for his part, admitted to 'being driven up the wall some-times' with the more visible signs of his striker's 'disco-man image': the soft hairstyle, suede boots, leather trousers, gold-chain necklace and rings.

McNeill may have been ultra-protective, but he had every reason to be so. Experienced in football, the manager had seen too many careers blighted too early through the inability to handle the instant success the sport offers its prodigies. The social whirl, the publicity in the newspapers, the sudden increase in spending money: all can contribute to youngsters disappearing from the game without a trace. Here was a player fast becoming the idol of the younger element of the Celtic support and with a personal magnetism that drew more fan-mail to the ground than the rest of the squad put together . . . and Billy McNeill spoke of the young man's 'special charisma', which he compared to that of another great Celtic player, the now legendary Charlie Tully. And like Tully, the young man was a cartoonist's delight, with a shock of black hair and sharp features. His popularity was by no means universal, however, as team-mate Frank McGarvey, indicated several years later. McGarvey, highly industrious and an ideal foil for the youngster, was understandably far from enamoured with a streak of selfishness in the young Nicholas's make-up, as he recalled several years later: 'I remember one day we were playing at Fir Park [in 1982]. We won 7–0 and Charlie scored a goal in a breakaway. I ran when he should have passed but I went offside, so I had to run back and then I ran again, but he still kept the ball. *Three times* it happened and I never got the pass. It's just as well he scored, because otherwise he would have got the biggest kick of his life up the backside. I did more work than he did and *he* got all the credit'. (*Mail on Sunday*: 15 July 1990)

In the early stages of 1982/83 Nicholas had added a new dimension to his game as he embarked on a goal-scoring spree, netting ten goals in eight matches prior to the first round of the European Cup. Before his leg-break he had relied on quickness of thought to outwit opponents, but now he had matured physically, adding the stamina that helped him come to terms with the challenges of the Premier League. Never noted as a strong player, however, he has always been irritated by the loophole in the rules that allows the tackle from behind in Scottish football.

EUROPA CUP 1

1e ronde
1982/198

AJAX

THE CELTIC FOOTBALL & ATHLETIC COY LTD
1888

YMPISCH ST ION

BETWEEN THE LINES

The often dour Jim McLean, manager of Dundee United, has long held a jaundiced view of media types. Interviewed by the Dutch soccer magazine, *Voetball International*, in 1982, he said it would be better if every journalist was a former player:

> That way they would take the game more seriously. When you hear journalists talking, they never talk about football. They are more interested in having fun.

The progress of 'the Cannonball Kid' – to dust off one of his nicknames – was to be given the strictest of tests with the renewal of Celtic's rivalry with one of the Continent's great names, Ajax of Amsterdam, three times winners of Europe's greatest prize.

Like Celtic, Ajax had been identified traditionally with a minority group, having always been the football team of the Dutch city's Jewish population. And now both organisations were in the same situation of trying to re-establish their reputations at an exalted level.

Celtic's manager, Billy McNeill, felt that it was time for Celtic to become a force in Europe again, and he was reasonably optimistic that, with a nucleus of experienced players and a clutch of youngsters, he might be able to strike a blow for the club in the first leg at Parkhead. For that occasion Ajax would be without their two international stars, the teenagers Frank Rijkaard and Wim Kieft; the latter was Europe's top scorer in 1981/82 and, at 19, the youngest player to win the coveted Golden Boot award, scoring 32 goals in 34 League matches. Celtic would also be handicapped by the absence of Roy Aitken, out through suspension.

Most intriguingly, Ajax were going to field the legendary Johan Cruyff, who had been the 'mega-star' of the 1970s. Now 35 years old, he was no longer viewed as a match winner, but rather as a playmaker operating from a deep position, where he would have a better chance of avoiding tackles and of protecting his legs. He had returned to Amsterdam after several lucrative years as a soccer mercenary. Five years after joining Barcelona for a record fee of £920,000, he had left Spain heavily in debt, having lost £1,500,000 in various business ventures and he was being hounded by the Spanish government for an alleged £200,000 in unpaid taxes. In an attempt to re-coup his losses, he had offered his services to the TV-dominated American market with the Washington Diplomats and Los Angeles Aztecs – and made further guest appearances around the world. Now, in 1982, he was involved in a sportswear company and, with his father-in-law running his affairs, earned his living in football by dint of 'appearance-bonuses' averaging £20,000 per match.

EUROPEAN CUP (FIRST ROUND)

15 September 1982   29 September 1982
Celtic Park (1st leg)   Olympic Stadium, Amsterdam (2nd leg)

CELTIC 2	**AJAX 2**	**AJAX 1**	**CELTIC 2**
Bonner	Galje	Schrijvers	Bonner
McGrain	Van Veen	Van Veen	McGrain
Reid	Ophof	Ophof	Reid
Moyes	Boeve	Boeve	Aitken
McAdam	Molby	Molby	McAdam
MacLeod	Lerby	Lerby	Sinclair
Provan	Olsen	Olsen	Provan (McCluskey)
McStay	Vanenburg	Vanenburg	McStay (Moyes)
McGarvey	Cruyff	Cruyff (Molenaar)	McGarvey
Burns (Sullivan)	Molenaar	Kieft	MacLeod
Nicholas	Schoenaker	Schoenaker	Nicholas

Scorers:

Nicholas (14. pen)	Olsen (4)	Vanenburg (65)	Nicholas (34)
McGarvey (27)	Lerby (18)		McCluskey (89)

Referee: E. Frederiksson (Sweden)   L. Agnolin (Italy)

Attendances: 56.299   62.000

Amid an excited buzz from the 56,000 crowd at Parkhead the Ajax trainers came on the field before the kick-off, and after prolonged conversation with the Dutch international keeper, Schrijvers, decided to replace him with the substitute Galje. Apparently, the former had been recovering from influenza, but in the moments before the start complained about feeling unwell again. A sensational start!

Sensing insecurity in the re-arranged Ajax defence, Celtic stormed into attack from the opening whistle; and the Dutchmen were rattled, looking very square at the back. Twice within the opening minutes Frank McGarvey had clear-cut chances. Put through by MacLeod's pass within a minute, he shot weakly at the advancing keeper, and shortly afterwards he took another fine pass, from McAdam this time, to shoot against the keeper again.

If Ajax appeared sluggish in deep defence, that was not the case up front. In four minutes the visitors took the lead. Cruyff, the focus of attention, took a throw-in on the left, and passed the ball to Olsen; slight of build and fleet of foot, Olsen was electric in his movements. He gathered the ball, made straight for goal and left McGrain and Moyes struggling in his wake before firing the shot past Bonner at the post. A brilliant goal; one that stilled the bedlam of Parkhead.

Celtic's characteristic response brought results in the 14th minute, after

Tommy Burns in 1982.

Hans Galje had turned aside a 30-yard free kick from Provan with straining fingertips; two minutes after that save the keeper had to admit defeat when Nicholas slotted home a penalty with admirable coolness. The culprit was Cruyff, who blatantly pulled Tommy burns down as the Celt swept past him.

another four minutes. Celtic had started to push forward, and Ajax punished their over-commitment to the maximum. Lerby, an elegant powerhouse in midfield, released the dangerous Olsen down the left. The sudden decrease in noise from the Celtic support warned of the danger, as Olsen sidestepped McGrain yet again. At the edge of the penalty area he checked up to swing over a ball in the direction of Cruyff, who 'killed' the ball coming to him at an awkward height, two feet above the ground, before flighting it between two Celtic defenders into the heart of the box. Lerby, who had started off the move more than 40 yards back, arrived into the space with perfect timing, and moved in on Bonner. The keeper had to commit himself, and Lerby waited that vital second before chipping the ball over him. Another wonderful goal, once again Celtic's weaknesses in defence appeared totally exposed. But consider the names involved in the move: Johan Cruyff, Jesper Olsen, Soren Lerby . . .

Again Celtic roared back into the match. MacLeod was fouled by Molenaar, who was booked by the referee; Nicholas found the net, but the 'score' was disallowed . . . then Celtic equalised in 27 minutes. Moyes headed clear from defence, the ball was flicked on by Nicholas' head, and Frank McGarvey raced in between a hesitant defender and his goalkeeper to tuck the ball away with understandably studied care. The match continued its frantic pace, as both teams abandoned defence and went all out for goals; Schoenaker rattled Celtic's bar with a header, and a fierce drive from MacLeod was deflected wide of Ajax's goal.

Probably it was the most exciting 45 minutes played in a European tie at Celtic Park . . . and the pace slackened in the second half. Celtic now needed goals desperately, having given up two already in the home leg, but Ajax were more than content to settle into a more solid defensive pattern. Nicholas remained the most dangerous Celtic forward, but he was being marked tightly – as was Tommy Burns, picked out by the Dutch champions as the playmaker. In fact, another scything tackle on Burns should have brought a second penalty kick to Celtic in 56 minutes, however the referee turned down the frantic appeals. Shots by Murdo MacLeod and young Paul McStay came close, but Ajax weathered the storm to settle for a highly satisfactory draw. At the end the Dutch champions lined up to receive waves of generous applause from the spectators, in recognition of their contribution to a thrilling occasion. Unlike most sides they had come to Celtic Park to win and entertain.

The consensus on the day after the match appeared inevitable: 'Celtic's European Cup ambitions once again look like coming apart at the first hurdle after last night's meeting with a Johan Cruyff-inspired Ajax at Parkhead,' (*Glasgow Herald*); 'Celtic will go to the Olympic Stadium in Amsterdam in two weeks' time chasing what appears to be a lost cause,' (*Daily Record*); 'I believe that Aberdeen and Rangers will survive, Dundee United have a chance but, miracles apart, Celtic are out . . . In the four years since Billy McNeill took over from Jock Stein, Celtic have failed to register a single European win away from home, even against mediocre opposition such as Dundalk, Miskolc, Timisoara and Partizani Tirana . . That's why contemplating victory in Amsterdam later this month really does enter the realms of fairy-tales and miracles.' (*Daily Express*)

The major talking-point was on the performance of the great Cruyff. Put under a microscope from the warm-up, the star had a mixed night: he attempted 52 passes and completed 41 of them successfully, he took seven free kicks and four corners, all of which posed a threat to Celtic's goal. He had been involved in both Ajax goals, but he had given up the penalty. In a match fought out at a hectic pace, Cruyff and the Swedish referee, Fredriksson, were observed deep in animated conversation no less than 15 times, and it was only on the 12th occasion that the official finally produced his yellow card for Cruyff's 'over-use of the tongue'.

Billy McNeill tried to hide his disappointment at the result, but felt irritated that too many Celtic players had stood back at times to admire the famous Dutchman, and had given him too much time and room to display his arsenal of talents. The Ajax manager, Aad de Mos, confessed to a confidence-trick. Just before the match, as the players were preparing to enter the tunnel, the manager turned to Cruyff and told him: 'I read in an article that Billy McNeill said you are an old man. Go out and show him.' After the match the manager expressed satisfaction with the outcome of his ploy, stating: 'I have never witnessed a player so desperate to go on to the field and do well in one particular match. The two goals we have scored should be enough.'

Cruyff, who had played against Celtic back in 1971 and was unaware that his manager's statement had been a fabrication designed solely to wind him up for the match, commented to Dutch journalists at the airport: 'Who is Mr McNeill? Oh, yes, I remember he was the big one in defence – but a poor player!'

GLASGOW BELONGS TO ME
An estimated 250,000 crowded into Glasgow's Bellahouston Park for the visit of Pope John Paul. It was the first visit to Scotland of a Pope; around 6,000 police and 7,000 stewards were needed to maintain order.

In the interval between the two legs of the tie, Celtic's scoring potential was evident at Motherwell in a 7–0 romp; Nicholas, in a superlative

Heroes in defence at the Olympic Stadium: Aitken (hidden), Sinclair,
McGrain and Bonner.

display, scored a hat-trick with laughable ease, signalling that he had become the hottest property in Britain. In their final matches before the renewal of hostilities at Amsterdam the clubs enjoyed different fortunes. Celtic stuttered to a 2–0 win over Hibs at Parkhead, but could draw consolation with the form of 17-year-old Paul McStay, exhibiting the maturity of a veteran. Ajax warmed up for Celtic's visit with a crushing 5–0 victory over Nijmegen, with Kieft – who had missed the Parkhead leg through injury – scoring three times on his return.

McNeill knew better than most the magnitude of Celtic's task in Amsterdam. Only once after drawing the first leg at Parkhead had Celtic come back from Europe with a victory in the second leg – against Vejle by 1–0 in 1973. However, he did indicate that Ajax's young players might struggle if Celtic went ahead, and he expressed hope that the club's recent experiences in Holland might stand them in good stead; Celtic had won the pre-season tournament organised by Feyenoord in 1981 and had lost narrowly in the 1982 final.

The match was scheduled for the Olympic Stadium, constructed in time for the 1928 games in Amsterdam – a stadium currently not too popular with spectators because it was starting to show signs of wear and tear. However, as Ajax's own ground held only 25,000 they had adopted the habit of playing their European ties at the larger Olympic Stadium. After the thrills at Parkhead two weeks earlier, and because of Cruyff's personal magnetism, the ground was filled to capacity for the first time in nine years.

McNeill, worried about the havoc that Cruyff could wreak playing before his adoring public, decided that he would have to be shadowed everywhere. He chose Graeme Sinclair, signed earlier in the season from lowly Dumbarton, for the task; Sinclair, about to play in only his third competitive game for Celtic, was remarkably unconcerned: 'I won't lose any sleep. I have done marking jobs before at Dumbarton.'

During the warm-up the Celtic players made for the end of the ground where 3,000 of their supporters had congregated; Charlie Nicholas expressed amazement at their enthusiasm: 'We came out early to practise, and ah saw this huge mass at the far end. Ah asked George McCluskey what it was. He said it wis the Celtic support. We jist stood there staring at it. It was unreal.'

To the delight of that travelling support Celtic started well, and indeed outplayed Ajax for much of the first half. Early on, Provan for Celtic and Lerby for Ajax were wayward in their finishing from long range, but Bonner was the first keeper to be tested when he dived full-length to save from Schoenaker.

In 34 minutes Celtic fashioned a remarkable goal to take the lead in both the leg and the overall tie. The move began with a devastating pass from Paul McStay, well back in defence, across the field for Sinclair to run on to up the left wing. The pass, delivered with perfect accuracy, must have

318

travelled 50 yards, and Sinclair fed the ball on to Nicholas; the young striker beat two men in his deceptively casual manner, before passing to McGarvey. He also moved smartly into position for a possible return, and when it reached him he swerved a delicate shot around the keeper . . .

The strike, classic in its simplicity, gave new heart to the players, and started the celebrations on the terracings – at least for 3,000 fans. It also stimulated Ajax into a concerted response: the full back, Van Veen was just too high with one shot from 30 yards, and Cruyff was encouraging his men to greater efforts.

Only three minutes after the interval every Celtic heart stopped when Cruyff took a free kick awarded for a foul against McStay 20 yards out; the famed striker bent the ball round the 'wall' and Bonner did well to see it at the last moment and play it on to the post, and eventually clear. The heat was on, similar to that which had caused a stronger Celtic team to crack for three goals back in 1971. But Celtic were defending with admirable resolution: Aitken and McAdam were twin pillars of strength in defence, and young Bonner was revealing exactly why he had replaced the more experienced Latchford, especially when he turned a close-in header over the crossbar. However, this was also a different Ajax and, perhaps lacking in the penetration of the earlier side, they were nevertheless causing all sorts of problems for Celtic's beleaguered defence. McGrain, given orders to come to grips with the speedy Olsen, was booked by the Italian referee Agnolin after a series of fouls on the winger, again looking dangerous whenever he received the ball.

Most encouraging for Celtic was the way the ball was being played out of defence; they still retained much of the composure of the first half, and troubled Ajax with the threat of a break-away. Shoenaker came close with a spectacular bicycle-kick in 59 minutes, and Celtic breathed again. But their celebrations were premature. Six minutes later Ajax scored, a simple, but sickening goal, deserved on the play. After a series of short passes the ball reached Vanenburg, who stabbed a shot into the net off the far post.

The score was tied, but the two goals scored at Parkhead by Ajax would be decisive if the game finished with no more scoring.

It was time for heroics – or honourable failure. In the dug-out McNeill decided on substitutions; off came Davie Provan, and on came the striker George McCluskey in 72 minutes . . . six minutes later off came young McStay, who had played a marvellous first half but was now tiring, and on came David Moyes, a central defender. Aitken was released from his defensive role, and a new factor, an elemental force, had been added to midfield. Celtic were committed to all-out attack in the remaining time . . .

Ajax were forced to defend, and such was Celtic's ascendancy that they could not spring any of their dangerous forwards loose. Frank McGarvey's brave header from a Sinclair cross rebounded from the bar with only seven minutes left, and some teams would have thrown in the towel then. But still

319

Celtic pressed forward, playing with pride and passion; they also were playing a superior brand of football that was thrilling to their supporters.

Under two minutes remained . . . as Ajax retreated in numbers before them, the ball was moved around as Celtic continued to look for a gap . . . from McGrain to MacLeod . . . to McGrain whose shot was partly blocked . . . to McGarvey . . . to Nicholas . . . and a quick-thinking switch to McCluskey found the substitute lurking free for a second on the left – 'and when my marker left me and went towards Charlie before he passed the ball, I had an opening. I took the ball on my right foot, drew it back to my left, and then hit it.'

The goalscorers: Nicholas and McCluskey.

It was a moment to celebrate so far from home – in a vast arena, playing before a foreign crowd, against a famous side. The ball rolled around the back of the net, the Celtic players hugged each other, the supporters roared with delight, and the substitutes, trainers, coaches, and manager leaped out of the dug-out to join in. Over on the Ajax bench Johan Cruyff sat with his head in his hands. Limping off the pitch three minutes before the end, he had stopped for a cautionary word with his captain Soren Lerby, pointing towards McCluskey: 'Watch out for that Celtic newcomer.' Beside him on the same bench, and looking at the Celtic celebrations with equal dismay was a striker, not used that night, in the person of a 17-year-old Marco van Basten.

Shortly afterwards the whistle went, and Celtic's euphoria was boundless as Billy McNeill and the backroom staff rushed on to the field to revel in a famous victory, while the supporters, mostly packed into one corner of the stadium, chanted and sang. For at least half an hour they remained rejoicing before they could be persuaded to leave the scene and return to the city centre to celebrate long into the night. Later the Amsterdam police and civic officials were to praise the fine behaviour of the Celtic fans; the Celtic Supporters' Association, who had sent over representatives to act as liaison officers with the police and their Ajax counterparts, was being justly singled out in the accolades.

Sadly, the victory, richly deserved and hard-won, did not become the stepping-stone for further triumphs. The hopes of a lengthy run in the competition, and perhaps eventual triumph, were dashed within a few weeks by the little-known Spanish side, Real Sociedad, who ousted Celtic in the next round by exposing those defensive frailties that were to haunt the Scots at home and abroad for most of the decade.

The boyhood dream of Charlie Nicholas in playing for Celtic had been realised, but the aftermath had to be disillusioning. He had heard the stories of the great nights in Europe but, as a player, he could see that the club was paying only lip-service to claims about being serious at the highest level of competition.

As a professional he had other – and legitimate – concerns. He would soon conclude that financial security lay elsewhere than at Parkhead, where he felt that Celtic still, in the 1980s, were indulging in the emotional blackmail of 'playing for the jersey'. Aware that he was a top attraction, that he was a valuable commodity, he tried for better terms; he became increasingly angry at what he perceived as the discrepancy between what he was being offered in private and the amounts being cited on the club's behalf in the newspapers.

His desire to leave Celtic was symptomatic of the shift in negotiating power in favour of the star performer that had occurred through freedom of contract. Alec Cameron observed in the *Daily Record*, when the Nicholas transfer saga was unfolding: 'There are no prizes in football for people who

THE ENGLISHMAN, THE IRISHMAN, THE SCOTSMAN . . .

The *Glasgow Herald* of 27 May 1983 expressed suitable indignation at the comments of John O'Neill, the Leicester City and Northern Ireland defender. After facing Charlie Nicholas in the British Home Championship at Hampden Park, O'Neill stated: 'I don't see how Nicholas can benefit by staying on in Scotland. The sooner he starts learning all about the English First Division game the better. Even a first year in the reserves at Old Trafford or Liverpool would do him more good than hanging on in Scotland.'

The *Herald* writer went on to illustrate the 'remarkable self-perpetuating myth that English football is the best' by citing the ignorance of the [unnamed] chairman of an English club who commented on his manager's interest in acquiring a Scottish first division player: 'But, he hasn't played senior football.'

A fortnight earlier, Aberdeen, who finished third in the Premier League, had won the European Cup-Winners' Cup with a marvellous display against Real Madrid in Gothenburg – a display that gained them continent-wide acclaim .

are loyal. Clubs have set the standard. When it suits them, they will sell.' (6 May 1983)

Many Celtic followers have complained over the years of the club's readiness to sell star players, raised and developed for little cost at Parkhead; they anticipated that Charlie Nicholas would soon be leaving at a vast profit to Celtic – and with little regret at the highest level within the club. It was rumoured that, when the chairman was informed that the manager's last attempts to persuade Nicholas to stay had failed, his only comment was a cryptic, 'Good'.

It was becoming increasingly clear in the early 1980s that clubs would have to treat the top-notch player in a fashion commensurate with his drawing power, and doubtless Nicholas would have been dumbfounded at the deal worked out for the benefit of the 35-year-old Cruyff; the Dutchman came from a working-class background like Nicholas, but it was revealed that he expected to pick up the astounding sum of £130,000 for his night's work against Celtic in the Olympic Stadium. His contract called for a personal 40 per cent of the takings, underlying how far his undoubted talents had taken him from the days when his mother cleaned the floors of the Ajax club.

Nicholas was in danger of becoming a victim of the schizophrenia which accompanies the fans' passion for his team, an obsession that would deny the player the basic right to better his lot financially – yet a restraint that the average supporter would find offensive if applied in his own place of work. The plea that Nicholas and others make – that they have to make the most of a short career – would hardly have met a sympathetic echo in a city already hit hard by the economic recession of the early Thatcher era in Britain. In Glasgow nearly a quarter of the population was dependent on Supplementary Benefit to meet his or her basic needs, and one male in three was out of work in districts such as Parkhead and Easterhouse.[4]

Another ancient, economic grievance was fuelling the resentment, as Peter Broughan wrote in the London magazine, *Time Out*:

> For a Scot, the most galling thing about English press and TV speculation concerning Charlie's future was the sheer, predictable arrogance of it all. As soon as a Scottish footballer achieves wide celebrity in England, the unthinking imperialism which has characterised the relationship of the two countries for centuries begins to grind into operation. Its ugliest manifestation was glimpsed on television in the person of Jimmy Greaves, *On the Ball*'s patronising idea of the voice of the people. The watery-eyed wind-up merchant encouraged Nicholas to 'Come South, Charlie, come South!' . . . Sitting at home you could practically hear the beer glasses hitting the screens in Glasgow pubs.
>
> (25–31 August 1983)

The last match Charlie Nicholas played for Celtic in Scotland was at Ibrox in the final League fixture of the season; in the second half a typical Nicholas performance helped Celtic to overcome a two-goal deficit and run out winners by 4–2. At the Broomloan Road end of the ground the players could see the banners imploring 'Don't Go, Charlie!'; and at the end Nicholas dashed round the goal to salute the fans with a wave – but it had the look of a farewell gesture.

THEY SAID IT . . .

'Gissa job!' – the despairing cry of Yosser Hughes, the main character in the BBC TV series *Boys from the Blackstuff*, based on the travails of a squad of asphalt-layers on Merseyside, currently unemployed. It was claimed in the Liverpool area that landing a job in the 1980s was the equivalent of winning the pools.

'Gotcha!' – the headline of the *Sun*, after the sinking of the Argentine battleship *Belgrano* by HMS *Conqueror* in May 1982 during the Falklands War.

The more embittered doubtless would have detected an element of poetic justice in the fact that this totally spontaneous, instinctive player moved away from the exhilarating style of Celtic to join up with the stultifyingly mechanical approach of Arsenal. It was not the club for a player of Charlie Nicholas' flair, and his experience in England has to be deemed as a failure in terms of the development of the most exciting prospect in British football.

In an interview with Kevin McCarra, printed in *Scotland on Sunday* on 21 January 1990, Nicholas admitted that he left Parkhead out of annoyance when Celtic were 'very foolish' about money in offering him a new contract. If it were only a matter of money, then for Celtic it has to be considered a misplaced economy, because Nicholas has never ceased to retain the imagination – and perhaps affection – of Celtic fans even when inflicting damage on his former club while in Aberdeen colours. When the journalist mentioned to an avid Celtic supporter that he was heading for Pittodrie to record the player's thoughts, he heard the heart-rending plea: 'Bring him back with you!'

✳   ✳   ✳

POSTSCRIPT

In July 1990 Charlie Nicholas returned to Parkhead, his spiritual home, for a £450,000 fee. He asserted that he was 'older and wiser now, much more of a team player', and Celtic manager, Billy McNeill was quick to observe that: 'I'm not anticipating that he'll be the Charlie Nicholas of seven years ago – I want him to be the Charlie Nicholas of today!

Footnotes

1 Charlie Nicholas still resents the tag, but the nickname does capture some of the youthful Nicholas' sparkle, a footballing vintage described by Kevin McCarra of *Scotland on Sunday* – as 'joyous, as immediate as sunshine, something to ricochet around your memory for ever.'

2 Arthur Hopcraft caught the mood of Liverpool at this time in his *The Football Man* (published in 1968), which remains one of the most perceptive books written about the sport: ' . . the city character, with its pervading harshness of waterfront life and bitterly combative Irish exile content, was given a sudden flowering of arrogant expression with the simultaneous rise of its pop musicians and of both its leading football teams. More than any other English city, Liverpool experiences its hope and its shame through its football.'

3 A reference to the signing of John Dowie from the English club in September, 1977 for an estimated fee of £25,000. The capture took place a month after Dalglish had been sold to Liverpool for an estimated £450,000.

4 While the debate about Nicholas' future was raging in the Scottish newspapers, the *Daily Record* in May 1983 revealed that 3,250,000 were unemployed in Britain. Nicholas could point out to his critics that he had personal experience of the effects of unemployment. His father had been made redundant once and the family had to subsist on dole-money. He could not afford to buy a new pair of football boots for his son, who had to play the game in 'gutties' (a form of sandshoes).

17

WHEN THE GOING GETS TOUGH . . .

TO THE CELTS (on the prospect of another Championship)

We who admire and wish you well,
We hope you conquer in the fight,
To many hearts, if Celtic fell,
'Twould bring delirious delight.
Yet though the Celts beat all their foes
We have no cause for jubilation,
They never suffered from the woes of training and inoculation.

Thus are flags lost in time of war.
The press its sympathy has stated
With Hearts, whom all feel sorry for;
How few the Celts congratulated.

Poem by J.C.
(This poem appeared in *Glasgow Star and Examiner*, 16 April 1915.
The parallels between 1915 and 1986 are intriguing.)[1]

IT WAS A TALE of two cities, really, that unforgettable afternoon in May 1986. The football matches may have been played at Paisley and Dundee that day, but the struggle for supremacy was yet another chapter in the age-old rivalry between Edinburgh and Glasgow.

Separated by only an hour's journey by train or bus, the two cities reflect striking differences in character that represent co-existing and complementary strands in Scottish life – and, by extension, football.

Edinburgh has long gloried in its impressive townscape and the Georgian elegance of its New Town which, when added to a reputation for intellect, gave it the title 'Athens of the North'. For centuries the capital has been the legal, administrative and financial centre of Scotland. Most ironically, in view of the rivalry between the cities, Edinburgh topped a survey by Glasgow University, conducted to determine 'the quality of life' in Britain's largest cities; Glasgow emerged a dismal 25th out of 38 in the 1989 poll.

Glasgow, while doing much to recover from its image as an academy of violence, has never established itself as a place for outsiders to live, the tag of 'European City of Culture in 1990' notwithstanding. *Fodor's Guide to Scotland* contains a decidedly ambivalent comment about the city: 'If you still feel that Glasgow is not for you, remember that the best urban expressway in Britain soars across the city, and you may traverse the whole conurbation east to west without meeting a stop light.' Glasgow remains a port city, vital and dynamic, engaged in trade and industry, a city alive and bustling with the vibrancy of making a living. One can never imagine the more reserved Edinburgh adopting a catchy slogan similar to 'Glasgow's miles better'.

GETTING THE MESSAGE
Some slogans of the 1980s:

Don't die of ignorance	(AIDS information campaign)
We're getting there	(British Rail)
Jesus is alive	(A postmark)
If it were a lady, it would get its bottom pinched	(Fiat 127 automobile)

Middle-class Edinburgh, that seems to hide its anonymous slums; working-class Glasgow that takes a nostalgic, indeed romantic, pride in the old, notorious Gorbals and the rough-and-ready democracy of the tenement close. If Edinburgh has songs written about it, they remain obscure; 'I Belong to Glasgow' could serve as the national anthem of every Saturday boozer in the world.

The poet Dan Wilton may have been taking a swipe at the capital when he recently characterised Glasgow as:

> *. . . no perfect, preening place*
> *It rains too much for paradise,*
> *Too many blotches scar a face*
> *Not merely pretty*
>
> *Here is a barking, mongrel town*
> *Where Scots and Irish coalesce.*
> *Dour dapper suburbs hedged around*
> *By crude graffiti.*

While the hard-nosed city of Glasgow lives and breathes its football through the ferociously competitive Old Firm, the citizens of Edinburgh often appear to look askance at such raucous obsession. As the late John

Fairgrieve, both a Rangers historian and a lifelong supporter of Heart of Midlothian, observed in 1972: 'At Ibrox or Parkhead self-esteem has to be continually fed by success – and appetites are voracious. At Tynecastle the quality is different, based on a tradition and a pride that approach smugness. The Hearts supporter has always tended to follow his side for fun, viewing the occasional cup or championship as a welcome bonus. Kindly outsiders see it as romantically aristocratic; others not so kind see it as obsolete amateurishness.'

To be equally unkind, the Heart of Midlothian Football Club has often been a metaphor for Edinburgh – a capital without a parliament, pomp and circumstance without the power. The very name suggests romance and pageantry, and invokes associations with Sir Walter Scott's novel. It has such a ring that wee boys across Scotland half-expect the club to play home games at Edinburgh Castle and not at Tynecastle; not entirely unfitting a thought, because shortly after the outbreak of World War One in 1914, when the Germans were threatening to sweep all before them, the entire Hearts team along with several hundred supporters enlisted in a battalion of the Royal Scots.[2]

This act, commemorated at the base of the clock on a roundabout adjacent to the Haymarket railway station, boosted recruitment at a period of national danger. Of the players, six never returned from the battlefields and trenches of Europe; and several others were wounded or gassed. The club's patriotism was praised rightly in Parliament for saving the collective honour of football – and thus preventing a threatened shutdown of the sport, as influential public voices wondered why fit, young athletes were not flocking to the colours. In a congratulatory letter to the club one MP stated: 'Edinburgh will only forget the Hearts when it agrees to root up the Heart of Midlothian [a design worked into the stonework] in the causeway near St Giles – and that is never.'

This selflessness helped cement the club and its teams in the affections of the city, where it has always enjoyed greater support and prestige than Hibernian – even in the latter's glorious era shortly after World War Two. It is no coincidence that the city's buses are painted in the maroon colours of the Tynecastle club, and have been for decades.

A club apart, and an institution even – but all too often fielding teams that have never quite managed to translate into success the respect in which most people in Scottish football have held them. The 'gentlemanly' ethos, identified by John Fairgrieve and others, may have proved its undoing as Celtic and Rangers piled up the honours between them. Although football is generally a working-class sport, Hearts teams have always presented a slightly 'soft' appearance, a suggestion of frailty. One critic noted that their nickname – 'the Jam Tarts' – does not inspire much confidence, with connotations of nursery rhymes and desserts rather than football.

Speaking back in 1931, at a time when Hearts had been champions twice (but runners up five times) in contrast to the Glasgow giants who had amassed 34 titles, John McCartney, the club's former manager, sighed that '[the Maroons] had never been blessed with much luck – that luck which is universally acknowledged as necessary in a season's campaign'.

Seven years later – with the club still in vain pursuit of the major trophies – Colm Brogan, a Glasgow author, delivered a harsher judgement:

> Hearts are the wealthiest team in Scotland and, for a generation, men turned their eyes towards Tynecastle in the hope of finding a formidable and permanent challenge to the Old Firm monopoly. Hearts are the deepest mystery in Scottish football. They fail not so much ingloriously as ridiculously. Their faithful supporters cheer frantically while they run rings around Rangers or bundle Celtic home ignominiously, and next Saturday there comes to Tynecastle the dismal news that the heroes have collapsed before the worried onslaught of some humble team struggling in the slums of the bottom of the League table. It used to be said that Hearts flattered to deceive, but that is no longer true. They flatter in vain; they deceive no more.
>
> (from *Scotland – 1938*, edited by J. R. Allan, 1938)

Hearts have long displayed an uncanny ability to snatch defeat from the jaws of victory; so often, throughout their history, a Hearts team, faced with the prospect of a major breakthrough, would fold under the pressure – and fail.

Even in the most prolific era in the club's history Hearts could still produce memorable failure. Their record in the late 1950s was a splendid one: the Scottish Cup once, the League Championship twice, and the League Cup three times. In 1956 Hearts, helped by the 'Terrible Trio' of Alfie Conn, Willie Bauld and Jimmy Wardhaugh – the three most gifted inside forwards of the period – won the Scottish Cup by beating a strangely dis-spirited, and much-changed, Celtic side by 3–1 in the final to end a 50-year hoodoo in the competition. Two years later Hearts ended another jinx, this time one of 60 years, by lifting the Championship, in the process scoring the astonishing total of 132 goals in 34 matches.

Yet, the season after the runaway triumph – in the course of a campaign that featured a strong challenge from Rangers – Hearts' lack of a killer instinct caused them to forfeit the chance to emulate their arch-rivals' (Hibernian) accomplishment of successive Championships in 1951 and 1952.

On the last day of the 1958/59 season Hearts needed two things to pip their Glasgow rivals on goal average: a victory over a mediocre Celtic at Parkhead, and for Rangers to lose at Ibrox to relegation-threatened Aberdeen. Rangers had a two-point advantage, but both aspirants had identical goals for-and-against tallies. Hearts started well, playing their accustomed brand of fast, attractive football to lead Celtic by 1–0 at half-time through a magnificent shot by Rankin from 25 yards that beat Haffey conclusively; meanwhile, Rangers and Aberdeen had settled for a 1–1 draw at the interval.

Unaccountably, although Hearts had to be aware of Rangers' continuing struggle at Ibrox, the Edinburgh men slumped in the second half, and yielded the momentum to an undistinguished Celtic side that managed to produce its best form of the season. The Championship was decided by a superb save from the often-maligned Frank Haffey who got his finger-tips to a fierce shot in 51 minutes; two minutes later a young Bertie Auld cheekily guided a long through-ball past keeper Marshall. In 67 minutes Eric Smith dived to head home, McGrory-style, a cross-ball only three feet above the ground.

Even with 23 minutes left, enough time to regroup and rally, Hearts failed to respond to the challenge. Shortly after leaving the pitch, losers by 1–2, they had to endure the further mortification of learning that Rangers had lost to Aberdeen, and the realisation that a routine victory at Parkhead would have given them the title. Perhaps 'routine' is not the word because it should be recalled that Hearts once went for a period of 45 years in the League without a win at Celtic Park.

Cyril Horne, the veteran correspondent of the *Glasgow Herald*, described that Ibrox side as 'the worst team I have ever seen wear the club's colours', and the *Daily Record* considered that the Rangers supporters, who booed the team from the field at the end, were 'in the mood to throw a grenade into the marble halls . . . until word came through that Rangers were the champions again, that Celtic had defeated Hearts'. (20 April 1959) Rather dubiously, the account in the *Daily Record* claimed that a number of Rangers supporters' buses passed Celtic ones on the way home, and 'believe it or not, they smiled joyously at one another and gleefully exchanged the thumbs-up sign'. To complete a bizarre day in Scottish football, Dunfermline Athletic managed to avoid relegation by defeating Partick Thistle, from the top half of the table, by the score of 10–1 – a result that would raise a few eyebrows, even at Firhill.

Strange things have been known to happen on the last day of a season.

Six years later, when even better placed to win the Championship, Hearts, again on the last day, failed to meet the challenge posed by Kilmarnock at Tynecastle. Kilmarnock, chasing their first title, came to Edinburgh needing to win by 2–0 to get the Championship; a draw would have suited Hearts, or even a defeat by 0–1. Kilmarnock showed little sign of nerves and played their normal, efficient game; Hearts appeared shaky throughout the match – before their own fans – and lost 0–2. Kilmarnock won the Championship on goal average – gaining the flag by the flimsiest of margins.

Little wonder then that Hearts were prime movers in advocating a change in the rules for determining champions when a tie in points occurs; from 1971, titles would be decided on goal difference – by subtracting the goals against from the goals for. In this way, Hearts felt, attacking football would be rewarded. They scarcely could have anticipated being the first prominent victims of the change . . .

That Saturday in 1965 the Hearts players slipped out of Tynecastle by the side exits to avoid the deflated supporters still milling around the stadium in shocked disbelief. Over in Glasgow, at Hampden Park, Billy McNeill and the rest of the Celtic players were celebrating the first trophy of the Stein era – a 3–2 victory over Dunfermline Athletic in the Scottish Cup.

It marked the springboard for Celtic's great success throughout the next decade, but Hearts seemed traumatised by that failure at Tynecastle. One observer felt that the club seemed resigned increasingly 'to accept the dominance of Celtic as a fact of football life'. Others shared the suspicion that Hearts were a club without effective leadership, preferring to look back at past glories while gradually edging closer and closer to the final ignominy of relegation – a punishment that occurred for the first time in their history in 1977.

Hearts were considered 'a sleeping giant' – sometimes literally so, because it was not unknown for elderly directors to nod off during board meetings. Far from being 'the talk o' the toon' and the team that 'Auld Reekie supports wi' pride' as the Hearts song boasted, the club had become mired in apathy, while one of the biggest and hitherto most loyal groups of supporters in Scotland simply stayed away in droves.

The reputation of the club was tarnished in this time by frequent sectarian outbursts from a section of the terracing; unfortunately, this pre-judice apparently found an echo in the club's boardroom. Those Celtic fans who growled that Hearts were little more than 'a branch office of Rangers' would point to an investigative series in the *Edinburgh Evening News* in the summer of 1981 with grim satisfaction. The articles revealed that, after Hearts had been relegated for the third time in five years, the club's 'once healthy financial position had deteriorated to a position of near-extinction'; worse, as contenders to take over Hearts appeared, one director insinuated that Kenny Waugh, a local bookmaker and businessman, was a Roman Catholic – and, that if he came in to rescue the club, the name would be changed to 'Sacred Heart of Midlothian'.

The 'danger' was averted when the victorious bidder, Wallace Mercer, took over and proved to be not so much the new 'King of Hearts' as their saviour. Mercer, an impressive entrepreneur and enthusiastic promoter of the club, presided over a rebirth at Tynecastle that saw 'gates' rise from an average of 5,000 to 20,000 within a seven-year period. Hearts revival contributed significantly to the staggering 80 per cent increase in overall Scottish League attendances in that time.

Sports writers, who always found him good 'copy', revelled in the joke that a card in Mercer's wallet bore the inscription: 'In the event of an accident, call a press conference.' Mercer's flair for public relations, allied

MONEY, MONEY, MONEY . . .

A number of British football clubs had to come to terms with a harsher economic climate in the 1980s, when revenue from the turnstiles was becoming insufficient to keep them afloat.

At the start of 1986/87 Middlesbrough FC was rescued from extinction by a consortium after a winding-up order was issued. The Official Receiver locked their ground, and sacked the manager, Bruce Rioch, together with others on the non-playing staff. Despite this trauma, Middlesbrough went on to gain promotion to Division Two that season – under the guidance of the reinstated Rioch.

In the autumn of 1986 Queen of the South announced that they had leased their car-park – apparently for a period of 125 years(!) – to a company which planned to build a supermarket on the site. It was reported that the revenue from the deal would bring the club more money annually than from their 'gates'.

to solid work in the backroom, did much to rekindle interest in the club's fortunes, and push it to the forefront of Scottish football in the mid-1980s.

The only thing missing was a major trophy to set the seal on the revival – the tangible evidence of success.

As the 1985/86 season neared its end, the old club appeared poised to achieve that target. Unbeaten in a run of 31 matches in the League and Scottish Cup, Hearts, on the morning of 3 May 1986, were getting ready to set off for Dundee to clinch the League Championship; a week later they were to meet Aberdeen in the final of the Scottish Cup at Hampden . . . Could the 1985/86 Hearts achieve the first 'double' in the club's history?

And yet Hearts had made a disastrous start to the season, amassing only eight points from their first ten matches – in contrast to Celtic's 14 points from nine games. The turning point for the Edinburgh team came with a gritty performance at Parkhead in October 1985 when, despite all Celtic's pressure in the second half, they hung on grimly to a one-goal lead, provided by a strike from Robertson; in the closing minutes Smith made a spectacular diving save to turn over a header from Roy Aitken.

Surprisingly, and gracefully, Wallace Mercer, at that point envisaged only one outcome to the League campaign: 'I sincerely hope that they [Celtic] win the League, and I think they will. I thought they were the most fluid side we have met this season. They played smooth attacking football with none of the hardness of other sides. I believe it would be a good thing for Scottish football if they won the League. They are exciting to watch, even if it is not so for the team they are playing.' *(Glasgow Herald:* 14 October 1985)

The resurgence of Hearts unquestionably pepped up a relatively lacklustre Scottish season, and boosted attendances wherever they played. An editorial in the *Edinburgh Evening News* rejoiced that the side's performances had 'tapped an emotional vein in the city which had lain dormant for much too long, put a fresh spring in the step of long-suffering soccer worthies, and inspired new generations of youngsters. Edinburgh is once more a soccer city.' In the same newspaper John Gibson – a regular columnist (and self-confessed Hibs supporter) – spoke for many in the East of Scotland when he stated that 'he badly wanted to see Hearts break the traditional Celtic/Rangers monopoly – anything to take the wind and the television-assisted propaganda out of the West'.

Celtic appeared to forfeit any right to the title with three successive, humiliating defeats in the autumn of 1985 by Dundee United (0–3), Aberdeen (1–4) and Rangers (0–3). The manager, David Hay, was scathing about his team's neglect of the basics: '. . . second to every ball, a leaky defence, wayward passing, and front men who can't shake off their markers.' It scarcely constituted a vote of confidence in the team's ability to mount a meaningful title challenge, but Celtic remained in nominal contention even after the dismissal from the Scottish Cup by Hibs in March 1986. Hay could not be happy with the attitude of his squad, as evidenced by that dismal performance at Easter Road where the tenacity which won the Cup in 1985 was sadly absent, and he clearly harboured doubts about his players' commitment to the League task when he said afterwards that 'No one here is indispensable' (a depressingly familiar refrain for Celtic managers in the 1980s). The manager conceded that Celtic still held an interest in the Championship, but it was only an outside chance.

At that late stage in the campaign Hearts were in the driving seat, five points ahead with only eight matches left to play; Celtic may have had two games in hand, but there was a decided lack of conviction about their play, even though they had been steadily gathering points. Their supporters remained largely unimpressed by Celtic as legitimate contenders; one letter-writer described the team in the *Celtic View* as 'Shockingly inconsistent, and lacking in team and fighting spirit'. Sir Winston Churchill once said that democracy had every fault attributed to it and more, but had at least one thing in its favour – that it was better than any of the alternatives. Similarly, the much-criticised Celtic continued to plug away and, relatively unnoticed, had embarked on an unbeaten run in the Championship from early in the New Year. After losing 2–4 at Tannadice to a rampant Dundee United (the second League defeat there within a fortnight), Celtic kept in contention, however unlikely their challenge appeared at times, with a series of commendable results. Facing up to the same series of matches which had dented their prospects earlier in the season, Celtic improved their points haul: Dundee United (1–1), Rangers (4–4) and Aberdeen (1–0). Three outright victories might have alerted Hearts to the threat posed by Celtic's late burst but, as the Edinburgh side continued on its splendid run,

Roy Aitken bars the way to goal.

few regarded Celtic as truly serious contenders, and their consistency was thus overlooked. In fact, Celtic had dropped only six points in 15 matches without defeat in a period stretching from 11 January to 30 April.

On that last day in April Celtic travelled to Motherwell, needing another victory to keep their title hopes alive, and accomplished their primary objective with a 2–0 victory, the third successive win by that margin, with the others coming against Hibs and Dundee. Unfortunately, it appeared that Celtic needed to score more goals to give themselves any chance of edging out Hearts in the event of goal difference deciding the destination of the Championship. David Hay did not hide his disappointment that the scoreline had not been at least doubled, and appeared to be putting a brave face on it when speaking of Celtic's last League fixture of the season, against St Mirren at Paisley only three days later: 'However, I know we will win against St Mirren at Love Street and, the way we are now playing, we are capable of making enough chances to get the target we need. We need a miracle, but now it is a smaller one than it looked a few days ago.'

For once, though, it seemed that the massive Celtic support had lost its collective belief in miracles. Fir Park, with the title still within their favourites' grasp, was only half-full and, on the Saturday, Love Street was not bursting at the seams, despite the Parkhead fans being greatly in the majority. If the odds quoted by the bookmakers reflected the cash placed, then Celtic supporters had not put their money where their hearts were, suggesting a certain resignation on the part of most supporters

333

about the final outcome: Hearts 1–10 on, Celtic 6–1 against.

But there was a chink of light for Celtic, for Hearts had not been too impressive latterly in the run-in.

After playing in spectacular fashion at Tannadice in mid-April to thrash Dundee United, they looked to have sealed the outcome, but some form of reaction had set in. Nerves had been fraying, most noticeably in two recent matches. They had dropped a vital point in a home match against Aberdeen, who had outplayed them throughout the encounter, scrambling a late goal to salvage a point. More indicative of the tension was a 1–0 win at Tynecastle over relegation-bound Clydebank on a day when a normal performance from the Maroons would have meant a barrowload of goals; Celtic on 29 March had recorded an ultimately impressive away 5–0 win over the same Clydebank.

Veteran Celtic supporters tried to draw some comfort from the 1953/54 season when Celtic and Hearts had fought it out head-to-head in the closing stages. In February 1954 Hearts scraped past Celtic by 3–2 at Tynecastle with a disputed goal scored in injury-time. The victory meant that Hearts were eight points ahead, although Celtic had three games in hand. The outcome of that campaign was a League Championship for Celtic as Hearts collapsed totally under the strain. Would history repeat itself?

THE TRUTH, THE WHOLE TRUTH . . .

The following exchange took place in an Australian court-room in January 1986, when Sir Robert Armstrong, representing the British Government, was arguing to impose a ban on *Spycatcher* – the memoirs of Peter Wright, represented by Malcolm Turnbull. The defence was exploring the differences between a lie and 'a misleading expression':

Turnbull: 'What's a misleading expression; a kind of bent untruth?'

Armstrong: 'As one person said, it is perhaps being economical with the truth .'

After 35 matches the 1985/86 standings were as follows:

	P	W	L	D	F	A	PTS	
Hearts	35	20	5	10	59	31	50	(+28 goals)
Celtic	35	19	6	10	62	38	48	(+24 goals)

Hearts were clear favourites in the title-race; they required only a single point at Dens Park against Dundee, while Celtic had to win by three clear goals at Paisley – and hope that Hearts lost.

At the back of Hearts' minds might have been the thought of the first game of the season on 10 August between the sides when Paul McStay equalised for Celtic with less than 30 seconds remaining. Had Hearts won that fixture, the matches on 3 May could well have been only of academic interest. And for Hearts supporters with a streak of masochism the other game at Tynecastle between the sides would have been significant; on 4 December Celtic again fought back to achieve a 1–1 draw, and the scorer was Mark McGhee, embarking on a one-man campaign to thwart Hearts' ambitions for the next few seasons.

Some Hearts' followers might have had twinges of anxiety in realising that Dundee had been a 'bogey' side for Hearts; in 11 Premier League encounters the Edinburgh side had won only twice – and had recorded one victory in five visits to Dens Park. The more superstitious among them – who might have considered buying a chicken to study its entrails for omens – might have pondered the fact that Dundee back in 1965 had inflicted an astonishing 7–1 defeat on Hearts at Tynecastle, a result that did much to cost Hearts that championship. Archie Knox, the manager of a Dundee side still with an outside chance of a place in Europe, stated boldly: 'Dens Park is the last place in the world Hearts would want to visit looking for the title.'

No guarantee existed that Celtic would win – and win well – at Love Street. Celtic have enjoyed a considerable edge over the Paisley side in the overall scheme of things, but that season the matches had been close: 2–0 for Celtic at Parkhead, and 2–1 for Celtic at Love Street, while the other game had been drawn 1–1 .

Both aspirants for the title were helped in that Dundee and St Mirren would be understrength for their last fixture: St Mirren would be without keeper Campbell Money and sweeper Steve Clarke, both out through injury; Dundee would have to play without their leading scorer, Ray Stephen, out through suspension, and also the injured defender, Stewart Forsyth.

Hearts did have a problem in deciding on a team. It appeared that a virus was affecting several regulars, although only the promising Craig Levein would miss the match. Some thought was given to asking the League for a postponement of the fixture, but it was decided to go ahead. On the brighter side, their hopes were bolstered by the return of the captain, Walter Kidd, back in the side after a suspension.

At Dens Park the atmosphere was one of a home game for Hearts; an army of 12,000 fans had journeyed to Dundee full of expectation – and sustained by the confidence that the long, unbroken run of matches had engendered. Many were wearing maroon scarves emblazoned with the word 'CHAMPIONS', while others carried banners with the same message. The night before they may have read in the *Edinburgh Evening News* the analysis by Stewart Brown of their favourites' chances on the eve of an historic encounter: 'There is no question of Hearts playing for a point at Dens. Sure, they will be cautious. But this is the day for a touch of class and a bit of style.' (2 May 1986)

Sandy Jardine, Hearts' assistant-manager but still capable of earning the accolade of the Scottish Football Writers' Player of the Year, took a similarly optimistic, if somewhat philosophical, approach: 'There is no pressure on us tomorrow. Pressure was three years ago when, if Hearts had not won promotion to the Premier Division, the club would probably have gone part-time.'

SCOTTISH PREMIER LEAGUE
3 May 1986
Love Street, Paisley

ST MIRREN 0	**CELTIC 5**
Stewart	Bonner
Wilson	McGrain (Grant)
D. Hamilton	Whyte
B. Hamilton	Aitken
Godfrey	McGugan
Cooper	MacLeod
Fitzpatrick	McClair
Abercromby	McStay
McGarvey	Johnston
Gallagher (Speirs)	Burns
Mackie	Archdeacon

Scorers:

McClair (6, 53)
Johnston (32, 33)
McStay (38)

Referee: A. Waddell (Edinburgh)

Attendance: 17,557

The weather at Love Street was overcast, the prelude to the inevitability of rain on a Saturday afternoon; fortunately, the temperature was high enough for the discomfort to be endured. The pitch was yielding, but did not present too many difficulties underfoot, and the dimensions of the playing surface – probably the largest in Scotland – were in favour of attractive, open play.

Both sides settled to a workmanlike rate in the opening minutes, and St Mirren looked dangerous in their first raids; one obvious temptation for Celtic to overcome was impatience, natural under the circumstances. However, in only six minutes Celtic got a vital break with a goal. Archdeacon, still trying to stake out a regular place in the side, took a corner on the right; Brian McClair rose virtually unchallenged to head the ball crisply into the net past the startled Stewart. It looked a simple goal,

---

FOUL PLAY

'The goal was scored a little bit by the hand of God, another bit by the head of Maradona.' This was Diego Maradona's assessment, after fisting the ball into the net for Argentina's first goal against England in the World Cup quarter-finals in Mexico, 1986. Neither the referee nor the linesmen spotted the infingement when the short Argentinian 'outjumped' the English keeper and a taller opponent to get to the ball.

'That was no game of football out there today. There were ten cheats and cowards, the scum of world football!' This was Ernie Walker's summing-up of the display of Uruguay, Scotland's last opponents in Mexico. The SFA secretary was speaking after a 0–0 draw in the group-play that meant elimination for Scotland; one Uruguayan (Batista) was ordered off after only 40 seconds following a foul on Strachan. The dismissal is believed to be the fastest ever in international football, and set the tone for much of the clash.

---

and it was; it had all the simplicity of a striker's goal – a clean, precise move that leaves defences bewildered.

The fans settled down in anticipation of more all-out attacks, but it was St Mirren who came closer with penetrating raids and Bonner had to be sharp to clear his lines from dangerous crosses. Still, one could sense a greater intensity on Celtic's part. A controlled persistence, a bustle in the midfield, the extra edge provided by motivation: all increased the longer the half went on, and as the rain started to come down.

In 32 minutes Mo Johnston scored another striker's goal, finishing off a splendid pass from Paul McStay; it was a goal that deflates defences, netted with the sort of shot that appears less than well-struck but is nevertheless impossible to save.

One minute later came a remarkable goal – and in the words of the *Glasgow Herald* one that 'ought to be preserved and exhibited in any coaching lesson'. Fortunately, it has been preserved, at least on video – and the majesty of the goal grows with each viewing. Danny McGrain, a venerable greybeard at right back, intercepted a cross in his own penalty area and cleared to another defender with an overhead kick; the ball was played back to McGrain as he moved out of strict defence. The full back, looking for an open Celtic player, found him in Paul McStay, still in his own half of the field; McStay, holding the ball momentarily, shielded it expertly and played it over to Roy Aitken. Another neat pass went to Danny McGrain, still moving upfield, who slipped it down the right wing to Brian McClair, running intelligently into space. Making ground, the striker looked for somebody in scoring position, could not spot anybody immediately, and settled for 'nutmegging' a defender. He moved menacingly on into the edge of the box before playing the ball across the face of the St Mirren goal – where Mo Johnston appeared behind the defence to slip the ball into the net.

Maurice Johnston takes on a St Mirren defender.

If any referee had yielded to the slight suggestion of offside about the conclusion of such an inspired move, it would have been a sin against aesthetics; fortunately, Mr Waddell and his linesman agreed that it was a goal to remember and savour.

It would be hard enough to duplicate those exact moves on a practice-field and with no opposition on the field; to do so, in a competitive match under increasingly difficult underfoot conditions remains a wonderful feat. To think that such a goal might decide a Championship adds an extra dimension to the memory.

Celtic had accomplished their task; they had scored the three goals required of them, and needed now to preserve that lead for the remaining 58 minutes. Even more important they had sent shock-waves reverberating around Scottish football grounds.

At Dens Park, urged on by the roars of their fans, Hearts had started well: in one early raid they had a legitimate claim for a penalty turned down when Clark was challenged in the box; a further spell of Hearts pressure brought four corners in a row, and from the last Roddy MacDonald came close with a header. 'News of Celtic's goal-burst at Paisley had a temporary silencing effect on the crowd, but Hearts knew nothing of these exploits and continued to work hard.' *(Edinburgh Evening News:* 3 May 1986)

At Ibrox, where Rangers were playing Motherwell and required a win for a place in Europe, the news was received in silence; but the Rangers fans took consolation in the fact that Hearts would still take the title by earning a draw at Dundee.

Back at Paisley, Celtic were now in rampant form: 'St Mirren continued to play some sparkling football on the occasions Celtic halted to take breath, but in the main there was nothing they could do about the Parkhead machine which flattened them in awesome fashion. I doubt if any team in the country could have done anything about it; I doubt if the entire Highland Light Infantry could have done anything about it. Flashing the ball about in breathtaking style reminiscent of the club's great team of the 1960s, Celtic were always going to score enough goals to keep up their end of the bargain.' (*Glasgow Herald*: 5 May 1986)

Paul McStay scores at Love Street.

Already the Celtic fans were chanting 'We're gonna win the League! We're gonna win the League!' One had to suspect that the chants were raised more in hope than genuine conviction, but Celtic's fourth goal, scored in 38 minutes by Paul McStay, had a touch of finality about it. Archdeacon made progress down the left, fighting gamely to retain possession and heading for the bye-line; he cut the ball back to MacLeod who smartly 'dummied' his marker, allowing McStay, racing in to the edge of the penalty area, to connect with the outside of his right foot. St Mirren's

At Paisley, the news starts to spread.

keeper, ex-Ranger Jim Stewart, was left completely helpless as the ball was driven sweetly past him. St Mirren's manager, another ex-Ranger, Alex Miller, commented afterwards: 'If that goal had been scored by a Brazilian, we would all be raving about it for months.'

That was the situation as the players headed for the pavilion at half-time. Celtic, now totally in command, although Bonner had had to make a couple of spectacular saves, could afford to play out time – and wait, hoping for a miracle.

At this point communications started to break down.

At Love Street the Celtic players were informed – wrongly, of course – that Hearts were losing at Dens Park. In the dressing-room the backroom staff found it difficult to hold the players' concentration, and to prepare them for the second half. Brian McClair, for one, was bewildered by the muted terracings at the start of the second half: 'I wondered why it was so quiet because we were sure Dundee were leading!'

At Dens Park the Hearts supporters had become more apprehensive, although they continued to encourage their team; but, increasingly, Hearts were being put on the defensive: 'Hearts fans had come in their thousands – some from as far away as the Continent – to cheer their side on to their first title win in 26 years. Even allowing for the fact that several Tynecastle men were the victims of a virus, the truth is that on the day when they really had to stand up and be counted, too many of them, probably because of the intense pressure, sat down to be counted out.' *(Glasgow Herald*: 5 May 1986)

Eight minutes after the interval Celtic scored another goal, an entirely irrelevant goal but the sort that is scored when a team is already four goals ahead. Johnston neatly cut the ball back to MacLeod who made a mess of his shot, but McClair, adjusting quickly to the situation, rerouted the ball past Stewart and accepted half-apologetically the congratulations of the other players. Again the Celtic fans on the terracing applauded dutifully, but their thoughts were elsewhere. On the terracing, and in the stand, thousands of ears strained to hear the commentary of the match at Dens Park through the tinny speakers of transistor radios. One despairing voice spoke on behalf of many: 'Hurry up and score, Dundee,' he wailed.

At Dundee, Hearts had settled nervously for a draw, and Dundee had started to come into the game as an attacking force; it still had not developed into a memorable contest: ' . . . and only the crowd of 20,000 made it a grand occasion. If the match had been played on Glasgow Green, most spectators would have left at half-time, or before.' *(Glasgow Herald*: 5 May 1986)

With 30 minutes to go Dundee made a substitution, putting on Albert Kidd, who had not played a first-team match in three months; on the Friday he had pleaded with his manager to be included in the 13 players chosen. His arrival on the field coincided with Dundee's best spell; Henry Smith made a spectacular save from John Brown, and Hearts breathed again. With about seven minutes left another piece of misinformation helped to change a remarkable day into a bizarre one. A rumour had started to spread throughout Dens Park, one which was communicated to the Dundee players – that Motherwell had equalised at Ibrox; a place in Europe was still possible for Dundee, who now made renewed efforts on Hearts' goal.

A corner to Dundee came over from the right, and John Brown leaped high to head the ball down, and from nowhere came Albert Kidd to hit the ball into the net.

At Ibrox Park, Graeme Souness experienced at first hand the bitterness of the Old Firm rivalry: hearing through transistor radios that Kidd had scored, Rangers fans assumed immediately that the scorer was Walter Kidd, and that Hearts had won the Championship. They burst into loud cheering – until the realisation slowly went round the stadium that Dundee were in the lead. The cheering gradually died down amid sullen mutterings.

Nothing much was happening on the field at Love Street, but thousands of Celtic supporters will remember it for the rest of their lives. St Mirren's goalkeeper was standing with the ball in his grasp, giving thought to clearing it downfield, until he was startled by 'the simultaneous roar from all around the ground in response to the opening goal at Dens Park . . . Celtic players scanned the dug-out, the sky, the terracings for guidance, afraid to believe the unbelievable'. The roar continued, minute after minute, as scarves, banners and colours were unfurled to be waved joyously in the pouring rain; not even the goals had provoked anything like this display of emotion. Nothing on the field was of any relevance as the fans celebrated.

At Dens Park, Hearts tried to rally, as they had done so often that season, but, emotionally drained, they had nothing left to give; legs and muscles could not obey messages from the brain, and it looked more likely that Dundee would score again. A minute or so later Kidd broke through Hearts' outer defence, employing a fast one-two with Harvey, before netting a second goal to end Hearts' title hopes.

Linked by radio throughout Scotland, fans reacted. At Love Street the Celtic supporters, appearing as extras in a plot that would have been rejected by Hans Christian Andersen, danced and sang, wept and shouted . . . Some Celtic players went through the closing minutes, playing with smiles on their faces, too jubilant to be able to hide their emotions; and '. . . when the roar was repeated a few minutes later, up a few decibels, even the players on the park could not mistake the meaning. And so we had the rare sight of a couple of Celtic players doing dances of joy while a game was going on around them.' (*Glasgow Herald*: 5 May 1986)

At Ibrox the spectators took consolation in the fact that Rangers had

It's all over! In the Paisley dug-out, Celtic players and officials react.

achieved a spot in Europe, and tried to shrug off the raising and the dashing of their hopes for Hearts. Apparently, the new manager, Graeme Souness, was surprised to find later that some of his players in the dressing-room were upset at the results from Dundee and Paisley.

At Easter Road, where Hibs were playing Dundee United, the home crowd went mad with joy at the news that Dundee had scored: '. . . their celebrations, similar in intensity to that which would acclaim a cup-winning goal, allowed them conveniently to ignore the shortcomings of their own players . . . The home players certainly looked bewildered as the terracings erupted in sea of dancing green, and their concentration lapsed . . .'

At Dens Park the Dundee supporters celebrated Kidd's goals, heralding them as a passport into European competition, but they could not help feel sorry for Hearts and their followers. 'The Hearts players were inconsolable, their fans – men, women and children – wept openly. Even those with the hardest of hearts must have had a lump in their throats.'

'Justice was done!' On the last page of the novel, *Tess of the d'Urbervilles,* by Thomas Hardy, the writer uses this expression ironically – and the sensitive reader has to scream out protest.

However, on 3 May 1986 a rough form of justice was done. Celtic *had* shown considerable fortitude in holding on and whittling away at Hearts' lead, and shown glimpses of the old flair. It was an achievement born of the Parkhead tradition of character and fighting spirit – and an outcome that once more defied belief.

And Hearts? *The Scotsman* managed to put the season into perspective for them: 'For Hearts, it may have been the saddest afternoon in the club's history. Perhaps it was also the cruellest . . . Even though Hearts again played well below their best, the forlorn quest for the title hardly deserved to end in such grievous circumstances. It was as if Lady Luck, who had bestowed any number of favours on the Edinburgh men in the last month, decided at the very last to cast a capricious spell over Hearts' fortunes.' (5 May 1986)

THE HAND OF 'GOD' ?

Celtic's Tommy Burns, interviewed on local radio after the League title was won so dramatically in 1986: '. . . and, I'd like to thank God for answering all my prayers.'

Two men emerged from the grief of Dens Park with massive dignity; the chairman, Wallace Mercer, and the manager, Alex MacDonald. Both turned up for the post-match press conference, and answered the questions courteously, if briefly. Later, after learning that many Hearts supporters were still waiting outside the ground, and calling for the players to appear, Mercer went out to speak to them. He explained: 'I had to speak to them because they have been absolutely wonderful this season. I thanked them for coming and for helping to get us this far, and told them to get themselves home in one piece.'

If they accomplished that, it was only on the surface; the broken pieces were all inside.

POST-MORTEM

Those sympathetic to Hearts would have to describe the events as a bitter anti-climax. Some journalists, searching for parallels in other sports, compared their failure to that of the flamboyant American golfer, Doug Sanders, on the last green at St Andrews in the 1970 Open. Needing only to hole a short putt to win the Championship – which would have been his only 'major' – he misread the break, and eventually lost a play-off to Jack Nicklaus, a man used to winning. Twenty years later a rueful Sanders admitted that he thought about the miss 'never more than twice a day!'

Others compared it to the sensational belly-flop of Devon Loch only 30 yards from the end of the 1956 Grand National; the Queen Mother's horse, ridden by Dick Francis, while leading to the cheers of the throngs at Aintree, inexplicably fell in the winning straight.

*　　*　　*

John Fairgrieve of the *Sunday Mail* took a jaundiced view of the events at Paisley, a view that ignored the fact that Hearts' eventual failure owed much to an abysmal performance there earlier in the season, a 2–6 defeat which carved a massive hole in the Edinburgh club's goal difference. 'Somehow, Celtic scored five goals against St Mirren. It is a score which pays tribute to the tenacity of the Glasgow club, but which pays no tribute whatsoever to the attitude of St Mirren.'

The journalist was unfair to St Mirren who, according to press reports, were not mere bystanders that day. TV coverage and repeated viewings of the video confirm that St Mirren were outplayed and outscored by a Celtic performance of genuine class. Alex Miller, St Mirren's manager, paid tribute to Celtic's lethal finishing, reckoning that Celtic had scored five times from only seven strikes – while St Mirren had done nothing with their four.

*　　*　　*

The events of that fateful day still haunt Alex MacDonald, the Hearts manager, as he revealed in an interview with Kevin McCarra: 'If I keel over with a heart attack, it'll be because of that game. Without a doubt it's still there in my mind. You keep going back to it. The only thing that has

344

changed is that if anybody asks me about it, I punch them on the chin.'
(*Scotland on Sunday*: 26 November 1989)

*   *   *

The letter of a Mr L. Trotter to his local newspaper, the *Edinburgh Evening News*, spoke volumes for the misery induced by Hearts' defeat: 'At Dundee on Saturday I felt my whole world collapse around me. When we lost the title, I cried. I cried when I came home. I couldn't talk to my wife about it. She was very understanding, and made me realise it was not the end of the world.' (8 May 1986)

*   *   *

The last word – and delivered not quite as harshly as it sounds. Referring to Hearts' sponsors at the time, one Celtic supporter summed up the situation: 'Aye, Hearts. Mita won the League; Mita won the Cup!'

Footnotes

1 Reference in poem to 'woes of training and inoculation' is apparently to the alleged effect of military training on the stamina of the enlisted Hearts players.

2 The origin of the name 'Heart of Midlothian' remains shrouded in mystery. Some believe the club was named after a jail, close to which football was played in the 19th century. Others contend that it was named after a dance hall frequented by youths who also had a passion for football. Nevertheless, the club is invariably linked with Sir Walter Scott's novel of that name. A fine outline of the club's history is contained in *The Heart of Midlothian Football Club, a pictorial history 1874-1984*, written by David Speed, Bill Smith and Graham Blackwood and published in 1984.

IN MEMORIAM

From the mid-1980s onwards a seemingly endless litany of disasters took a terrible toll on human life. Among them the following tragedies:

May 1985:	Fire at Bradford City football ground (56 dead)
May 1985:	'Riot' at Heysel Stadium, Brussels (41 dead)
August 1985:	Manchester Airport jet blaze (55 dead)
January 1986:	*Challenger* explodes over Cape Kennedy (7 dead)
November 1986:	North Sea helicopter crash (45 dead)
March 1987:	*Herald of Free Enterprise* sinks off Zeebrugge (193 dead)
November 1987:	Fire at King's Cross tube station, London (31 dead)
July 1988:	'Piper Alpha' explosion in North Sea (167 dead)
December 1988:	Rail crash at Clapham, London (36 dead)
December 1988:	Pan Am 747 explosion over Lockerbie (270 dead)
January 1989:	M1 Motorway plane crash (47 dead)
April 1989:	Disaster at Hillsborough Stadium (95 dead)

18

THE WORLD TURNED UPSIDE DOWN

A GRAND OLD TEAM

Sure it's a grand old team to play for,
Sure it's a grand old team to see,
And if you know its history,
It's enough to make your heart go o–o–o–o,
We don't care what the Rangers say,
What the hell do we care?
For we only know that there's going to be a show,
And the Glasgow Celtic will be there.

Sure it's the best darn team in Scotland,
And the players all are grand,
We support the Celtic as they are the finest
In the land, God bless them!
We'll be there to give the Bhoys a cheer
When the League flag flies,
And the cheers go up when we know the Scottish Cup
Is coming home to rest in Paradise.

(One version of a supporters' song dating from late 1960s)

THE OLD FIRM have always had an infinite capacity for the sensational –
and never more so than in the 1980s.

The decade had begun controversially for them with the Scottish Cup
final of 1980 when George McCluskey's goal in extra time proved the
margin of victory for Celtic, and provided an excuse for bands of spectators
to invade the pitch after the match and engage each other in a riot.

The spurious 'excitement' of that occasion, however, could not compare
with the genuine wave of interest and speculation sweeping through
Scottish football in the wake of the arrival of Graeme Souness from
Sampdoria to become player-manager of Rangers in 1986. The

consequences of his free-spending – and sometimes imaginative – approach to his responsibilities at Ibrox not only have altered the sport in Scotland, but have not yet run their full course.

Celtic, for example, retaliated a year later with the appointment of Billy McNeill as manager, after an exile of four seasons, rehired despite the bitterness which had surrounded his departure. He was able to revive the club for the 1987/88 campaign after a disappointing last season under Davie Hay. The tangible results were the League Championship and Scottish Cup 'double' in the official centenary season to the accompaniment of swelling euphoria from directors, players and supporters.

However, all these events were eclipsed, surely, in terms of world-wide attention by the bizarre saga which started to unfold in public on Friday, 12 May 1989.

The story had its origins in the discontent of Celtic's striker, Frank McAvennie, who left Parkhead in March 1989, to rejoin West Ham United less than 18 months after coming to Celtic Park from the London club for a fee of £750,000. The player, restless for some time, had sought a move since the start of the season – a fact that Celtic covered up by repeated denials, reasonably so on the grounds that they wanted to protect the player from adverse reactions from supporters unable to comprehend the thought that anyone wearing a Celtic jersey might be unhappy. Anxious to return south, McAvennie later cited his experience of the uncomfortable life of an Old Firm player in Glasgow. Perhaps he should have had an inkling of what was in store when, on the day that he signed for Celtic, somebody shouted to him at Heathrow Airport: 'McAvennie, you're nothing but a Fenian bastard!'

Virtually unnoticed in the media coverage of the prolonged episode was Billy McNeill's revelation that, having accepted McAvennie's departure as a certainty, he had his mind set on spending a large chunk of the fee on a suitable replacement. The transfer-fee came to a remarkable £1,250,000 for a player nearing 30 years of age, albeit one whose unselfish, hard-working approach had never been fully appreciated.

For nearly six months the manager had been contemplating McAvennie's successor – but, even so, the parading of Maurice Johnston on that Friday in May before the assembled press corps came as a shock. Most supporters were delighted because the signing, at a club record fee of £1,250,000, indicated a welcome sign of ambition and positive thinking; a minority, recalling Johnston's acrimonious departure from Celtic Park two years earlier, expressed doubts about his suitability.

McNeill was acutely aware of the goalscoring aptitude of the quicksilver forward, who had scored in every match of Scotland's current World Cup campaign. Some saw it as further proof of the manager's astute trading in the transfer market; he had sold one player at a considerable profit and replaced him with another, certainly three years younger and possibly more gifted – a forward with skills honed by Continental experience in France.

One Celtic director, unable to forget the bitterness surrounding Johnston's departure for Nantes under freedom of contract for a fee, set by a tribunal, at £30,000 less than the £400,000 paid by Celtic to Watford in November 1984, remained unhappy about the project. However, Billy McNeill and director Tom Grant, entered into negotiations with Johnston, and later the club's chairman, Jack McGinn, flew secretly to France to conclude the financial end of the deal. The upshot, according to one newspaper account, was that Johnston had agreed verbally to join Celtic at least six weeks before the player became the subject of concentrated media attention.

His return to Celtic was all the more ironic since Johnston had claimed to have been hounded out of Glasgow two years earlier after his experiences of life in the 'goldfish bowl' of an Old Firm player, and aggravation which included taunts from Rangers fans in clubs and discos. 'Mo' would doubtless have subscribed to the complaint of his friend Frank McAvennie: 'One half of the city hates you, and the other half thinks it owns you.' Still, Billy McNeill stressed he was unworried by Johnston's 'playboy' reputation: 'I didn't want to sign a choirboy. Angels with dirty faces will do for me.'

Regardless of any qualms, the affair constituted both a major signing coup and a superbly stage-managed piece of public relations at a crucial time for Celtic. Many in Celtic's support had been questioning openly the club's ambition and commitment *viz-a-viz* the free-spending Rangers, their opponents in the Scottish Cup final due to be held eight days after the 'acquisition' of Johnston, who – it was indicated – would officially sign for Celtic when he completed his spell with Nantes at the end of June. The *Daily Record,* Scotland's biggest-selling newspaper, devoted four pages in all (including the front and back pages) to the signing, whilst Rangers were relegated to a mere one-third of an inside page. Rangers had cause to feel aggrieved, as they were due to collect the Championship trophy at Ibrox that same day. However, it marked one of the rare occasions that Rangers were up-staged in the publicity stakes in the late 1980s .

Whatever the reason, Rangers gave a lacklustre performance against Aberdeen at Ibrox as they slumped to a 0–3 defeat; at Love Street, Johnston sat in the stand and watched his 'new team-mates' win by 1–0 over St Mirren, and basked in the adulation as his name was chanted repeatedly by fans desperate to believe once more in the aspirations of the club.

The dramatic swoop seemed to alter the complexion of the debate then raging among their downhearted supporters about the very future of Celtic, an argument to be renewed with full vigour a year later when the club experienced similar problems on the playing field. It should be noted that the Celtic support has been expressing disquiet for some years about every aspect of the running of the club, and has been perturbed by what many followers – and sections of the press – perceived as a certain lethargy on the Board's part in making Celtic a modern football organisation again, though

Roy Aitken collects the Championship trophy in 1988. Tommy Craig and Billy McNeill look on.

McNeill's return brought a temporary respite from the criticism.

When Celtic landed that double in 1988, Billy McNeill and his assistant Tommy Craig had imposed a more developed sense of teamwork and discipline on to the normal Parkhead style once described memorably by Rob Hughes of *The Sunday Times* as 'that terrific old Celtic flavour, the relish with which they ping the ball around from feet to feet, the long rein given to their instincts, above all the effervescence with which little men chase and scurry into forward positions as if the opposition is non-existent.'

Celtic's long-standing vulnerability in defence was remedied by an emphasis on possession, a practice which put an increased premium on teamwork. During the 1987/88 season the opposition teams were harried mercilessly when in possession even in their own half. This restriction on enemy operations certainly benefitted Celtic's front men because opposing defenders, kept under constant pressure, became increasingly liable to make mistakes the longer the match went on. No player had been more valuable on the field in carrying out this policy than the tireless Frank McAvennie.

However, Celtic's abysmal start to season 1988/89, with five defeats in the initial nine matches that constituted a quarter of the League Championship, tended to undermine the cohesion.

What went wrong?

Certainly the club suffered from injuries, most notably that to Pat Bonner whose absence served to underline his value to the team; other players had to absent themselves for extended periods, such as the promising young defender Derek Whyte, out for 16 weeks with a tendon injury, combative midfielder Peter Grant, sidelined for 14 weeks with a form of hepatitis, and forward Joe Miller, severely troubled with a lingering virus for 19 weeks.

In the Premier League, where clubs play each other four times a season, it does not take long for coaching staff to work out strategies to combat tactical ploys. The other sides had learned to counter Celtic's successful method of the previous season . . . and, deprived of key personnel through injury, Celtic had little new to offer. Some alleged that a certain unrest behind the scenes, perhaps sparked by McAvennie's ill-concealed desire to leave, lay behind the poor start.

Other critics saw a more fundamental problem. After the unqualified joy of the 1987/88 triumphs no real attempt was made to strengthen the squad, no recognition of the need to improve in order to compete in Europe. Those critics saw that *laissez faire* attitude as lack of ambition. The discontent, first voiced as murmurings, rapidly swelled into a noisy chorus as it became clear that Celtic could not retain the Championship.

Unfortunately for Celtic, the club destined to win the Championship would be Rangers, and many were prepared to make forthright and perhaps unjustified comparisons between the two organisations. Rangers had developed, it appeared, an unstoppable momentum both on and off the field. The genuine fear for Scottish football was that the Ibrox club was set on a course to dominate every aspect of the game, and that their traditional rivals, Celtic, were being left far behind, very much the poor relations. It was perceived that Celtic had slumped in comparison with Rangers in terms of commercial enterprise. Rangers' business acumen, since the 'Ibrox revolution' heralded by Souness' arrival in 1986, had transformed the club into a major marketing force in British sport, with every avenue of income being pursued aggressively to consolidate its position as the richest football power in the United Kingdom.

THE GOOD, THE BAD, AND THE UGLY . . .

Ian Jack had mixed feelings about the flowering of Glasgow's civic pride in the late 1980s. He was impressed by the 'epidemics of stone-cleaning and tree-planting [which] have transformed its former blackness into chequer-works of salmon pink, yellow and green. Old buildings have been burnished and refitted. Museums, delicatessens and wine bars have been opened. There are business centres, sports centres, heritage centres, art centres . . .'

However, not everything in the garden was rosy, for in 'peripheral' housing estates such as Possilpark (where in the 1950s there had been a choice of dancehalls, cafes and cinemas) unemployment figures could now rise as high as 50-60 per cent, since nearly every local factory had closed 'leaving nothing but pubs and bookies; shops'. To the residents of such estates, where teenagers wandered aimlessly about the streets to vent '[a] frustration bred from the lack of hope and solved, temporarily, by alcohol, vandalism, theft, and heroin', the Citizens' Theatre and the Scottish Opera seemed like 'hopeless fripperies, possibly located on Mars'. (*Before the Oil Ran Out: Britain 1977-1986*, 1988)

Rangers had come a long way from the early 1880s, when the president, George Goudie, had to loan the club £30 from his own pocket to stave off the threat of extinction and, as *Scottish Sport* recalled in 1894, the club had fallen on such 'hard times' that 'office had almost to go a'begging.' Now, an insatiable curiosity surrounded the activities of Rangers Football Club, an organisation being viewed increasingly – and approvingly – as the epitome of go-getting 1980s Thatcherite entrepreneurship.

The general attitude towards Celtic could be labelled as 'patronising' at best, and the directors were described uncharitably as 'cocooned in the traditions of the club, refusing to go public to raise much needed capital' in order to compete. The verdict could have been construed as harsh and unsympathetic to a group of individuals caught on the horns of a genuine dilemma, having to come to terms with a series of crises: the upgrading of the stadium to meet minimum standards and needs for the 21st century, the assembling of a side worthy of the club's proud heritage, the realisation that traditional penny-pinching attitudes would have to be revised in order to become competitive . . . And all this had to be done while operating for historical reasons from a lower financial base than the other half of the Old Firm.

The French sporting daily *L'Equipe* revealed the magnitude of the task facing Celtic if the club was to rejoin the European elite. Twenty years after Nereo Rocco, the coach of AC Milan, unhesitatingly ranked Celtic as one of the top three clubs in the world, that newspaper brought into focus two decades of descent into the also-rans of European competition. Its survey of the top clubs of the Continent at the end of the 1980s was based on a wider range of criteria than mere football accomplishment, although that was included; it contained such items as finance, stadia, and past performance at the higher levels. Celtic FC was placed in 28th position, a sort of Third Division; Rangers, rated as Britain's top club, held down 11th place, on the brink of promotion to the prestigious first ten, a roll which included such names as Real Madrid, Barcelona, Inter Milan, AC Milan, Juventus, Benfica, Bayern Munich . . . all clubs for which Celtic had once been a match.

Scotland on Sunday splashed a report in February 1990 of a proposed 16-team European Super League, predicted to get underway in 1991/92 with Liverpool, Arsenal, and Rangers as the sole British participants in a scheme devised by Silvio Berlusconi. Ironically, the magnate, involved with Italian media and football, has said that his favourite team was Celtic's 'Lisbon Lions'. Few could doubt which club Rangers chairman David Murray was referring to when he stated: 'I suppose if you're not invited to the party, you won't be interested.'[1]

It sounded like another manifestation of the old Ibrox arrogance, a by-product of the self-confidence detected by Simon Barnes of *The Times* only two months before the 1989 Scottish Cup final, when he noted that 'the players have that air of finely-honed smugness you associate with Liverpool'. (13 March) Billy McNeill's frequent references to Celtic as 'the underdogs' of Scottish football only has validity in the context of the advantages accruing from the wealth and power enjoyed by Rangers. Now he had to prepare his men for battle with a grim determination to wipe the self-assured smiles off the Ibrox faces . . .

Both sides had incentives to win the match – apart from the unstated, built-in motivation of beating the other half of the Old Firm. Celtic, as holders of the trophy, were anxious to retain it and make up for a disappointing season in which they had got off to a poor start and never made much of an impression. Rangers, on the other hand, wanted the Cup to scotch the talk of a hoodoo, and to complete a splendid 'treble'; they had won the

Skol/League Cup by beating Aberdeen 3–2 in a thrilling match, and had gained the League title with a comfortable six-point margin over Aberdeen.

Desperate though they might have been to prevent an Ibrox 'treble', Celtic came to Hampden with an unmatched pedigree in the Scottish Cup. That factor should have been enough to give the bookies pause for thought before they offered the odds of Rangers as 5–4 favourites and Celtic as 11–5 outsiders. After all, Celtic had established themselves as the greatest Scottish Cup fighters of them all, the record holders of the trophy with 28 triumphs (as opposed to Rangers' 24). In the early 1960s Rangers had drawn level and briefly surpassed Celtic's haul of final victories, but under Jock Stein's management Celtic had recovered their pre-eminence in the competition.

Celtic, too, were indelibly associated with the romance and folk-lore of the Scottish Cup, boasting a colourful history of dramatic wins, remarkable comebacks and late victories, underlined as recently as 1985 and 1988 with triumphs against Dundee United in which Celtic had snatched the Cup in the dying minutes after trailing in the latter stages.

Rangers' successes in the competition had been characterised more by dourness and efficiency than by flair and drama . . . but, despite their frequent success, at times the history of Rangers in the Cup had been marked by a curious fallibility. Remarkably, it had taken Rangers 20 years to win the trophy for the first time, and it should be remembered that Rangers participated 14 times in the competition before Celtic made their impressive debut in 1888/89. Later on, and astonishingly so in view of the fine calibre of the Ibrox teams of the period, another lengthy drought, erroneously called 'a 25-year hoodoo' ensued, ending only in 1928 with a famous victory by 4–0 over Celtic.[2] Then there was Berwick in 1967 . . .

And in the 1980s the indications were that yet another prolonged hoodoo was in effect. Only once in the decade had Rangers won the Scottish Cup, defeating the hapless Dundee United in the 1981 replay by 4–1; on three other occasions – against Celtic in 1980 (0–1), and against Aberdeen in 1982 (1–4) and in 1983 (0–1) – they had lost in the final.

The jinx had led to their international striker Ally McCoist despairing of ever completing a set of winners' medals. Since his arrival at Ibrox from Sunderland in 1983 he had picked up five League Cup medals and two League Championship medals, but one major trophy had proved irritatingly elusive. In a series for the *Scottish Daily Express* in April 1990, McCoist revealed how palpable the frustration had been for Rangers and the supporters in the period between 1984 and 1988, during which his club had failed to reach at least one final. Recalling how Dundee had bundled Rangers out of the Cup at Ibrox in 1984, McCoist shakes his head: '. . . the fans were screaming for my blood and I was in a terrible state in the dressing-room. Derek Johnstone and Colin McAdam told me to get my head up and face the crowd outside. I did so, and headed for the car. When I turned around, they [Johnstone and McAdam] had fans pinned against the wall, giving them pelters for shouting at me!'

Some of Celtic's hopes resided in the fact that Rangers' hoodoo was continuing, and manifesting itself in bizarre ways. In Graeme Souness' three seasons as manager Rangers had won the League Cup three times, the League Championship twice . . . but had achieved very little in the Scottish Cup.

In fact, their Scottish Cup record was dismal, because in those three years they had defeated only one side from the Premier Division, and had been eliminated by relegation-bound Hamilton at Ibrox in 1987, then by lowly Dunfermline at East End Park in 1988. Even the victories gained had been often less than convincing: a 4–1 win over Raith Rovers followed a 0–0 draw at Kirkcaldy in 1988; another win in 1989 – by 3–0 – over Raith Rovers came on the heels of a fortunate 1–1 draw at Starks Park; another replay at Tannadice ended in a 1–0 win after a 2–2 draw at Ibrox with Dundee United; and in the semi-final at neutral Celtic Park, St Johnstone were eliminated 4–0 after a 0–0 draw. Their only uncomplicated result in 1989 was an 8–0 romp over Stranraer.

The defeats merit examination in detail. Against Hamilton, Rangers dominated the match, but a combination of poor finishing and the luck enjoyed by a gallant Hamilton defence ensured that Adrian Sprott's goal put Hamilton through to the next round. It appeared that a lack of discipline cost Rangers dearly; too many Ibrox players appeared to allow the memories of a previous League match – in which two Rangers players were ordered off – to affect their concentration. However, nothing could alter the fact that Rangers had lost at home to a Hamilton Academical side that had gained only seven points at the halfway stage of the Premier League campaign – and that Chris Woods' British record of 1,196 minutes without conceding a goal had come to an abrupt end.

A year later, at Dunfermline, Rangers were swept aside at an early stage in the competition by an enthusiastic side free from the restraints of relegation worries for the day. After Rangers' full back John Brown was ordered off, perhaps unluckily, they could not mount an effective counter-attack to threaten Dunfermline's two-goal lead. Allegations of damage to furniture in a dispirited visitors' dressing-room followed the defeat.

However, in 1989, Rangers had advanced to the final, admittedly with replays against Raith Rovers, Dundee United and St Johnstone. If this was the year to end a hoodoo, Rangers were going about it the hard way – but they had survived.

Sportswriters had called into question the temperament of the Ibrox side, and doubts still remained three years into the new regime. Souness had been at pains to develop a system, and he had largely accomplished that primary task. His way at Ibrox was based on a patient build-up from the back and from midfield, characterised by methodical possession play. It had been an educational experience, and one which met with some resistance from the more 'redneck' Rangers fans and from the less sophisticated among the players.

In League competition, where patience and consistency are richly rewarded, Rangers' approach had been successful; in Cup football it had been less so. The discrepancy lies in the fact that knock-out Cup-ties have a dynamism of their own.

The smaller clubs relish a Cup-tie and revel in the opportunity to grab the headlines for once. In the course of the 90 minutes of one match, inspiration can produce remarkable performances that might never be repeated. That is why the law of averages suggests that Rangers and Celtic have a considerable advantage in any replayed Cup-tie. The same regard for percentages prompted Jock Stein to state that he preferred to play Italian clubs only once, rather than in the customary two legs of European football.

Rangers' new approach was geared to League football; in Cup-ties they would start invariably as favourites but . . .

There was also a question mark about their disciplinary record. During the early years of Souness' tenure, Rangers' on-field discipline was at odds with their new-found style; the patient approach rested uneasily on spirits thirsting for the rough-and-tumble of physical play.

Besides, the player-manager was not regarded as having set a clear example. In his League debut for Rangers, against Hibs at Easter Road, Souness was ordered off in the first half after a foul on McCluskey; in the last match of the same campaign, against Aberdeen at Pittodrie when Rangers clinched the title, Souness was again banished; against Celtic in the opening Old Firm clash of the following season, once more Souness was ordered from the field after a tackle on Billy Stark . . . And critics could point out other occasions – notably an early incident in a European Cup match against Steaua Bucharest – when he was fortunate to escape dismissal.

Even Rangers' goalkeeper, Chris Woods, had raised a few eyebrows. Normally, goalkeepers are passive onlookers when trouble breaks out. But the Englishman had raced 40 yards from his goal to add his protests to Souness' dismissal at Easter Road – and had been booked; at Parkhead a year later photographs capture Souness being red-carded and Woods is revealed yet again some 40 yards out of his goalmouth . . . and, of course, he had achieved the rare notoriety for a goalkeeper in being ordered off in an Old Firm match, at Ibrox in 1987.

Prior to one of the early Rangers-Celtic matches in which he played, Terry Butcher, Rangers' captain, expressed the opinion that the presence of so many English players on the field might have a 'calming' effect on the frenzied atmosphere. Along with Chris Woods, Graham Roberts and Frank McAvennie – experienced in England with West Ham – he might have

355

consoled himself with that thought during his time in the Govan Sheriff Court while on trial for 'disreputable behaviour'.

The hopes of the Celtic supporters rested on those flimsy premises: that Rangers' recent record in the Cup had been undistinguished, that a doubt existed about the temperament of the Ibrox side, and on the Glasgow folk-wisdom that it is preferable to bet on the underdogs in Old Firm matches.

For an upset to occur in the 1989 final, two things would have to happen. Celtic would require an infusion of traditional inspiration to raise their game; Rangers' methodical football would have to disintegrate for them to drop a level.

Nobody would have wagered too much on those assumptions.

SCOTTISH CUP FINAL
20 May 1989
Hampden Park

CELTIC 1	**RANGERS 0**
Bonner	Woods
Morris	Stevens
Rogan	Munro (Souness)
Aitken	Gough
McCarthy	Sterland (Cooper)
Whyte	Butcher
Grant	Drinkell
McStay	I. Ferguson
Miller	McCoist
McGhee	Brown
Burns	Walters

Scorer:
Miller (42)
Referee: R. B. Valentine (Dundee)

Attendance: 72,069

Some observers claim to have detected a sense of unease in the Rangers camp a week prior to the final, although the Ibrox announcer sounded jaunty enough as he read out Celtic's full-time result at Love Street at half-time to the crowd attending the Rangers-Aberdeen fixture. The match at Paisley had kicked off an hour earlier than usual to avoid traffic congestion and potential clashes between rival fans outside Ibrox, and it was reported that the announcer explained that the Celtic game had finished early, adding light-heartedly 'just like their season'. (Or words to that effect.)

Rangers' defeat by 0–3 to Aberdeen put a damper on the celebrations for the League title, already overshadowed in the newspapers by the 'signing'

RABBLE ROUSERS

After the Rous Cup between Scotland and England at Hampden Park, soccer hooligans embarked on a six-hour rampage of injury and destruction in a trail from the city centre to the stadium and back. Alec Cameron described the 'street villains', allegedly visiting supporters who had to be escorted to and from the match, as 'snarling, snapping crocodiles in a conga line of hate'. (*Daily Record*: 29 May 1989)

Glaswegians could scarcely cast the first stone at the 250 arrests, half of whom were English, because after the Scottish Cup final 700 victims had been treated in the Accident and Emergency Departments of the city's three major hospitals between 5p.m. on the Saturday and 5a.m. on the Sunday morning. Most of the patients had been involved in soccer violence in the aftermath of the Old Firm Cup final, and drew this comment from Ian Anderson, consultant at the Victoria Infirmary: 'They carved each other up with knives and bottles, then came into us, drunk as monkeys, and still full of fight, expecting to be put back together again.' (*Evening Times*: 23 May 1989)

of Mo Johnston for Celtic. Their captain, Terry Butcher, appeared at a loss for words when he was handed a microphone to address the crowd after being presented with the Championship trophy. Deflated perhaps by this anti-climax to a hitherto triumphant season, Butcher put up his hands in a gesture of apology on behalf of his team: 'It's not often you set off on a lap of honour as champions with your heads on the floor, when you should be happy and looking back over a memorable campaign . . .'

That result was not the confidence-booster that the Ibrox men might have anticipated at the end of a League season in which they had established a psychological advantage over their Parkhead rivals by winning three out of the four matches. In the process they had inflicted two defeats of such proportions – by 5–1 and 4–1 in the games at Ibrox – that Paul McStay, Celtic's midfielder, still found it painful to discuss them in an interview with Jim Traynor of the *Glasgow Herald* on the eve of the final: '. . . the way things went this season . . . they gave us a couple of heavy defeats, but beating them in the final would be a great way of ending the season. It might help wipe out the bad memories.'

Celtic could field a team close to full strength, and one player looking forward to the clash was Joe Miller, now restored to fitness through training and a special diet of steaks and pasta. Back in the first team, he had displayed his goalscoring flair by netting the winning goals in Celtic's last two League matches – against Hibernian at Parkhead and St Mirren at Paisley. He appeared to be relishing the opportunity to play through the middle, a role he had filled successfully with his previous club, Aberdeen.

Rangers, on the other hand, would have to play the match without the influence of the veteran midfielder Ray Wilkins, sidelined by an injury to his Achilles' tendon; Ian Durrant, badly injured at Aberdeen earlier in the season, could not play – and a further blow dented the Ibrox morale with the late withdrawal of Derek Ferguson, a victim of a mishap at training. The worst aspect for Rangers was that all these players were midfielders . . .

Celtic, despite the underdog tag, looked confident and relaxed as they arrived at Hampden Park for the final. Billy McNeill and his backroom staff had got the players in the right frame of mind for the task by taking the squad down to Seamill for some days away from the emotional turmoil that can disrupt preparations for a Cup final. The clamour for tickets was proving exceptional even by Old Firm standards; one Glasgow business-man, a Rangers season-ticket holder for half a century, was unable to get his hands on one; yet touts in London were selling the coveted briefs for up to 15 times the face-value.

Celtic's preparation was a judicious mixture of relaxation – including some uninhibited horseplay – and thorough tactical discussion. One important tactic worked out in those days was to devise yet another role for Roy Aitken. Celtic's captain, throughout his career, had often been a victim of his own versatility; he could perform competently in several positions and was called upon frequently to shore up weaknesses in Celtic's lineup. Once more in a Scottish Cup final he was required to play a pivotal role. Rangers' danger man was Mark Walters, a skilled winger with a fine turn of speed, and Celtic remembered that in Rangers' decisive wins earlier in the season he had run riot. The strategy was simple: play Roy Aitken on the right side of midfield with the option of moving forward down the wing; thus, the supply of passes to the feet of Walters could be cut off, and the danger of overlapping runs by either John Brown or Stuart Munro would be curtailed . . . and those with long memories could recall that a young Roy Aitken had scored both Celtic's goals from a similar position in a 2–2 draw at Ibrox in 1977 .

The Celtic party was so wound up for victory that it took in its stride Rangers' blatant attempt to steal the headlines on Cup final day with the announcement that the highly successful partnership of Graeme Souness and his assistant, Walter Smith, had been signed up for another five years at Ibrox.

They paid no attention to the observations of the more superstitious who wondered if this 13th Old Firm Scottish Cup final would cap a wretched season for the men in green and white.[3]

Nobody expects classic football in a Rangers-Celtic match; the tension generated by more than a hundred years of ferocious rivalry guarantees that the arts and crafts of the game will be set aside in exchange for physical effort. More often than not the match evolves into a grim war of attrition, a battle of wills marked by physical challenges that frequently threatens to boil over into warfare.

Paul McStay.

Some journalists find a satisfaction in that tension:

What a game. What an atmosphere. What a day for it. What a pity there had to be a loser. As a matter of fact, I'd go as far as saying this is as good a match as I've seen all season. In my eyes there's no finer sight than seeing two sides going at it hammer and tongs from the word go, both with but one thought in mind – victory. I, along with one particular set of punters, loved every nail-biting minute of the whole pulsating affair.

(Sunday Post: 21 May 1989)

But others are not so easily impressed:

The poignant display of contrasting emotions [at the end] made it easy to forget the final had been a colourless contest between two teams who found it impossible to break free of the shackles fastened around legs by a stultifying tension. Players lived in fear of making the error which could win and lose the prize.

(Glasgow Herald: 22 May 1989)

And the truth? Probably it lies somewhere between the two reports.

Tommy Burns, after playing in his last final as a Celtic player, spoke frankly to Alan Davidson of the *Evening Times*: 'In ten years time I don't think people will be talking about the quality of the match. They will be looking at the record books and having it confirmed to them that Celtic won 1–0.'

HE SAID IT

The match was also the last Cup final under the control of SFA secretary Ernie Walker. Before leaving Hampden, he said: 'It was a brilliant day on which even the weather played its part, and the huge crowd behaved themselves. We can ask for no more than that.'

Some people might have wanted a game of football too.

Winning was the important thing, and Celtic set out to do so by putting into practice their commendable planning; once more Tommy Burns explains: 'We set out to close them down, but still allow ourselves to play. And I think that over the piece we were more aggressive and created the better chances.'

Burns had every reason to be proud of his personal contribution; in a crowded midfield he always tried to be constructive, to create rather than destroy – and, because it marked another chapter in the Old Firm's on-going war, he was prepared to run himself into the ground, even at the age of 32 on an emotional, stamina-draining, sultry afternoon. It should be remembered, however, that Burns, generally more recognised as a silky performer, is admired unreservedly by that archetypal Ranger, Jock Wallace.

In a first half devoid of sustained football, and punctuated by stoppages, apart from a goal a few minutes before half-time, the major talking points among the fans were the fouls – calculated, cynical and intimidating.

Three such fouls, excluding the over-zealous tackling employed by both teams, stick in the mind; the perpetrators were Drinkell, Sterland and Grant, the victims Tommy Burns, Paul McStay and Mark Walters.

Drinkell had come back into the midfield area to help out; he raced at least ten yards to tackle Tommy Burns as the Celtic player gathered a pass. Drinkell won the ball, but swept Burns to the ground as he followed through, making little or no effort to avoid a collision . . .

A few minutes later Sterland challenged Paul McStay for a 50-50 ball and won it; like Drinkell earlier, he followed through to catch McStay dangerously high with his boot . The incident raised howls of outrage from the Celtic support, and brought McNeill out on to the track in angry protest . . .

Mark Walters had been quiet throughout the first 15 minutes but, when he did display his considerable footwork for the first time, Grant raced down Rangers' left touchline alongside him. The Celtic defender clearly attempted to bodycheck the Ranger; at the same instant as the collision Grant seemed to land a blow on the winger's face . . .

Three fouls not out of place in South American football – but the most important fact remained that the victims were probably the three most talented players on the pitch. The message had to be clear even to the simplest intelligence; nobody, specially the more gifted, was going to be allowed time to display skill, to play the game, to create danger . . .

The reactions of the fouled players foreshadowed the eventual outcome of the final.

Tommy Burns gritted his teeth in pain, picked himself up slowly, and rejoined the match. He contented himself with some pointed words to the referee, Mr Valentine, who ignored the comments with the same tolerance as he had shown in allowing the tackle . . .

Paul McStay had to receive prolonged treatment on the field from the Celtic trainer, while his manager continued to gesture from the touchline. The Celtic midfielder too picked himself up, and attempted to walk off the bruises. His expression remained poker-faced, but determined, as he resumed his position . . .

Of the three, Mark Walters was the one who reacted most theatrically – although, in his defence, a player in a football match might expect to be kicked rather than punched. The referee had awarded a free kick rightly for the tackle; as Grant escaped further punishment, Mr Valentine could not have seen the activity on his blind side, and the linesman, positioned 50 yards down the line behind the play, was equally unsighted. Walters rose to

Joe Miller outpaces Terry Butcher.

his feet, rightly aggrieved, but for the rest of the match he appeared to allow the incident to affect him. Frustrated by the close and generally fair marking of Morris and Aitken, he gave way to flashes of petulance . . .

Neither goalkeeper was troubled much by shots in the first half, although both indicated their confidence with crisp handling of the ball and a brisk command of the penalty areas. Defences were clearly on top, but hasty clearances and frequent bailing out to the keepers revealed the nerves barely under control.

The only goal was scored shortly before the interval, and it was a disaster for Rangers. Gary Stevens, an expensive buy from Everton, moved in confidently to clear up a loose ball on the edge of the box; he controlled the bouncing ball, and then passed it back to Woods, who was starting to advance from his goal, but the full back may have taken his eyes off the ball

362

momentarily. His pass back was not struck crisply enough, and Joe Miller, racing in from the left behind Stevens, picked up the botched attempt and fired a low shot just inside Woods' left-hand post; photographs show the goalkeeper, six yards out of his goal, still diving as the ball crosses the line behind him.

Nobody could claim it as a spectacular goal, but the youngster deserved great credit for his quick reflexes. He came buzzing in at right angles to the path of the ball, turned sharply about 14 yards out, and released his shot without hesitation. At Hampden in this latest episode of the long-running saga between forwards and keepers, reminiscent of the last gun-fight in a deserted street in Western movies, the striker had won. It was a moment of redemption for him; seven weeks earlier, in the final League match of the season between the Old Firm, Miller had volunteered to take a penalty kick for Celtic with the score at 2–1 for Rangers. Woods guessed correctly, and dived left to block Miller's weak shot. The save did much to seal the Championship for Rangers, and signalled the end of Celtic's faltering challenge.

In personal terms it marked a moment of satisfaction for the youngster. Burdened with the expectations aroused by the transfer-fee of £650,000 paid to Aberdeen in November 1987, Miller had found it difficult to settle at Celtic Park after a promising start. Throughout much of the miserable 1988/89 season he had been hampered with injury and illness, but in that Cup final against the club's oldest rivals he appeared to come of age. He has ascribed some of his difficulties in settling down to a change of position; Celtic had been playing him in a wider zone, rather than the through-the-middle role preferred by the free-running Miller.[4]

Apart from Steven's obvious gaffe, the goal left a sour taste in Rangers' mouths.

Roy Aitken, in challenging for the ball in his own half of the field, certainly appeared to have touched the ball last before it crossed the touchline. However, displaying that aggression and confidence necessary to survive in an Old Firm Cup final, Aitken picked up the ball for the throw-in with such authority that the referee, Mr Valentine, who had ordered Aitken off in the 1984 final against Aberdeen, apparently gave him the benefit of the doubt.

From the throw-in Grant crossed a hopeful ball into the penalty area where Gough headed clear, but not emphatically; Butcher and McGhee made for it, and Rangers' central defender could have been penalised for his attentions to Celtic's 'born-again striker'. When Butcher 'won' the duel with McGhee, the ball was played across the pitch towards Stevens and . . . Celtic had gained the important goal only three minutes from half-time.

Graeme Souness later absolved his full back from the blame for the defeat, graciously allowing that Stevens had been the best Rangers player afield. But he remained bitter about the throw-in, claiming that two Rangers had moved out of position, anticipating that, understandably, the award would be theirs. Souness' indignation at Aitken's gamesmanship lost much of its moral credibility, however, when one recalls that the same Souness had confounded the visiting Dynamo Kiev recently by reducing the playing dimensions of the Ibrox pitch for a European Cup-tie.

Within a minute of Miller's strike, even as the Celtic supporters behind Bonner's goal were still celebrating noisily, Rangers came within a whisker of equalising. Walters picked up a pass, found space within the penalty area and placed his shot behind the Celtic keeper; Derek Whyte, outstanding in Celtic's defence, anticipated the development and backed into the six-yard box to scramble the ball past for a corner.

The critical period after the interval – the first 15 minutes – belonged to Celtic, and the Parkhead midfield established control. With Paul McStay and Tommy Burns there, Celtic would have the advantage in pure football; both men attempted to hold the ball, to use it positively, and gave warning to Rangers that any looseness in the Ibrox defence would be punished to the full. Alongside them, Peter Grant and Roy Aitken played in the more defensive and combative positions, although both were prepared to move forward, with Aitken in particular revelling in the freedom of the right wing.

Early in the half, Miller, still exulting in his goal, embarked on a long run of almost 50 yards and had a choice of Celts for his final pass; with McGhee and Morris also moving into space, Miller released McStay whose shot narrowly missed the left post.

Rangers' depleted midfield was suffering in comparison. Mel Sterland, signed from Sheffield Wednesday as a full back, looked out of place when called upon to be constructive – and his only memorable contribution to the match was in fouling McStay in the first half. John Brown, another player better known as a full back, tried hard and won several loose balls, but his distribution was erratic. Ian Ferguson frequently looked dangerous, but was crowded out whenever he threatened too much.

Rangers' anticipated rally started midway through the half after Davie Cooper came on in 57 minutes as a substitute for Sterland, and, in 68 minutes, Souness, at the age of 36, came on as a second substitute to replace Munro.

Clearly Rangers were trying to be more constructive in the closing stages, but the match had been slipping away from them. Statistics give a clear indication of Celtic's superiority: Celtic had six corners to Rangers' two, a suggestion of Celtic's command – and Celtic were awarded 18 free kicks to Rangers' four, a clear statement of Celtic's greater self-discipline.

Before the match Celtic's fears had centred on the ability of the defence to handle Rangers' powerful strike-force of Kevin Drinkell, Ally McCoist and Mark Walters. Walters' contribution had been vastly curtailed by the effective use of Aitken; the impact the other two made was negligible

Derek Whyte keeps an eye on Ian Ferguson (then of St Mirren) in 1986.

because of the sterling work of Mick McCarthy and Derek Whyte in the heart of defence. Their job became easier when Rangers started to abandon the studied build-up, and sent long, high balls down the middle for McCoist or Drinkell. McCarthy won everything in the air and Rangers lacked the subtlety to exploit McCoist's advantage in speed and mobility. Young Derek Whyte had a superb match, commanding in the air against the dangerous Drinkell and mobile enough to win on the ground.

The extent of Rangers' desperation was indicated by both Gough and Butcher moving up among the forwards; that decision left gaps in defence – without adding sharpness to attack – and Celtic almost punished them in 70 minutes. Aitken ran freely down the right and his well-flighted cross found Burns making a run beyond the far post; the powerful header from Burns beat Woods but was cleared off the line by Stevens, making partial atonement for his error.

Rangers' pressure continued but Celtic's defence remained confident; Bonner, still not overworked, left his goal boldly to clutch in fine style a dangerous cross from Walters, now operating on the right in a futile attempt to get into the game. Controversy broke out five minutes from the end when Rangers did get the ball into the net, but the referee, having seen that Bonner had been impeded by Cooper in going for the ball, had blown for a free kick.

In the last minute Celtic were awarded a free kick near the corner flag on the right; the situation posed a problem in ethics.

Celtic, traditionally a team devoted to attack, would be given another opportunity to mount a dangerous thrust into Rangers' penalty area . . . an 'insurance' goal could ensue . . . However, what might happen if the ball were cleared quickly, and too many Celts had committed themselves to attack?

Perhaps, a short free kick could be taken and the ball sheltered and held in the vicinity of the corner flag for several seconds? If only Bertie Auld were still out there to waste time and frustrate opponents.

Roy Aitken took the responsibility of captaincy; he called for the short pass, wasted no time at all, and drove the ball deliberately wide of Rangers' goal – and moved downfield to take up a semi-defensive position with great satisfaction.

Seconds later the whistle went – and Celtic's celebrations began:

> . . . they emerged from an ominous shadow cast by Rangers and basked in the warming glow of the summer sun, not to mention football glory. Many of them looked as though they wanted to frolic on the old stage all night. They saluted their supporters and took turns at holding up the shiny cup as though it were the Holy Grail. The faithful roared their affirmation.
>
> Things were different for Rangers: none of them able to bear the weight of defeat. The captain, Terry Butcher, sank to his knees and held his head in his hands. Ian Ferguson [who had won a medal when playing for St Mirren against Dundee United] . . . stood before the Rangers end, head bowed and clutching one of the goalposts for support. The manager, Graeme Souness, persuaded the young midfield player to let go and leave the scene of his despair, but as he trudged towards the tunnel he took off his boots and tossed them away . . . He was inconsolable. And still we will say it is only a game.
>
> (*Glasgow Herald*: 22 May 1989)

WINNING WAYS

Celtic's victory in the 1989 Scottish Cup final continued Billy McNeill's remarkable run as the club's manager:

Celtic had won all four major Cup finals under his management:
> Scottish Cup: 1980, 1988, 1989
> League Cup: 1982

Celtic had won all three Old Firm finals:
> Scottish Cup: 1980, 1989
> League Cup: 1982

Celtic had won a major trophy in each of the manager's seven seasons in charge:
> League Championship: 1978/79, 1980/81, 1981/82, 1987/88
> Scottish Cup: 1980, 1988, 1989
> League Cup: 1982

On top of the world – Joe Miller is hoisted by Roy Aitken.

A strange Scottish Cup final – and one that featured two Irishmen, seven Englishmen, a Singaporean, a Swede and 13 Scots.[5] Both sides had spent considerable sums – a fortune in the case of Rangers – in order to strengthen their squads. Despite the money spent, the best players on the field were those who cost little: Paul McStay, Tommy Burns and Roy Aitken. Perhaps the most encouraging aspect of the result was that it restored football to the level of a game again, where money could not guarantee success on the field.

It may not be a rich man's world after all . . .

POSTSCRIPT

With a startling suddenness the Mo Johnston affair turned sour for Celtic when ominous hints surfaced on the day after the Cup final that he would not be joining them after all. 'Personal contractual obligations' were cited as the stumbling block in the *Sunday Mail* of 25 June 1989, and it was an irate Celtic chairman, Jack McGinn, exasperated by the Byzantine developments, who ended any interest that the club still had left in the player by stating bluntly: 'There is no place at Celtic Park for someone who does not want to play for the club.' He continued to maintain that Johnston had signed a binding agreement with Celtic – and his stance was supported by FIFA. Johnston signed for Rangers in July 1989.

Most intriguingly, Ally McCoist of Rangers has since revealed the secret of his new team-mate's abrupt change of allegiance:

> We were sharing the Tom Weiskopf Suite at the Marine Hotel in Troon during the build-up to the Scotland-England game at Hampden [on 27 May 1989, one week after the Scottish Cup final]. Mo had to tell someone because he had been bottling up the situation and nerves were getting the better of him. It would have to be me he told! He started dropping subtle hints just before we went down for dinner one evening. We were sitting back with our feet up watching television when he told me what a nice house the gaffer, Graeme Souness, had, and said he was there the other week. I thought he was winding me up and then he eventually said: 'I've signed for Rangers.' I replied: 'Queen's Park, Berwick, Kilsyth?' Mo eventually convinced me and swore me to secrecy.
>
> (*Scottish Daily Express*: 11 April 1990)

The affair remains shrouded in mystery. It may have been only a nine-day wonder for Celtic, but it helped write yet another glorious chapter in their history!

Footnotes

1 Celtic were quoted as being sceptical about Berlusconi's scheme. Note also the comments of Graeme Souness in his *A Manager's Diary* (1989), when writing on Maurice Johnston's reasons for joining Rangers: 'He wanted to play back home, he wanted to be with a BIG club and he wanted to play in the European Cup as well as the World Cup.'

2 Although Rangers' period of failure lasted from 1903 until 1928, it should be remembered that during the First World War seasons, from 1915 to 1919, the Scottish Cup competition was abandoned.

3 Celtic had won six Old Firm finals to Rangers' five, and the Cup had been withheld in 1909 after the 'Hampden Riot'. Given the clubs' dominance of the competition, those who favour the conspiracy theory delighted in the draw for the 1989 semi-finals which allowed the teams to avoid each other again. This had been the 12th time since 1960 that the 'luck of the draw' had kept the Old Firm apart at that stage, and the *Sunday Post* of 26 March 1989 reckoned that the odds for such an occurrence were 140–1 against.

4 A few months after the 1989 Scottish Cup final Miller made his feelings about the situation abundantly clear in a fit of anger during the Skol/League Cup semi-final against his former club Aberdeen at Hampden. Having become that rarity, a substituted substitute, he came close to hurling his jersey in disgust at the dug-out. Miller, once described rather enigmatically by manager Billy McNeill as 'a little boy in a big man's suit', sought a transfer after the incident.

5 The 24 participants (including the two substitutes) were of the following nationalities, as defined by birthplace:

Scots: Aitken, Whyte, Grant, McStay, Miller, McGhee, Burns, Munro, Souness, Cooper, Ferguson, McCoist, Brown (13)

Irish: Bonner, Rogan (2)

English: Morris, McCarthy, Woods, Stevens, Sterland, Drinkell, Walters (7)
(NB: Morris and McCarthy eligible to play for Eire)

Singaporean: Butcher (though born in Singapore, he is eligible to play for England)

TOP OF THE POPS

According to a survey of British taste in the *Today* newspaper of 26 December 1989, the following topped the charts in the decade:

FILMS	ALBUMS
1 *Crocodile Dundee*	*Brothers in Arms:* Dire Straits
2 *ET: the Extra Terrestrial*	*Thriller:* Michael Jackson
3 *Indiana Jones and the Last Crusade*	*Bad:* Michael Jackson
4 *Who Framed Roger Rabbit?*	*Queen's Greatest Hits:* Queen
5 *Fatal Attraction*	*Whitney:* Whitney Houston
6 *Return of the Jedi*	*Kylie:* Kylie Minogue
7 *Ghostbusters*	*True Blue:* Madonna
8 *Crocodile Dundee II*	*The Joshua Tree:* U2
9 *Batman*	*No Jacket Required:* Phil Collins
10 *The Empire Strikes Back*	*Tango in the Night:* Fleetwood Mac